Language Planning and Policy in Africa, Vol. 2

LANGUAGE PLANNING AND POLICY
Series Editors: Dr Richard B. Baldauf Jr., *University of Queensland, Brisbane, Australia*
and Professor Robert B. Kaplan, *University of Southern California, USA*

Other Books in the Series
Language Planning and Policy in Africa, Vol.1: Botswana, Malawi, Mozambique and South Africa
  Richard B. Baldauf Jr. and Robert B. Kaplan (eds)
Language Planning and Policy in Europe, Vol. 1: Hungary, Finland and Sweden
  Robert B. Kaplan and Richard B. Baldauf Jr. (eds)
Language Planning and Policy in Europe, Vol. 2: The Czech Republic, The European Union and Northern Ireland
  Richard B. Baldauf Jr. and Robert B. Kaplan (eds)
Language Planning and Policy in Pacific, Vol. 1: Fiji, The Philippines and Vanuatu
  Richard B. Baldauf Jr. and Robert B. Kaplan (eds)
Language Planning and Policy: Issues in Language Planning and Literacy
  Anthony J. Liddicoat (ed.)
Language Planning and Policy in Latin America, Vol. 1: Ecuador, Mexico and Paraguay
  Richard B. Baldauf Jr. and Robert B. Kaplan (eds)

Other Books of Interest
Directions in Applied Linguistics
  Paul Bruthiaux, Dwight Atkinson, William G. Eggington, William Grabe and Vaidehi Ramanathan (eds)
English in Africa: After the Cold War
  Alamin M. Mazrui
Language Decline and Death in Africa: Causes, Consequences and Challenges
  Herman M. Batibo
Language Diversity in the Pacific: Endangerment and Survival
  Denis Cunningham, D.E. Ingram and Kenneth Sumbuk (eds)
Language in Jewish Society: Towards a New Understanding
  John Myhill
Language Planning: From Practice to Theory
  Robert B. Kaplan and Richard B. Baldauf Jr. (eds)
Linguistic Landscapes: A Comparative Study of Urban Multilingualism in Tokyo
  Peter Backhaus
Multilingualism in European Bilingual Contexts: Language Use and Attitudes
  David Lasagabaster and Ángel Huguet (eds)
Politeness in Europe
  Leo Hickey and Miranda Stewart (eds)
The Defence of French: A Language in Crisis?
  Robin Adamson
Urban Multilingualism in Europe
  Guus Extra and Kutlay Yagmur (eds)
Where East Looks West: Success in English in Goa and on the Konkan Coast
  Dennis Kurzon

For more details of these or any other of our publications, please contact:
Multilingual Matters, Frankfurt Lodge, Clevedon Hall,
Victoria Road, Clevedon, BS21 7HH, England
http://www.multilingual-matters.com

LANGUAGE PLANNING AND POLICY

Language Planning and Policy in Africa, Vol. 2

Algeria, Côte d'Ivoire, Nigeria and Tunisia

Edited by

Robert B. Kaplan and Richard B. Baldauf Jr.

MULTILINGUAL MATTERS LTD
Clevedon • Buffalo • Toronto

Library of Congress Cataloging in Publication Data
A catalog record for this book is available from the Library of Congress.

British Library Cataloguing in Publication Data
A catalogue entry for this book is available from the British Library.

ISBN-13: 978-1-84769-011-1 (hbk)

Multilingual Matters Ltd
UK: Frankfurt Lodge, Clevedon Hall, Victoria Road, Clevedon BS21 7HH.
USA: UTP, 2250 Military Road, Tonawanda, NY 14150, USA.
Canada: UTP, 5201 Dufferin Street, North York, Ontario M3H 5T8, Canada.

The articles in this book also appeared in the journal of *Current Issues in Language Planning* Vol. 1 (1), 2000; Vol. 2 (1), 2001, Vol. 5 (3), 2004 and Vol. 6 (4), 2005

The policy of Multilingual Matters/Channel View Publications is to use papers that are natural, renewable and recyclable products, made from wood grown in sustainable forests. In the manufacturing process of our books, and to further support our policy, preference is given to printers that have FSC and PEFC Chain of Custody certification. The FSC and/or PEFC logos will appear on those books where full certification has been granted to the printer concerned.

Typeset by Archetype-IT Ltd (http://www.archetype-it.com).
Printed and bound in Great Britain by the Cromwell Press Ltd.

Contents

Series Overview

Since 1998 when the first polity studies on Language Policy and Planning – addressing the language situation in a particular polity – were published in the *Journal of Multilingual and Multicultural Development*, 25* studies have been published there and, since 1999, in *Current Issues in Language Planning*. These studies have all addressed, to a greater or lesser extent, 22 common questions or issues (Appendix A), thus giving them some degree of consistency. However, we are keenly aware that these studies have been published in the order in which they were completed. While such an arrangement is reasonable for journal publication, the result does not serve the needs of area specialists nor are the various monographs easily accessible to the wider public. As the number of available polity studies has grown, we have planned to update (where necessary) and republish these studies in coherent areal volumes.

The first such volume was concerned with Africa, both because a significant number of studies has become available and because Africa constitutes an area that is significantly under-represented in the language planning literature and yet is marked by extremely interesting language policy and planning issues. In the first areal volume, we reprinted four polity studies – Botswana, Malawi, Mozambique and South Africa – as:

> **Language Planning and Policy in Africa, Vol. 1: Botswana, Malawi, Mozambique and South Africa (2004).**

We hope that the first areal volume has served the needs of specialists more effectively. It is our intent to continue to publish other areal volumes as sufficient studies are completed. This volume – Africa 2 – is one such volume:

> **Language Planning and Policy in Africa, Vol. 2: Algeria, Côte d'Ivoire, Nigeria and Tunisia (2007).**

We will continue to do so in the hope that such volumes will be of interest to areal scholars and others interested in language policies and language planning in geographically coherent regions. We have already been able to produce four areal volumes in addition to Africa 1:

> **Language Planning and Policy in Europe, Vol. 1: Finland, Hungary, Sweden (2005);**
> **Language Planning and Policy in Europe, Vol. 2: The Czech Republic, The European Union and Northern Ireland (2006);**
> **Language Planning and Policy in the Pacific, Vol. 1: Fiji, The Philippines and Vanuatu (2006);**
> **Language Planning and Policy in Latin America, Vol. 1: Ecuador, Mexico and Paraguay (2007).**

The areas in which we are planning to produce additional volumes, and some of the polities which may be included are:

> **Europe**, including The Baltic States, Cyprus, Ireland, Italy and Luxembourg.

1

Asia, including Bangladesh, Chinese Characters, Hong Kong, Japan, Nepal, Sri Lanka, and Taiwan.

Africa, including Cameroon, Senagal and Zimbabwe.

In the meantime, we will continue to bring out *Current Issues in Language Planning*, adding to the list of polities available for inclusion in areal volumes. At this point, we cannot predict the intervals over which such volumes will appear, since those intervals will be defined by the ability of contributors to complete work on already contracted polity studies.

Assumptions Relating to Polity Studies

We have made a number of assumptions about the nature of language policy and planning that have influenced the nature of the studies presented. First, we do not believe that there is, yet, a broader and more coherent paradigm to address the complex questions of language policy/planning development. On the other hand, we do believe that the collection of a large body of more or less comparable data and the careful analysis of that data will give rise to a more coherent paradigm. Therefore, in soliciting the polity studies, we have asked each of the contributors to address some two-dozen questions (to the extent that such questions were pertinent to each particular polity); the questions were offered as suggestions of topics that might be covered. (See Appendix A.) Some contributors have followed the questions rather closely; others have been more independent in approaching the task. It should be obvious that, in framing those questions, we were moving from a perhaps inchoate notion of an underlying theory. The reality that our notion was inchoate becomes clear in each of the polity studies.

Second, we have sought to find authors who had an intimate involvement with the language planning and policy decisions made in the polity they were writing about; i.e., we were looking for insider knowledge and perspectives about the polities. However, as insiders are part of the process, they may find it difficult to take the part of the 'other' – to be critical of that process. But it is not necessary or even appropriate that they should be – this can be left to others. As Pennycook (1998: 126) argues:

> One of the lessons we need to draw from this account of colonial language policy [i.e. Hong Kong] is that, in order to make sense of language policies we need to understand both their location historically and their location contextually. What I mean by this is that we cannot assume that the promotion of local languages instead of a dominant language, or the promotion of a dominant language at the expense of a local language, are in themselves good or bad. Too often we view these things through the lenses of liberalism, pluralism or anti-imperialism, without understanding the actual location of such policies.

While some authors do take a critical stance, or one based on a theoretical approach to the data, many of the studies are primarily descriptive, bringing together and revealing, we hope, the nature of the language development experience in the particular polity. We believe this is a valuable contribution to the theoretical/paradigmatic development of the field. As interesting and challenging as it may be to provide a priori descriptions of the nature of the field based on specific paradigms (e.g., language management, language rights, linguistic imperialism) or to provide more general frameworks (e.g., Hornberger, 2006; Spolsky 2004) – nor have we been completely immune from the latter ourselves (e.g., Kaplan & Baldauf, 2003, Chapter 12) – we believe that our current state of knowledge about language planning and policy is still partial and the development of a sufficient database is an important prerequisite for adequate paradigm development.

Furthermore, we recognise that the paradigm, on the basis of which language policy and planning is conventionally undertaken, may be inadequate to the task. Much more is involved in developing successful language policy than is commonly recognised or acknowledged. Language policy development is a highly political activity. Given its political nature, traditional linguistic research is necessary, but not in itself sufficient, and the publication of scholarly studies in academic journals is really only the first step in the process. Indeed, scholarly research itself may need to be expanded, to consider not only the language at issue but also the social landscape in which that language exists – the ecology of language and its social system. A critical step in policy development involves making research evidence understandable to the lay public; research scholars are not generally the ideal messengers in this context (Kaplan & Baldauf, 2007). We hope this series also may contribute to that end.

An Invitation to Contribute

We welcome additional polity contributions. Our views on a number of the issues can be found in Kaplan and Baldauf (1997); sample polity monographs have appeared in the extant issues of *Current Issues in Language Planning* and in the volumes in this series. Interested authors should contact the editors, present a proposal for a monograph, and provide a sample list of references. It is also useful to provide a brief biographical note, indicating any personal involvement in language planning activities in the polity proposed for study as well as any relevant research/publication in LPP. All contributions should, of course, be original, unpublished works. We expect to work closely with contributors during the preparation of monographs. All monographs will, of course, be reviewed for quality, completeness, accuracy and style. Experience suggests that co-authored contributions may be very successful, but we want to stress that we are seeking a unified monograph on the polity, not an edited compilation of various authors' efforts. Questions may be addressed to either of us.

Robert B. Kaplan   **Richard B. Baldauf, Jr.**
rkaplan@olypen.com   rbaldauf4@bigpond.com

Note

*Polities in print include: 1. Algeria, 2. Botswana, 3. Côte d'Ivoire, 4. Czech Republic, 5. Ecuador, 6. European Union, 7. Fiji, 8. Finland, 9. Hungary, 10. Ireland, 11. Italy, 12. Malawi, 13. Mexico, 14. Mozambique, 15. Nepal, 16. Nigeria, 17. North Ireland, 18. Paraguay, 19. Philippines, 20. South Africa, 21. Sweden, 22. Taiwan, 23. Tunisia, 24. Vanuatu, and 25. Zimbabwe. A 26th monograph on Chinese Characters is also available.

References

Hornberger, N. H. (2006) Frameworks and models in language policy and planning. In T. Ricento (ed.) *An Introduction to Language Policy: Theory and Method* (pp. 24–41). Oxford: Blackwell.

Kaplan, R. B. and Baldauf, R. B., Jr. (2007) Language policy spread: Learning from health and social policy models. *Language Problems & Language Planning* 31 (2), 107–129.

Kaplan, R. B. and Baldauf, R. B., Jr. (2003) *Language and Language-in-Education Planning in the Pacific Basin*. Dordrecht: Kluwer.

Kaplan, R. B. and Baldauf, R. B., Jr. (1997) *Language Planning From Practice to Theory*. Clevedon: Multilingual Matters.

Pennycook, A. (1998) *English and the Discourses of Colonialism*. London and New York: Routledge.

Spolsky, B. (2004) *Language Policy*. Cambridge: Cambridge University Press.

APPENDIX A

Part I: The Language Profile of . . .

1. Name and briefly describe the national/official language(s) (*de jure* or *de facto*).

2. Name and describe the major minority language(s).

3. *Name and describe the lesser minority language(s) (include 'dialects', pidgins, creoles and other important aspects of language variation)*; the definition of minority language/dialect/pidgin will need to be discussed in terms of the sociolinguistic context.

4. *Name and describe the major religious language(s)*; In some polities religious languages and/or missionary policies have had a major impact on the language situation and provide *de facto* language planning. In some contexts religion has been a vehicle for introducing exogenous languages while in other cases it has served to promote indigenous languages.

5. Name and describe the major language(s) of literacy, assuming that it is/ they are not one of those described above.

6. Provide a table indicating the number of speakers of each of the above languages, what percentage of the population they constitute and whether those speakers are largely urban or rural.

7. Where appropriate, provide a map(s) showing the distribution of speakers, key cities and other features referenced in the text.

Part II: Language Spread

8. Specify which languages are taught through the educational system, to whom they are taught, when they are taught and for how long they are taught.

9. Discuss the objectives of language education and the methods of assessment to determine whether the objectives are met.

10. To the extent possible, trace the historical development of the policies/ practices identified in items 8 and 9 (may be integrated with 8/9).

11. Name and discuss the major media language(s) and the distribution of media by socio-economic class, ethnic group, urban/rural distinction (including the historical context where possible). For minority

languages, note the extent that any literature is (has been) available in the language.

12. How has immigration affected language distribution and what measures are in place to cater for learning the national language(s) and / or to support the use of immigrant languages.

Part III: Language Policy and Planning

13. Describe any language planning legislation, policy or implementation that is currently in place.
14. Describe any literacy planning legislation, policy or implementation that is currently in place.
15. To the extent possible, trace the historical development of the policies/ practices identified in items 13 and 14 (may be integrated with these items).
16. Describe and discuss any language planning agencies/organisations operating in the polity (both formal and informal).
17. Describe and discuss any regional/international influences affecting language planning and policy in the polity (include any external language promotion efforts).
18. To the extent possible, trace the historical development of the policies/ practices identified in items 16 and 17 (may be integrated with these items).

Part IV: Language Maintenance and Prospects

19. Describe and discuss intergenerational transmission of the major languages and whether this is changing over time.
20. Describe and discuss the probabilities of language death among any of the languages/language varieties in the polity, any language revival efforts as well as any emerging pidgins or creoles.
21. Add anything you wish to clarify about the language situation and its probable direction of change over the next generation or two.
22. Add pertinent references/bibliography and any necessary appendices (e.g., a general plan of the educational system to clarify the answers to questions 8, 9 and 14).

Language Policy and Planning in Algeria, Côte d'Ivoire, Nigeria and Tunisia: Some Common Issues

Robert B. Kaplan
Professor Emeritus, Applied Linguistics, University of Southern California.
Mailing Address: PO Box 577, Port Angeles, WA 98362 USA <rkaplan@
olypen.com>

Richard B. Baldauf Jr.
Associate Professor of TESOL, School of Education, University of Queens-
land, QLD 4072 Australia <rbaldauf4@bigpond.com>

Introduction

This volume brings together four language policy and planning studies related to Africa.[1] (See the 'Series Overview' for a more general discussion of the nature of the series, Appendix A for the 22 questions each study set out to address, and Kaplan *et al.* 2000 for a discussion of the underlying concepts for the studies themselves.) In this paper, in addition to providing an introductory summary of the material covered in these studies, we want to draw out and discuss some of the more general issues raised by them.

Although Algeria, Côte d'Ivoire, Nigeria and Tunisia do not represent a geographic cluster, they do have in common a number of factors:

- all four of the countries are participants in *francophonie*, the association of French speaking nations;
- following global trends, in the three francophone countries, there is evidence that language shift is occurring away from French as a lingua franca (Wright, 2006) to a greater use of English;
- Arabicisation is a national issue in Algeria and Tunisia (Sirles, 1999) and Arabic use is a regional and religious issue in the north of Côte d'Ivoire and Nigeria;
- geographically, they represent two distinct clusters: Algeria and Tunisia in the Maghreb in the northwest corner of the continent, and Côte d'Ivoire and Nigeria in Central West Africa. Thus, the group is not geographically coherent except in the sense that all the polities lie in western Africa;
- Algeria and Tunisia (see, Daoud, this volume) are in fact part of a coherent grouping – Morocco (see, Marley, 2000) is the remaining major member of this Magrhebian group, and all have French as a major exogenous language.
- Côte d'Ivoire is also a French-speaking polity, and Nigeria – where

French has been made the second official language (Omoniyi, 2003) – has joined the *francophonie*.

French has been maintained as an important language in many of France's former colonies, especially in Africa. In post-independence Africa, there has developed a sharp rivalry between Arabic and French, and ongoing competition between these two languages and national/ethnic languages for the position of official language. The role of the French language in the Francophone world must be set in the context of the preoccupations that Francophones themselves have about the importance of their own languages, about their relationship to France and about post-independence governments not only from a postcolonial point of view but also from the standpoint of an understanding that national/ethnic languages are also an essential dimension of their development. Consequently, French has become a language of communication between cultures as well as a vehicle for transmitting French culture. (See, Salhi, 2002 for further discussion of French language in the Francophone world; Breton, 2003 for some discussion of sub-Saharan Africa).

Algeria

Algeria constitutes an interesting subject for the study of language policy and language planning thanks to its almost unique history in the Arabic-speaking world: it is the only Arab country which lived under French assimilationist colonial rule for 132 years. Less than four years after Algeria's independence (1962), Gordon (1966: 246) wrote: 'Algeria's future will remain a fascinating case-study for Orientalists and for those interested in "development" and "modernisation".' The language issue during both the pre-independence and post-independence eras further marks this uniqueness within Africa and the Maghreb, as Djité has pointed out: 'Nowhere else in Africa has the language issue been so central in the fight against colonialism [as in Algeria]' (1992: 16). In short, the most severe problem that Algeria has had to cope with since its independence lies in language.

After the three countries of the Maghreb achieved their independence – Morocco on 2 March 1956, Tunisia on 20 March 1956, and Algeria on 5 July 1962 – it was the Algerian leadership who demonstrated ideological intransigence in recovering both language and identity. Algeria has emerged as 'the most vociferous in proclaiming its Arab Muslim identity' (Gordon, 1978: 151). The language planning activities, more systematic and assertive in Algeria than in the other two Maghrebi countries, have been carried out with revolutionary zeal. A number of observers (Abu-Haidar, 2000: 161; Grandguillaume, 2004: 33–34) have identified in this zeal a major cause of the rise of Islamic fundamentalism in Algeria and of the civil war that has ravaged the country since the early 1990s. Ephraim Tabory and Mala Tabory (1987: 64) have summarised Algeria's interest in language planning and policy as follows:

> The Algerian situation is complex, as it is at a crossroad of tensions between French, the colonial language, and Arabic, the new national language; Classical Arabic versus colloquial Algerian Arabic; and the

various Berber dialects versus Arabic. The lessons from the Algerian situation may be usefully applied to analogous situations by states planning their linguistic, educational and cultural policies.

Through the decade of the 1990s, Algeria frequently made headlines because of its internal instability and the civil war. Recent developments have allowed the country to overcome this chaotic state; they have gradually put an end to the hostilities and, at the same time, have almost obliterated the language-in-education planning activities (Arabisation) current since independence.

On 8 April 2004, Abdelaziz Bouteflika, the outgoing President of Algeria, was re-elected in a 'landslide victory.' Although there were reports of irregularities, foreign journalists qualified this election, which was endorsed by some foreign monitors, as a 'proper contest' (*Guardian Weekly*, 2004: 12). According to *The Economist* (2004: 40), the election was 'the cleanest that Algeria, or, for that matter, any Arab country, has ever seen'; thus, the 'first legitimate election' since the country got its independence from France in 1962.

Abdelaziz Bouteflika, a former diplomat, was also a member of the hardline clique that seized power in 1965, three years after the end of the Algerian war of independence. In 1999, handpicked by the military – who have, since liberation, always held the real power in Algeria – he was elected as the sole candidate after all his rivals withdrew from the competition as a protest against massive fraud. For five years, the lack of legitimacy in his administration prevented him from carrying out long-awaited social and economic reforms. However, despite his weak performance, President Bouteflika was returned to power in April 2004, probably because he had managed to reduce the violence that had plagued Algeria since the beginning of the 1990s.

After the success of the religious fundamentalists of the Islamic Salvation Army (FIS) in the 1991 parliamentary elections, the authorities cancelled the electoral process and the FIS's response took the form of an armed struggle against the secular state apparatus. In the ensuing decade, Algerians suffered from a bloody civil war in which the death toll has been estimated at between 120,000 and 200,000 victims. At the present time, displaced populations are estimated at between 1 and 1.5 million persons, and the Algerian security forces are believed to have arrested and 'disappeared' more than 7,000 persons. Furthermore, thousands of highly skilled and qualified mainly francophone Algerians were forced into exile, with the majority settling in France.

During his first term in office, President Bouteflika promoted national reconciliation; he brokered an amnesty programme in the form of the 'Law on Civil Harmony' as the result of which 25,000 Islamists agreed to stop their armed struggle. Since then, violence has fallen off, and the presumably outgoing presidential candidate reaped the benefit of that strategy in the election of April 2004. Part of the electorate may well have chosen to retain Bouteflika in office for the stability that he had managed to bring to the country and that he promised to maintain if he were re-elected. Exhausted by a decade of indescribable violence and also probably tired of constant changes of governments and leaders – Algeria had had five presidents between 1991 and 1999 – the population may have preferred Bouteflika to continue the programme of reforms to which he had committed his country during his first term in office. According to *The Economist* (2004: 41) 'Algeria has become a far gentler place. [. . .] The country's economic fortunes have also brightened. [. . .] [But] Mr Bouteflika has plenty of work on his hands.'

Between 1999 and 2004, President Bouteflika initiated a number of reforms most of which were not implemented because of the lack of legitimacy in his administration: opposition from within the power circles (conservatives) and without (Islamic Fundamentalists) prevented the initiation of major educational reforms that might have undermined the official language policy in place since the independence of the country. However, Bouteflika did succeed in launching a national debate over a number of sensitive issues that had previously been considered anathema. While none of his predecessors had had the courage to tackle such issues, he had, in his frequent speeches, dared to break a number of taboos. He raised such sensitive issues as those related to Algerian history, religious practices and the linguistic reality of the country. This new political discourse on language has to be seen in the light of the language policies implemented after 1962. Algerian experience with language-in-education planning can roughly be considered in two major periods: the first from 1962 to the 1970s, characterised by bilingualism in French and Standard/Literary Arabic, and the second from the 1970s to the present, characterised by monolingualism in Standard Arabic for the majority of the population and French-Arabic bilingualism for a small minority, mainly for the children of those in power.

Soon after he was elected in April 1999, Bouteflika took everyone by surprise when he suddenly started dealing with the language issue in public. In May 1999, he declared: 'It is unthinkable . . . to spend ten years study in Arabic pure sciences when it would only take one year in English' (*Le Matin*, 1999). The President thus appeared to have tacitly acknowledged the failure of Arabisation, at least in science and technology teaching, and to envisage a return to bilingualism in these fields. For him 'There has never been a language problem in Algeria, but simply rivalry and fights for French-trained executives' positions' (*El Watan*, 1999a). Not only did Bouteflika make such comments, but at the same time he constantly spoke in French in his public speeches, and he also demonstrated his skill in Literary Arabic. He adopted the bilingual fluency in French and Arabic in imitation of the Moroccan leadership as exemplified by the late king, Hasan II; he wanted to project a role model for bilingual Algerian citizen.

Bouteflika's public use of language was clearly opposed to the practice of his predecessors; indeed, he purposefully violated the law known as 'Act N° 91–05' (implemented on 5 July 1998) which prohibited any and all official public use of any language other than Arabic. Bouteflika did not hide his own awareness that he was infringing the law. In an interview with a French magazine, he said: 'When I speak French, some people write in the press that I am in breach of the Constitution.' (*Paris Match*, 1999: 35) Furthermore, Bouteflika admitted publicly that 'our [Algerian] culture is plural,' in sharp contrast to his predecessors' insistence on Algerians being solely 'Arabs and Moslems'. Bouteflika even went so far as to claim a French contribution to

Algeria's cultural heritage. In a press conference that he gave at the Crans Montana Summit in Switzerland in autumn 1999, he said: 'We attended French school and we are thus heavily influenced by Descartes' (Benrabah, 2004: 96). In addition, Bouteflika attended the *Francophonie* Summit in Beirut in October 2002, even though Algerian authorities had rejected the whole idea of an institutionalised *Francophonie*, considering it to be potentially 'neo-colonialist'. In the summer of 1999, Bouteflika declared:

> Algeria does not belong to *Francophonie*, but there is no reason for us to have a frozen attitude towards the French language which taught us so many things and which, at any rate, opened [for us] the window of French culture (Cherrad-Benchefra & Derradji, 2004: 168).

Bouteflika's constant use of French created an uproar among those of the elite who were in favour of total Arabisation and of total eradication of French. In the autumn of 1999, the President of the Committee for Foreign Affairs at the People's National Assembly (the Algerian Parliament) wrote privately to Bouteflika, then the newly elected president, reproaching him for his use of French in public; in answer, Bouteflika made the criticism public, and the deputy was forced to resign from the Assembly. Bouteflika also received a letter signed by several members of the High Council for the Arabic Language, warning him against his public use of French and taking strong exception to 'the francophone lobby in the presidency.' In a televised speech, Bouteflika reminded the authors of that message that it was not the mission of the High Council for the Arabic Language to choose the president's entourage for him (*El Watan*, 2000: 23); further, he declared: 'For Algeria, I will speak French, Spanish and English, and, if necessary, Hebrew.' In August, 1999, he declared on live television:

> Let it be known that Algeria is part of the world and must adapt to it and that Arabic is the national and official language. This being said, let it be known that an uninhibited opening up to other international languages – at least to those used in the United Nations – does not constitute perjury. In this domain, we are neither more Arab nor more intelligent than our brothers in Morocco, Tunisia, Egypt, Jordan, Syria, Lebanon, or Palestine or anywhere else. To move forward, one must break taboos. This is the price we have to pay to modernise our identity. Chauvinism and withdrawal are over. They are sterile. They are destructive (*El Watan*, 1999b: 3).

Thus, the language situation in Algeria continues to be confused, though there seems to be evidence of a reasonable resolution to the arguments and the arrival of a more rational language (and language-in-education) policy. The Algerian situation provides a good example of individual agency in language planning (Abdelaziz Bouteflika), illustrating yet again the impact that an individual can have on language choice in a particular polity.

Côte d'Ivoire

Côte d'Ivoire is a multilingual polity, encompassing some 60 African languages, but it has retained the French language as the sole official language of education and administration, as per Article 2 of its constitution. Many inaccurate descriptions of the language situation were disseminated during the colonial period, and these inaccuracies have perpetuated the notion that the language situation there may involve literally hundreds of languages. As a consequence, it is widely believed that, in such a complex linguistic situation, the selection of any African language as the official national language would trigger tribal warfare. Thus, the complex language situation cannot lend itself to the development of a workable language (or language-in-education) plan. It is argued that the only hope for peace and national unity, and the only way to provide access to science and technology (i.e., to modernisation) lies in maintaining French as the sole official language. Such a position commits the government to inaction – that is, to maintain the linguistic status quo. On the other hand, there is evidence that the traditional descriptions of the language situation exaggerate the degree of linguistic diversity and give the false impression of divisiveness within the population. In part, this difficulty stems from the fact that national boundaries in Africa were not drawn up on the basis of linguistic and cultural criteria, but rather reflect European colonialist ambitions. Thus, the languages spoken in Côte d'Ivoire are shared with other neighbouring polities; e.g.:

- the Kwa languages are shared with Ghana;
- the Kru languages are shared with Liberia;
- the Mandè languages are shared with Guinea, Mali and Burkina Faso, and
- the Gur languages are shared with Burkino Faso.

An analysis of day-to-day communication suggests two ideas: (1) from the perspective of their functions, it is possible to distinguish four language types, and (2) an examination of individual and group patterns of communication shows a language repertoire that makes language demarcation an essentially irrelevant exercise. The four language types are:

- languages of interethnic communication (e.g., Anyi, Dida, Gouro, Lobi),
- regionally dominant languages (e.g., Baulé, Bété, Dyula),
- national linguas franca (e.g., Dyula),
- the official language (French).

As a result, the typical Ivorian will have a language repertoire consisting of at least the first language (for intra-ethnic communication), the regionally dominant language, and one of the national lingua francas. An educated Ivorian will have standard French in addition while young Ivorians in the major cities may speak 'Popular French' or Nouchi, local pidgins providing a local identity.

When the colonial administrators decided to impose Standard French on the population, they assumed that it would spread quickly and, having spread, would unify the different ethnic groups. However, the initial élitist educational system, the desire of the administrators to keep the number of literate locals to a minimum and the selective system of education in place since independence created a communication crisis by producing graduates whose talents did not fit the economic and social needs of the country and at the same time by disempowering women, farmers, labourers and other relevant sectors of the population who constituted the workers who produced the polity's goods and services. Educational statistics demonstrate high drop-out rates and an inability to absorb even educated individuals into employment. It is now clear that mastery of Standard French alone is not sufficient to repair the dysfunctional aspects of the educational system. When the population concentrated in large cities like Abidjan has becomes aware that it cannot communicate adequately in Standard French for reasons beyond its control, the population resorts to the use of two dominant lingua francas – Dyula and Popular French (a local, simplified, non-élite variety of Standard French). Dyula has not enjoyed prestige until relatively recently. It is perceived as an easy language to learn and an overt symbol of group membership. The frequent use of Dyula by the political élite and by advertising agencies on radio and television has accelerated its spread. Popular French has spread rapidly through the population, well beyond urban centres, and its use is not necessarily characterised by illiteracy. The resulting condition – language development contrary to the intent of government sponsored language planning – has resulted in a situation promoting the spread of Dyula and Popular French, an example of unplanned language planning.

The language situation in Côte d'Ivoire has, however, changed somewhat since 2000. While the pidginisation and nativisation of French has further deepened through a variety known as Nouchi, the socio-political strife that has gripped the country since the coup d'état of 1999 may have significant effects on the potential of Dyula as a national lingua franca.

The situation in Côte d'Ivoire demonstrates the significance of cross-border languages and the need for approaches based on ecology of language rather than limited by the political boundaries of individual polities. Further, this situation demonstrates the ways in which language planning may become self-contradictory and may result in unplanned language planning producing results quite different from what the original planners actually had in mind. Unlike the important role of Abdelaziz Bouteflika in Algeria, no charismatic leader has emerged in Côte d'Ivoire; on the contrary, the linguistic history is marked by the absence of such a leader. It is also marked by the absence of the political will to act in the language environment.

Nigeria

Nigeria is not French speaking (although there has been some attempt to bring it into the French-speaking world in the past several years). Nigeria has used English as the *de jure* national official language, but it is a vastly heterogeneous community linguistically, with over 400 languages, making it the most multilingual country in Africa. Three of the multitude of languages – Hausa, Yoruba and Igbo, all Nigerian indigenous languages – are constitutionally expected to be co-official with English, but they serve largely regional functions de facto. In addition, Nigerian Pidgin English plays a major role, though it receives no official recognition. Religious worship – Christian, Moslem and African traditional – in many Nigerian churches and mosques, especially in urban centres, functions in several different linguistic modes – i.e., fully in English, or fully in indigenous language, or bilingually (or multilingually). There is, in addition, diversity in the language of literacy from one State to another with an inequality in languages in basic literacy and post-literacy education.

The predominant role of English in the Nigerian educational system reflects both policy stipulation and the dichotomy between reality and policy in the educational sector, especially at the pre-primary and primary school levels. From the secondary school level of education onwards, English dominates, especially in formal and official interactions. In informal and unofficial inter-actions, however, the indigenous languages are very much in evidence from the primary school to the university level, except in interethnic interactions where a common language is not available to participants. The objectives of language education as they relate to each level of education illustrate the supremacy of English. English is the language of the media; most of the indig-enous languages are relegated to the background. On radio and TV and in the print media as well as in local level publications, pamphlets and religious publications, Hausa, Yoruba and Igbo (as well as other indigenous languages) are almost totally neglected. Although statistics are not easily available, immigration has had an important impact on language distribution.

The planning and management of Nigeria's languages and the problems of language policy-making are characterised by:

- the negative attitudes to, and ideologies about, the Nigerian indigenous languages, historically;
- the existing official overwhelming bias in favour of English – because of its prestige, its ego-boosting potential, its susceptibility to upward social mobility and its official functions;
- the reliance on sentiment rather than on objective data (e.g., statistics of language use);
- the elite-domination of language policy-making and the equation of elite-interest with public interest, and
- the public's general ignorance about language.

The complex and intriguing context of language policy in Nigeria has resulted in the challenges deriving from language policy, the resulting missed opportunities and constraints, including:

- the failure to accord priority to language policy-making,
- the absence of implementation strategies,
- the instability in politics and administration,
- the frequent changes among policy-makers and the consequent changes in policy,
- the failure to seek out and consult language experts, and
- the lack of political will.

As a result of these several shortcomings, no single document can be found that might be construed as a statement of language policy in Nigeria. The nearest pertinent document one can locate lies in the language provisions of the National Policy on Education (1977, 1981). Aspects of the National Policy on Education relating to language policy-making or related legislation with respect to language planning, literacy planning and education planning may be identified, but as Kaplan and Baldauf (1997) point out, relegating the entire responsibility for national language planning to the education sector is an invitation to policy failure. The activities of the National Language Development Centre, the indigenous language-training institute, and numerous other language promotion agencies for major and minority languages all have a role to play, though sometimes they contradict each other. Note the absence of a charismatic leader.

Tunisia

Tunisian linguistic history has developed over three millennia; the oldest language spoken by the indigenous people was designated *Berber* (barbarous) by the Romans. With the arrival of the Phoenicians from Tyre (Lebanon) and the eventual founding of the Carthaginian Empire (814–146 BCE), Libyc-Punic bilingualism began to develop evolving into Libyc-Latin during the Roman domination of the area (146 BCE–349 CE). (Punic survived for 600 years after the destruction of Carthage.)

The Vandals dominated from 438 to 533 CE followed by the Byzantine Empire (533–647 CE) which revived Roman culture and thus permitted Greek to take hold. Arabic was introduced in 647 CE, and Arabic-speaking Muslims took about 50 years to gain control of the area. Linguistically, the region became multilingual with substrates of Berber, Greek, Latin and Punic still preserved in the dialectal vocabulary and in place names throughout contemporary Tunisia. To complicate the situation further, Arabic-Berber bilingualism developed in the period 1050–1052, partly resulting from the near total conversion of the Berbers to Islam. At present Berber is considered a dying language, spoken by less than 0.5% of the population. From the 11th century, Arabic became the dominant, and eventually the official, language of Tunisia. In the period from the 11th to the 14th centuries, Spain reclaimed its territory from the Arab-Berber Moors. For the three ensuing centuries, Christians (i.e., Spanish) and Muslims (i.e., Turks) competed for control of the Mediterranean basin. In the 19th century yet another linguistic conflict developed, this time between French and Italian, with significant interference from Arabic and Maltese. Intense trade competition across the basin with Tunis as the southern hub helped to consolidate a pidgin called *Lingua Franca*, in development since the 14th century. French became embedded in Tunisia when France took advantage of a protectorate in 1881 and turned it into a colonial structure that endured until 1956 when Tunisia gained its independence. French has (after 50 years of independence) unquestionably importantly influenced Tunisian Arabic, particularly in its written mode. Thus, the current situation in Tunisia may be described as diglossic and bilingual:

- diglossic in the uses of various forms of Arabic along a written/spoken continuum ([HIGH/WRITTEN] classical Arabic/Literary Arabic/Modern Standard Arabic/Educated Arabic/Tunisian Arabic [LOW/SPOKEN]);
- bilingual in the uses of French (Metropolitan French/North African. French/Other European languages [i.e., English]). French and Arabic are commonly mixed, ranging from simply code switching to extensive code mixing.

When Arab Muslims first came to the North Africa in the 7th century, they established the *Zaituna Mosque* in Tunis; it constituted the first university in the Muslim world, offering Qur'anic studies, Islamic law, reading and writing of classical Arabic and some science. The *Zaituna Mosque* supported the development of a statewide network of *kuttab* – classes held in mosques – designed to teach young boys the *Qur'an* as well as basic literacy skills in Arabic. This system has persisted into the present. On the other hand, secular bilingual education dates from 1875, the founding of *al-Madrassa al-Sadiqiyya*, an Arabic-French bilingual school providing a European (i.e., 'modern') curriculum to the children of the social élite. A system of French-medium schools was established during the colonial period (1881–1956), implanting the French curriculum surviving into the 1970s. Following independence, educational reform began with the Educational Reform Law of 1958, laying out a ten-year plan intended to:

- unify the several school systems (*kattab*, French, bilingual schools) into a bilingual system administered and controlled by the Ministry of Education;
- establish a new organisational structure – 6-year primary cycle, 6-year secondary cycle (like the French baccalaureate), and a 3- to 5-year university cycle;
- nationalise the curriculum and restore the primacy of Arabic as the medium of instruction;
- establish education as public and free at all levels, and
- increase enrolment at all areas, especially of girls and in rural areas.

Further reform of primary and secondary education occurred in the period from 1987 to 1997 under the influence of the World Bank and the European Union intended to correct the problems in the system stemming from the irrelevancy of the curriculum, the inadequacy of the learning materials, poor teacher preparation and questionable assessment tools collectively resulting in high drop-out rates and dubious literacy skills. Arabisation of all language use has continued unbroken since independence, but increasingly after the National Pact 1988 (which stressed the national character of Arabic), and even more so after the 1999 Prime Minister's circular (which, in eight specific regulations, banned any foreign language in all correspondence addressed to Tunisians and in all internal documents of the government, and established deadlines – by December 2000 – for the Arabisation of all software and all administrative forms – and by December 2001 – for work on dictionaries to provide Arabic lexicon in all areas of knowledge). Only three of the specific requirements were reiterated in a follow-up circular from the Prime Minister's office in November 2000. Many people felt that the deadlines were unrealistic, and indeed the dictionary work has fallen far behind the timetable. Additionally, no training programme was implemented to prepare people to use the new lexicon. It seems unrealistic to assume that the only thing necessary to Arabise academic disciplines is an appropriate lexicon. The French government did not take a favourable view of Arabisation and the consequent threat to French, nor did it react well to the closing down of the TV channel *France 2* nor to the closing down of several French newspapers and magazines; tension developed in relations between Tunisia and France. The French government devotes vast resources as well as economic pressure to the promotion of French while US and British promotion of English pales by comparison.

While Arabic/French rivalry continues, English has begun to spread – in education, business, and those areas where Arabic is not likely to spread in the foreseeable future.

Thus, Berber is unlikely to survive. Despite enormous efforts at Arabisation, the rivalry between Arabic and French continues; it is, perhaps, unrealistic to predict the successful development of lexicon, texts, academic materials, and teaching skills to support Arabisation across all areas of knowledge. An increasing rivalry between French and English is developing. Other foreign languages are perceived to have a role to play in Tunisia in the context of globalisation.

Conclusions

Of these four African polities, three use French – Algeria, Côte d'Ivoire and Tunisia; two are located in the Maghreb, and all are linguistically highly diverse. Algeria and Tunisia have declared Arabic to be their national languages, while Côte d'Ivoire has opted for French. Nigeria has used English as the *de jure* national official language, but in light of the fact that it is surrounded by French-speaking polities it has considered adding French, especially because of the Cameroonian sectors with which it shares borders (see, e.g., Kouega, 2007). All four polities have avoided promoting the use of African languages. To varying degrees, all four polities have been influenced by the global spread of English, particularly in such areas as science and technology. Tunisia in particular has struggled with the need to develop the capacity of indigenous languages (i.e., Arabic) to open access to science and technology; although Arabic has been designated the only language through which education may be disseminated, to some significant extent French is being used to teach a variety of technical subjects.

In Algeria, the influence of one popular charismatic individual is clearly a significant factor; in the other polities, where the initial élitist educational system, the desire of the administrators to keep the number of literate locals to a minimum and the selective system of education in place since independence, have created the communication crisis by producing graduates whose talents do not fit the economic and social needs of the country and at the same time by disempowering women, farmers, labourers and other relevant sectors of the population who constitute the workers who produced the polity's goods and services. Somewhat traditional arguments against language planning have been advanced: i.e., in such complex linguistic situations, the selection of any African language as the official national language would trigger tribal warfare. Thus, the complex language situation cannot lend itself to the development of a workable language (or language-in-education) plan. The only hope for peace and national unity, and the only way to provide access to science and technology (i.e., to modernisation) lies in maintaining French as the sole official language. In some cases, the Constitution (or other seminal document) specifies that all (or some) indigenous languages are equal to the Official (foreign) language, in fact, despite the rhetoric, it is very clear that indigenous languages do not share such status with the official language. It is equally clear that, in this group of polities, serious language planning has not occurred, despite the fact that government has, at least to some extent, mustered the will to focus on the chaotic situation. In short, the language situation remains complex, governments remain paralysed and unable to act, and 'popular' and new varieties (e.g., Nouchi) emerge and spread, producing unplanned language planning and a set of unexpected developments at variance from the official language plan (whatever it may be).

Note

1. The studies in this volume were previously published as follows: Benrabah, M. (2005) Language planning in Algeria. *Current Issues in Language Planning* 6 (4), 379–502; Djité, P.G. (2000) Language planning in Côte d'Ivoire. *Current Issues in Language Planning* 1 (1), 11–50; Adegbija, E. (2004) Language policy and planning in Nigeria. *Current Issues in Language Planning* 5 (3), 181–246; Daoud, M. (2001) The language planning situation in Tunisia. *Current Issues in Language Planning* 2 (1), 1–52.

References

Abu-Haidar, F. (2000) Arabisation in Algeria. *International Journal of Francophone Studies* 3 (3), 151–163.

Benrabah, M. (2004) La question linguistique [The language Issue]. In Y. Belaskri and C. Chaulet-Achour (eds) *L'Epreuve d'une décennie 1992–2002. Algérie arts et culture* (pp. 83–108). Paris: Editions Paris-Méditerranée.

Breton, R. J.-L. (2003) Sub-Saharan Africa. In J. Maurais and M. A. Morris (eds) *Languages in a Globalising World* (pp. 203–16). Cambridge: Cambridge University Press.

Cherrad-Benchefra, Y. and Derradji, Y. (2004) La politique linguistique en Algérie [Language Policy in Algeria]. *Revue d'aménagement linguistique* 107, 145–170.

Djité, P.G. (1992) The Arabization of Algeria: Linguistic and sociopolitical motivations. *International Journal of the Sociology of Language* 98, 15–28.

El Watan (1999a) 22 May. On www at http://www.elwatan.com

El Watan (1999b) 3 August, 3.

El Watan (2000) 1 March, 23.

Guardian Weekly (2004) Landslide poll win for Algerian president. 15–21 April, 12.

Gordon, D.C. (1966) *The Passing of French Algeria*. London: Oxford University Press.

Gordon, D.C. (1978) *The French Language and National Identity*. The Hague: Mouton.

Grandguillaume, G. (2004) L'Arabisation au Maghreb [Arabisation in the Maghreb]. *Revue d'Aménagement Linguistique* 107, 15–39.

Kaplan, R. B. and Baldauf, R. B., Jr. (1997) *Language Planning from Practice to Theory*. Clevedon: Multilingual Matters.
Kaplan, R. B., Baldauf, R. B., Jr., Liddicoat, A. J., Bryant, P., Barbaux, M.-T. and Pütz, M. (2000) Current Issues in language planning. *Current Issues in Language Planning* 1, 135–144.
Kouega, J. P. (2007) Language planning in the Cameroon. *Current Issues in Language Planning* 8 (1), 3–94.
Le Matin (1999) 22 May. On www at http://www.lematin-dz.com
Marley, D. (2000) Language policy in Morocco. *International Journal of Francophone Studies* 3 (2), 68–88.
Omoniyi, T. (2003) Language ideology and politics: A critical appraisal of French as a second official foreign language in Nigeria. *AILA Review* 16, 13–25.
Paris Match (1999) N° 2624, 9 September, 28–35.
Sahli, K. (2002) Critical imperatives of the French language in the francophone world: Colonial legacy and post-colonial policy at odds. *Current Issues in Language Planning* 3 (3), 317–345.
Sirles, C. A. (1999) Politics and Arabization: The evolution of the postindependence North Africa. *International Journal of the Sociology of Language* 137, 115–129.
Tabory, E. and Tabory, M. (1987) Berber unrest in Algeria: Lessons for language policy. *International Journal of the Sociology of Language* 63, 63–79.
The Economist (2004) Freer and more peaceful: An Arab state slouches towards democracy. *The Economist*, 17–23 April, 40–41.
Wright, S. (2006) French as a lingua franca. In M. McGroarty *et al.* (eds) *Annual Review of Applied Linguistics*, 26 (pp. 35–60). Cambridge: Cambridge University Press.

Further Reading

Algeria

Al-Kahtany, A. H. (2004) Retrieving the irretrievable: Indigenous literacies and post-colonial impact. *Geolinguistics* 30, 15–31.
Bensalem, S. (1999) Algerie: retrouvailles en français [Algeria: Together again with French]. *Français dans le Monde* 307 (Nov-Dec), 10–11.
Judy, R. A. T. (1997) On the politics of global language, or unfungible local value. *Boundary 2-An International Journal of Literature & Culture* 24 (2), 101–143.
Ouabbou, N. (1998) [Integrismo islamico o el sable contra la palabra] Islamic integration or the war against the word. *Kanina* 22(2), 143–151.
Pantucek, S. (1993) Prozess der Arabisierung in Algerien [The process of Arabization in Algeria]. *Archiv Orientalni* 61 (4), 347–362.
Sarter, H. and Sefta, K. (1992) La Glottopolitique algerienne: Faits et discourse [Algerian glottopolitics: Actions and speech]. *Franzosisch Heute* 23(2), 107–117.
Tigziri, N. (2004) Les langues dans les constitutions algeriennes [Languages in the Algerian constitutions]. *Cahiers de l' ILSL* 17, 289–299
Zouaghi Keime, M. A. (1991) Bilinguisme et enseignement du français [Bilingualism and the teaching of French]. *Français dans le Monde* supplement 18(Apr), 41–44.

Côte d'Ivoire

Adopo, F. (1996) Le Projet-Nord aujourd'hui et demain [The Northern Project today and tomorrow]. *Travaux neuchatelois de linguistique (TRANEL)* 26 (Apr), 103–115.
Adopo, F., Caummaueth, R., Ehivet, S. and Tera, K. (1986) Langue d'enseignement, langue officielle et langue vernaculaire dans les systemes educatifs: le cas de la Côte d'Ivoire [Language of instruction, official language, and vernacular language in educational systems: The case of the Ivory Coast]. *Cahiers Ivoiriens de Recherche Linguistique (CIRL)* 19 (Apr), 69–95.
Boone, D., Lamine, S. and Augustin, M.-A. (1998–1999) L'Utilisation du français et de l'adioukrou par les aizi [French and Adioukrou language use by the Aizi people]. *The Journal of West African Languages* 27 (2), 103–115.

Chumbow, B. S. and Bobda, A. S. (2000) French in West Africa: A sociolinguistic perspective. *International Journal of the Sociology of Language* 141, 39–60.

Djamou, B. M. (2006) Living on borrowed languages: College students' perceptions of French as a national language in Côte d'Ivoire. PhD dissertation, Pennsylvania State University. *Dissertation Abstracts International, A: The Humanities and Social Sciences* 66, 8, Feb, 2811-A

Djité, P. G. (1988) Correcting errors in language classification: Monolingual nuclei and multilingual satellites. *Language Problems & Language Planning* 12 (1), 1–13.

Djité, P. G. (1989) French in the Ivory Coast. *French Review* 62 (3), 494–504.

Djité, P. G. (1993) Language and development in Africa. *International Journal of the Sociology of Language* 100–101, 149–166.

Duponchel, L. (1976) L'Enseignement des langues etrangeres vivantes en Côte-d'Ivoire: situation et perspectives [Teaching modern foreign languages in the Ivory Coast: Situation and perspectives]. *West African Journal of Modern Languages* 1 (Jan), 89–92.

Halaoui, N. (1991) De l'organisation nationale de la terminologie [Concerning a national organization for terminology development]. *Terminologies Nouvelles* 6 (Dec), 60–67.

Hebrard, J. (1996) Scolarisation et culture de l'ecrit: le cas de la Côte-d'Ivoire [Schooling and the written culture: The case of Ivory Coast]. *Diagonales* 40 (Nov), 29–30.

Kodjo, C. (1987) Le Champ d'utilisation du français en Afrique: le cas de la Côte d'Ivoire [The domain of usage of French in Africa: The case of the Ivory Coast]. *Cahiers Ivoiriens de Recherche Linguistique (CIRL)* 22 (Oct), 127–137.

Kwofie, E. N. (1978) La Langue française en Afrique occidentale: son emploi, son acquisition et les attitudes des sujets parlants en pays francophones [The French language in West Africa: Its use, learning, and informant reactions in francophone countries]. *West African Journal of Modern Languages* 3 (June), 38–47.

Tchagbale, Z. (1986) Maitriser le français pour maitriser la science [Mastering French to master science]. *Cahiers Ivoiriens de Recherche Linguistique (CIRL)* 20(Oct), 103–118.

Tchagbale, Z. (1995) Plaidoyer pour l'emploi des langues nationals [An appeal for the use of national languages]. *Diagonales* 35 (Aug), 39–42.

Turcotte, D. (1979) La Planification linguistique en Côte d'Ivoire: faire du français le vehiculaire national par excellence [Linguistic planning in the Ivory Coast: making French a national means of communication par excellence]. *Revue canadienne des etudes africaines/Canadian Journal of African Studies* 13 (3), 423–439.

Nigeria

Aaron, M. (1998) A way to improve literacy in primary education in Nigeria. *Notes on Literacy* 24 (2), 1–57.

Adamo, G. E. (2005) Globalization, terrorism, and the English language in Nigeria. *English Today* 21 (4(84)), 21–26.

Adegbija, E. (1994) The candidature of Nigerian Pidgin as a national language: Some initial hurdles. *ITL: Review of Applied Linguistics* 105–106 (Sept), 1–23.

Adegbija, E. (1994) Survival strategies of minority languages: A case study of Oko (Ogori) in Nigeria. *ITL: Review of Applied Linguistics* 103–104, 19–38.

Adegbija, E. (1995) Marketing new lexical terminology in Nigeria: Some practical considerations. In M. Pütz (ed.) *Discrimination Through Language in Africa? Perspectives on the Nambian Experience* (pp. 101–122). Berlin: Mouton de Gruyter.

Adegbija, E. (2001) Language and attitude change in sub-Saharan Africa: An overview. *ITL, Review of Applied Linguistics* 133–134 (May), 271–301.

Adegbite, W. (2000) Sequential bilingualism and the teaching of language skills to early primary school pupils in Nigeria. *Glottodidactica* 28, 5–17.

Adegbite, W. (2003) Enlightenment and attitudes of the Nigerian elite on the roles of languages in Nigeria. *Language, Culture and Curriculum* 16 (2), 185–196.

Adekunle, M. (1997) English in Nigeria: Attitudes, policy and communicative realities. In A. Bamgbose, A. Banjo and A. Thomas (eds) *New Englishes: A West African Perspective* (pp. 57–86). Trenton, NJ: Africa World Press.

Adekunle, M. A. (1978) Language choice and the Nigerian linguistic repertoire. *West African Journal of Modern Languages* 3 (June), 114–127.

Adeniran, A. (1979) Personalities and policies in the establishment of English in Northern Nigeria (1900–1943). *International Journal of the Sociology of Language* 22, 57–77.

Adeyanju, T. K. (1983) Language needs of Nigerian post-primary students. *T.E.S.L. Talk* 14 (3), 3–14.

Afolayan, A. (1984) The English language in Nigerian education as an agent of proper multilingual and multicultural development. *Journal of Multilingual and Multicultural Development* 5 (1), 1–22.

Akere, F. (1981) Sociolinguistic consequences of language contact: English vs Nigerian languages. *Language Sciences* 3, 283–304.

Akere, F. (1997) Languages in the curriculum: An assessment of the role of English and other languages in the education delivery process in Nigeria. In A. Bamgbose, A. Banjo and A. Thomas (eds) *New Englishes: A West African Perspective* (pp. 178–199). Trenton, NJ: Africa World Press.

Akinnaso, F. N. (1989) One nation, four hundred languages: Unity and diversity in Nigeria's language policy. *Language Problems & Language Planning* 13 (2), 133–146.

Akinnaso, F. N. (1990) The politics of language planning in education in Nigeria. *Word-Journal of the International Linguistic Association* 41 (3), 337–367.

Akinnaso, F. N. (1993) Policy and experiment in mother tongue literacy in Nigeria. *International Review of Education/Internationale Zeitschrift fur Erziehungswissenschaft/ Revue Internationale de pedagogie* 39 (4), 255–285.

Akinnaso, F. N. (1994) Linguistic unification and language rights. *Applied Linguistics* 15 (2), 139–168.

Akinnaso, F. N. (1996) Vernacular literacy in modern Nigeria. *International Journal of the Sociology of Language* 119, 43–68.

Akinnaso, F. N. and Ogunbiyi, I. A. (1990) The place of Arabic in language education and language planning in Nigeria. *Language Problems & Language Planning* 14 (1), 1–19.

Allan, K. (1978) Nation, tribalism and national language: Nigeria's case. *Cahiers d'Etudes Africaines* 18 (3(71)), 397–415.

Amani, L. (1991) Terminologie et langues nationales au Niger. [Terminology and national languages in Nigeria] *Terminologies Nouvelles* 6 (Dec), 72–77.

Annamalai, E. (1992) The National language question in Nigeria: A place for Pidgin? *New Language Planning Newsletter* 7(1), 1–4.

Anyaehie, E. O. (1994) Language status and translation studies: A Nigerian perspective. In C. Dollerup and A. Lindegaard (eds) *Teaching Translation and Interpreting, II: Insights, Aims, Visions* (pp. 19–24). Amsterdam: Benjamins.

Arasanyin, O. F. (1998) Surplus agenda, deficit culture: Language and the class-divide in Nigeria. *Journal of West African Languages* 27 (2), 81–101.

Attah, M. O. (1987) The national language problem in Nigeria. *Revue canadienne des etudes africaines/Canadian Journal of African Studies* 21 (3), 393–401.

Awoniyi, T. A. (1975) Problems related to curriculum development and teaching the mother tongues in Nigeria: A historical survey 1800–1974. *Audio Visual Language Journal* 13 (1), 31–41.

Awonusi, V. O. (1985) Issues in language planning: An examination of the continued role of English as Nigeria's lingua franca. *Sociolinguistics* 15 (1), 25–30.

Awonusi, V. O. (1990) Whose standard, which model? Towards the definition of a standard Nigerian spoken English for teaching, learning and testing in Nigerian schools. *ITL: Review of Applied Linguistics* 89–90 (Sept), 91–106.

Babalola, E. T. (2002) The development and preservation of Nigerian languages and cultures: The role of the local government. *Studia Anglica Posnaniensia* 37, 161–171.

Bamgbose, A. (1984) Mother-tongue medium and scholastic attainment in Nigeria. *Prospects* 14 (1), 87–93.

Bamiro, E. O. (1988) What is Nigerian English? *ICU Language Research Bulletin* 3 (1), 65–80.

Banjo, A. (1976) The university and the standardization of the English language in Nigeria. *West African Journal of Modern Languages* 1 (Jan), 93–98.

Bowers, R. (1997) You can never plan the future by the past: Where do we go with English? In A. Bamgbose, A. Banjo and A. Thomas (eds) *New Englishes: A West African Perspective* (pp. 87–96). Trenton, NJ: Africa World Press.

Brann, C. M. B. (1979) Multilingualism in Nigerian education. In W. Mackey and J. Ornstein (eds) *Sociolinguistic Studies in Language Contact*. The Hague: Mouton.

Brann, C. M. B. (1979) A typology of language education in Nigeria. In W. McCormack and S. Wurm (eds) *Language and Society: Anthropological Issues*. The Hague: Mouton.

Brann, C. M. B. (1985) Language policy, planning and management in Nigeria: A bird's eye view. *Sociolinguistics* 15 (1), 30–32.

Brann, C. M. B. (1986) Triglossia in Nigerian education. *NABE Journal* 10 (2), 169–178.

Brann, C. M. B. (1991) National language policy and planning: France 1789, Nigeria 1989. *History of European Ideas* 13(1–2), 97–120.

Brann, C. M. B. (1993) Democratisation of language use in public domains in Nigeria. *Journal of Modern African Studies* 31(4), 639–656.

Brann, C. M. B. (1997) Language choice in the Nigerian State Houses of Assembly. *Afrika und Ubersee: Sprachen-Kulturen* 80 (2), 255–278.

Capo, H. C. (1982) The codification of Nigerian languages. *Jolan* 1, 129–139.

Dada, A. and Ogunyemi, O. (1988) Education at the crossroads: Bilingualism in Nigerian elementary classrooms. *Working Papers in Educational Linguistics* 4 (2), 93–103.

Ejieh, M. U. C. (2004) Attitudes of student teachers towards teaching in mother tongue in Nigerian primary schools: Implications for planning. *Language, Culture and Curriculum* 17 (1), 73–81.

Elugbe, B. (1997) Nigerian Pidgin: Problems and prospects. In A. Bamgbose, A. Banjo and A. Thomas (eds) *New Englishes: A West African Perspective* (pp. 284–299). Trenton, NJ: Africa World Press.

Emenanjo, E. N. (1985) Nigerian language policy: Perspective and prospective. *Jolan: Journal of the Linguistic Association of Nigeria* 3, 123–134.

Emenyonu, E. N. (1983) National language policy in Nigeria: Implications for English teaching. In M. A. Clarke and J. Handscombe (eds) *On TESOL '82: Pacific Perspectives on Language Learning and Teaching* (pp. 25–33). Washington, DC: Teachers of English to Speakers of Other Languages.

Emordi, F. I. (1990) La Situation linguistique actuelle au Nigeria: la place et le statut de la langue française. [The current linguistic situation in Nigeria: The place and status of the French language] *Cahiers de l'Institut de Linguistique de Louvain* 16 (2–4), 59–76.

Ezeani, E. O. (2002) Learning the sciences in the Igbo language. *Journal of West African Languages* 29 (2), 3–9.

Fagborun, J. G. (1994) *The Yoruba Koine-Its History and Linguistic Innovations*. Munich: Federal Republic Germany: Lincom Europa.

Fakuade, G. (1992) Guosa: An unknown linguistic code in Nigeria. *Language Problems & Language Planning* 16(3), 260–263.

Fakuade, G. (1994) Lingua franca from African sources in Nigeria: The journey so far. *Language Problems & Language Planning* 18(1), 38–46.

Fasold, R. W., Carr Hill, R. A., Gerbault, J. and Ndukwe, P. (1997) Motivations and attitudes influencing vernacular literacy: Four African assessments. In A. Tabouret Keller, R. B. Le Page, P. Gardner Chloros and G. Varro (eds) *Vernacular Literacy: A Re-Evaluation* (pp. 246–270). New York: Oxford University Press.

Glick, C. and Hige-Glick, M. (1999) English and the development of language policies in India and Nigeria. *Language & Culture* 35, 61–80.

Goke-Pariola, B. (1987) Language transfer and the Nigerian writer of English. *World Englishes* 6 (2), 127–136.

Harnischfeger, J. (1998) Sprachpolitik und 'Nation Building' in Nigeria [Language policy and 'nation building' in Nigeria]. *Afrikanistische Arbeitspapiere* 56 (Dec), 61–109.

Haruna, A. (2003) An endangered language: The Gurdu(eng) language of the Southern Bauchi Area, Nigeria. In M. Janse and S. Tol (eds) *Language Death and Language Maintenance: Theoretical, Practical and Descriptive Approaches* (pp. 189–213). Amsterdam: John Benjamins.

Herms, I. (1975) Zur Rolle der nigerianischen Sprachen bei nationalen Prozessen in Nigeria [The role of Nigerian languages in the national processes in Nigeria]. *Zeitschrift fur Phonetik, Sprachwissenschaft und Kommunikationsforschung* 28, 349–354.

Ibekwe, J. O. (2006) Educational language policy in Nigeria: A critical analysis. PhD dissertation, University of Connecticut. *Dissertation Abstracts International, A: The Humanities and Social Sciences* 66, 11, May, 3929

Ikwue, I. O. (1984) Effective educational language planning in Nigeria. *International Education Journal* 1 (1), 39–60.

Isong Uyo, N. J. (1998) A paradigm / model for rhetorical communication and language planning in the state development: Annag and Ibibio perceptions of bidialectalism in Akwa Ibom State, Nigeria. *Dissertation Abstracts International, A: The Humanities and Social Sciences* 58 (8), 2904–2905.

Jibril, M. (1987) Language in Nigerian education. *Indian Journal of Applied Linguistics* 13(1), 37–51.

Jowitt, D. (1997) Nigeria's national language question: Choices and constraints. In A. Bamgbose, A. Banjo and A. Thomas (eds) *New Englishes: A West African Perspective* (pp. 34–56). Trenton, NJ: Africa World Press.

Kwa, S. N. (1999) Le Français, deuxieme langue officielle [French, second official language]. *Français dans le Monde* 307 (Nov-Dec), 15.

Mann, C. (1990) Choosing an indigenous official language for Nigeria: Perspectives and procedures. *Work in Progress* 23, 118–139.

Mann, C. C. (1993) The sociolinguistic status of Anglo-Nigerian Pidgin: An overview. *International Journal of the Sociology of Language* 167–178.

Mann, C. C. (2000) Reviewing ethnolinguistic vitality: The case of Anglo-Nigerian Pidgin. *Journal of Sociolinguistics* 4 (3), 458–474.

Mgbo Elue, C. N. (1987) Social psychological and linguistic impediments to the acquisition of a second Nigerian language among Yoruba and Ibo. *Journal of Language and Social Psychology* 6 (3–4), 309–317.

Mohammed, A. (1976) The search for a lingua franca and standards in Nigerian education. In A. G. S. Momodu and U. Schild (eds) *Nigerian Writing: Nigeria as Seen by Her Own Writers as Well as by German Authors* (pp. 153–166). Tubingen: Erdmann.

Ndolo, I. (1988) Radio broadcasting and the language problems of sociopolitical integration in Nigeria. *Dissertation Abstracts International, A: The Humanities and Social Sciences* 49 (3), 371-A–372-A.

Ndolo, I. S. (1989) The case for promoting the Nigerian pidgin language. *Journal of Modern African Studies* 27 (4), 679–684.

Ndukwe, P. (1982) Standardizing Nigerian languages. *Jolan* 1, 141–146.

Obanya, P. (1975) French language teaching curriculum research and development in Nigeria. *Audio Visual Language Journal* 13 (2), 111–115.

Okedara, J. T. and Okedara, C. A. (1992) Mother-tongue literacy in Nigeria. *Annals of the American Academy of Political and Social Science* 520 (Mar), 91–102.

Okoh, N. (1979) Survey of the language situation in Nigeria. *Polyglot* 1(fiche 2), B1-B22.

Okonkwo, J. I. (1994) Nationalism and nationism: The sociolinguistic cross-roads of the Nigerian national language policy. *Afrikanistische Arbeitspapiere* 40 (Dec), 115–130.

Oladejo, J. A. (1990) The teacher factor in the implementation of language policy in the developing English world: The case of Nigeria. *Journal of English and Foreign Languages* 5(June), 11–25.

Oladejo, J. A. (1993) How not to embark on a bilingual education policy in a developing nation: The case of Nigeria. *Journal of Multilingual and Multicultural Development* 14 (1–2), 91–102.

Olagoke, D. O. (1982) Choosing a national language for Nigeria. *Jolan: Journal of the Linguistic Association of Nigeria* 1, 197–206.

Omodiaogbe, S. A. (1997) A crisis of policy, poverty and pedagogy. *English Today* 13(4), 36–39.

Omojuwa, R. A. (1978) The primary education improvement project (Nigeria). *International Review of Education/Internationale Zeitschrift Fuer Erziehungswissenschaft/Revue Internationale de Pedagogie* 24(3), 365–370.

Omoniyi, T. (1994) English and the other tongues in official communicative interaction in Nigeria. *ITL: Review of Applied Linguistics* 103–104 (Apr), 57–75.

Omoniyi, T. (2003) Language ideology and politics: A critical appraisal of French as second official language in Nigeria. *AILA Review* 16, 13–25.

Omoniyi, T. (2003) Local policies and global forces: Multiliteracy and Africa's indigenous languages. *Language Policy* 2 (2), 133–152.

Osa, O. (1986) English in Nigeria: 1914–1985. *English Journal* 75 (3), 38–40.

Osisanwo, W. (1985) Language skills and the designing of learning objectives: The example of English language in Nigeria. *Journal of Teacher Education* 1 (1), 225–238.

Oumarou, I. A. (1996) Linguistique et alphabetization [Linguistics and literacy]. *Bulletin de l'Institut de Linguistique et des Sciences du Langage de l'Universite de Lausanne* 16–17, 77–97.

Oyewole, A. (1977) Toward a language policy for Nigeria. *Odu* 15, 74–90.

Paden, J. (1968) Language problems of national integration in Nigeria: The special position of Hausa. In J. A. Fishman, C. A. Ferguson and J. Das Gupta (eds) *Language Problems of Developing Nations*. New York: Wiley.

Parry, K. (1992) English in Nigeria. *Geolinguistics* 18, 49–65.

Rufai, A. (1977) The question of a national language in Nigeria: Problems and prospects. In P. F. Kotey, A. and H. Der-Houssikian (eds) *Language and Linguistic Problems in Africa: Proceedings of the VII Conference on African Linguistics* (pp. 68–83). Columbia, SC: Hornbeam.

Salami, L. O. (2004) 'Other tongue' policy and ethnic nationalism in Nigeria. *Language Policy* 3 (3), 271–287.

Salami, S. A. (1996) Strategies for the development of standard orthographies of Nigerian languages. *Research in Yoruba Language and Literature* 5, 33–42.

Simire, G. O. (2003) Developing and promoting multilingualism in public life and society in Nigeria. *Language, Culture and Curriculum* 16 (2), 231–243.

Ubahakwe, E. (1980) The dilemma in teaching English in Nigeria as a language of international communication. *English Language* 34, 156–163.

Ure, J. (1976) Mother tongue and other tongue: Bridges and transitions. *West African Journal of Modern Languages/Revue Ouest-Africaine des Langues Vivantes* 1, 79–88.

Zima, P. (1968) Hausa in West Africa: Remarks on contemporary role and function. In J. A. Fishman, C. A. Ferguson and J. Das Gupta (eds) *Language Problems of Developing Nations*). New York: Wiley.

Tunisia

Abdesslem, H. (1996) Communication strategies or discourse strategies in foreign language performance? *IRAL* 34 (1), 49–61.

Battenburg, J. (1997) A Fulbrighter's experience with English language teaching in Tunisia: The land of mosaics. *CATESOL Journal* 10 (1), 113–119.

Dhaouadi, M. (1996) Un essai de théorisation sur le penchant vers l'accent parisien chez la femme tunisienne [A theoretical essay on the tendency to use a Parisian accent in Tunisian women's homes]. *International Journal of the Sociology of Language* 122, 107–125.

Fitouri, C. (1984) Bilinguisme et education en Tunisie [Bilingualism and education in Tunisia]. *Franzosisch Heute* 15 (2), 111–117.

Ghrib, E. M. (1983) The introduction of Arabic as a medium of instruction in the

Tunisian educational system. *Al-'Arabiyya: Journal of the American Association of Teachers of Arabic* 16 (1–2), 109–130.

Hawkins, S. (2004) Globalization vs. civilization: The ideologies of foreign language learning in Tunisia. PhD dissertation, University of Chicago. *Dissertation Abstracts International, A: The Humanities and Social Sciences* 64, 7, Jan, 2539-A–2540-A

Payne, R. M. (1983) *Language in Tunisia.* Tunis: Bourguiba Institute of Modern Languages.

Sirles, C. A. (1999) Politics and Arabization: The evolution of postindependence North Africa. *International Journal of the Sociology of Language* 137, 115–129.

Stevens, P. B. (1983) Ambivalence, modernisation and language attitudes: French and Arabic in Tunisia. *Journal of Multilingual and Multicultural Development* 4 (2–3), 101–114.

Zouaghi Keime, M. A. (1991) Bilinguisme et enseignement du français [Bilingualism and the teaching of French]. *Français dans le Monde* supplement 18 (Apr), 41–44.

The Language Planning Situation in Algeria

Mohamed Benrabah
UFR d'Etudes Anglophones, Université Stendhal Grenoble III, Grenoble, France

This monograph describes the language planning situation in Algeria. It uses a historical perspective to understand the processes involved in language change, language policies and language-in-education practices of the polity. The monograph is divided into six parts. The first one presents a background on the country and the people to show its geographical and ethnic diversity on which linguistic plurality is grounded. The second part deals with the evolution of the economic situation – from centralised economic nationalism to market economy – and its repercussion on the issues mentioned above. The third part examines the language profile of Algeria and the diachronic evolution that led to it. Language policy and planning, described in the fourth part, considers, first, the unilingual demand of the nationalist period (in favour of Arabisation), then, the new language policy which promotes multilingualism within a democratising structure. The fifth part examines planned language spread and use via language-in-education, the milieu and the media in its first section, and unplanned developments in its second section. The final part of the monograph focuses on future prospects against the background of past practices and Algeria's new language policy. It argues that Arabisation led to crises and that recent policy decisions may produce changes that are more in tune with the country's linguistic situation.

Keywords: Algeria, Arabic, Arabisation, bilingualism, diglossia, French, multilingualism, Tamazight

Introduction

Algeria makes an interesting object for study on language policy and language planning (LPLP) thanks to its almost unique history in the Arabic-speaking world: it is the only country which lived under French assimilationist colonial rule for 132 years.[1] Less than four years after Algeria's independence, Gordon (1966: 246) wrote: 'Algeria's future will remain a fascinating case-study for Orientalists and for those interested in "development" and "modernization"'. The language issue during both the pre-independence and post-independence eras further marks this uniqueness within Africa and the Maghreb, as Djité (1992: 16) has pointed out: 'Nowhere else in Africa has the language issue been so central in the fight against colonialism [as in Algeria].' As Berger (2002: 8) puts it, the language issue represents 'the most severe problem of Algeria in its present and troubled state.'

After the three countries of the Maghreb got their independence – Morocco on 2 March 1956, Tunisia on 20 March 1956, and Algeria on 5 July 1962 – it was the Algerian leadership that showed ideological intransigence in recovering both language and identity. Algeria has come out as 'the most vociferous in proclaiming its Arab Muslim identity' (Gordon, 1978: 151). The language planning activities, more systematic and assertive in Algeria than in the other two Maghrebi countries,[2] have been carried out with some kind of 'revolutionary zeal' (Sirles, 1999: 122–3). A number of observers have seen in this fervour a major cause of the rise of Islamic fundamentalism in Algeria (Abu-Haidar, 2000: 161; Grandguillaume, 2004a: 33–4) and of the civil war ravaging the country since the early 1990s (Miliani, 2000: 16; Thomas, 1999: 32). Like many other cases around the world, the language situation in Algeria is quite complex and lessons could be learnt from it. In 1987, Ephraim and Mala Tabory presented Algeria's interest for LPLP as follows:

> [t]he Algerian situation is complex, as it is at a crossroad of tensions between French, the colonial language, and Arabic, the new national language; Classical Arabic versus colloquial Algerian Arabic; and the various Berber dialects versus Arabic. The lessons from the Algerian situation may be usefully applied to analogous situations by states planning their linguistic, educational and cultural policies. (Tabory & Tabory, 1987: 64)

Until the early 2000s, Algeria made headline news because of its internal instability and civil war (Martinez, 1998). The recent developments have allowed the country to overcome this unstable state. They are gradually putting an end to the hostilities and, at the same time, almost making obsolete the language (-in-education) planning activities (Arabicisation) current since the independence of the country. It would be interesting, first, to focus on these recent developments, particularly the 2004 presidential election.

Recent developments

On 8 April 2004, Abdelaziz Bouteflika, the outgoing President of Algeria, secured re-election with a 'landslide victory' (*Guardian Weekly*, 2004: 12). Although there were reports of irregularities, foreign journalists qualified this election, which was endorsed by some foreign monitors, as a 'proper contest' (*Guardian Weekly*, 2004: 12). According to *The Economist* (2004a: 40), the poll was 'the cleanest that Algeria, or, for that matter, any Arab country, has ever seen': this makes it the 'first legitimate election' since the country got its independence from France in 1962.

Abdelaziz Bouteflika, a former diplomat, was also a member of the hardline clique that seized power three years after the end of the Algerian war of independence. In 1999, handpicked by the military – who have always held real power in Algeria since the liberation of the country – he was elected as the sole candidate after all his rivals withdrew from the poll to protest against massive fraud. For five years, his lack of legitimacy prevented him from carrying out long-awaited social and economic reforms. However, despite his weak performance, President Bouteflika was returned to power in April 2004 probably because he had somehow managed to reduce the violence that had substantially plagued Algeria since the beginning of the 1990s.

After the success of the religious fundamentalists of the Islamic Salvation Army (FIS) in the 1991 parliamentary polls, the authorities cancelled the electoral process and the FIS's response was an armed struggle against the secular state apparatus. In the ensuing decade, Algerians suffered a bloody civil war with a death toll estimated between 120,000 and 200,000 victims (Aggoun & Rivoire, 2004: 17; *Guardian Weekly*, 2004: 7). At the present time, displaced populations are estimated at between 1 and 1.5 million (Garçon, 2004: 9) and the number of people arrested and made to 'disappear' by Algerian security forces and their allies corresponds to more than 7000 (HRW, 2003: 3). Furthermore, thousands of highly skilled and qualified mainly francophone Algerians were forced into exile, with the majority settling in France (PNUD, 2002: 78; Vermeren, 2004: 320).

During his first term in office, President Bouteflika promoted national reconciliation – he brokered an amnesty programme: 'Law on Civil Harmony' – and 25,000 Islamists agreed to stop their armed struggle (*CIA, World Factbook*, 2005; *The Economist*, 2004a: 41). Since then, violence has fallen off and the outgoing presidential candidate reaped the benefit of that strategy at the poll of April 2004. Part of the electorate may well have chosen to maintain Abdelaziz Bouteflika in office for the stability he had somehow managed to bring to the country and which he promised to maintain if he were re-elected. Exhausted by a decade of indescribable violence and also probably tired of constant changes of governments and leaders – Algerians had five presidents between 1991 and 1999 – the population may have preferred president Bouteflika to continue the programme of reforms to which he had committed his country during his first term in office (Ben Yahmed, 2004: 36). According to *The Economist* (2004a: 41) 'Algeria has become a far gentler place. [. . .] The country's economic fortunes have also brightened. [. . .] [But] Mr Bouteflika has plenty of work on his hands.'

New discourse on language

Between 1999 and 2004, President Bouteflika initiated a number of reforms, but most of them could not be implemented because of his lack of legitimacy: opposition from within the power circles (conservatives) and without (Islamic Fundamentalists) prevented the initiation of major educational reforms that might undermine the official language policy implemented since the independence of the country. However, he did succeed in launching a national debate over sensitive issues which had, so far, always been considered anathema. None of his predecessors had ever done it. He, thus, dared to break a number of taboos in his numerous speeches. He raised such sensitive issues as those related to Algerian history, religious practices and the linguistic reality of the country. This new political discourse on language has to be seen in the light of the language policies implemented after 1962. For example, Algerians' experience with language-in-education planning roughly corresponds to two major periods: the first one, from 1962 to the 1970s, characterised by bilingualism in French and Standard/Literary Arabic; and the second one, from the 1970s to the present, characterised by monolingualism in Standard Arabic for the majority of the population and French-Arabic bilingualism for a small minority, mainly the children of those in power.

Soon after he was elected in April 1999, Abdelaziz Bouteflika took everyone by surprise when he suddenly started dealing with the language issue in public (Bensalem, 1999: 11). In May 1999, he declared: 'It is unthinkable . . . to spend ten years study in Arabic pure sciences when it would only take one year in English'[3] (*Le Matin*, 1999). The President thus appears to acknowledge tacitly the failure of Arabisation at least in the area of science and technology teaching and to envisage a return to bilingualism in this field. For him 'There has never been a language problem in Algeria, but simply rivalry and fights for French-trained executives' positions' (*El Watan*, 1999a). While making these comments, the new President was also constantly using French in his public speeches showing at the same time his rhetorical skills in Literary Arabic. He adopted the Moroccan leadership's fluency in both languages – as exemplified by the late king, Hasan II. He wanted to project the perfect role model of the bilingual Algerian citizen.[4]

President Bouteflika's language use in public is in complete opposition with his predecessors'. In fact, he was violating the legislation implemented on 5 July 1998, known as 'Act N° 91-05', which prohibits all official public use of languages other than Arabic.[5] Abdelaziz Bouteflika made it known that he was aware he was infringing the law. In an interview with a French magazine, he said: 'When I speak French, some people write in the press that I am in breach of the Constitution' (*Paris Match*, 1999: 35). Another first for the Algerian president: he admits publicly that 'our culture is plural'. Again, his attitude contrasts significantly with his predecessors' insistence on Algerians being solely 'Arabs and Moslems'. Bouteflika even goes as far as claiming a French contribution to Algeria's cultural heritage. In a press conference that he gave at the Crans Montana Summit in Switzerland in autumn 1999, he said: 'We attended French school and we are thus heavily influenced by Descartes' (Benrabah, 2004a: 96). What was also new was Abdelaziz Bouteflika's decision to attend the Francophonia Summit held in Beirut in October 2002 (Métaoui, 2002). So far, the Algerian authorities had rejected the whole idea of an institutionalised Francophonia, considered as potentially 'neo-colonialist' (Gordon, 1978: 172). The new president declared in the summer of 1999:

> Algeria does not belong to Francophonia but there is no reason for us to have a frozen attitude towards the French language which taught us so many things and which, at any rate, opened [for us] the window of French culture. (Cherrad-Benchefra & Derradji, 2004: 168; Morsly, 2004: 181)

The constant use of French by President Bouteflika created an uproar among those of the elite who were in favour of the hegemony of Standard Arabic (Arabisation) and the eradication of French. In the autumn of 1999, the President of the Committee for Foreign Affairs at the People's National Assembly (the Algerian Parliament) wrote privately to the newly elected president reproaching him for his use of French in public. As an answer, the Head of State made the parliamentarian's message public, and the deputy resigned from his Assembly post. Abdelaziz Bouteflika also received a letter from members of the High Council for the Arabic Language warning him against his public use of French and 'the francophone lobby in the presidency'. During a televised speech, the President reminded the authors of the message that it was not the mission of the High Council for the Arabic Language to choose the president's entourage for him (*El Watan*, 2000: 23). He even declared: 'For Algeria, I will speak French, Spanish and English, and, if necessary, Hebrew.' In August, 1999, he declared on live television:

> Let it be known that Algeria is part of the world and must adapt to it and that Arabic is the national and official language. This being said, let it be

known that an uninhibited opening up to other international languages – at least to those used in the United Nations – does not constitute perjury. In this domain, we are neither more Arab nor more intelligent than our brothers in Morocco, Tunisia, Egypt, Jordan, Syria, Lebanon, or Palestine or anywhere else. To move forward, one must break taboos. This is the price we have to pay to modernize our identity. Chauvinism and withdrawal are over. They are sterile. They are destructive. (*El Watan*, 1999b: 3)

Since the independence of the country, the various governments have tended to exacerbate the language issue to the point of making it highly politicised. The new President's discourse can first be understood as an attempt to make the language issue less emotionally charged, to diminish the intensity of disputes on linguistic issues and to adopt a more pragmatic orientation. According to Vermeren (2004: 321–2), the new government's language policies in favour of bilingualism aim at, among other things, bringing back some Algerian Francophone intellectuals who went into exile. But it could also be the sign of a new language policy and the decline of Arabisation as a result of changes in the economic and political spheres (Bouhadiba, 2004: 500; Cherrad-Benchefra & Derradji, 2004: 168; Morsly, 2004: 181; Queffélec *et al.*, 2002: 33). Furthermore, his use of French in public seems to have freed Algerians from guilt: a phenomenon described by a number of Algerian sociolinguists as the 'Bouteflika effect' (Bouhadiba, 2004: 500; Elimam, 2004: 115; Morsly, 2004: 181). As an illustration of this significant attitudinal change, here is the reflection of a well-known Algerian lawyer:

I have just made the best address to the Court of my career in the trial involving the Local Development Bank. You cannot imagine how pleased I was to see that I did not have to look for words, idiomatic expressions: I have been obliged to plead in [Classical/Standard] Arabic for thirty years. It has been a permanent clash with magistrates. As soon as I uttered three words in French: 'Maitre, use the national language!' Last week, a witness spoke with an impeccable French accent. The president wanted him to speak Arabic. I told him since the Head of State had broken this taboo, we would imitate him. He accepted my argument. (Schemla, 2000: 217)

This incident illustrates the importance of 'the role of political leaders in shaping public discussion of language issue'. (Tollefson, 2002: 424). Abdelaziz Bouteflika's acknowledgement of French as part of Algeria's language profile is part of his strategy to modernise Algerian institutions such as the educational system, described by many as a 'real failure' (Grandguillaume, 1997b: 3). It is clear that the educational reforms are meant to accompany Algeria's development and modernisation, encouraged by Bouteflika's government and the international community. The main reform concerns the return to bilingual education and the end of monolingualism. According to Baker (2002: 237):

Wherever bilingual education exists, politics is close by. To assume that bilingual education is educationally justified and therefore, *ipso facto*, will enjoy strong support is naive. Bilingual education is not simply an educational issue. Behind bilingual education there are always expressions of political ideology, tides of political change, and political initiative.

One can argue then that, in Algeria, a need is felt for new language policies and language-in-education planning. The political elites' apparent change of attitudes in favour of bilingualism – at least at the level of political discourse – shows a shift in ideology regarding language policy and national identity. The 'one language-one nation' ideology has led to a deadlock and, to put an end to this stalemate, the authorities seem ready to recognise ethnic and linguistic plurality as a resource for nation-building (Benrabah, 2004d: 50–3). The attempt to move away from homogenising and assimilationist policies comes from the pressure of democratisation and globalisation. In other words, structural economic reforms need to move from an era of Soviet-like central planning to one of free market enterprise with integration in world economies. In fact, the Algerian economy is in urgent need of modernisation for at least one reason: to reduce social unrest due to the high rate of unemployment. In June 2000, the then Minister of Economics wrote an article in the weekly journal *Jeune Afrique-L'Intelligent* in which he encouraged French investors to come to Algeria. One of his arguments was that French was widely used by Algerians: 'For the vast majority of Algerians, French remains the code to enable them to have access to technologies. This absence of a linguistic barrier is a definite advantage for French companies' (Benachenhou, 2000: 31). The Minister thus admits that the French language can serve as a tool to open up to the world economy and for Algerians to meet the demands of globalisation. But the current changes also come from ethnic diversity: since April 1980, Berber unrest has led to instability that has weakened the regime's authority and could lead to separatism (Chaker, 2002; Sekaï, 1995). These social, political and economic openings are likely to put an end to the stagnation that has characterised Algeria for the last three decades – a stagnation that is also characteristic of the entire Arab world (*Economist*, 2004b: 13). But before dealing with economic issues, it is necessary first to consider Algeria's background briefly.

Part I: Background on Algeria

The country

Algeria is officially designated locally as *Al Jumhuriyah al Jaza'iriyah al Dimuqratiyah ash-Sha'biya* (the People's Democratic Republic of Algeria), with Algiers (in Arabic, *Al Jaza'ir*) as its capital. It is part of North Africa or the Maghreb which in Arabic means 'west'. It is midway along the Mediterranean coastline and bounded by the Mediterranean Sea to the north, Morocco to the west, Mauritania and Mali to the southwest, Niger to the southeast, Libya to the east and Tunisia to the northeast (see map in Figure 1). With an area of 2,381,741 square kilometres (919,595 square miles), it is the largest country of the Maghreb and the second largest in Africa after the Sudan. The mountain ranges of the Tell Atlas and Sahara Atlas divide the country into three topographical regions: a narrow fertile littoral; the High Plateaus which comprise a steppe plain delimited by the Tell and Sahara Atlases; and the Sahara Desert in the south which represents approximately 80–85% of the total land area of the country. Most of the Sahara consists of rocky plateaus (*Hamadas*) and two great sand deserts: the Great

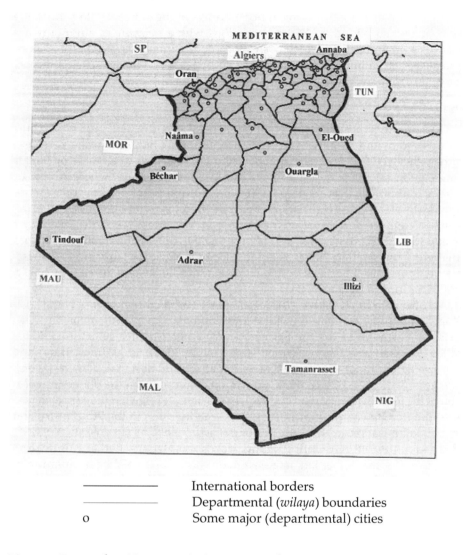

————————— International borders
————————— Departmental (*wilaya*) boundaries
o Some major (departmental) cities

Figure 1 Geographical location of Algeria in North Africa

Western Erg and the Great Eastern Erg. The River Chelif is the only permanent river (Atlapedia, 2003; *CIA, World Factbook*, 2005).

In July 2003, the population was estimated at 32,818,500. For demographic density, there are 11 people per square kilometre (28 people per square mile), and because of the fertile northern littoral, this density declines progressively in the High Plateaus and in the Saharan Atlas Mountains. The major urban centres extend about 80 kilometres (50 miles) from the coast and stretch from the Moroccan to the Tunisian borders. The estimated populations of the major cities are: Algiers (3,000,000), Oran (610,000), Constantine (500,000), Annaba (400,000), Batna (182,000). The rate of urbanisation is 61.7% (Atlapedia, 2003; *CIA, World Factbook*, 2005; Gillet, 2004c: 1313).

Algeria inherited a hierarchical organisation of the entire territory from the French colonial period (1830–1962). Regions with a measure of autonomy are *wilaya,*[6] *daira* and *baladia* which correspond to the French *préfecture* (province), *arrondissement* (administrative division) and *commune* (village, district) respectively (see map in Figure 1).

The people

Customarily, the Algerian population has been divided into two ethnic groups, Arabs and Berbers. However, these terms are not used in a racial sense; rather, they refer to groups of people who are raised in the Arabic or Berber language respectively and who grow up in an environment where Arabic or Berber traditional customs prevail. From a cultural point of view, one cannot oppose an 'Arab culture' to a 'Berber culture' because symbols, modes of representation and models are often the same from one Algerian border to another (Haddadou, 1997: 81). As such, it is preferable to speak of 'Arabophones' and 'Berberophones' rather than Berbers and Arabs because the latter group consists mainly of Arabised Berbers: very few have a Middle Eastern ancestry (Chaker, 1998: 16; Gordon, 1966: 8).

According to Ibn Khaldun (2003: 125), the great Maghrebi historian and sociologist of the 14th century, the oldest and original people living in the northern coast of North Africa are the Berbers. These white Mediterranean inhabitants called themselves *Imazighen* which is the plural for *Amazigh* (masculine) and *Tamazight* (feminine). They were later stigmatised and designated by the pejorative term *Berbers* – a 14th century innovation resulting from the phonetic evolution of the Roman/Greek word *barbari*: 'barbarians, foreign language speakers' – after the Roman conquest in 146 BCE, the Arab invasion in the 7th century and French colonisation in the 19th century (Dalby, 1998: 88; El Aissati, 1993: 92; Haddadou, 1997: 72–3). Until 1945, the words *Amazigh* (for Berber culture) and *Tamazight* (for the Berber language) were unknown to the Kabylian community in Algeria. Both terms are recent borrowings from Moroccan Berberophones. *Amazigh,* which goes back to antiquity, means 'free man, noble man', a clear break from the traditional denotation meaning a barbarian human being with an unintelligible idiom (Chaker, 1998: 86–7; Haddadou, 1997: 81). The terms *Amazigh* and *Imazighen* rehabilitate the Berbers and their language. As a generic name *Tamazight* also serves as a means of drawing together and uniting various Berber-speaking groups of people.

By July 2005, Algeria's total population was estimated at 32,531,853 and projections for 2006 give 33,200,000 (Belabes, 2005b: 1; *CIA, World Factbook,* 2005). Arabophones represent the principal ethnic group that constitutes approximately 70–75% of the population, and the remaining 25–30% are Berberophone. While the number of Berberophones in Algeria has been a matter of estimates rather than of a linguistic/population census, they are roughly estimated at around 6–7 million out of Algeria's 32 million inhabitants (Chaker, 1998: 16; Maddy-Weitzman, 2001: 23, 37). The Arabo-Berber population represents 99%, and the non-Arabo-Berber community accounts for 100,000 people (less than 1%), mainly of European descent, predominantly French, although there are minorities of Italian, Spanish, Maltese and Corsican extraction (Atlapedia, 2003). Before briefly describing the other minority group – the Berber or

Berberophones – another minority is worth noting because it played an important role in Algerian history: the Jewish community. The number of Algerian Jews is now insignificant as a result of their mass exodus in 1962 – there were only 500 in 1972. Before 1962, there were around 130,000 (in 1948), roughly half of Arabo-Berber origin and half being the descendants of Jews expelled from Spain in 1391 and 1492 (Abitbol, 1999: 429; Bar-Asher, 1992: 16–20; Gordon, 1966: 8).

Berberophones are made up of four groups, and population figures are largely guesswork owing to the lack of official recognition of Berber languages. The Tuaregs, desert nomads estimated at a few thousand, live around the Hoggar Mountains near the southeast and southwest borders of Algeria. The second distinct Berberophone group are the Mozabites (estimated between 80,000 and 100,000) centring on Ghardaïa and enclosed bastion cities in the Mzab region in the Sahara. The Chaouias represent the third Berber community, with their heartland being the Aures Mountains, further east, south of Constantine. Between 500,000 and 1 million Berbers are Chaouia. The final and most important Berber group is represented by the Kabylians (about two-thirds of Berberophones). Kabylia is an isolated and relatively barren area along the Mediterranean coast, east of Algiers (Chaker, 1998: 14–15; Dalby, 1998: 89). It should be noted that there are large numbers of Kabylians in urban centres like Algiers, Oran and Constantine (Chaker, 1998: 173; El Aissati, 1993: 93). Not only do Kabylians form the largest group among contemporary Berberophones in Algeria, but they have distinguished themselves by their ideological minority views against mainstream 'official' ideology within the Algerian nationalist movement and in post-independent Algeria. The following lengthy quotation sums up quite well this uniqueness in Algerian history.

> The Kabylians are unique among the Berbers in that they have a long history of corporate identity and have been intimately involved in major developments throughout Algerian history, since the time of the French conquest – from their fierce resistance to French rule, to being the subject of sustained French attention in an effort to wean them away from Algeria's Arab Muslims (far more so than in Morocco), to their over-representation among both immigrant workers in France and in the Algerian state apparatus, to their essential role in the struggle for independence, at both the elite and mass levels. No less significant, from a contemporary perspective, is the fact that from the late 1940s, Kabylian intellectuals tendered an alternative, minority view to the dominant stream promoting an Arab-Muslim Algeria. They instead emphasised the need for an 'Algerian Algeria', whose identity was, and should remain, intimately linked with the population's employment of Berber dialects and Algerian colloquial Arabic, and not the modern standard Arabic being imported from the Arab East. Although their ideas fell on deaf ears, they served as a precursor to post-independence developments. (Maddy-Weitzman, 2001: 37)

For detailed information on the linguistic characterisation of Arabic and Berber languages, see sections on Arabic and Tamazight in Part III (The Languages of Algeria).

Part II: The Economy of Algeria

Analysts described Algeria's economy in 2004 as healthy at the macro-economic level and bankrupt at the micro-economic one (Benderra, 2003; Byrd, 2003; Gillet, 2004a; Martín, 2003; Moatti, 2004). Government finances have improved due to substantial trade surpluses, record foreign exchange reserves, and reductions in foreign debt (*CIA, World Factbook*, 2005). The strong money growth comes from hydrocarbon revenues: since 2000 rising crude prices have led to state coffers overflowing and excess liquidity in the banking system (Algeria Interface, 2004; IMF, 2004: 4). In 2003, government earnings reached US$24 billion (Sahar, 2004: 4) representing 60% of the state budget revenue and 30% of GDP with a value of US$53.8 billion (*CIA, World Factbook*, 2005; World Bank, 2004). In 2002, non-petroleum exports brought to state budget a mere US$722 million and consisted of semi-finished products (for a total value of US$593 million), capital goods (US$49 million) and customer items (US$25 million). During the same year, the total value for imports stood at US$11.75 billion. They included industrial and capital goods for a total value of US$4.466 billion, semi-finished products for US$2.344 billion, food produce for US$2.678 billion, and consumer commodities for US$1.59 billion including medical goods for US$593.1 million (Algeria Interface, 2004).

In 2002, Algeria's main trading partners were France, Italy and the USA. For exports, the country traded with Italy (20.1%), the USA (14.2%) and France (13.6%) and it imported commodities from France (22.7%), the USA (9.8%), and Italy (9.6%) (Boniface, 2005: 364). The balance of trade recorded a surplus of US$6.67 billion in 2002 (Algeria Interface, 2004). Algeria's foreign currency reserves, which fell to US$4.4 billion in 1999 leaving the polity on the edge of bankruptcy, rose to US$22.5 billion in 2002 (Martín, 2003: 42). The foreign debt was reduced by a third, from US$33.7 billion in 1996 to US$22 billion in 2002, and the total debt service decreased from US$9.331 million in 1992 to US$4.166 million in 2002 (Martín, 2003: 42; World Bank, 2004). Inflation, which rose to 32% in 1992 (Byrd, 2003: 68) went down to 3% in 2002 (*CIA, World Factbook*, 2005). In 2004, GDP amounted to US$212.3 billion (purchasing power parity) and GDP per capita (purchasing power parity) was estimated at US$6,600 (*CIA, World Factbook*, 2005; World Bank, 2004). GNP was US$2083 in 2003 (Giret *et al.*, 2004: 40). Real GDP has improved as a result of high oil production and an increase in government spending (*CIA, World Factbook*, 2005).

Hydrocarbons represent the main pillar of Algeria's economy and their part in the total value of exports stood at 95–7% in 2003 (Algeria Interface, 2004; *CIA, World Factbook*, 2005; Martín, 2003: 39). Oil proved reserves rose from 1.2 billion tons in 1982 to 11.87 billion barrels in 2004 (*CIA, World Factbook*, 2005; Stora, 2001: 46). These reserves, estimated to last for 45 years of consumption and exportation (Aïssaoui, 2001: 278–82), place Algeria 14th in world rank, producing 1.2 million barrels per day in 2004 (*CIA, World Factbook*, 2005). With 3 trillion cubic metres in the 1980s (Stora, 2001: 46), Algerian reserves of natural gas rose to 4.739 trillion cubic metres in 2004 (*CIA, World Factbook*, 2005). Algeria's stocks represent 4% of world reserves (the fifth-largest). With natural gas production estimated at 80.3 billion cubic metres in 2001, Algeria exported 57.98 billion cubic metres and became the second-largest exporter (*CIA, World Factbook*, 2005). Besides petroleum and natural gas industries, the industrial sector also includes light and heavy industries such as steel, metallurgy, engineering, electric and electronic industries, textiles, mining, petrochemicals and food processing. As to agricultural products, Algeria produces wheat, barley, oats, grapes, olives, citrus-fruit, fruit, sheep and cattle. The industrial production growth rate was 6% in 2004 (*CIA, World Factbook*, 2005) and the growth rate stood at 6.7% in 2003 (Giret *et al.*, 2004: 40). The labour force, estimated at 9.91 million in 2004, was engaged, according to 2003 estimates, by government (32%), agriculture (14%), construction and public works (10%), industry (13.4%), trade (14.6%) and other (16%) (*CIA, World Factbook*, 2005). On average, monthly salaries in the industrial sector stand at US$300 and the guaranteed national minimum wage allocated to 13% (waged workers) is around 100 Euros per month (Martín, 2003: 44).

The development of Algeria's economy has undergone three main phases. The first one corresponds to the period following independence (Destanne de Bernis, 1971: 546; Goumeziane, 1994: 52; Ollivier, 1992: 113; Si Ameur & Sidhoum, 1992: 146) with colonial legacies such as illiteracy at around 90%[7] (Bennoune, 2000: 12; Heggoy, 1984: 111; Lacheraf, 1978: 313). The second phase, called 'post-colonial transition' ('economic nationalism'), lasted until the 1980s (Goumeziane, 1994: 18–19) and came under the influence of 'developmentalist' economists and the Soviet Union (Dahmani, 1999: 31; Goumeziane, 1994: 38; Ollivier, 1992: 130). Developmentalists favoured the state-led strategy of the 'industrialising industries' (heavy industry) (Destanne de Bernis, 1966, 1971). They also viewed hydrocarbons as the 'real riches' of the country and the source of economic and social power (Hidouci, 1995: 42–3, 52). But Algeria's economic model differed from that of the USSR on at least one very important issue, which is telling for the field of language policy. Planning, which was fundamental to the Soviet economy, played a marginal role in the Algerian case and very few economic and social activities were planned (Dahmani, 1999: 39; Hidouci, 1995: 35). Algeria became a highly centralised 'administered' distributive socioeconomic system characterising 'rentier' states (Beblawi & Luciani, 1987; Dillman, 2000; Talahite, 2000; Vieille, 1984) and mass loyalty was secured via high oil budget revenues (Dahmani, 1999: 6–20; Goumeziane, 1994: 51; IMF, 2004: 8). Within a decade, Algeria's economy changed from an agricultural mono-exporting state into a petroleum mono-exporting one[8] (Hidouci, 1995: 52). High levels of investment in industry led to substantial social gains: between 1966 and 1977 the number of jobs created increased by 1,400,000 (Goumeziane, 1994: 68) and educational reforms undertaken in the 1970s provided universal schooling in Arabic (see Part V) reaching substantial results: in 1962–1963, only 777,636 pupils attended primary schools, by 1970 the figure reached 1,851,416, and 5 million by 1987 (Chabane, 1987: 5–6; Khalloufi Sellam, 1983: 44). Algeria was described then as the 'Algerian miracle', an 'example' and 'a model to be followed' (Dahmani, 1999: 30; Martín, 2003: 34; Stora, 2001: 53). As to Algeria's language-in-education planning (Arabisation), some observers hailed the 'revolution in Arabic' (Berri, 1973).

Unfavourable economic developments and high population growth hampered these gains. Algeria suffered from the *Dutch disease* effect in the 1980s following the high rise of international oil prices of the 1970s. Industrial investment got Algeria into debt with foreign financial institutions[9] especially after oil prices in the international market collapsed and the dollar was devalued in 1986. Meanwhile, population growth rose unchecked: in 1975, the fertility rate almost reached the world record with 8.1 children born per woman[10] (Stora, 2001: 62); and from 10 million inhabitants in 1952, it grew to 23 million in 1987 and 29.5 million in 1997 (ADBG, 2004; Si Ameur & Sidhoum, 1992: 148). Demography and lack of investment led to social tensions and the October 1988 uprisings. A multi-party (pre-democratic) system was set up followed by a civil war opposing the Islamist armed groups and the government forces.[11]

When the government was unable to repay its external debt in the mid-1990s, the International Monetary Fund (IMF) imposed the implementation of a structural adjustment programme – from April 1994 to March 1995 and from April 1995 to March 1998 – to encourage the transition to a market economy which marks the third economic phase (Dahmani, 1999: 184–92; Martín, 2003: 40). With macro-economic stabilisation the government launched, in April 2001, a multi-million dollar economic growth programme, the National Plan for Re-launching the Economy (NPRE), allocating US$7 billion which represented 13% of the GDP for the year 2000 (Martín, 2003: 47). The National Agricultural Development Plan was also implemented and proved fairly successful: in October 2004, the agricultural growth rate reached 6.41% (Algeria Interface, 2004; Boudedja, 2004: 5). By contrast, the NPRE 'has had only insignificant effects on the economic growth rate' (Martín, 2003: 48). The reason for this stagnation was the government's failure to implement the three objectives it set itself in 1999: develop the private sector, promote trade liberalisation and implement a series of 'structural reforms'. The government made progress in modernising trade legislation and made multilateral trade liberalisation irreversible (Martín, 2003: 42). In April 2002, Algeria signed the Euro-Mediterranean Association Agreement with the European Union (Martín, 2003: 53), and negotiations are under way to join the World Trade Organisation (Yemloul, 2004: 28). But old statist nationalist quarters stalled the other two government's objectives (Gillet, 2004b: 1338–9; Moatti, 2004: 61; Werenfels, 2002: 1). It is this deadlock situation which is largely responsible for the failure to transform the oil bonanza and excellent macro-economic health into wealth and wealth directed into the population's well-being.[12] Youth and women, being in the majority, suffer the most from this situation. For example, the illiteracy rate among those aged 15 and over stands at 31% to 33.4% and affects women disproportionately: according to 2003 estimates, literate females represented 61% of the total female population while literate men represented 78.8% of the total male population[13] (*CIA, World Factbook*, 2005; Giret *et al.*, 2004: 40; PNUD, 2002: 167). Within the Algerian age structure, those under 30 represent 62.7% at the present time and the majority cannot find a job: two thirds of the unemployed population are below 30 years old (Riols, 2004: 50–1).

For the 'structural reforms', the Algerian government set itself, among other things, a goal of 'ending State intervention in pedagogical orientations and eradicating religious fanaticism, revising school cycles, curricula and textbooks, as well as legalizing the nearly 600 private schools that exist in a legal vacuum, and promoting teaching formation' (Martín, 2003: 41). Algeria's education has been detrimental to quality and great open-mindedness (Si Ameur & Sidhoum, 1992: 167). An illustration is the high level of dropouts. In May 1997, the High Council for Education reported a 32% yearly dropout rate with only 25% completing a full nine-year course ('Fundamental School') (*El Watan*, 1997a: 1). Moreover, the success rate for the Baccalaureate exam, around 70% in the 1970s, dropped to 10% in 1993[14] (Benrabah, 1999a: 170). With limited horizons, many young Algerians joined Islamic armed groups in the 1990s and, in 1995, 60% of all those enrolled in these groups were illiterate and aged between 18 and 20 (*Le Monde*, 1995: 5). In the 2000s, the youth chose exile: more than 1 million people applied for a French visa in 2003 while only 200,000 had obtained one in 2002 (Gillet, 2004c: 1315).

Failure to make real political and economic reforms consolidates the material bases of social discontent and instability.[15] But unless these reforms are put into practice, foreign polities (Europeans in particular) have every reason to fear that 'a demographic bomb' (Riols, 2004: 50) made up of young Algerians in despair will storm their borders in search of better living conditions. Not only will they begin to emigrate massively, but they will also create trans-boundary mayhem as a result of massive migration and the reinforcement of international fundamentalist terrorism that the Algerian 'system continues to produce and export . . . and the international institutions are becoming more and more aware of the serious drift of this system' (Byrd, 2003: 78). The government is sensitive to international pressure for advancing reforms because 'the consciousness of the [Algerian] power circles that their own survival in the government depends to a large extent on international support. And this international support mainly depends, in turn, on the implementation of the market reforms' (Martín, 2003: 48). It is within this context imposed by economic and political agendas (internationalisation and democratisation) that one should understand President Bouteflika's initiatives in the fields of language policy and language-in-education planning.

Part III: The Languages of Algeria

The context in which language policies (Arabicisation) were implemented in Algeria requires an understanding of the people and their language(s). These are presented in the following section in terms of the historical and sociolinguistic factors that have led to the present situation.

Historical approach

In Antiquity, the natives of the region, the Berbers, dominated Northern Africa and the Sahara (from the Atlantic to the Egyptian borders). Geography and the climate of Berberia determined the way of life of its people and influenced their history. With only a few centres of civilisation located along the coast – all of foreign origin – Algeria was a vast rural area peopled by agriculturists and nomads. The geographical isolation reinforced a tribal structure and cultural divisiveness. Sporadically or for relatively short periods of time, these indigenous populations were able to unite into a coherent state and even managed to develop a rich and prosperous civilisation (Djité, 1992: 16). In general, Berbers were unsuccessful as rulers of their own lands and hence allowed several foreign groups to dominate the region. But they resisted the various conquerors and remained a people difficult to rule. At times, when they submitted to civilisations from without, the Berbers of the interior kept to themselves and remained monolingual. In urban zones, bilingualism and multilingualism – Berber-Punic, Berber-Punic-Roman, etc. – became the norm (Elimam, 2004: 300–1; Morsly, 1996: 77).

Phoenicians were the first invaders to allow the rise of a local civilisation in North Africa. They spoke Punic, a Semitic language. In 860 BCE, they settled mainly in Carthage, near modern Tunis, and in many other trading posts along the Mediterranean coast. For eight centuries, the Carthaginians were allies of the Berber leaders of the interior, and important inroads were made by the Punic language and civilisation. Bilingualism prevailed: Numidic kings and elites spoke and used Punic as the official language while peasants spoke Berber. The Carthaginian idiom was in use until the third century CE (Ageron, 1993: 766; Basset, 1921: 373; Camps, 1987: 113; Elimam, 2003: 25–34; Jaïdi, 2004: 24–33).

During the second century BCE, the Romans destroyed Carthage and occupied all of North Africa. Many Punic-speaking Carthaginians fled to other towns and rural zones and the language went with them. Italian and Mediterranean immigrants as well as transhumants settled in newly created military garrisons and in old Berber and Phoenician towns and cities. The number of Roman cities exceeded 500 (Lancel, 2003: 98–125). In these centres grew a new class of acculturated people called *Romani* opposed to non-Romanised peoples, the *Mauri* ('Moors') (Hamman, 1979: 22). According to Benabou (1975: 488), the sociolinguistic profile of Roman North Africa was marked by multilingualism. Romani spoke Latin, used exclusively in towns. Punic remained at the periphery, and the *Mauri* were monolingual Berber speakers living in mountainous areas (Benabou, 1975: 60). The Romans dominated Algeria by force for almost six centuries. Long after the Romans left Algeria, the Christian community continued to utilise Latin, and Latin-inscribed remnants attest to the use of this language during the 11th and 12th centuries (Marçais, 1938: 8).

In 429 CE, the Vandals invaded North Africa. They celebrated their heretic religious doctrines in the Gothic language but maintained the Roman customs and Latin as the language of legislation and diplomacy. A century later (in 533 CE), the Romanised Byzantines re-conquered the northern part of Africa and re-instated the social organisation imposed by Rome in the past. Linguistic traces of the Vandal and Byzantine periods are almost non-existent (Morsly, 1996: 54). In 647/ 648 CE, the Byzantines were defeated by the Arabs who came from the east to spread Islam. North Africans gradually converted to Islam and by the 12th century the majority became 'orthodox' Sunni Moslems. The Arabic language spread progressively, and more and more Berbers became arabophones (Ageron, 1993: 766–7; Julien, 1994: 341–66).

The process of linguistic Arabisation took place during two periods. The first wave of Arabs (perhaps 150,000) spread their religion with a fair degree of Arabisation (Gallagher, 1968: 131). Up to the 11th century, the diffusion of Arabic was superficial (Lewicki, 1936: 274; Marçais, G., 1913: 37). The indigenous populations acquired their knowledge of Arabic through reading the Koran and listening to missionaries from the East. This is how, right from the beginning, Arabic came to be strongly associated with Islam in North Africa (Gellner, 1973). In 1045 CE, the Muslim dynasty of the Zirids settled in present-day Tunisia, repudiating their allegiance to the Fatimids in Cairo. As a response, the Cairene caliph sent westward the turbulent nomadic tribes of the Banu Hillal who had come from the Arabian Peninsula and were stationed in Egypt. Around 200,000 tribesmen (Gallagher, 1968: 131) were left to roam and plunder at will. Ibn Khaldun, the great North African scholar of the 14th century, described these tribes as 'a plague of locusts devastating everything on their way' (Servier, 1994: 60). The Banu Hillal reshaped the cultural boundaries in North Africa, at the same time extending Arabisation of culture and language in the region. The first period of Arabisation was mainly an ideological process of Islamisation. The incursion of Arabic was limited, sometimes even resisted by those opposed to the new masters. By contrast, in the post-Hillali period, Arab civilisation and Islam made a profound impact on the local people because of the mental similarity between Berbers and Arabs. Both groups had the same life style and similar symbolic or feudal relationships which emerged between them. With the Hillalis, the spread of Arabic was vast and profound (Benabdi, 1980: 18; Julien, 1994: 412–15; Kaddache, 1992: 84–8).

The two periods of Arabisation have given rise to two distinct types of Arabic. One variety known as 'pre-Hillali' or 'Baldi' brought from urban areas of Medine, Syria and Palestine and spoken in North African long-established towns (Algiers, Tlemcen, Cherchell, Tenes, etc.) and villages in Little Kabylia in the east and Ghazaouet and its surroundings in the west. The Hillalis' variety is 'rural', 'Bedouin' or 'Barani' Arabic spoken in most of the rural areas of Algeria today, especially in the High Plateaus, the Tell mountains (North), the *Ksours* or rural hamlets and in the Sahara (Benallou, 2002: 38; Bouamrane, 1986: 31; Marçais, 1960: 388). In most Arabic-speaking areas, Berber is the substratum, but some regional variants of Arabic descend from Punic, especially in the north-eastern part of Algeria (Chaker, 1998: 19–20; Elimam, 1997: 36–40, 2003: 33–52).

The Hillali invasion led to the development of urban centres along the coast which did not interest the Bedouin Arabs who were plains and steppes people. Trade between these towns and southern European states developed, increasing the diversity of their ethnic composition and contact between languages (Abun-Nasr, 1975: 153–5; Benabdi, 1980: 30–1; Brunschvig, 1940–1947: 431). The coastal urban ethnic make-up increased further with the seizure of a number of towns by the Spaniards who established fortified posts at Mers el Kebir, Oran, Tlemcen, Honaïn, Mostaganem, Dellys, Tenes, Cherchell, Bougie (Bejaia) and the Peñon of Algiers, a small harbour island facing the future capital of Algeria (300 metres only). For example, Mers el Kebir (occupied in 1505) and Oran (in 1509) were Spanish possessions until 1791 (Gordon, 1966: 12; Julien, 1994: 627–9; Kaddache, 1998: 4–5; Llabador, 1948: 185–7; Queffélec *et al.*, 2002: 13; Ruff, 1998: 15–16; Vincent, 2004: 107). Ottoman rule in Algeria began in 1529. The Turks were allowed to marry local women but their offspring, called *Kouloughlis*, could not hold positions of authority (government or army). Leaders (*deys*) preferred to look to the sea and the lucrative practice of piracy instead of developing the country. They did not provide the necessary climate for the development of artistic or literary creativity (Abun-Nasr, 1975: 175). Ottoman rulers encouraged divisions between numerous tribes as a way of controlling them (Harbi, 1994: 226; Julien, 1994: 679).

The absence of Turkish control over the diverse communities of Algeria was reinforced at the linguistic level. For three centuries, Turks turned Algeria into a pirate state open to multiple cultural models: a 'mosaic' of ethnic groups and languages (Kaye & Zoubir, 1990: 69). If Classical Arabic remained the common liturgical language, the Berber oral varieties represented a strong symbol of collective identity used for a defiant opposition towards the central Ottoman authority (Harbi, 1994: 225–6). The sociolinguistic structure in cities and towns was as complex and varied as the population: multilingualism involving approximately 15 languages prevailed. Turks and some Kouloughlis used the official language, Osmanli Turkish. Spoken Arabic remained important: not only was it spoken by the old townspeople (*Baldis*) and Spanish/Andalucian immigrants, but it was also the only tongue understood by the tribesmen in the surrounding country where Berber remained in force; when interacting with the local populations, Turks also used spoken Arabic (de Haëdo, 1998: 125–6; Meouak, 2004: 304; Morsly, 1996: 57). There was also the medieval Mediterranean pidgin, the lingua franca, which contained a simplified grammar and words coming from Arabic, Spanish, Turkish, Italian, Provençal and Portuguese (Calvet, 1999b: 121–8; Kahane *et al.*, 1958: 38; Lanly, 1970; Meouak, 2004: 313–18). According to Kahane *et al.* (1958: 38), it is thanks to the lingua franca that the North African varieties of Arabic adopted many Greek and Romance words pertaining to navigation, naval artillery and fishing.

   One ethnic group that best characterises the hybrid nature of 16th century Algeria's urban centres is the Jewish community. A former Spanish Christian slave, Diego de Haëdo (enslaved in Algiers between 1578 and 1581), described the Jewish linguistic practices in the Regency: in schools, Jewish children learned to read and write in Hebrew, sometimes in Arabic, and they also wrote Hebrew in Arabic (de Haëdo, 1998: 122, 140). Before the French occupation in 1830, most of the Algerian Jews spoke dialectal Arabic sometimes called *yahudi* (Dalby, 1998: 28). Many Jews had two names, one Hebrew, used in the Jewish community and home, the other Arabic, used when interacting with Muslims. In rural areas, Jews were sometimes completely assimilated and spoke the language of their neighbours exclusively (Benabdi, 1980: 31). Those who were literate wrote Arabic in Hebrew script (Laskier, 1994: 15–16; Valensi, 1969: 28) as a way to reflect ethnic/ religious identity in the use of orthography (Hary, 2003: 73). The large number of Hebrew and Aramaic grammatical and lexical elements inserted in this form of Arabic and the use of the Hebrew-Aramaic alphabet rather than the Arabic one justify the use of the term 'Judeo-Arabic' as an ethnolect (Hary, 2003: 62; Myhill, 2004: 118–22; Thomas, 1999: 3).

   When the French took over on 5 July 1830, most Turks (around 15,000) returned to Turkey. Within a relatively short period of time (132 years), the French occupation made a profound impact on Algeria's culture and linguistic profile. The influence was so deep that Algerian society was never the same again. In 1830, the total population was estimated at 3 million (Quefféléc *et al.*, 2002: 23; Valensi, 1969: 20) and was mainly rural (Nouschi, 1986: 197). At the time, literacy in Arabic was estimated at 40 to 50% (Gordon, 1978: 151). Valensi (1969: 29) estimates that, before the French takeover, the Berber-speaking community represented about 50% of Algeria's population. By the time of independence, there were 10 million Algerians, a quarter of whom lived in towns. The illiteracy rate stood at around 90% with only 5.5% of the population literate only in Literary Arabic (around 300,000). In 1966, the Berber-speaking population amounted to 18.6% – the only time in the history of post-independence Algeria when the language issue was included in a population census

(Bennoune, 2000: 12; Chaker, 1998: 13; Gordon, 1978: 151; Heggoy, 1984: 111; Lacheraf, 1978: 313). Such are the results of a methodical policy of deracination and deculturisation implemented by colonial France between 1830 and 1962. To realise their 'civilising mission' (*mission civilisatrice*), the French imposed an assimilationist policy on millions of recalcitrant Algerians (Gallagher, 1968: 132–3).

Assimilationist colonial policies

Long before the military conquest ('pacification') was complete – lasting from 1830 to 1871 – there was talk of French schools. The latter were opened, as early as 1831, for the children of European settlers, or *pieds noirs* as they came to be called, and for the conquered Algerians.

The French imperial ('civilising') mission was symbolised by the supremacy of French culture and language over other cultures and languages no matter what their historicity (Wardhaugh, 1987: 7–8). For example, here is how a military general and Governor of Algeria (1832–1833) believed in the promotion of French at the expense of Arabic: 'The remarkable feat would be to gradually replace Arabic by French ... which can only spread among the natives, especially if the new generation will come in numbers to be educated in our schools' (Turin, 1983: 40–1). What the Governor ignored is that Algerians had their own idea about education and civilisation. In 1834, a French general paid tribute to the Algerians' level of education when he said: 'nearly all the Arabs can read and write; in each village there are two schools' (Horne, 1987: 29). Unlike education in France which became laicised after the expropriation in 1789 of clerical properties by French revolutionaries, Algerians had a somewhat traditional 'rudimentary' and 'archaic' system (Bennoune, 2000: 146–7; Horne, 1987: 29). Undoubtedly, there was no separation between the schooling system and religious institutions: in the curriculum, religion and education were inseparable, and any thinking required Islam as its focal point (Valensi, 1969: 18). Furthermore, the schooling system was completely autonomous from the central authorities and depended on mosques or headquarters of religious brotherhoods – *Zawiya* (Heggoy, 1984: 99).

Twenty years after the seizure of Algiers, the literacy rate had been almost halved (Colonna, 1975: 30). Turin describes the deterioration of the situation in Algiers as follows: before 1830, 'primary schools [*mcids*] were numerous with many pupils; in 1840, out of a population of 12,000 Moors, there were 24 *mcids* with 600 pupils; in February 1846, there was no more than 14 *mcids* for the teaching of 400 children' (1983: 130). In fact, the traditional educational system collapsed during the last quarter of the 19th century (Colonna, 1975: 29). Algerians were subjected to the most extreme forms of cultural aggression by the French rulers, a form of conquest they had never experienced with preceding conquerors.

The 'instruct to conquer' ideology (Turin, 1983: 17) took on another form. French colonial administrators and academics created the 'Berber/Kabylian myth'. They claimed that the Algerian people comprised two separate races, Berbers and Arabs, the former being the real indigenous populations, superior to the latter because they were descendants of Europeans. The 'Berber/Kabylian myth' implied that Berbers were susceptible to assimilation into French culture ('Frenchification') while Arabs were not (Eickelman, 1985: 219–20; Favret, 1973:

323; Sivan, 1979: 24). Colonna found that, by the end of the 19th century, the colonial authorities used French schools to attract rural Kabylians and that '89% of rural teacher-trainees were of Kabylian origin' (1975: 106). According to Roberts, the colonisers also encouraged Kabylian migrant workers away from the Arabic-speaking interior to factories in metropolitan France (1980: 118). The 'Berber policy of France' (Chaker, 1998: 111) was an attempt to 'pacify' a region where the last major uprisings took place in 1871, and the revolt came as a blow to the 'Berber/Kabylian myth'. After this insurrection, European settler elites (politicians, journalists and novelists) considered all *Ismaelites* hopeless for Frenchification: they remained 'Arabs' or *indigènes* – as all Muslim Algerians were called, hence 'lumping together all natives under one generic noun [which] effaces not only ethnic-cultural distinctions but also individual ones' (Sivan, 1979: 25).

The term *indigènes* also included the Jewish community that, in 1830, represented 2% (15,000) of the total native population of Algeria (Abitbol, 1999: 152; Thomas, 1999: 3). After 1830, the number of Jews increased as a result of immigration from neighbouring Tunisia and Morocco: 15,000 in 1830, 21,000 in 1851, 33,000 in 1871 and 130,000 in 1948[16] (Abitbol, 1999: 160, 429). In 1870, the French government granted full French citizenship to all Algerian Jews (by the *Crémieux* decree) and, thus, created a rift between the two 'indigenous' communities because the Jews tended to identify themselves with the *pieds noirs* (Gordon, 1966: 8). Jews were highly represented in the school population. Unlike their Muslim compatriots, Jewish parents reacted swiftly by accepting colonial schools for their children. Moreover, by the beginning of the 1860s, the *Alliance Israélite Universelle* based in Paris set up a network of schools in Algeria to offer modern education in French to the great majority of young Jews. Consequently, many Jews accepted French as the principal language with or without the maintenance of Judeo-Arabic and/or Hebrew (Bar-Asher, 1992: 13; Laskier, 1994: 15–16).

Algerians also suffered the brutality of the French army's methods of pacification. The fierce Algerian resistance was met with a scorched-earth policy. Fifteen years after the beginning of the conquest, the native population, estimated at approximately 3 million in 1830, had diminished by 1 million. Brutal retaliation was accompanied by land expropriation for punitive measures. Through seizure, forced purchase or the division of tribal land held in common, the conquering armies of soldiers sequestered properties to create a public domain and colonial settlements. The number of European settlers (French, Italians, Maltese), who were always in the shadow of the military forces, increased rapidly: it rose from 37,374 in 1841 to 245,000 in 1871, 781,000 in 1940 and around 1 million in the early 1960s (Halvorsen, 1978: 338; Horne, 1987: 30; Mansouri, 1991: 42; Sirles, 1999: 119).

Land expropriation resulted in the destruction of the tribal system and a completely fragmented Algerian society. The vast majority of landless peasants migrated to the outskirts of towns and cities created for the *pieds noirs* mainly along the fertile Mediterranean coast. European colonialism in Algeria was in fact a coastal phenomenon. Thus Algerian migrants who did not leave the country came to live close to French-speaking regions and to be in contact with the French language (Sirles, 1999: 119–20). What is more, the degree of urbanisation also affected the spread of the French language. On the eve of French occupation, the total urban population in Algeria represented less than 5% (Nouschi, 1986: 197). The first major socio-demographic transformations took place during the second half of the 19th century: from 5% in 1830, the urban population rose to 13.9% in 1886, 16.6% in 1906, 20.2% in 1926 and 25% in 1954 (Khiar, 1991, 1992).

In the meantime, colonial brutality and cultural aggression pushed Algerians into systematic passive cultural 'resistance-refusal' which lasted almost five decades. Algerian parents viewed with suspicion the secular education offered by the colonisers and were distrustful of its religious agenda: they considered the offer as an evangelist effort to drive their offspring away from Islam (Saad, 1992: 24). Algerians preferred their children to remain illiterate rather than sending them to French schools. The few who did attend these institutions were considered 'renegades' (Djeghloul, 1986: 39–40; Harbi, 1984: 79). All types of schools offered by the colonial authorities were rejected by the majority of the population. The situation worsened during the last quarter of the 19th century. While the traditional educational system was collapsing, the number of Algerian students in French secondary schools was diminishing: 216 students in 1877, 198 in 1882, 144 in 1884, 115 in 1886, 111 in 1888, 81 in 1889 and 69 in 1892 (Djeghloul, 1986: 53). At the primary level, the situation improved slowly but not significantly in comparison with the total number of children of Primary school age: there were 3200 native students in 23 schools in 1883, 12,300 in 124 schools in 1892, and 25,300 in 228 schools in 1901 (Heggoy, 1984: 101).

Following the last major uprising (in Kabylia) in 1871, the administrative control which had been held by the military fell into the hands of civilian officials. The latter were adamantly opposed to any schooling for the natives beyond low level vocational training (Ageron, 1968: 339). Under civilian authorities, cultural aggression was intensified. The control of the indigenous population required the establishment of a registry office. The law promulgated on 23 March 1882, imposed Gallicised names. The 'hybrid' Latinised names represented a break- away from previous Algerian naming systems (Yermèche, 2004: 489–90, 497). What is more, land expropriation and deracination of indigenous populations produced dramatic results on the Berber language. In 1830, Berber tribes were present almost all over the country (the Tell, plains, Sahara Atlases, etc.) and there was a linguistic continuum between all the different Berber regions. By dispossessing peasants of their land, French colonialism emptied entire areas of Berber-speaking populations. These zones were later repopulated by Arabophones (Grandguillaume, 1996: 38; Kahlouche, 1996: 36; Rahal-Sidhoum, 2001; Vermeren, 2004: 51–2). In the 19th century, some western and eastern areas of Algeria were deserted by Berber-speaking populations and later Arabised (Benabdi, 1980: 31; Chaker, 1998: 115–16).

Changing attitudes towards French

In 1910, metropolitan officials imposed conscription for Muslim natives. During the 1914–1918 war, 173,000 Algerians served in the French army and some 25,000 died for France. Another 119,000 were mobilised in the Hexagon to replace French workers who had been conscripted (Knapp, 1977: 69). Both Algerian conscripts and expatriate workers quickly realised the importance of modern education for social advancement. By 1920–1922, Algerians' cultural resistance turned into an acceptance of the colonial school system which quickly changed into a demand for more education in French (Colonna, 1975: 26; Heggoy, 1984: 103), a change that would lead to ambivalent attitudes towards the French after independence, when there was both dissatisfaction with and attraction to the colonial language (Morsly, 1984: 26; Tounsi, 1997: 107). French was both the carrier of modern universal values (French Revolution and Declaration of Human Rights) and the instrument of brutal colonialism that had to be condemned (Stora, 1998: 27–8).

However, in spite of more favourable attitudes towards French and European education, progress in the education of young Muslims was slow (Colonna, 1975: 33; Knapp, 1977: 68). Compared with schooling figures for European children, the number of Arabic- and Berber-speaking pupils remained very low (Bennoune, 2000: 164; Colonna, 1975: 50). The vast majority of the young generation were not getting any education at all (Heggoy, 1984: 104). For example, in the University of Algiers, there were only 386 Algerian students (including 31 female students) in 1950–1951 and 589 (including 51 females) in 1954–1955. Outside Algeria, 553 studied in the universities of metropolitan France in 1950 and 1270 in the three traditional Islamic universities of al-Qarawiyyin in Fez, al-Zaituna in Tunis and al-Azhar in Cairo (Bennoune, 2000: 170).

With respect to education for Algerians in Arabic, progress was even worse. Jacobean ideology applied to Algeria simply meant the disqualification of anything but French. The Arabic language had no status, and only French was considered the language of culture and learning. For example, French linguists, who considered Classical/Literary Arabic as a dead language not worth teaching and studying, described the various Arabic and Berber varieties using the Latin alphabet. They even taught dialects at the secondary and tertiary levels (Algiers University) to *pieds noirs* students (Thomas, 1999: 4). Some colonial academics used the diglossic situation of Arabic, among other things, to disqualify Literary Arabic and, hence planned its death (Marçais, W., 1913: 7; Saadi-Mokrane, 2002: 45). Literary Arabic was decreed a foreign language – by the Decree of 8 March 1938 (Grandguillaume, 1983: 96). It was not until 1961 that the French authorities admitted that the 1938 decree was an error. The Decree of 25 July 1961, signed by Charles de Gaulle, cancelled the latter and imposed the obligation of teaching Arabic in the primary cycle (Grandguillaume, 1983: 96). The Maspétiol Report published in the winter of 1954 stated that about three-quarters of the Algerian population were illiterate in Arabic and 90% in French (Horne, 1987: 110). The 1954 census shows that only 13.7% of the total adult Muslim population could read and write: 55% in French, 20% in French and Arabic, and a mere 25% in Arabic (Bennoune, 2000: 170). Consequently, skills in Literary Arabic remained modest and the liberation struggle was fought mainly in French (Gordon, 1978: 149). A study on the formation of the Algerian revolutionary elite found that out of 69 leaders only five had an Arabic educational background, and the rest (64) were trained in French (Mansouri, 1991: 60).

Nevertheless, the teaching of the banned idiom had been maintained albeit in difficult conditions. In some regions some traditional Koranic schools and *Zawiyas* still managed to exist. With the rise of the nationalist movements, by the end of the 1920s (see Part V), the *Association of the Ulemas* set up a network of free private schools (*medersa*) across the country to provide education in Arabic

(Smati, 1999: 185–7). These learning institutions valued the teaching of Arabic, the revival of Islamic cultural identity and the Pan-Arab ideals. They neglected the teaching of scientific disciplines but allowed pupils and students to acquire written and oral competence in Literary Arabic (Bennoune, 2000: 169). Between 1931 and 1947, there were 174 *medersas* employing 274 teachers. In 1947, the Ben Badis Institute was opened in Constantine to prepare future teachers for the *Association*'s school network and those students who wished to continue their studies in the Islamic universities of al-Zaituna in Tunis and al-Azhar in Cairo (Bennoune, 2000: 168). During the 1950s, the Ulemas created 441 educational centres (with branches in Paris and Cairo) as well as 181 to 193 schools and 58 *medersas* (Bennoune, 2000: 169; Gordon, 1966: 32). By 1950, 16,286 students were enrolled, including 5696 girls. Staffed by 700 Algerian teachers, the Ulema schools provided Arabic language teaching for 75,000 students by 1955 (Assous, 1985: 100). At the same time, there were around 700 students in the Ben Badis Institute (Bennoune, 2000: 169).

Paradoxically, events linked to the War of Algeria (1954–1962) were going to reinforce the status of French among Algerians and have a major impact on language attitudes in post-independence Algeria. When De Gaulle rose to power in May 1958, he introduced an ambitious Five-Year Plan (the Constantine Plan) to develop industrialisation and give Algeria an economic solution to its turmoil. In the years 1959 and 1960 substantial amounts of money were invested in the creation of industrial enterprises and jobs, and 400,000 acres of arable land were handed over to Algerian peasants (Horne, 1987: 340–1). Training administrative cadres was also provided for 100,000 Algerians who were to become the backbone of independent Algeria's administration (Grandguillaume, 1983: 105). Vast new horizons of schooling were to be opened to children who had been excluded so far from learning. Between 1954 and the beginning of 1960, school attendance for Algerian children more than doubled: 386,585 in 1954, 510,000 in 1958, and 840,000 in 1960 (Horne, 1987: 341; Mansouri, 1991: 56). However, despite De Gaulle's efforts, only 14% of the Algerian children were in school, and only 557 Muslims, compared to 4548 Europeans, attended the University of Algiers by the time of independence (Gordon, 1978: 152).

The vast majority of the peasantry was not influenced by literacy and ideals of rational culture and democracy. The Algerian war of liberation changed all this. In fact, one of the major paradoxes of this armed struggle was a quantitative and qualitative increase in the spread of francophonia in Algeria. Such a phenomenon, described as a 'delayed Frenchifying process' (Vermeren, 2004: 139), was to have far-reaching effects on the Algerian population's language attitudes and representations in post-independence Algeria. In the military field, the French counter-revolutionary strategy aimed at draining away the 'water' to asphyxiate the 'fish' and, thus, deprive Algerian fighters of contact with the population which provided them with food and shelter. So 'regroupment camps' and 'pacification zones' were created in 1954 and then generalised in 1957–1958. By 1960, the French army had relocated around 2 million villagers – representing 24% of the total Muslim population (Pervillé, 2003: 40). These uprooted rural populations, which had had no contact with the *présence française* previously, discovered the French language and culture in schools provided by the military who favoured poor populations living in remote areas. After liberation, the majority of displaced people preferred to settle in urban centres deserted by the *pieds noirs* who had left the country (Vermeren, 2004: 137–8). They swelled the population in towns and cities which had been in contact with French for many years. Their sons and daughters were to take part in reinforcing French acculturation intensified by the 'delayed Frenchifying process' of the end of the War of Algeria.

Conclusion

The preceding historical overview shows that Algeria was marked by cultural hybridity and multilingualism: it was bilingual (Berber-Punic) during the Phoenician period, trilingual (Latin-Punic-Berber) under the Roman occupation, and multilingual since the Ottoman presence. The Jacobean centralist hegemonic model of French colonialism aimed at dismantling the polyglot aspect of Algeria and reproducing another France, a linguistically and culturally homogeneous Algeria (Frenchification). It was a particularly destructive tool in the hands of French colonialists which was soon to 'colour' the new elites of independent Algeria in their nation-building endeavour.

The language profile of Algeria

Since its independence in 1962 and the first Constitution promulgated in 1963, Algeria has had one official language: Arabic, which is the *de facto* language of government. Arabic also remained the unique national language until the beginning of the 21st century: the authorities made Tamazight the second national language on 8 April 2002. The terms 'Arabic' and 'Tamazight' denote a language family of Afro-Asiatic descent, and of Hamito-Semitic origin.

Arabic

As the national language of 22 countries, Arabic is spoken in one form or another by more than 200 million people (Comrie *et al.*, 1997: 76; Elkhafaifi, 2002: 254). The word 'Arabic' covers a whole variety of meanings (Laroussi & Madray-Lesigne, 1998) but, for the purposes of the present monograph, three senses will be considered. The first sense refers to what is called Literary Arabic or Modern Standard Arabic, a written form of Arabic more readily associated with the modern media which was developed in the 19th century as part of the cultural Revival, or *Nahda*, in the Middle East (Arkoun, 1984; Gordon, 1985; Grandguillaume, 1989, 1996). Literary or Standard Arabic is essentially a modernised form of Classical Arabic known in Arabic as *'al'arabiyya alfusha* (the 'pure' or 'clear' language). It is the written language of the Koran. Some writers make a distinction between Classical Arabic and Standard Arabic. But the differences between the two varieties are relatively small and Standard Arabic generally follows the same rules as Classical Arabic (Bentahila, 1983: 3; Grandguillaume, 1990: 159). In this monograph, this difference is not recognised; the terms (Modern) Standard Arabic, Literary Arabic, Classical Arabic, etc. are used synonymously. Classical Arabic grew out of the ancient poetic language of Pre-Islamic Arabia. With the spread of Islam, it became the language of the Koran. The Arabic script developed in the 6th century CE; which comes from the Nabatean alphabet which was, in turn, borrowed from an early Aramaic alphabet, derived from Phoenician (Dalby, 1998: 30; Grandguillaume, 1996: 40; Kaye, 1987: 673).

Figure 2 Geographical location of Berber and Algerian Arabic varieties in Algeria (adapted from *Ethnologue*, 2004)

In the second sense, the word *Arabic* also applies to a language that is depreciated by the majority of its speakers who consider it as devoid of grammar. It refers to the colloquial language known as '*amma, darija* or *lahja* ('dialects'). The colloquial varieties number in the hundreds. Being spoken and not written, they are distinguishable from Classical Arabic as a result of a general grammatical simplification in structure with fewer grammatical categories (Kaye, 1987: 667). In the third sense, the term *Arabic* also refers to a new 'intermediate' form (between *alfusha* and *darija*) which has been in the making since the 1970s when Algerians started to use Classical Arabic in the media, the educational system, government, etc. It is a kind of compromise which lies half-way between the written and spoken forms of Arabic, and is known as Educated Spoken Arabic (Benali-Mohamed, 2002: 56; Benallou, 2002: 37; Mahmoud, 1986: 239; Queffélec *et al.*, 2002: 34–5).

From a phonetic and phonological viewpoint, the pre-Hillali (*Baldi*) and Hillali (Bedouin / *Barani*) distinction mentioned for Arabic varieties is characterised by the presence of [q]-[ʔ]-[k] in the former and [g] in the latter (Cantineau, 1960: 69; Marçais, 1902: 17). The two groups can also be separated by the presence or absence of the inter-dentals /θ/ and /ð/ which are typically Bedouin (Cantineau, 1960: 44). However, the socio-demographic changes in Algerian society (urbanisation) have disrupted this distinction (Belkaïd, 1976: 126; Benallou, 2002: 39). Moreover, spoken Arabic in Algeria, which is the first language of 80–85% of the population, is spread over four major geographical areas each with its own linguistic features (see map in Figure 2):

(1)   Western Algerian Arabic used in an area which extends from the Moroccan border to Tenes.
(2)   Central Algerian Arabic spoken in the central zone which extends to Bejaia and includes Algiers and its surroundings.
(3)   Eastern Algerian Arabic spoken in the High Plateaus around Setif, Constantine, Annaba and extends to the Tunisian border.
(4)   Saharan Algerian Arabic spoken by around 100,000 inhabitants in the Sahara Desert (Ethnologue, 2004; Queffélec *et al.*, 2002: 35; Taleb Ibrahimi, 1995: 31).

What distinguishes the Maghrebi or North African Arabic from the other Arabic language groups is the influence of Tamazight. Since Arabic and Tamazight belong to the same language family, the Afro-Asiatic group of languages, each has a predisposition to take in features from the other. Over the centuries, Tamazight influenced Arabic and vice versa. Tamazight traces in Arabic can be found at the lexical, phonological, morphological and syntactic levels (Benali-Mohamed, 2003: 208; Chafik, 1999: 64, 78, 120, 142; Lacheraf, 1998: 151; Vermeren, 2004: 54–5). Hence, the Maghrebi Arabic varieties in general and the Algerian ones in particular can be described as 'Berberised dialects' (Chtatou, 1997: 104). Some academics reject this substratum-based theory and prefer a more 'dynamic' approach: the 'linguistic fusion' (*Sprachbund*) theory. According to this hypothesis, both Arabic and Berber accommodated to each other by adapting their internal linguistic structures which had become very similar (Maas, 2002: 211). Within this approach, the phonological level – prosody and syllabification in particular – is of paramount importance. According to Maas (2002: 212), a speaker of Middle Eastern Arabic will find Maghreban Arabic varieties unintelligible whereas a Berber-speaking monolingual has no difficulty understanding *darija* (for example, Algerian Arabic). The influence of Berber on the Maghrebi varieties of Arabic is such that many words are of Arabic origin but their structure is Berber (Chafik, 1984: 103). Algerian Arabic is thus closer to Tamazight than to the Arabic dialects of the Middle East to the extent that one feels as if he / she is faced with two distinct language groups (Chtatou, 1997: 115).

This linguistic nativisation is noticeable with almost all the lexical items borrowed from the languages that Algerians came into contact with over the centuries. A small number of Greek words were introduced by the Romans and / or the Turks (Ben Cheneb, 1922: 9; Hamdoun, 2004): e.g. *fnâr* ('lighthouse'), *bromich* ('bait for catching fish'). The Romans left Latin words like *pullus* ('chick') Berberised as *fullus* which became *fllûs* in Algerian Arabic. Among the other

Latin lexical items, one finds *qalmun* ('hood'), *harkas* ('espadrille') (Benrabah, 1999a: 71). Disregarding proper names, the number of Turkish words has been estimated at 634 (Ben Cheneb, 1922: 9; Benzaghou, 1978: 29) among which the following common lexical items can be mentioned: *braniya* ('aubergine'), *bukraj* ('kettle') (Ben Cheneb, 1922: 20, 22). From Judeo-Arabic, Algerian Arabic has kept *bestel* ('a dish') and *sdaka* ('charity') (Bar-Asher, 1992: 178; Duclos, 1995: 124). Among the traces of the lingua franca, there are *sourdi* ('money') and *babor* ('ship') (Perego, 1960: 95). The Spaniards also left linguistic traces, and more than 300 lexical items have survived in Algerian Arabic, especially in the west of the country (Benallou, 1992: 6, 2002: 133). Some of these loan words have been indigenised to the point of being considered non-Spanish/Catalan. Among the latter words, one can find: *trabendo* ('smuggling'), *bogado* ('lawyer'), *mariou* ('cupboard'), *capsa* ('tin'), *fechta* ('celebration') (Benallou, 1992, 2002). Finally, the other major European linguistic traces found in the Arabic spoken in Algeria come from French. Such influence is important because it is recent and results from the deep socio-economic impact of French colonialism as a modernising factor. This impact is apparent in the vocabulary in almost all semantic fields: agriculture, fishing, urbanisation, industry, etc. For example, common Arabic words such as *mekteb* ('office'), *tawila* ('table'), *mistara* ('ruler') and *siyara* ('car') were replaced by their French counterpart pronounced [biro], [tabla], [rigla], [tomobil] respectively (Hadj-Sadok, 1955: 61–97; Queffélec *et al.*, 2002: 27; Sayad, 1967: 214–17).

Tamazight

The existence of Tamazight in the northern part of Africa west of Egypt dates back to at least 2000 years BCE. The earliest documentation is provided by the Libyan inscriptions (with only one dated from 139 BCE). There is linguistic evidence to show that Berber languages are closest to the oldest form of Afro-Asian: they have changed least grammatically (Hetzron, 1987: 648; Weber, 1987: 12). In North African polities (Algeria, Morocco, Tunisia, Libya, etc.), the Berber languages are in the minority everywhere. There are four major languages of the Berber branch in Algeria (see map in Figure 2). 'Tamashek' is the language of the Tuaregs of the Sahara (near the Niger border). The Mozabites and Chaouias speak 'Mzab' and 'Shawia' respectively. Kabylians speak 'Kabyle' known locally as 'Takbaylit' (Dalby, 1998: 89; El Aissati, 1993: 92). But there are other small isolated Berber-speaking communities scattered around the country. 'Chenoua' is spoken around the Chenoua mountain between the coastal towns of Cherchell and Tipaza, west of Algiers; 'Tarifit' in coastal towns such as Arzew and Beni Saf in the west of Algeria; 'Korandje' and 'Tachelhit' around Tabelbala oasis near the Moroccan border; 'Tagargrent' south of Constantine; 'Tamazight of Central Atlas' in the south of Oran; 'Taznatit' around Timimoun, near the Touat region; 'Temacine Tamazight' in the vicinity of Touggourt; 'Tidikelt Tamazight' in Salah and Tit in southern Algeria (Ethnologue, 2004). Berber diversity is not specific to regional entities sometimes representing the expression of tribal structures (Queffélec *et al.*, 2002: 33). Most languages of the Berber branch are mutually unintelligible (Hetzron, 1987: 648; Weber, 1987: 12).

Tamashek, the language spoken by the Tuareg nomads in the Sahara Desert, is the only Berber variety to have maintained the old script called *Tifinagh* with its letters known as *Isekkil*. It is an unusual consonantal alphabet which descends from the ancient Libyan script developed from a late form of the Egyptian hieroglyphs (Dalby, 1998: 89; Hetzron, 1987: 648; Weber, 1987: 12). Today, almost all Berber languages use Arabic or Latin scripts for everyday use. But with the rise of Berber nationalism in the 1970s, berberophone militants have adopted Tifinagh as a symbol of Berber authenticity. Since the late 1980s, three scripts have been in use for Berber: Arabic, Latin and Tifinagh (Tilmatine, 1992: 156).

Across all of North Africa, place names are largely of Berber origin easily recognisable by the double mark of feminine nouns *t- -t*. For example, in Tamashek, the word *barar* for 'son' is pronounced *tabarart* for 'daughter'. This specifically Berber form is found in the language names *Tamazight*, *Tachelhit* and *Tagargrent* as well as place names such as Touggourt and Tamanrasset (Dalby, 1998: 89). Furthermore, the various invaders of North Africa left cultural traces which are still visible today in the presence of many loanwords. For example, in the Kabylian lexicon, there are words remaining from an early influence from Greek, Phoenician, Punic/Carthaginian and Roman/Latin (Tilmatine, 1992: 159). From the Punic/Carthaginian language, Berber has borrowed words like *agadir* ('wall'), and from Latin *asnus* ('donkey foal'), *urtu* ('orchard'), *iger* ('field'), *tayuyya* ('harness') (Taifi, 1997: 62). The strongest influence comes from Arabic and French. As noted, linguistic proximity (Afro-Asian origin) and prolonged contact made Berber influence Algerian Arabic morpho phonology and lexis. As a result of the homogenising effect of Islam, Arabic left major traces in the vocabulary of all Berber languages with the exception of Tamashek (Chaker, 1991: 216; Taifi, 1997: 63; Tilmatine, 1992: 156). For example, out of 6000 entries in his Kabyle-French dictionary, Dallet (1982) gives 1590 words of Arabic origin. According to Chaker (1984: 58), Arabic loanwords represent 35% of the total Kabyle lexis and relate to the following major semantic-lexical fields: numerals, generic terms (animal, human, body, bird, tree), intellectual life (writing, thinking, understanding, book, letter), religious and spiritual lives (belief, prayer, mosque, saints), socio-economic life (work, money) (Chaker, 1991: 226). Among these borrowings, one finds *ddin* ('religion'), *nnbi* ('prophet'), *ttesbiq* ('deposit'), *ssalaf* ('loan'), *tti ara* ('trade'). Numerals were among the first to be Arabised. For example, in Berber languages such as Kabyle which has had prolonged contact with Arabic only two numerals out of 10 have not been arabised. By contrast, all 10 numerals have kept the old Berber form in Tamashek (Chaker, 1991: 226; Taifi, 1997: 65). The influence of French is also important, especially in technical and administrative fields (Chaker, 1991: 227). Following the French conquest, Berber borrowed many French words either directly or via Arabic. Among these loans, there are *fesyan* ('army officer'), *kmandar* ('army major'), *lkufa* ('convoy'), *ttebla* ('table'), *ibiru* ('office'), *ttumubil* ('automobile'), *ajenyur* ('engineer'), *timmarksit* ('Marxism') (Kahlouche, 1991: 101–4; Taifi, 1997: 62; Tilmatine, 1992: 159).

French

French is officially considered a foreign language in Algeria, a status which is 'absolutely theoretical and fictitious' (Queffélec *et al.*, 2002: 36). Algerian French was born in the midst of a highly complex multilingual context. During the colonial era, interaction occurred between speakers with multiple linguistic structures and systems that interpenetrated each other: French, Provençal, Castillan, Catalan, Italian (southern), Corsican, Maltese, Judeo-Arabic, Arabic and Berber

(Morsly, 2004: 173). The extension and development of the colonial educational system allowed Standard French to spread mainly among the population of European descent and a minority of Arabo-Berber Algerians. This situation gave birth to the 'latest among the regional French varieties' (Lanly, 1970: 197; Perego, 1960: 91) which was shared by both Europeans and Arabo-Berbers (Queffélec, 1995: 814). French varieties during colonisation can be schematised along a dialect continuum (Queffélec *et al.*, 2002: 25–6). At one end of the continuum is found the basilect known as *pataouète* mainly used in the port towns of Algiers, Oran, Skikda, Annaba and Mostaganem. It was spoken by French and European Algerians from low social classes as well as a minority of urban Arabo-Berbers who interacted with the former (Duclos, 1995: 121; Queffélec *et al.*, 2002: 25). At the other end of the continuum, there was an acrolect which is mainly written, strongly influenced by the French norm and used by teachers, journalists, writers, colonial administrators, etc.

By 1900, the basilectal variety, which served as a vernacular language, disappeared under the influence of the French schooling system and language standardisation. An intermediate form (mesolect) arose and maintained many features of the basilect (Queffélec, 1995: 809). The original basilectal aspects exist at the level of phonetics, morpho-syntax, vocabulary and phraseology (Duclos, 1992; Lanly, 1970; Perego, 1960). These features still appear today in the words and expressions used by Algerian speakers of French. For example, it is typically Algerian to use *piment* instead of *poivron* in *Une salade de piments et tomates* ('A pepper and tomato salad'), *chaîne* instead of *queue* in *Faire la chaîne* ('queue up'). Interjections such as *Je te jure, ma parole, ma fille, poh poh poh* are remnants of *pieds noirs* speech (Duclos, 1995: 123–4; Queffélec *et al.*, 2002: 455). Algerian French still contains words of Corsican/Italian origin like *ch'koumoun* ('misfortune'), Catalan/Spanish origin like *kalentika* ('a dish'), *melva* ('type of bonito fish'), *mouna* ('large brioche') (Queffélec *et al.*, 2002: 372, 415, 427).

The spectrum of French varieties described above for the colonial period is still valid at present even though the vast majority of Algerians of European descent left the country in 1962. The basilectal form is used by two social categories within the population. First, there are Algerians who hold low-ranking positions in the administrative sector, educated before Arabisation was implemented, with an elementary education in French. The second group includes Arabised monolinguals trained after the implementation of Arabisation who did not have access to French for one reason or another (nationalism, lack of teachers, etc.). Both groups consist of civil servants in town halls, courts of justice, etc. (Queffélec *et al.*, 2002: 119–20). The acrolectal variety is used by the francophone elite in their work on a daily basis (university science teachers, senior civil servants, etc.). However, these social categories use the mesolectal form for social interaction instead. It is by far the most widespread variety of French spoken in Algeria. It is used by Arabic-French or Berber-French bilinguals who had a long school-training with prolonged and stable contact with French. The term *mesolect* covers a wide range of varieties intermediate in form between basilect and acrolect. Such variety, which is undergoing a process of standardisation (phonetic/phonological, morpho-syntactic and lexical), is currently being indigenised under the influence of the three local languages: Algerian Arabic, Classical/Literary Arabic and Tamazight (Queffélec *et al.*, 2002: 119–21). One notable phonetic/phonological influence from Arabic and Berber is the use of emphatic /θ/ and /ð/ for /t/ and /d/ respectively. The use of emphatics is common in the context of back vowels as in: /Tɑpi/ for *tapis* ('carpet') and /Domaž/ for *dommage* ('it's a shame') (Aouad-Elmentfakh, 1980: 78; Dekkak, 1979: 44). Morpho-syntactic differentiation is less important, but one can find, among other things, gender-differentiations which are unacceptable in metropolitan French. For example, the expression *agente policière* refers to a policewoman and adjectives such as *concerné* ('concerned') and *mis en cause* ('implicated in an enquiry') have been converted into nouns (Queffélec *et al.*, 2002: 156, 255, 419–20). Furthermore, Algerian French tends to simplify the verbal system involving the future tense (Cherrad-Benchefra, 1995: 105).

When compared with metropolitan French, the transformations within the lexis of Algerian French have been 'spectacular' and quantitatively important (Cherrad-Benchefra, 1995: 89). In fact, the number of 'Algerianisms' has been estimated at 1500 by Queffélec *et al.* (2002: 140). Loan words come either from Arabic or Berber and concern several lexical semantic fields: religion and holidays (e.g. *Achoura, fatwa, yennayer*), education (e.g. *cheikh, taleb*), administration (e.g. *darki, djoundi*), politics (e.g. *dawla, houkouma*), behaviour (e.g. *hogra, rahma, radjel*), dressing and food (e.g. *burnous, amane, tabzimt*), etc. (Queffélec *et al.*, 2002: 147–560). Morphological processes play a major role in word-formation: (1) compounding: *hizb frança* ('The Party of France', a term used derisively by Arabist zealots to disqualify Algerian Francophones), *café-goudron* (strong black espresso café), *babor-Australia* ('Boat from Australia': a mythical boat from Australia that young desperate Algerians with limited horizons yearn for to emigrate to the West) (Queffélec *et al.*, 2002: 138); (2) suffixation involves either an Arabic/Berber base or a French one followed by a French suffix: *dégoûtage* ('despair and boredom'), *cravaté* ('someone wearing a tie'), *taxieur* ('taxi-driver'), *khobziste* ('an opportunist and profiteer who takes advantage of any situation to make gains symbolised by the word *khobz* which means 'bread' in Arabic') (Derradji, 1995: 114–17; Kadi, 1995: 154–61; Queffélec *et al.*, 2002: 136–7)

Diglossia, bilingualism and literacy

McFerren (1984: 5) states that diglossia 'remains the single greatest impediment to Arabisation in the Maghreb'. Diglossia involves a situation in which two varieties of the same language live side by side in a complementary relationship, each performing a different function in society. Charles Ferguson described a diglossic community as having a prestigious standard or 'High' (or H) variety used formally (literature, the media, formal speech-making, education, prayer) and is linguistically related to but significantly different from the vernacular or 'Low' (or L) varieties used colloquially and usually informally (Fasold, 1984; Ferguson, 1959). The former is learned through formal education in school while the latter is an acquired system with a community of native speakers. Arabic in the Arab world has been cited as an exemplar of diglossia. It is the ideal of *al-'arabiyya* 'the pure Arabic' (Hary, 2003: 65) and the set of myths about the 'High' language held by many native speakers, regardless of the level of education, that bring about the obstacle mentioned (Kaye, 1987: 675).

The belief that only the 'High' variety is 'appropriate' for use in the classroom – dialectal Arabic is usually stigmatised and regarded as a degenerate form of Arabic – has long been entrenched in Arabic-speaking polities (El-Dash & Tucker, 1976; Ennaji, 1999; Ferguson, 1959; Taha, 1990). Such conviction is even more marked in the Maghreb in general and Algeria in particular (Grandguillaume, 1997a: 9–10). As in the rest of the Arab world, diglossia as a major sociolinguistic and educational barrier – social, psychological and educational problems and difficulties that hamper the socioeconomic development of learners (Ezzaki & Wagner, 1992: 217–8; Ibrahim, 1983: 511, 1989: 42; Marley, 2004: 28; Talmoudi, 1984: 32) – has not received enough objective attention in Algeria. The major source of the problem is these myths that people and the elite closely associate with religious and nationalist issues. Orientalists and Arabists were among the first to draw attention to the (teaching) problems created by diglossia (Ferguson, 1963; Marçais, 1930). Immediately after Algeria's independence, the latter arguments were often refuted by the authorities on nationalist grounds – conspiracy theories[17] (Saad, 1992: 74; Taleb Ibrahimi, 1981: 19). However, there were Arab educators/linguists who also considered the issue of diglossia and its negative effects on Arab personality. For example, as early as 1955, Furayhah, a Lebanese scholar, described the two varieties of Arabic as the expression of two separate selves (1955: 33). But, as forecast by Ferguson in 1959, the process of bridging the gap between the 'High' and 'Low' forms has been under way in Algeria since 1962. The following major factors, mentioned by the American sociolinguist, have favoured the destabilisation of diglossia: linguistic urbanisation as a result of population mobility (rural depopulation), mass instruction in Classical Arabic and the Arabisation of the milieu (see Part VI 'Language maintenance and future prospects'). These ecological factors give rise to a *Koiné* that several Algerian linguists call Algerian Arabic (Benrabah, 1993; Bouamrane, 1986; Queffélec *et al.*, 2002).

However, linguistic urbanisation as a result of rural depopulation has not always been in favour of Algerian Arabic since the independence of the country. Until the 1960s, the indigenous population of Tizi Ouzou, the administrative centre of Kabylia, was largely arabophone. Post-independent rural depopulation in the Kabylian region has allowed Tamazight to become the major language of communication in Tizi Ouzou. In the latter city, Arabophones are bilingual: they use Algerian Arabic at home and Tamazight when interacting with Berber-speaking compatriots outside (Kahlouche, 1996: 42–3). Tizi Ouzou represents, in fact, a miniature replica of the language profile of the entire country marked by societal bilingualism and polyglossia (Blanc, 1999; Platt, 1977).

As a complex multilingual society, Algeria presents at least two H, several L languages and an intermediate set of M (or mid) varieties. Algerian Arabic represents the main M form of Arabic and, with the exception of a few elderly monolingual Berber speakers, is used by almost all groups (Queffélec *et al.*, 2002: 34–5). Moreover, a cosmopolitan city like Algiers with different Berber-speaking communities (Kabylian, Shawia, Tamashek, etc.) will probably produce a Berber Koiné (M variety) in the future, especially after having acquired, in April 2002, the status of national language and finally official status (Kahlouche, 1996: 43). The L forms are all the other rural and urban varieties of Arabic and Berber (all first languages). The two H forms are Standard Arabic and French. The former colonial idiom remains in a privileged position: it is the first obligatory foreign language in schools, it is the working language in government besides Arabic, and it is also used in the homes, etc. (Bouhadiba, 2002: 16; Morsly, 1980: 131–5, 1984: 23–4; Queffélec et al., 2002: 36). It has the status of a major language in Ferguson's terminology (Ferguson, 1966: 311). Both are acquired languages even though a few Algerian families of European descent have French as their first language (Morsly, 1996: 71–2). Since independence, English has been gaining dominance in a number of sectors: the oil industry, computing and scientific and technological documentation (Bouhadiba, 2002: 16). In the 1980s and early 1990s, an ESP resource-centre project was established to set up advisory units for in-service teacher training and materials design (Bencherif, 1993) but the project faded in the mid-1990s (Daoud, 2000: 79; Lakhdar Barka, 2002). Between 1993 and 2003, a small number of schoolchildren were taught English as the first oblig- atory foreign language, starting from the Fourth grade. Thus, the Algerian child grows up in a multilingual environment. If she/he follows the nine-year long compulsory school curriculum, and depending on whether her/his first language is Algerian Arabic or Tamazight, she/he will acquire one of the two following combinations of languages presented in the order of acquisition/ learning (adapted from Queffélec et al., 2002: 86–7): Type 1: L1: Algerian Arabic, (L2: Tamazight), L3: Literary Arabic, L4: French, L5: English. Type 2: L1: Tamazight, L2: Algerian Arabic, L3: Literary Arabic, L4: French, L5: English.

For the native speaker of Algerian Arabic (Type 1) who grows up in Tizi Ouzou, for example, Tamazight represents the second language of socialisation. But this is the case for a minority of Arabophones; for the majority in most parts of the country, the first language learned at school is Literary Arabic – hence the brackets showing Tamazight as optional. For the child who chooses English instead of French as the first foreign language, French is almost always present in her/his environment (the media, family, streets, etc.) while the reverse is not necessarily true since English is learned at school only. For the child whose first language is Tamazight (Type 2), Algerian Arabic is almost always the second language of socialisation, then comes Literary Arabic as the imposed institu- tional language at school, then French and English in that order. Of the two combinations presented above, Type 1 is probably the most widespread in Alge- ria. As a matter of fact, when Tamazight is part of a bilingual or multilingual competence, it almost always involves speakers whose first language is Berber (Taifi, 1997: 73). In addition to the above possible combinations of (acquired and learned) languages, the Algerian child, who reaches the secondary level at the age of 16, is likely to learn one of the following foreign languages: German, Span- ish, Russian (Lachachi, 2003: 75).

A final aspect of Algeria's polyglossia pertains to code-switching, that is, instances when speakers alternate between languages or language varieties (Swann, 2000: 148). Algerians switch back and forth between Standard Arabic and French, dialectal/Algerian Arabic and a Berber variety (Kabyle et Mzab, Shawia, Tamashek, etc.), French and dialectal/Algerian Arabic, a Berber variety (Kabyle, Mzabite, Shawia, Tamashek, etc.) and French, etc. (Bouamrane, 1986: 108–11, 181–2; Bouhadiba, 2002: 18–26; Kahlouche, 1993: 73; Queffélec et al., 2002: 121). Although code-switching is officially stigmatised, it is in fact an expression of an aspiration to be competent in the language of social promotion and, in Alge- ria, this language is French. Code-switching is widespread among young people, especially girls who, because of overt prestige, use code-switching even if they have an elementary competence in French (Caubet, 2002: 234).

Standard Arabic and French are the major languages of literacy in Algeria. Governmental documents, the media, literature(s), etc. are produced in both languages. The substantial gains obtained through Arabisation are visible in literacy rates: a very high number of Algerians are literate in Standard Arabic. Among the literate population (around 20–23 million), three quarters are more or less competent in French (Queffélec *et al.*, 2002: 118). Literary Arabic and French thus remain the languages of social and economic promotion. And this is reflected in young Algerians' attitudes towards the various languages that are in competition in Algeria.

In April/May 2004, this author carried out a large survey among secondary school students in three cities in the west of Algeria.[18] A total of 1051 subjects filled out a written direct closed-choice questionnaire. They were all aged between 14–15 and 20; the majority (55.6%) were 17–18 years old. In terms of gender, 42.5% were male and 57.5% female. The survey revealed that the most valued languages among young students are Literary Arabic and French. For example, to the statement 'The most useful language for studies is . . . ', 1028 respondents gave the following answers: (1) Algerian Arabic: 3.2%, (2) Literary Arabic: 38.1%, (3) French: 58.1%, (4) Tamazight: 0.6%. The above results show that a very small proportion of informants chose the 'Low' varieties as languages for instruction – 3.2% for Algerian Arabic and 0.6% for Tamazight. This supports the trend current in the Arab world and discussed elsewhere. Furthermore, the presence of two 'High' varieties makes the situation more complex: the results obtained for the activity show that French has an edge on the national official language. Literary Arabic alone is not sufficient for social mobility as the results for two other statements show. One thousand and forty-two informants responded as follows to the statement 'Literary Arabic is necessary for finding a job in Algeria': (1) Agree completely: 8.5%, (2) Agree: 19.3%, (3) Neither agree nor disagree: 17.5%, (4) Disagree: 32.8%, (5) Disagree completely: 21.9%. The majority (54.7%) disagree with the statement. Literacy in Arabic alone does not secure a job in Algeria. By contrast, Arabic-French bilingualism is highly valued as confirmed by the high percentage (82.4%) of respondents who agree with the statement 'Being bilingual in Arabic and French is an advantage and allows one to live and prosper in Algeria'. The results show that 1044 subjects responded as follows: (1) Agree completely: 40.5%, (2) Agree: 41.9%, (3) Neither agree nor disagree: 9.9%, (4) Disagree: 4.7%, (5) Disagree completely: 3.1%. (For other results of this survey, see Part VI: Language Maintenance and Future Prospects.)

Part IV: Language Policy and Planning

Language policy and planning can be defined as conscious intervention to change the future of language and its use in a community (Mesthrie *et al.*, 2000: 384; Rubin & Jernudd, 1971: xvi). It is a process which involves both the choice of one variety/language among alternatives (Daoust, 1997: 438; Fasold, 1984: 248) and some kind of organised body (usually, government authorities) to take charge of such a planning change (Weinstein, 1983: 37). This endeavour requires the achievement of linguistic, political and social goals by means of a body of ideas, laws and regulations: language policy (Kaplan & Baldauf, 1997: 3; Mesthrie *et al.*, 2000: 384). Up to the present time, four dimensions of language planning have been identified: (1) 'status planning' refers to most of the legal process of making a language national and/or official (Kloss, 1967, 1969); (2) 'corpus planning', being the technical side of the enterprise, attempts to fix or modify the linguistic characteristics (internal structure) of the language in question (Kloss, 1967, 1969); (3) 'acquisition planning' ensures that the planned language is spread and promoted by being taught and learned in the educational system (Cooper, 1989); (4) 'prestige planning' involves the development of a favourable psychological background which is necessary for the future success of language planning activities (Haarmann, 1990). This neat but oversimplified division does not account for the fact that it is nearly impossible, in practice, to separate these various interdependent activities (Kaplan & Baldauf, 1997: 28, 49).

As in other developing countries, the Algerian government plays a major role in language planning activities. After Algeria got its independence from France in 1962, its leadership formulated a language policy for the post-colonial age known as the policy of Arabisation or Arabisation for short.

The policy of Arabisation: 'Arabicisation' *vs.* 'Arabisation'

The Arabic term *ta'rib* is sometimes translated interchangeably as 'Arabicisation' or 'Arabisation', although the difference between these terms is not insignificant (Benabdi, 1980; Elkhafaifi, 2002; Ennaji, 1999; Ibrahim, 1989; Suleiman, 1999). The first sense applies mostly in the Arab Middle East and to two countries of North Africa (Libya and Egypt) referring to both status/acquisition and corpus planning activities – planners replace some other (usually colonial) language by Arabic as the medium of instruction in all cycles of the educational system, and they enrich the language by incorporating into it newly borrowed or derived/revived words. In North African countries (Algeria, Morocco, Tunisia), which were former French colonies, *ta'rib* means the replacement of French by Arabic in all walks of life (education, administration, milieu, media, etc.) as well as the use of the latter language as an instrument for national unity and the affirmation of an identity that is exclusively Arab. Hence, while 'Arabicisation' is a linguistic process, 'Arabisation', is both cultural and linguistic and has a much wider application with profound implications for modern Arab society (Cherrad-Benchefra & Derradji, 2004: 153; Grandguillaume, 1990: 155–6; Saadi-Mokrane, 2002: 49; Vermeren, 2004: 201; Yahiatene, 1997: 66).

In Algeria, the language policy chosen by planners had both linguistic and cultural/ideological aims. For Algerian supporters of Arabisation as a linguistic process, French, the colonial language, must serve as a model for planners. A process described by Gilbert Grandguillaume as 'Arabisation-translation', when he claims that newly created words 'can only be understood through the French words that they translate and not through Arabic's own semantic context' (Grandguillaume, 1990: 159). For example, the Modern Arabic expressions *luughat xashab* and *maa'ida mustadiira* are direct translations of French terms *langue de bois* ('political cant') and *table ronde* ('round table (talks)') respectively. In other words, it consists of saying in Arabic the same thing one might have said in French. Supporters of the cultural/ideological project insist on the national/official language to convey other things than French. Arabisation-translation is seen as the 'Trojan horse of Westernization' (Grandguillaume, 1983: 25, 1990: 159–60). They rather prefer what Grandguillaume calls 'Arabisation-conversion' which aims at establishing a mentality that is non-French but exclusively Arabo-Islamic or nationalist with Classical/Standard Arabic as its linguistic vehicle – non-Arab groups must be assimilated. Arabisation-conversion is thus synonymous with the Islamisation of society while Arabisation-translation aims at restoring a language and not a faith. If the former process can only be accompanied by monolingualism with Classical/Standard Arabic and total Arabisation, the latter comes with bilingualism (Grandguillaume, 1983: 31, 1990: 156, 1996: 42).

Immediately after independence, supporters of Arabisation-translation, who were secular and progressive, held power in the first government (1962–1965). When the latter was removed by a *coup d'état* in June 1965, nationalist conservatives and supporters of Arabisation-conversion tilted the balance of power in their favour. Their ideology was to be part and parcel of the totalitarian socio-political model implemented after the 1965 military overthrow. Systematic Arabisation or Arabisation 'at all cost' starts with the military coup in 1965. Language-in-education planning may be one of the key strategies used by governments to achieve their grand designs.

The newly appointed Minister of Education was in favour of a systematic and immediate arabising process (Grandguillaume, 1995: 18) while his predecessor would have preferred a gradual realisation of Arabisation (Gordon, 1966: 200). In November 1965, the new Minister of Education asked the question: 'What kind of man do we want to train (in schools)?' (Taleb Ibrahimi, 1981: 72). In a report drawn up in August 1966, he writes: 'National Education is, in some respects, like a business firm which needs to plan its production according to its forecasts/ perspectives mapped out not only for a few years, but for almost a generation' (Taleb Ibrahimi, 1981: 101). The Minister of Education also writes 'School, is the silent revolution' (Taleb Ibrahimi, 1981: 76) and even goes so far as to quote T.S. Eliot's definition of the word *culture*: 'Culture is something that needs to be developed. It is not in man's power to build a tree. All he can do is plant it, take care of it and wait until it grows little by little' (Taleb Ibrahimi, 1981: 66). The preceding quotations are characteristic of discourse in totalitarian regimes: the need to transform the governed, it is dominated by the idea of creating a 'new man' and a 'new society'. For example, the newly appointed Minister of Education, who used the expressions 'a new Algerian' and 'a new Algeria', talked about the necessary emergence of a new generation that needs to 'learn to think in Arabic' (Taleb Ibrahimi, 1981: 98). Other Algerian nationalist-conservatives consider the linguistic aspects of Arabisation as 'secondary' and prefer the new school to 'arabise thinking first' or to aim at 'the arabisation of minds and hearts before that of languages' (Grandguillaume, 1983: 117; Rakibi, 1975/1982: 137). After 1965, the balance of power being in the nationalists' favour allowed them to implement Arabisation as a comprehensive (linguistic and cultural) ideology.

Schiffman argues that every language policy is embedded in and proceeds from 'linguistic culture',[19] that is the sum total of 'behaviours, assumptions, cultural forms, prejudices, folk belief systems, attitudes, stereotypes, ways of thinking about language, and religio-historical circumstances associated with a particular language' (Schiffman, 1996: 5). Algeria's leaders' language choices are grounded on and proceed from a linguistic culture that is the product of history and the Algerian national movement. It is thus necessary to understand the development of Algerian nationalism in relation to the language issue.

The dual nature of Algerian nationalism

Mobilisation towards the task of nation-building involves the notion of identity as a source of symbols and legitimacy. Among the central components of national identity there is culture, religion and language. The latter represents 'an outward sign of a group's peculiar identity and a significant means of ensuring its continuation' (Kedourie, 1961: 71). With other Arab nationalist movements around the world, Algerian nationalism shares the view that the constituent parts of national identity comprise Arab-Islamic tradition (culture), Islam (religion) and Classical Arabic which is the carrier of the Koran, the holy book of Muslims (language).

The dual nature of Algerian nationalism stems from the intellectual and political formation of the Algerian elite. Those trained in France came into contact with French ideas and thinking as students (under the influence of professors, universities, etc.) or as workers influenced by trade unions, socialist and communist militants, etc. (Vermeren, 2004: 92, 100). French linguistic culture considers language as a defining 'core value', that is, a feature that characterises culture (Smolicz, 1979). The long tradition of mythologising about French has deep roots and an almost religious impact as the following quotation dated in 1925 by a French public official shows: 'the French God has always been a jealous God. He can be worshipped only in French . . . [a language] whose jealous cult can never have too many altars' (Weber, 1984: 73). There is an ironic paradox with French linguistic culture: inspired by democratic Jacobinism and an enlightenment social conscience, French language policy has come to resemble models hardly inspired by democratic impulses. The French sociolinguist Calvet argues that some of the methods adopted in France to deal with the language issue are similar to those associated with fascist countries. He mentions four such approaches: (1) xenophobic purism on the level of the national language, illustrated by attempts to remove 'foreign' elements; (2) cultural centralism directed against dialects; (3) nationalist centralism directed against national minorities; and (4) colonialism or linguistic expansionism beyond the frontiers of the country (1999a: 261–2).

The other linguistic culture that influenced Algerian intellectuals comes from the Middle East where many nationalists lived in exile during colonisation and the War of Algeria. In the Middle East, they discovered Pan-Arabism and Arab linguistic nationalism. The principal founding father of Arab (linguistic) nationalism was Sati Al-Husri (1880–1963) (Carré, 1996: 13; Suleiman, 1994: 7). Educated in the West, in France in particular, Al-Husri's ideas can be described as 'acculturationist': they remain 'the product of an imitative adaptation of Western culture' (Tibi, 1981: 23). Al-Husri, who spoke Turkish as his first language, was an Ottoman Iraqi subject and a government official who promoted Classical Arabic as the most important index among the various affiliative bonds which exist in the Arab world. At the same time he fought the local varieties considered to have a divisive role in Arab life (Suleiman, 1994: 10). His uncompromising pronouncement, borrowed from the Prophetic tradition[20] (Gadant,

1988: 52; Suleiman, 1994: 22), states: 'Every Arabic-speaking people is an Arab people. Every individual belonging to one of these Arabic-speaking peoples is an Arab' (Tibi, 1981: 163). He thus turns linguistic identity into an ethnic one (Grandguillaume, 1983: 40), a self-identification that will have far-reaching effects on people's representations in the Maghreb in general and Algeria in particular (Vermeren, 2004: 20).

Al-Husri's ideas were to be used later by the founding fathers of the Arab Resurrection Party *Ba'th*. The major theorists of Ba'thist ideology (Pan-Arabism) were enthusiasts of the traditional Arab mythology which revered religious texts. In this tradition, 'religion was as much the conveyor of the language as the language the conveyor of religion' (Polk, 1970: xiv). Its purity, beauty, timelessness, and *i'jaz al Qur'ān* (the inimitability of the Koran) have turned Classical Arabic into a 'miraculous language' (Calvet, 1999a: 38; Carré, 1996: 72). Furthermore, there is a widespread belief in the oneness of Arabic (spoken and written varieties) in the entire Arab world (Ma'mouri *et al.*, 1983: 12–13). The latter aspect legitimises the constant return to origins and the quest for linguistic purism and authenticity of long ago.

Another illustration of the significance of Classical Arabic for Arab-Muslim society is the emotion it gives rise to as a unifying force and symbol for all Arabic-speaking peoples. There is a belief that a form of organic unity exists between Arabism and the Arabic language (Garrison, 1975); that is a relationship reinforced by ideas developed by the Ba'th. The founding Congress of Ba'th in April 1947 set up a Constitution which extended further the concept of Arab 'nation' – Pan-Arab community defined, henceforth, as 'one nation from the Atlantic to the Gulf' (Article 7). Article 10 reads: 'An Arab is a person whose mother tongue is Arabic, who has lived or who lived or who looks forward to living on Arab soil, and who believes in being a member of the Arab nation' (Sharabi, 1966: 96). According to a prominent Coptic Pan-Arab nationalist leader, 'Arab nationalism is synonymous with the Arabic language' (quoted in Suleiman, 1994: 18). Ba'th also took up Al-Husri's belief that ethno-regional, or even national, linguistic sentiments would lead to divisiveness. Another major founding member of Ba'th, Michel Aflak, a Christian who idealised Islam, believed that non-Arabic-speaking communities such as Berbers in North Africa (as well as Christians in the Middle East and Kurds in Iraq) will be automatically diluted into the 'Arab nation'. The curt tone of Articles 11 and 15 in the Ba'th Constitution describes illegal and as of no right any 'schismatic' ethno-regional community which rejects the Pan-Arab nationalist ideal (Carré, 1996: 57–8; Saint-Prot, 1995: 25). For example, Berbers in North Africa, who demand linguistic rights and reject Pan-Arabism, are considered as divisive and their demands illegitimate. There are even Iraqi Ba'th militants who, in the past and on an official visit to Morocco, encouraged their Moroccan Ba'thist friends to simply eradicate their Berber-speaking compatriots (*Thawiza*, 2002: 5).

The Maghrebi scholar Abdallah Bounfour describes Ba'th ideology as expansionist and considers Pan-Arab pronouncements on cultural unity and the rejection of multilingualism as a return to the basics of (Arab-Islamic) imperial ideology which idealises the primacy of the 'Unique [God] against multiplicity' (Bounfour, 1994: 8). Compared with French linguistic culture – which was familiar to Al-Husri and major Ba'th theorists because most of them studied in

France – Pan-Arab linguistic culture is not only imperialist but founded on undemocratic and extremely elitist principles. Ba'th ideologues seek socio-political structures based on a 'single Arab state' – with Egypt the natural 'leader of the Arab world' (Cleveland, 1971: 131) – and promote an 'Arab nation' led by a strong charismatic person (Carré, 1996: 53). As to civil liberties, Ba'th partisans simply took up Al-Husri's rejection of the freedom of the individual, a thought inspired by totalitarian doctrines. The extent of his disposition to totalitarianism is indicated in the following intransigent declaration: 'I say continuously and without hesitation: "Patriotism and nationalism above and before all else, even above and before freedom"' (Cleveland, 1971: 170). In fact, the educational policies that Al-Husri introduced in 1923 and 1944 as Director General of Education in both Iraq and Syria were focused inward. To achieve 'cultural independence', he eliminated the study of foreign languages in primary schools (Cleveland, 1971: 63, 79). He also knowingly subjected history to the demands of his pan-Arab ideology by employing a judiciously selected history syllabus while at the same time acknowledging that such practices characterised modern dictatorships (Cleveland, 1971: 147).

Both French and Arabic linguistic cultures have a number of elements in common:

(1)   The idea of 'nation' is totally identified with one single language.
(2)   Linguistic purism and 'fixedness': 'language was 'fixed' once and for all in the past, and cannot be changed now by mere mortals' (Schiffman, 1996: 71).
(3)   Expansionism and a 'war' against dialects and local languages.
(4)   Centrist language policies.

It is probably the added effect of these two linguistic cultural traditions which lies behind the zeal of Algeria's language planners formed in the major parties that represented the backbone of Algerian nationalism.

Growth of Algerian nationalism

On 1st November 1954, the National Liberation Front Party (FLN) declared war on the French in Algeria. That historic All Saints' Day of 1954 represented the final stage in the development of Algerian nationalism which had come into the open in the late 1920s. The national movement grew out of three separate strands each associated with a particular leader and characterised as either reformist or independence-oriented. If all these parties were diluted in 1954 into a conglomeration to liberate the country, all those who created the FLN came from the independence-oriented party, with Reformists having almost no role in this endeavour (Yefsah, 1990: 24). In this section, the emphasis will rest on the independence-oriented nationalist group and one Reformist ideology. In fact, these two nationalist brands will influence language planning in post-independence Algeria. The discussion will begin with the presentation of the two major Reformist parties with their conception of the 'Algerian nation' and respective programmes (with regard to the issue of language and identity).

The Democratic Union of the Algerian Manifesto (UDMA) was founded in April 1946 by a group of liberals, the central figure being Ferhat Abbas (1899–1985). He was the son of a *caïd* (indigenous local governor) and Commander of the French Legion of Honour. He epitomised the Westernised middle-class (*évolué*) and his social milieu oriented him towards bourgeois France (Horne, 1987: 40). The UDMA had a very restricted following among the rank and file (Harbi, 1984: 44) and its members (mainly doctors, lawyers, pharmacists and other liberal functionaries) demanded like the *pieds noirs* an equal access to political and economic posts (Yefsah, 1990: 27). Abbas equated Franco-Algerian equality and assimilation with metropolitan France because he did not believe in a separate Algerian identity (Collot & Henry, 1978: 66–7). However, if he demanded equality with Algerians of European descent, he remained secular but attached to his Islamic faith (Stora, 1991: 75; 2004: 58). As for the language issue, Abbas' demand for the study of Arabic is clearly stated in a 1936 editorial:

> This [Arabic] language is to the Muslim religion what the Church is to the Catholic religion. It could not live without it. The belief of an illiterate Muslim is a web of indigestible superstitions. For us the Mosque is nothing. The reading of the Sacred Book is everything. It stands as the cement of our faith. Is it then necessary to declare our commitment to the teaching of the Arabic language, the basis of our belief? (Collot & Henry, 1978: 66)

Moreover, the programme of the Algerian Popular Union, a party created by Abbas in July 1938, called for the 'teaching of the Arabic language' (Stora & Daoud, 1995: 92). In the Manifesto of the Algerian people (*Manifeste du Peuple Algérien*), which emerged in 1943, he made a number of demands, among which the following pertain to language and education: 'free and compulsory instruction for the children of both sexes', 'the recognition of Arabic as an official language in the same capacity as the French language' (Stora & Daoud, 1995: 121).

In May 1931, Sheikh Abdelhamid Ben Badis (1889–1940) founded a religious movement, as embodied by the *Association of the Ulemas*.[21] Ben Badis descended from a rich bourgeois family of Berber (Kabylian) origin settled in Constantine (in Eastern Algeria). He became a scholar at the religious Zitouna University in Tunisia. As an ascetic and deeply conservative theologian, he believed in Islamic reformism (*Islah*) emanating from the Middle East. According to Ben Badis, the regeneration of Algeria needed a return to the first principles of Islam. He accused the Algerian rural traditional brand of Islam, represented by the *marabouts* (holy men), as a corruption of the Muslim faith which served colonialism (Horne, 1987: 38). The Ulema's programme was both religious and cultural. It considered education as a means to achieve *Islah*, and the *Association of the Ulemas* set up a network of free schools (*medersa*) across the country (see Part III). These institutions valued the revival of Islamic cultural identity, Pan-Arab ideals and the teaching of Arabic. Ben Badis' famous creed was: 'Arabic is my language, Algeria is my country, Islam is my religion' (Stora, 1991: 74). Hence, it is to the Ulemas' credit that they pushed the Algerian elite, attracted by assimilation, to value their (Arab-Islamic) identity and not to ignore their past.

According to Gadant, 'the Ulemas were a national movement which produced makers of ideology, but in politics, they were always, no pun intended, reformists' (Gadant, 1988: 28). For example, Article 3 of the rules and regulations of the *Association of the Ulemas* banned any debating of political issues (Collot & Henry, 1978: 45; Yefsah, 1990: 25). If Ben Badis opposed the assimilation called for by Ferhat Abbas, he nevertheless advocated the integration of the 'Algerian Muslim community within the great French family' (Stora, 1991: 75). The Ulemas mistake their own social position (religious, urban, bourgeois) for that of the entire country: they have a Jacobean definition of Algerian identity assimilated with towns and cities (Harbi, 1984: 117). Moreover, they had close ties with Middle Eastern Pan-Islamic/Pan-Arab ideologies, and they remained docile to their directives (Ageron, 1969: 88; Bessis, 1978: 473, 475). Their inability to dissociate language from religion leads them to equate Arabisation with Islamisation (in its *Islah* version):

> The Arabic language is not thought of as a means of transmitting knowledge but as a support for religion which must hold the highest influence over ideas. The revival of Arabic is both put in competition with French and used as a barrier erected against 'foreign influences'. (Harbi, 1984: 117–18).

The Ulemas undervalue the people's culture, the peasants' traditional rural Islamic faith and, consequently, their modes of expression (Petit, 1971: 262). The French historian Meynier recalls a telling event about the Ulemas' failure to bridge the gap that separates them from the population. After a public speech made by Ben Badis in El Eulma (Eastern Algeria) in the 1930s, people in the audience asked: *wach qâl?* ('What did he say?') (Meynier, 2002: 53). Moreover, the Arabic expressions used by the religio-conservatives to refer to the common man show their contempt: *Salafat al'amma* (despicable masses), *Al-ra'iyya* (imitators), *Al-sùqa* (people of the marketplace), *Al-ça'âlik* (people of the street) (Harbi, 1984: 119). And the Ulemas had suspicious attitudes towards Berber-speaking populations' faith and languages. In 1948, the Ulemas demanded that the colonial authorities close down the Kabylian radio station. They also wrote in the organ of their party (*El-Baçaïr*) that the Kabylians would become really Algerian when they would 'cease to whisper their jargon (Kabyle language) which grates on our ears' (Ouerdane, 2003: 80).

The independence-oriented (revolutionary) movement as embodied by the *Étoile Nord-Africaine* emerged in France in 1926 and was presided over by Messali Hadj (1898–1974). This charismatic leader of poor parentage (the son of a shoemaker) had received little formal education before he was conscripted into the French army during the First World War. He then settled as a migrant worker in the slums surrounding Paris and joined the French Communist Party which would support the founding of the *Étoile*. Messali's ideals were a mix of populist socialism coupled with nationalist and religious doctrines based on rural traditional Islamic dogma (Horne, 1987: 39). The *Étoile* rejected assimilation and demanded Algeria's self-determination. Messali's brand of nationalism took over all the major symbols and values of the 'glorious' Arab-Islamic past: 'The Muslim Algerian people have a glorious historical past, a religion and a language totally different from those of France, and there is no apparent reason why one should go back on one's opinions' (Stora, 1994: 85). In 1927, the *Étoile*'s political platform called, among other things, for 'The total independence of Algeria', and 'access to education at all levels; the creation of schools in Arabic' (Collot & Henry, 1978: 39). Item 8 of its political programme adopted in May 1933 advocated 'Compulsory education in the Arabic language. Access to education at all levels. The creation of schools in Arabic. All official documents must be published simultaneously in Arabic and French' (Collot & Henry, 1978: 52).

The French authorities dissolved the *Étoile* in 1929 and Messali spent several spells in prison or exile. As an expatriate, he lived six months in Switzerland (1935–1936) where he met Emir Chekib Arslan – a Pan-Arabist from the Lebanese aristocracy, well known for his sympathy for Nazi ideology and a yearning for the re-creation of an Arab kingdom led by a 'King of all the Arabs' (Bessis, 1978: 473–5). Messali's association with Arslan strengthened the former's adherence to Pan-Arabism and Arab-Islamic ideology (Meynier, 2002: 57–8). And this is how he came to share the Ulema's Jacobean definition of Algerian identity (Yefsah, 1990: 34). It is, then, thanks to Messali that the two populations of migrant Algerian nationalists (living in France and the Levant respectively) merged the two brands of nationalism: French Jacobinism and Pan-Arabism (Vermeren, 2004: 92).

In 1937, Messali Hadj recreated his political organisation as *Parti du Peuple Algérien* (PPA) with roughly the same programme but concerned almost exclusively with Algeria. During a general assembly held in Paris in August 1938, a motion was passed in favour of extending public education in Algeria. Among the claims, there were (1) the creation of a faculty of Arabic language and literature in Algiers University (similar to the ones in Morocco and Tunisia), (2) the development of Muslim universities for Muslim professors to teach Arabic language and literature, (3) making compulsory the teaching of Arabic at all levels – primary, secondary and higher education (Collot & Henry, 1978: 136). After another ban, Messali founded in 1946 a successor to the PPA called the *Mouvement pour le Triomphe des Libertés Démocratiques* (MTLD). It is from the ranks of PPA/MTLD that the radicals of the FLN were to emerge to launch the war and free the country from colonial rule. But before 1954, the members of the PPA/MTLD were divided on the cultural and linguistic identity of the future 'Algerian nation'. There were, on the one hand, moderates, headed by Messali himself, who believed that the birth of Algeria coincided with the Arab invasion and the spread of Islam – their slogan: an 'Arab-Islamic Algeria'. On the other hand, there were secular Marxist radical nationalists – most of them of Kabylian origin – who rejected such a national conception as simplistic, racist and imperialist. They called for more secularism and an 'Algerian Algeria'. They believed that, in addition to the Arabic and Islamic constituent parts, Algerianness should also include Berber, Turkish and, why not – though not openly declared – French elements (Meynier, 2002: 94). The first conception of Algeria favoured Classical Arabic over all other idioms, while the latter defended equality between all Algeria's languages and cultures (Yefsah, 1990: 35). The conflict between the two factions intensified and led to the 'Berberist crisis' of April 1949 (Harbi, 1993: 63–4).

Messali Hadj decided against linguistic-cultural pluralism and in favour of centralised Jacobinism and Unitarianism which overestimated Algeria's linguistic-cultural homogeneity and ignored the reality (Harbi, 1993: 59). Messali's decision would be taken over by all post-independence FLN leaders and successive governments (Benrabah, 1995: 36). But if the 1949 crisis ended in favour of the party moderates and the suppression of the Berber issue in the Kabylians' collective subconscious for a long time (Ouerdane, 2003: 85; Yahiatene, 1997: 66), it had far-reaching consequences for pre- and post-independence Algeria. The

'Berberist crisis' engendered wounds that would not heal. It also aroused suspicion and wariness between the Arabic-speaking and Berber-speaking leadership
(Harbi, 1980: 33).

Despite their differences – on the status of the 'Algerian nation', independence, integration, etc. – all three major nationalist strands shared a common
denominator: the language demand stood out as an important element in all
parties' programmes and manifestos. Arabic and Islam had a unifying role that
served the resistance against colonialism and during the War of Liberation
(Ennaji, 1999: 384; Grandguillaume, 1996: 40; Holt, 1994: 33; Sarter & Sefta, 1992:
109). A focus on Arabic and Islam was simply unavoidable for at least two major
reasons. First, like Classical Greek and Irish Gaelic in pre-independence Greece
and Ireland respectively, Classical Arabic aroused the type of strong symbolism
associated with ancient idioms to liberate dominated populations. Such symbolic
value was further strengthened by the link that exists between Classical Arabic
and Islamic culture and religion which served as the *patrie* of resistance throughout the colonial era. 'Islam and the Arabic language were effective forces of resistance against the attempt of the colonial regime to depersonalize Algeria'
(Gordon, 1966: 137). And this is probably what prevented the grass roots of the
PPA/MTLD party in Kabylia from supporting the Kabylian mutineers during
the 'Berberist crisis' in the late 1940s (Addi, 1994: 23; Mahé, 2001: 432; Meynier,
2002: 96). Second, the imposition of assimilationism as well as centralised Jacobean language policy, typical of French linguistic culture, turned the Koranic
idiom into a 'martyr' language (Benrabah, 1999a: 58–9) – status that was further
enhanced by a colonialist piece of legislation in the 1930s: on 8 March 1938, Standard Arabic was decreed a foreign language.

Demands of Nationalism

The hegemony of the FLN party during the war of liberation and the dilution
of pre-war political pluralism (PPA/MTLD, UDMA, *Association of the Ulemas*,
etc.) made real political power lie in the hands of the military who have, since,
discredited civilian politics (Addi, 1994: 55–74; Stora, 1998: 30; Vermeren, 2004:
111–12). While neighbouring Morocco and Tunisia saw their urban bourgeoisie
rise to power, independent Algeria was to be led by 'the plebeian elite'. They
came from the peasantry and were strongly influenced by religious ideals and
'hostile to the possibility of letting non-Moslem indigenous Europeans or Jews be
Algerian . . . The idea of citisenship rarely disqualifies the duty of the believer'
(Harbi, 2002: 14).

Less than three months before independence on 12 April 1962 at Tunis airport,
the president-to-be Ahmed Ben Bella made a triple assertion of Algeria's
Arabness: 'We are Arabs, we are Arabs, we are Arabs'. On 20 September 1962, the
constituent assembly declared Ahmed Ben Bella the first President of Algeria,
and soon after he declared that Arabic was to be introduced in the educational
system. (For language-in-education planning, see Part V: Language Spread in
Algeria.) A month later (1 November 1962), Ben Bella said: 'Our national
language, Arabic, will resume its rightful place . . . ' (Vermeren, 2004: 143).
Adopted on 10 September 1963, the first Constitution described Algeria as an
'integral part of the Arab Maghreb, of the Arab World, and of Africa' (Article 2).
In its preamble, it declares 'Algeria must affirm that Arabic is the national and

official language and that it derives its spiritual strength from Islam essentially'. Article 5 states that 'Arabic is the national and official language of the state'. However, under the provisions of Article 73 'French can be used provisionally along with Arabic' (Gallagher, 1968: 130; Khalfoune, 2002: 172). In August 1963, the National Assembly called for 'the use of Arabic in all administrations at the same level as French' (Gallagher, 1968: 130). It was introduced as a working language in the Parliament in 1964 and, in June 1964, the first volume of the Official Journal was published in Arabic (Grandguillaume, 2004a: 28). But French remained widely in use to the point where Ben Bella addressed MPs in French in spring 1964 (Gallagher, 1968: 130). It was a reality that the Algerian authorities had to reckon with. Despite his revolutionary slogans, the first president proved to be tentative and less sure of the wisdom of arabising 'at all cost' which would sacrifice the French language (Gordon, 1978: 152).

Meanwhile, the Ulemas' call for more Arabic and more Islam put the government under so much pressure that Ben Bella declared: 'Arabisation is not Islamisation' (Granguillaume, 1983: 184). On 30 September 1964, the Minister of Religious Affairs, Tewfik El Madani, opened the (first) Islamic Institute in Kabylia, a religious institution completely arabised with a clearly stated religious character (Granguillaume, 1983: 97). With the exception of individuals such as the Minister of Religious Affairs, the Ulemas as a political movement did not join in Ben Bella's government. However, Tewfik El Madani's views on Arabisation were typically representative of the ideology of the *Association of the Ulemas*. In his discourse as Minister, he clearly stated that the language of Arabisation could only be the Koranic idiom; that Arabisation was motivated by the Islamic faith which remained the most fundamental component of Algerians' identity, and that Arabisation must be correlated with the Islamisation of Algerian society (Grandguillaume, 1983: 130; Holt, 1994: 38). Thus, Kabylians viewed the foundation of the first Islamic Institute in 1964 as 'aggressive Arab-Islamism' and as central to Ben Bella's programme (Ouerdane, 2003: 143). It aimed to impose forced Arabisation onto Kabylians through Islam with the help of 'token Kabylians': for instance, Ben Bella named a Kabylian Arabist (Mohammedi Saïd) as the member of the FLN Political Bureau in charge of Arabisation (Ouerdane, 2003: 132, 155; Tabory & Tabory, 1987: 66).

Resistance came also from liberal and secular intellectual quarters: the 5th Congress of Algerian Students, held in August 1963, voiced their dissatisfaction with Arabisation as did the Union of Algerian Writers and the French-speaking media (Grandguillaume, 2004a: 28). One well-known French-language writer, Kateb Yacine, was to become the major symbol against the implementation of Standard Arabic as the sole national/official language and the rejection of native languages, namely Algerian Arabic and Berber. He also defended bilingualism and considered the French language 'war booty'. He rejected Classical Arabic on the grounds that it was 'liturgical, the language of pedants and religious zealots' (Grandguillaume, 1983: 131).

But the leadership of Algeria had something else on their agenda, as their reactions to a sociolinguistic survey show. In 1963/1964, the Algerian government hired a team of American sociolinguists (University of California, Berkeley) to draw up the sociolinguistic profile of the country. As a conclusion to their survey, the researchers recommended the institutionalisation of Algerian

Arabic and Berber as inter-regional languages because they were the most widely used and most consensual. The Algerian authorities signed a contract with this group of sociolinguists under the terms of which the conclusions of their survey of Algeria should never be made public (Elimam, 1997: 158). As pointed out by Grandguillaume, the attention the colonial authorities had given to Algerian Arabic and Berber (research and teaching at secondary and higher levels) was seen by many as a deliberate attempt to sow divisions among the indigenous people and to block the emergence of national consciousness. The scientific study and the teaching of first languages were rejected on the grounds that they represented a danger to national unity (Grandguillaume, 1983: 27, 1996: 38–9). For example, the Berber radio often came under attack from conservative/ nationalist quarters. As another example, in January 1963, there was controversy over a newspaper article in which the author demanded the closing down of the Kabylian programme (Grandguillaume, 1983: 118) because of the 'Berber danger' to national unity (Chaker, 1998: 128).

The 1962–1965 period corresponds to Algeria's option for revolutionary 'socialism'. During Ben Bella's regime, the left wing of the FLN party favoured a decentralised economic system and called for a reform of the party towards a labour-type organisation with unions (the National Union of Algerian Students or UNEA, and the General Union of Algerian Workers or UGTA, etc.) playing a major role. Confronted with the religio-conservatives who favoured rapid and systematic Arabisation, the first Minister of Education Abderrahmane Benhamida warned that Arabisation would only be implemented gradually. It would be better, he said, to wait 20 years for a solid solution than to opt immediately for Arabisation that might collapse in a couple of years (Altoma, 1971: 699). Expert foreign observers tended to agree with Abderrahmane Benhamida that overhasty Arabisation would lead to undesirable results, a position that was sanctioned by other Arab states at the Third Conference of Arab Teachers held in Algiers in August 1963 (Gordon, 1966: 200). As to Arabisation-Islamisation as advocated by the Ulemas, their opponents called for 'an Arabisation that needs to be rein-vented without falling under the control of ideological or spiritual enslavement of any sort' (Déjeux, 1965: 6). The military coup of June 1965 put an end to all this. The putchist leader, Colonel Houari Boumediene, ensured that actual power remained – as it has remained ever since – in the military establishment. He thus imposed an authoritarian top-down process with state capitalism run by techno-crats (Gordon, 1966: 158). The military also used the secret police to control the administration and the economy and the economic policy of the 'industrializing industries' reinforced the army's position (Harbi, 2002: 15). Unsurprisingly, Boumediene's period of office began with a dissolved parliament, a suspended constitution and general mistrust and suspicion among the population. The FLN became a mere political instrument with no real power. Other mass organisa-tions such as the UNEA and UGTA were soon to be brought under control.

The cautious approach to Arabisation of Ben Bella's era was definitively aban-doned by the new authorities following the military putch in June 1965. Just after the coup, Houari Boumediene committed himself fully to the Ulemas' slogan (Arabisation and Islamisation) and declared that his presidency was to be guided by Islamic ideals (Abu-Haidar, 2000: 156). Consequently, the Ulemas joined his government in July 1965. The determination of the new leadership is best illustrated by the following declaration made during a government session by the first Minister of Education in Boumediene's government, Ahmed Taleb Ibrahimi (son of Sheikh Ibrahimi, leader of the Ulemas after the death of Ben Badis): 'This [Arabisation] will not work, but we have to do it . . .' (Grandguillaume, 1995: 18). Political developments after June 1965 were certainly responsible for the authorities' assertive attitudes towards systematic Arabisation. For one, the military regime yearned for legitimacy (Benrabah, 2004b: 60–61).

More assertive policies

Islam and nationalism, among other things, served as instruments to compensate for the unconstitutional authority of Algerian leadership (Cubertafond, 1995: 94). In a society where the majority of the population is Muslim, Islam is legitimising – this is one of the main characteristics of Arab-Muslim countries (Grandguillaume, 1982: 55, 1990: 156–8). As to nationalism, Arabisation is essential because the language issue stood high on the agenda of the Algerian national movement. Moreover, the link between Islam and nationalism in Algeria was the Arabic language (Cubertafond, 1995: 109). The way in which the first Minister of Religious Affairs described the Arabic language has already been described. After the military coup, one of his disciples, Mouloud Kassim Naït Belkacem, who would later hold major posts in the administration and would prove to be a fervent advocate of Arabisation 'at all costs', repeated almost the same words when he said:

> The Arabic language and Islam are inseparable. Arabic has a privileged position as it is the language of the Koran and the Prophet, and the shared language of all Muslims in the world, language of science, language of culture. (Rouadjia, 1991: 111)

The view stated above is largely held by all members of the religio-conservative movement of the Ulemas who joined the new government and thus agreed to use their ideology to legitimise the unconstitutional regime born of the military overthrow. The Ulemas do not advocate an ideology that is capable of integrating Algeria's past in its entirety: their insistence on the Arab-Islamic dimension alone prevents any harmonious integration of other constituent parts of Algerian identity (the Berber and French in particular). And their Jacobean identification of Algeria's linguistic landscape is inherently confrontational. In the aftermath of the *coup d'état*, they were in charge of the Ministry of Religious Affairs, the Ministry of Information and, most important of all, the Ministry of Education (El-Kenz, 1994: 83–4). The Ulemas were now free to generalise Arabisation, at least in the educational sphere. Their endeavour was to be encouraged by another event, an international one but with a knock-on effect on the Arab world in general and Algeria in particular. The Arab armies' defeat in the Arab-Israeli war of June 1967 created among the populations a sense of trauma and abandonment from their respective regimes defeated by the tiny Jewish state (Vermeren, 2004: 193). Against all odds, the military setback led Marxists in the Maghreb and Algeria to drop their internationalist ideology in favour of Pan-Arab nationalism. Left-wing intellectuals and student populations then got involved in populist demands, among which were more Arabic-language teaching in schools and a quest to return to 'national values' such as

Islam ('authenticity'). Confronted with these demands, spurred by political and ideological motivations, the authorities responded by abandoning the cautious realisation of Arabisation (Vermeren, 2004: 195–6). In fact, the severity of Algeria's internal discord made its leaders more prone to try radical policies. Algeria's zeal even made Moroccans have doubts about their moderation and under-hasty approach. At a conference in Tunis on language problems in March 1975, a Moroccan delegate declared: 'We talk about Arabisation; the Algerians are doing something about it' (Gordon, 1978: 174). Unlike neighbouring Morocco and Tunisia, the authorities could not ensure that the language issue did not monopolise the political scene (Thomas, 1999: 38, 26).

After June 1965, the educational authorities were to remain faithful to Pan-Arabist practices found in the Middle East: the curriculum was focused inward, beginning with history which would be subjected to the demands of nationalism. The teaching of history in the Sixth Grade was the first to be Arabised both in form and content. In form, from September 1966, history was taught in Classical Arabic. This is how a former official of the Algerian Ministry of Education described the Arabisation of content: 'for that particular year [1966], schoolchildren tackled history starting not from Antiquity but from the beginnings of Islam. These measures were symbolic of the new direction taken by the educational policy' (Haouati, 1995: 56). To provide his regime with constitutional legitimacy, Colonel Boumediene finally brought the country to elections in the year 1976 (the National Charter, the Constitution and the Presidency). He was elected president with a huge majority and the new constitution was acclaimed overwhelmingly (Grandguillaume, 1983: 190, 2004a: 31; Vermeren, 2004: 401). Article 3 of the Constitution declared Arabic the sole national and official language of Algeria, but this time, unlike the preceding and following constitutions, Article 3 also reads: 'The State must generalise the use of the national language in all institutions'. During the same year, the authorities also organised public televised debates around the National Charter approved by referendum with 98.5% of the votes on 27 June 1976. Among demands made by the public before the referendum, conservatives asked for the weekend to become Thursday–Friday, instead of Saturday–Sunday. This was meant to kow-tow to the Middle East and impose Friday as the Islamic holy day. Berber militants posed the problem of the teaching of Tamazight. By the end of August 1976, the authorities appeased the conservatives by decreeing Thursday–Friday as the weekend in Algeria while neighbouring Morocco and Tunisia maintained Saturday–Sunday (Abu-Haidar, 2000: 156; Grandguillaume, 1983: 190). In his speech closing the debate on the National Charter, President Boumediene responded to the Berbers' demand as follows: 'How would our children make themselves understood by their brothers in Cairo and Bagdad if, instead of learning Arabic, they were to learn Berber?' (Sadi, 1991: 189). Pan-Arabist ideology was part and parcel of Colonel Boumediene's regime and even affected activities related to corpus planning.

By the late 1960s, language planners from the three countries of the Maghreb, linked by a common heritage (similar cultural and colonial background), decided to handle, in a joint effort, problems related to the standardisation of the lexis used in elementary school textbooks. Among the first joint decisions, there was one pertaining to the development of a corpus of basic words which would serve as the sole source for textbooks in the first three years of primary education. Lists were to be drawn up from two sources: (1) spontaneous conversational recordings of five to nine-year-olds from different dialect areas in the Maghreb; (2) Arabic language textbooks already in use (by the end of the 1960s) in the three countries in Grade One and Two at the primary level. For the final selection of words, linguists, educators and planners preferred the lexis that was 'common to all three countries or, failing this, to two of the three' (Benabdi, 1980: 181). The final compilation, called *The Official Linguistic Corpus for the First Stage of Elementary School*, contained approximately 4800 words. Even though this corpus is based in large part on oral usage, major alterations were introduced to turn it into an artificial list. In an attempt to level linguistic differences, words were modified phonologically and morphologically in order to make them fit patterns acceptable in Literary Arabic and 'free from regional characteristics'. Moreover, the list also contained items not belonging to the speech of five to nine-year-olds (Benabdi, 1986: 66–8). The great majority of entries are shared with Classical Arabic. Approximately 3.5% of words on the list differed from their counterparts in the latter language, including borrowings and colloquialisms. Numerous examples of words shared by all three countries of the Maghreb were discarded. They were replaced by Literary equivalents or terms used in the Middle East. For example, two words for common food items are illustrative. The first, the word /hût/ 'fish', found in Literary Arabic and used in all three Maghreb countries, was superseded by /samak/, the current word for 'fish' in the Middle East. The second lexical item /čina/ 'orange', common to all Maghreb dialects was replaced by the Middle Eastern/Classical counterpart /burtuqâl/.

The above examples clearly show that the overriding consideration of the planners was not real language use but ideology: 'the aim of linguistic unity with the rest of the Arab World should be the dominant goal of the lexicon as a whole' (Benabdi, 1986: 76). In fact, the Maghrebi compilers were tuned in to practices of the Arab language academies which reject colloquial words as divisive (Altoma, 1971: 710). By the end of the 1980s, a pro-Arabist university teacher wrote that Algerian Arabic varieties were incapable of transmitting science and high culture and were divisive for an 'Arab nation which yearns for a total and global unity' (Cheriet, 1983: 28). As for foreign loanwords, Algerian compilers did not take people's feelings and practices into consideration: instead of *ordinateur* and *SIDA*, French loans currently used by the population, planners preferred the use of *computer* and *AIDS*, English borrowings used in the Middle East (Benrabah, 1995: 45). Furthermore, the compilation of an 'artificial' lexicon through a process of classicised colloquial Arabic can be described as a refusal to allow Algerian Arabic access to writing and as a way of fossilising the relationship between speech and writing. According to Calvet (1999b: 236) 'we have thus the most anti-democratic situation that is imaginable: a people decreed the speakers of a vulgar dialect and denied access to knowledge in their own language.'

Other pieces of legislation were passed by the end of the 1960s. In April 1968, a circular required all civil servants to learn the national official language by the year 1971. The Arabisation process also concerned the media and publishing (Assous, 1985: 110–17; Gordon, 1978: 152–3; Grandguillaume, 2004a: 28–9). (See Part V Language Spread in Algeria.) The 1970–1977 era corresponds to systematic Arabisation. The authorities declared 1971 the 'year of Arabisation'. Several institutions were created to monitor language planning: the Permanent Committee for Higher Education (established in 1971), and the National Commission for Arabisation created under the auspices of the FLN party in January 1973 (Grandguillaume, 1983: 108; Torki, 1984: 101). In May 1975, the First National Conference for Arabisation was convened by the government to accelerate the Arabisation process (Assous, 1985: 123–6; Grandguillaume, 2004a: 30). On 12–20 December 1973, Algeria was chosen as the site for the second Pan-Arab Congress for Arabisation. The congress decided on the creation of standardised scientific and technological terminology for all Arabic-speaking polities. Besides the Pan-Arab Congress, other supra-national bodies exist to monitor the Arabisation process: the Arab League, the Bureau for the Coordination of Arabisation, the Institute for Research and Studies on Arabisation, the Congress of Arab Ministers for Higher Education, the Congress of Arab Universities, and the Conference for the Teaching of Arabic (Kadi, 2004: 134).

After the death of President Boumediene in December 1978, his successor, Chadli Bendjedid, authorised even more radical policies demanded by the Arabist/Islamist wing of the FLN party. This conservative group supported total arabisation and the implementation of an Islamic (theocratic) society in Algeria (Grandguillaume, 2004a: 31–3). In November, 1979, arabised students at the University of Algiers began a strike at the Faculty of Law which spread to other arabised sections and then to other Algerian universities. Strikers complained about the lack of job opportunities for arabised graduates and demanded immediate arabisation of the administration (Ruedy, 1992: 228). Some demonstrators' posters read: 'We are boycotting classes as we did in 1956,[22] and we will not go back until full arabisation is implemented', 'Unity of language is unity of mind', and 'The Arabic language is part of the 1954 revolution' (Assous, 1985: 133–4). The strike lasted until 20 January 1980. But less than three months later, another major event was to shake the regime to its very foundations: the convulsions known as the 'Berber Spring' (see 'Demands of democratisation'). In the meantime, and after the arabised students' strike ended, the Ministry of the Interior sent a circular (dated 19 January 1980) to all government agencies and administrations concerned with employment urging them to consider arabised candidates for job recruitment. The Commission for Education and Culture of the FLN party announced, in February 1980, its national plan for the Arabisation of the administration. The authorities decreed the full Arabisation of the judicial system and many new jobs were created (Ruedy, 1992: 228). On 14 August 1980, the Ministry of Higher Education ordered the arabisation of university departments of social sciences and humanities and, on 11 November the same year, it created the Permanent Commission for Arabisation (Assous, 1985: 137).

In the intervening time, other bodies had been established to monitor the Arabisation process: the High Council for the National Language (in 1980), Centres for the Intensive Teaching of Languages (in 1981). By the end of the 1980s, two other institutions emerged: the Algerian Academy for the Arabic Language in 1986 and the Algerian Association for Arabisation in 1989 (Kadi, 2004: 134–5). As far as legislation was concerned, President Chadli Bendjedid promulgated in 1986 the new National Charter which asserted on page 51: 'the Arabic language is an essential constituent part of the cultural identity of the Algerian people'. The government also passed by referendum a new Constitution, in

February 1989. In Article 3, Arabic remained the single national official language but the obligation upon the State imposed under President Boumediene's rule was removed (Benrabah, 1999a: 288; Cherrad-Benchefra & Derradji, 2004: 163).

Probably the most important (French-style Jacobean) piece of legislature ever to be enacted since the independence of the country came in the early 1990s. As a final move towards total Arabisation of the country, the Algerian parliament enacted the law known as 'Act N° 91-05 of 16 January 1991, on the generalisation of the use of the Arabic language'. In its Article 4, the act imposes Arabic as the unique language for all educational and administrative institutions, organisations and associations in all their commercial, financial, technical and artistic dealings. It fixes 5 July 1992 as the deadline for total Arabisation of the administration. Court cases and proceedings were to be conducted in Arabic only (Article 7). No language other than Arabic was to be used in the educational system (Article 15). All disciplines taught in universities had to be totally Arabised by 5 July 1997 (Article 37). As of 5 July 1992, any official document written in any language other than Arabic would be considered null and void (Article 29). The law also applied to all public meetings and debates in both public and private sectors of the society. Imports of hardware and software technology (typewriters, computers, photocopying machines, etc.) in languages other than Arabic were forbidden (Article 39). Standard Arabic was to be exclusively used in the media (with the exception of French-language newspapers already in existence), road signs, sign posts, films and documentaries, billboards, etc. (Article 19). Repressive measures are best illustrated in Article 32 which fixed fines for any offending party. It read: 'Anyone who signs a document written in any other language than Arabic, while on duty, is liable for a fine between 1000 and 5000 Algerian Dinars [approximately between US$40 and US$200]'. It is worth noting how Algerian language planners seem to kowtow to French practices. The initiator of 'Act N° 91-05 of 16 January 1991', Mouloud Kacim Naït-Belkacem, declared in a newspaper interview that he had used, as his model, the French piece of legislation: 'Act N°75-1349 of 31 December 1975' passed by the French Parliament to counter the spread of the English language before the United Kingdom entered the European Union (*El Moudjahid*, 1990: 5).

From February to June 1992, during the brief presidency of Mohamed Boudiaf – his predecessor, President Chadli had had to resign after the FIS won the elections cancelled by the military –, the law of total compulsory Arabisation was postponed by 'Decree 92-02 of 4 July 1992'. Another project that was postponed in 1992 concerned the teaching of French at the elementary level. The Minister of Education decided against delaying French language teaching from the Fourth to the Fifth Grade in the primary cycle as demanded by the pro-Arabisation lobby (Laib, 1993: 7). But to give the latter group something in return, the government decided that, starting from September 1993, parents could choose between French and English for the children entering the Fourth Grade (Bennoune, 2000: 303; Benrabah, 2004a: 95–6). Official discourse justified this choice on the grounds that English was 'the language of scientific knowledge' (HCF, 1999: 28) and French being 'in essence imperialist and colonialist' (Goumeziane, 1994: 258). In July 1996, the new government cancelled President Boudiaf's decree and revived 'Act N° 91-05 of 16 January 1991' and, in November 1996, a new Constitution was passed by referendum with Article 3 unchanged.

Table 1 Chronology of events, political developments and decisions concerning language planning in Algeria (1962–2005)

Year	Events, political developments and decisions/declarations
1962	• 18 March, the Evian Agreements signed by the French government and the Algerian revolutionary leadership. • June, the Tripoli Programme declares: '[The role of the Revolution] is above all [. . .] to restore to Arabic – the very expression of the cultural values of our country – its dignity and its efficacy as a language of civilisation.' • 21 August, the Ulemas demanded that Islam and the Arabic language be the major constituent parts of the Algerian people's identity. • 5 October, Ben Bella declared that Arabic was to be introduced in the educational system (primary cycle) during the next school year. • November–December, Arabisation gives rise to controversy in the press. • 15 December, the High Commission for Educational Reform met for the first time: one of its recommendations was gradual Arabisation.
1963	• 12 June, the National Assembly passed a motion in favour of Arabisation: Arabic introduced as the working language for the parliament (development of translation). • 20 June, the Minister of Education declared open literacy campaign in French. He was criticised by a Ulema member (Mohamed El Mili). • August, the National Assembly called for 'the use of Arabic in all administrations at the same level as French'. • 5–12 August, the Third Conference of Arab Teachers held in Algiers. Delegates approved of Algeria's gradual approach to Arabising the educational system and declared that an overhasty Arabisation would lead to undesirable results. • September, Arabic became obligatory in all school programmes and at all levels: 10 hours a week (of a total of 30 hours) in primary cycle. • 10 September, the first Constitution Adopted; Article 5 states: 'Arabic is the national and official language of the state'; Article 73: 'French can be used provisionally along with Arabic'. • 29 September, Hocine Aït Ahmed formed an opposition party, the Socialist Forces Front (FFS), and led fellow Kabylians into an armed struggle against the government.
1964	• Arabic is introduced as a working language in Parliament. • 5 January, meeting in Algiers of the first Islamist association: the Association Al-Qiyam. • January, controversy over the status of Arabic in the University of Algiers: creation of the Islamic Institute, and modification of the structure of the Bachelor's degree in Arabic which had given rise to controversy. • 22 May, creation by decree of the High School of Interpreting and Translation. • 1 June, the first volume of the Official Journal published in Arabic. • September, creation of the National Centre for Literacy. • September, Arabisation of the First Grade in primary cycle and the volume of Arabic teaching rose to 10 hours in all other levels. • September, implementation of the educational system of religious instruction. • 30 September, the Minister of Religious Affairs opened the first Islamic Institute in Kabylia. • 21 October, the Ministry of Education recruits 1000 Egyptian teachers.
1965	• 19 June, Military *coup d'état* led by Colonel Houari Boumediene: Ahmed Taleb Ibrahimi (Ulema member) became Minister of National Education.
1966	• February, the foundation of the national publishing house named SNED. • 8 June, Rulings N° 66-154 and N° 66-155 specified the role and place of the Arabic language in the judiciary. • 10 August, a group of Berberist militants living in Paris set up the statutes for the Berber Academy or the Berber Association for Cultural Exchange and Research (known by its French initials ABERC).

Table 1 (contd.) Chronology of events, political developments and decisions concerning language planning in Algeria (1962–2005)

1967	• 11 August, the Minister of National Education denounced the teachers' opposition to Arabisation. • September, total arabisation of Grade Two in primary education. • September, Mouloud Mammeri is informally allowed to restore the Chair of the Berber studies at Algiers University. • October, newsreel in cinemas are Arabised. • Ruling N° 67-191 introduced tax exemption for the edition and importation of books in Arabic. • A survey carried out by the University of Berkeley under the auspices of the Department of Planning shows that 80% of the youth are against the Arabisation of university learning.
1968	• 26 April, Decree N° 68-95 required all civil servants to learn the national official language by the 1st January 1971. • April, creation of the Circle for Berber Studies (CEB) in the University of Algiers. • 15 October, Decree N° 68-588 makes obligatory evaluation in Arabic for all exams in university Faculties of Letters and Human Sciences.
1969	• 2 May, a group of Berberist militants living in France form the Berber Academy (*Agraw Imazighen*). • September, the University of Algiers opened an arabised section in the Faculty of Law and an Arabised Bachelor's course in history. • 5 December, creation of the National Commission for the Reform of the educational system and a sub-commission for Arabisation.
1970	• 12 February, Ministerial decree 'setting the levels of competence in the national language needed by personnel in public administration, local authorities and various institutions'. • 11 April, a presidential circular reminding civil servants not to refuse circulars in Arabic. • 21 July, the Ministry of Education split into three ministries: the Ministry of Primary and Secondary Education, the Ministry of Higher Education, and the Ministry of Islamic Education.
1971	• 7 January, meeting of the Council of Ministers: decree for the implementation of Arabisation was discussed. 1971 was declared as the 'year of Arabisation'. • 20 January, Ruling 71-2 extends the 26 April 1968 Decree (N° 68-95) for all personnel of public administrations to be arabised. • April, the yearly Colloquium of senior executives of the Ministry of Education on Arabisation; three decisions: (1) total arabisation of Third and Fourth Grades in primary cycle; (2) total Arabisation of one-third of courses in the First year in Middle school; (3) total Arabisation of one third of courses in scientific disciplines in secondary schools. • 27 June, the Ministry of Justice issued a decree making Arabic the unique language of the judicial system. • 25 August, Ministerial decree for the Arabisation of institutions of the Ministry of Higher Education. • September, creation of the Permanent Committee for Higher Education. • September, the Ministry of Islamic Education opened 20 Islamic High Schools and creates the degree (Baccalaureate) of original Islamic education.
1972	• May-June, a group of Berber militants proposed the teaching of Tamazight in the University of Paris-Vincennes: birth of the Group of Berber Studies (known by its French initials GEB). • 29 January, the teaching of Tamazight began in the University of Paris-Vincennes.

Table 1 (contd.) Chronology of events, political developments and decisions concerning language planning in Algeria (1962–2005)

1973	• Year 1973: increasing popularity for the Berber militant song; most popular singer: Aït Menguellet. • 21 March, decision requiring competence in Arabic by civil servants in the Ministry of Primary and Secondary Education, and the Ministry of the Interior. • September, Mouloud Mammeri's teaching of Berber language and culture in the University of Algiers, tolerated since October 1965, was abolished by the Ministry of Higher Education. • 1 October, Ruling N° 73-55 turned all national seals in Arabic in the administration. • 6 November, the National Commission for Arabisation was created under the auspices of the FLN party. • 12–20 December, Algiers is the site for the 2nd Pan-Arab Congress for Arabisation.
1974	• 5 December, report of the National Commission for Arabisation on the state of Arabisation in Algeria.
1975	• 14–17 May, the government convened the First National Conference for Arabisation to accelerate the Arabisation process. • May, total Arabisation of the judicial system was implemented. • September, Arabisation of humanity subjects (geography, history and philosophy) in the secondary cycle.
1976	• 1 March, all public signs (streets, highways, stores, administrative buildings) and car licence plates were Arabised. • 16 April, private and religious schools banned by decree. • 23 April, Algeria's Official Journal published the re-organisation of the educational system based on 'Arabo-Islamic values and the socialist conscience'. • June, the police affixed seals on the Berber publication known as the 'Fichier berbère' (created in 1946 and was mainly concerned with the study of the Kabylian language). • 27 June, the National Charter approved by referendum with 98.5% of the votes. On page 65, centralisation and monolingualism in Arabic are reaffirmed, Tamazight is totally ignored and French is referred to as a 'foreign language'. • July, inauguration of the first promotion of completely Arabised magistrates. • 27 August, Thursday-Friday becomes weekend, instead of Saturday–Sunday. • September, reform of the educational system and implementation of an experimental schooling system ('Fundamental School'). • 19 November, the second Constitution of Algeria was acclaimed by referendum (99.18%). Article 3 reads: 'Arabic is the national and official language. The state must see to generalise its use.' • 21 December, the Ministry of the Interior recruited 50 Arabised female police inspectors.
1977	• January, total Arabisation of the regional daily (Oran) paper *El Djoumhouria*. • 25 February, election of the Popular National Assembly (parliament). • 21–27 April, cabinet reshuffle and Mostefa Lacheraf became Minister of Primary and Secondary Education: pause in the overhasty process of Arabisation. • 19 June, demonstration of Kabylian football supporters in Algiers stadium in the presence of President H. Boumediene; among slogans chanted: 'The Berber language will live', 'Down with dictatorship', 'Long live democracy'.
1979	• March, the old opposition party, the FFS, reactivated in 1977, demanded in its 'Political Platform Pre-Project': 'The Berber language has the right of citizenship in the Berber polity, an inalienable right that neither internal colonialism nor foreign colonialism can ban. It must be institutionalised and developed as a national language [. . .]. Only obscurantist's apprentices and mercenary flunkeys would like to oppose the Arabic language to the Berber language.' • 8 March, cabinet reshuffle: Mohamed Cherif Kharroubi replaced Mostefa Lacheraf as Minister of Primary and Secondary Education: implementation of total Arabisation, religious instruction and the Fundamental School. • June, violent incidents among the Berber-speaking community. • September, French was taught as the first obligatory foreign language in the Fourth Grade and English in the Eighth Grade. • November, Arabised students at the University of Algiers go on strike: they demand immediate Arabisation of administration.

Table 1 (contd.) Chronology of events, political developments and decisions concerning language planning in Algeria (1962–2005)

1980	• 3 January, the FLN Central Committee made public its decisions on education: it re-launched Arabisation. • 19 January, the Ministry of the Interior sent a circular to all government agencies and administrations concerned with employment urging them to consider Arabised candidates for job recruitments. • 9–22 February 1980, the Commission for Education and Culture of the FLN party announced its national plan for the Arabisation of the administration. • 10 March, the authorities banned Mouloud Mammeri's conference on ancient Berber poetry to be held in the university of Tizi Ouzou (the administrative centre of Kabylia). • 16 April, general strike in Tizi Ouzou and Kabylia ('Berber Spring'). • 1–31 August, many militants of democracy and the Berber cultural movement organised the first independent meeting on the issue of language and identity in Algeria (Seminar in Yakouren, Kabylia); the platform demanded, among other things, the 'institutionalisation of the people's languages (Algerian Arabic and Tamazight) as national languages'. • 14 September, Decree for the Arabisation of the first year in the following university disciplines: social sciences, law and administration, political sciences, and economic information; • 11 November, the Ministry of Higher Education created the Permanent Commission for Arabisation. • December, creation of the High Council for the National Language following the recommendation of the Central Committee of the FLN Party (meeting of June 1980).
1981	• 7 March, Decree N° 81-28 relating to the transcription of proper names in Arabic. • 14 March, the Arabisation of the milieu was decreed (Decree N° 81-36). • May, the transcription of names of towns and localities in Latin letters based on Arabic pronunciation (Decree N° 81-27). • 23 September, the Minister of Higher Education announced the creation of four university Departments for the study of popular cultures and dialects (Algiers, Oran, Constantine and Annaba).
1982	• 7 July, a Master's degree on popular culture was established in the Institutes of Arabic Language and Culture in the universities of Algiers, Oran, Constantine and Annaba.
1984	• 9 June, the National Assembly passed the Family Code based on Shari'a.
1986	• 1986, new National Charter was promulgated which read: 'the Arabic language is an essential constituent part of the cultural identity of the Algerian people' (p. 51); 'Algerians are Arab and Moslem people' (p. 109). • 19 August, foundation of the Algerian Academy for the Arabic Language under the patronage of the President of the Republic (Law N° 86–10). • September, 'minority foreign languages' (German, Italian, Russian, Spanish) were removed from Middle Schools.
1987	• February, the Ministry of Higher Education opened the Higher National Institute for Popular Culture in Tlemcen. • November, foundation of Bendali School (private institution) for the education of political military and educational elites' children.
1988	• September, government's banning of Algerians' enrolment in educational institutions controlled by the *Office Universitaire et Culturel Français*. • 4–10 October, riots in Algiers and other large cities (600 dead) followed by political liberalisation.
1989	• 23 February, new (third) Constitution passed by referendum; in Article 3, Arabic remained the single national official language.
1990	• 24 January, the Department of Amazigh language and culture was opened in the University of Tizi Ouzou. • 20 April, 100,000 FIS members demonstrated in the streets of Algiers demanding the dismantlement of bilingualism and the implementation of Shari'a. • 27 December, 400,000 people demonstrated in the streets of Algiers calling for democracy and against the law of total Arabisation scheduled to be passed by parliament.

Table 1 (contd.) Chronology of events, political developments and decisions concerning language planning in Algeria (1962–2005)

1991	• 16 January, National Assembly voted 'Act N° 91–05 of 16 January 1991' for total Arabisation. • October, a second Department of Amazigh Language and Culture was opened in the University of Bejaia. • 4 November – 23 December, the strike of university teachers against the implementation of 'Act N° 91–05 of 16 January 1991', and the government's recruitment of 1500 Iraqi professors.
1992	• 4 July, 'Act N° 91-05' aiming at total compulsory Arabisation is postponed ('Decree 92-02 of 4 July 1992').
1993	• September, the Ministry of Education introduced English in the primary cycle to compete with French (Fourth grade).
1994	• 24 September, the Berber Cultural Movement (MCB) called for general strikes in the educational sector ('satchels' strike').
1995	• 28 May, the High Commission for Amazigh Affairs (known by its French initials HCA) was created by decree under the patronage of the President of the Republic.
1996	• July, the new government cancelled 'Decree 92-02 of 4 July 1992': 'Act N° 91-05' was revived. • 28 November, the third Constitution was passed by referendum with Article 3 unchanged. But in its preamble, it read: 'the fundamental constituent parts of [Algeria's] identity [. . .] are Islam, Arabism and Amazighism'. • 17 December, 'Act N° 91–05' is revoked setting new deadlines for its nation-wide implementation: the administrative sectors were to be Arabised by 5 July 1998 and tertiary education by 5 July 2000.
1997	• 10 May, the two Departments of Amazigh Language and Culture in the Universities of Tizi Ouzou and Bejaia, became Institutes or Faculties (Ruling N° 97-40) starting from September 1997.
1998	• 25 June, the assassination of a popular Kabylian singer, Matoub Lounes, followed by riots in Kabylia (June-July). • 26 September, the High Council for Arabic Language was founded to oversee that total Arabisation was implemented gradually.
1999	• 15 April, election of Abdelaziz Bouteflika as President of the Republic. • May, President Bouteflika declared: 'It is unthinkable . . . to spend ten years study in Arabic pure sciences when it would only take one year in English'. • 3 September, during a meeting with the Kabylian civil society in Tizi Ouzou, President Bouteflika declared: 'Tamazight would never be consecrated in law as an Algerian official language and if it were to be a national language, it is up to the entire Algerian people to decide by referendum'.
2000	• 13 May, President Bouteflika set up the National Commission for the Reform of the Educational System (known by its French initials CNRSE).
2001	• March, the president of the CNRSE handed in the final report on educational reform. • 21 April, riots in Kabylia after the assassination of a Secondary school student in a Kabylian village and the creation of a spontaneous movement called 'citizens' movement' (*Archs*). • May 2001, Ali Ben Mohamed, former Minister of Education, founded the National Coordination for the Support of the Authentic and Open School. He was backed by leaders of Islamist parties, some teachers' and parents' unions, religious groups and a number of politicians. • 11 June, the representatives of Kabylia's Citizens' movement drew up a list of 15 vindications known as the El Kseur Platform. • 3 September, the Ministry of the Interior announced the suspension of the implementation of the educational reform. • 24 September, President Bouteflika declared that Tamazight was to become a national language.
2002	• 8 April, Article 3 of the Constitution was modified to include Tamazight as the second national language of the State of Algeria. • Creation by decree of the National Centre for Tamazight Language Planning.

Table 1 (contd.) Chronology of events, political developments and decisions concerning language planning in Algeria (1962–2005)

2003	• March, creation of the National Association for the Defence of Francophonia in Algeria. • 13 August, Article 6 of Ruling No. 03-09 legalised private schools which had existed in a legal vacuum. • September, implementation of parts of the recommendations made by the CNRSE: French introduced as the 1st obligatory foreign language in 2nd year in primary cycle, English in 1st year in Middle School as the 2nd obligatory foreign language.
2004	• 26 December, Abderrazak Dourari became Head of the Institute for the Planning of Tamazight
2005	• August, after the last round of talks between Kabylia's representatives and the Prime Minister: agreement on making Tamazight official without resorting to a referendum.

Updated from Chaker, 1998: 209; Cherrad-Benchefra & Derradji, 2004: 160–4; Grandguillaume, 1983: 184–93; Guenoun, 1999: 14–89; Mansouri, 1991: 167–173; Vermeren, 2004: 395–407

On 17 December 1996, the 'transitional parliament' voted unanimously for this law and set new deadlines for its nation-wide implementation: the administrative sectors were to be arabised by 5 July 1998 and tertiary education by 5 July 2000 (Benrabah, 1998: 4; Grandguillaume, 1997b: 3). But following another wave of Berber unrest due to the assassination of the Berberist singer Matoub Lounes, the authorities created, on 26 September 1998, the High Council for Arabic Language to oversee that total Arabisation should be implemented gradually (Benrabah, 1999a: 263; Bensalem, 1999: 10–11). Meanwhile, two other monitoring bodies had already been founded in 1996: the Algerian Agency for Terminology and the High Council for Education (Kadi, 2004: 135). A summary chronology of these changes (1962–2005) can be found in Table 1.

Demands of democratisation and internationalism

Eighteen years after achieving independence, Algeria was shaken by the first and most serious rioting of its independent history. On 10 March 1980, the newly created university of Tizi Ouzou (the administrative centre of Kabylia) invited the writer and academic Mouloud Mammeri to give a conference on his newly published collection of ancient Berber poetry. The meeting was banned by the authorities in Algiers and the entire Kabylian region went into civil disobedience. Kabylians defied the central government, and demonstrators cried in Berber '*Tamazight di llakul*' ('Berber in school') and in French 'Le berbère et l'arabe parlé = langues officielles' ('*Berber and spoken Arabic = official languages*'), 'Le berbère est notre langue – à bas l'oppression culturelle' ('*Berber is our language – down with cultural oppression*') among other slogans (Gordon, 1985: 138; Kahlouche, 2004: 105). They called for the recognition of their language and culture and made four major claims:

(1) Children should be literate in Tamazight.
(2) Tamazight should be a subject of study at university level.
(3) Tamazight should be given more importance in the media.
(4) Tamazight should be the medium of publications of different sorts. (El Aissati, 1993: 100)

The police crackdown on striking students and workers led to the death of 30 to 50 people and the wounding of hundreds (Maddy-Weitzman, 2001: 38; Tabory & Tabory, 1987: 63). According to Ephraim and Mala Tabory 'the excessive speed of the Arabisation policy kindled the unrest in Kabylia' (Tabory & Tabory, 1987: 76).

Following these convulsions, which have come to be known in Berber as *tafsut imazighen* ('Berber Spring'), the socio-political panorama was never to be the same again (Chaker, 1998: 51–64). The language issue got the better of the regime which had felt invincible since the military coup in June 1965. In fact, the 'Berber Spring' was the final stage of a long process of resistance by the Kabylian community starting immediately after independence. About 50% of the population in Kabylia boycotted the first presidential elections held on 15 September 1963 and won by Ben Bella with 95% of the votes (Ouerdane, 2003: 142). Ben Bella was autocratic and did not hide his anti-Berberist feelings; in fact, subsequent governments remained clearly hostile to Berbers and their aspirations (Chaker, 1997: 87). A highly symbolic illustration of such opposition is the Ben Bella government's abolition in October 1962 of the only existing chair of Berber studies at the University of Algiers (Chaker, 1998: 42). Then, Hocine Aït Ahmed, one of the FLN's 'historic chiefs', led fellow Kabylians into an armed struggle against the central authorities under the banner of the newly formed party, Socialist Forces Front (known by its French initials, FFS). This front united various, and sometimes opposed ideological strands: they were unanimous in their opposition to the policy of Arabisation. In fact, all members of the FFS were former nationalist militants and adhered to Arabo-Islamism as a way of transcending divisions and fighting French colonialism. But they were not ready to accept for independent Algeria the Arab-Islamic ideology as an official dogma that ignored manifestations of Berber language and culture (Mahé, 2001: 442). The armed revolt lasted from September 1963 until October 1964 and ended in complete failure: Aït Ahmed went into exile in Europe, and the authorities felt legitimised in their uncompromising attitudes towards a monolithic view of Algeria's linguistic and cultural identity.

The period between the armed resistance of 1963–1964 and the 'Berber Spring' of 1980 is characterised by a form of peaceful opposition and an increase in the Berber collective consciousness. Following the post-independence violent uprising, a number of Kabylians settled abroad, primarily in France which has a large community of Berber expatriates. Chaker estimates the current Diaspora at around 700,000 (Chaker, 1998: 69). The establishment on 10 August 1966 of the Berber Association for Cultural Exchange and Research (known by its French initials ABERC), the Berber Academy (*Agraw Imazighen*) on 2 May 1969 and the Berber Study Group (*Groupe d'Etudes Berbères*) at the University of Paris-VIII-Vincennes in May–June 1972 (Chaker, 1998: 44–5; Guenoun, 1999: 29, 31–2; Mahé, 2001: 435) were vital to the spread of Berber collective consciousness among Diaspora Berbers and in Algeria (Kahlouche, 2004: 105; Maddy-Weitzman, 2001: 42). The political discourse of Berberist exiles was strongly 'anti-Arab' and in favour of pan-Berber and the creation of a 'Berber nation' (Guenoun, 1999: 10). In the meantime, in Algeria, the government installed after the military coup of June 1965 had allowed the reintroduction of Berber in the University of Algiers lasting for seven years (October 1965–June

1973). Consequently, a moderate pole of cultural resistance grew within Algeria around the writer and academic Mouloud Mammeri who secretly taught Amazigh language and culture in the University of Algiers. By the beginning of the 1973/1974 academic year, the Algerian authorities had abolished the teaching of Mouloud Mammeri (Chaker, 1998: 147; Guenoun, 1999: 10–11; Kahlouche, 2004: 104–5). During the 1970s, another Amazigh voice, the Berber language broadcasting channel ('Chaîne II') in existence since colonial times, was constantly threatened with extinction (Chaker, 1997: 95).

As a reaction to these repressive methods, passive resistance spilled over into the streets of Algiers. For example, Berberophones deliberately used French or Berber in cafes, restaurants, hotels and even certain administrations (Harbi, 1980: 32). Following the 'Berber Spring', ideological guidance came from the Berber Cultural Movement (known by its French initials, MCB) whose roots go back to the 'Berberist Crisis' of 1949. The agenda of this movement is both national and regional. The MCB called for a Western-style socio-political system: Berberist militants believed that only liberalisation and democratisation could guarantee their linguistic and cultural rights within Algeria (Maddy-Weitzman, 2001: 38). They opposed compulsory Arabisation and insisted on the official recognition of the people's languages (Algerian Arabic and Berber). In addition to calls for democratisation, the MCB also demanded the advent of a secular state largely transmitted through the French language and culture. They refused the Arabisation of the educational system because of its 'de-Frenchifying' objectives and its inability to transmit democratic and secular ideals (Mahé, 2001: 471). In February 1985 seven Berberist activists were imprisoned and, in November 1985, several MCB militants were arrested by the police after they had created the first Algerian League of Human Rights (Chaker, 1998: 59–60). According to Chaker, more than 300 arrests were made for 'Berberist activities' (1998: 103).

The *intifada* of October 1988 was followed by a genuine democratic era which lasted from 1989 to 1992 (Mahé, 2001: 471). The single-party system gave way to a new constitution (of 23 February 1989) and the right to form parties, associations, etc. Political pluralism was accompanied by freedom of speech with an opening up in the only national TV channel (ENTV) and the creation of several independent newspapers. Subjects which had previously been taboo (religion, history, Arabisation and the educational system) were openly discussed. The language policy implemented since independence was freely debated with scholars popularising their academic work published in the national independent press. Political tolerance enabled university professors to take a stand against imposed Arabisation. Between 4 November and 23 December 1991, university teachers went on strike against the implementation of 'Act N° 91-05 of 16 January 1991' for total Arabisation. They also rejected the government's recruitment of 1500 Iraqi professors to implement the law at the university level and thus disqualify the majority of Algerian teachers (Aggoun & Rivoire, 2004: 234; Maghreb Machrek, 1992: 109). Following the opening up of Algerian political life in 1989, MCB activists operated under the banner of the old Socialist Forces Front (FFS) headed by Hocine Aït Ahmed and the newly formed party – Rally for Culture and Democracy (RCD) – headed by one of the leading Berberist activists, Saïd Sadi. The agenda of the former is more national while that of the latter is more communal and ethnic. But both parties give high priority to Berberist demands. For example, by the end of 1990, the FFS organised huge demonstrations against the law of total Arabisation scheduled to go into effect on 5 July 1992. Advances made by the Berber language began in the university. In January 1990, the Department of Amazigh Language and Culture was created at the University of Tizi Ouzou, the first in post-independent Algeria. A year later, in October 1991, a similar section was to be opened in the University of Bejaia. The main objective for the two Departments was to provide Master's training ('Magister') in Berber studies (Chaker, 1998: 150; Kahlouche, 2000: 158; Tigziri, 2002: 61).

After the implosion of the Algerian state in early 1992, demands for the official recognition of Berber language and culture fell onto deaf ears. Then on 24 September 1994, the MCB called for three general strikes that affected the entire educational sector. Among the slogans chanted by demonstrators, there was one in Berber *ulac llakul ma wlac tamazight* ('No school without Berber'). Known as the 'satchels' strike' ('grève des cartables'), it lasted until 9 April 1995 when President Liamine Zeroual's government held conciliatory talks with the MCB leadership. On 28 May 1995, the authorities passed a presidential decree (N° 95–147) enacting the creation of an administrative structure, the High Commission for Berber Affairs (known by its French initials, HCA) to be attached to the president's office (Cherrad-Benchefra & Derradji, 2004: 166; Kahlouche, 2000: 160; Yahiatene, 1997: 75–76). The mission of the HCA was 'the rehabilitation of Tamazight [culture] . . . one of the foundations of the national identity, and the introduction of the Tamazight language in the systems of education and communication' (Maddy-Weitzman, 2001: 39). According to Mahé (2001: 537), the role of the HCA has been more symbolic than anything else – organizing cultural manifestations such as poetry and theatre competitions – and the national press has often questioned this role. The introduction of Tamazight in the educational system (see Part V – Language Spread in Algeria) was a historical achievement, but its teaching remained characterised by a great deal of haste and improvisation because of the lack of an official status for the language and proper planning institutions (Kahlouche, 2000: 161–2; Tigziri, 2002: 64). The Departments of Amazigh language and culture in the universities of Tizi Ouzou and Bejaia became Institutes of Amazigh language and culture after the Ministry of Higher Education had issued circular N° 97-40 on the 10 May 1997. The following September, a four-year Bachelor's degree on Amazigh language and culture was opened. The number of students rose from 25 in 1997 to 300 in 2001/2002 and 2004 (Kahlouche, 2004: 108; Tigziri, 2002: 61). The first group of graduates (20 students) obtained their BAs in Amazigh language and culture in 2000/2001 (Tigziri, 2002: 62).

But the revival of 'Act N° 91-05' in 1996 would prove to be another source of anger for Kabylians. According to Abu-Haidar (2000: 161), the government's aim was to appease the religious fundamentalists and the Pan-Arabists. The RCD declared the law of total Arabisation to be racist and a prelude to bringing the Islamists of the FIS to power. Ten days before its implementation, the singer and Berberist militant Lounes Matoub was assassinated, on 25 June 1998. The artist's death was followed by a several weeks' long outburst of demonstrations and violence in Kabylia as well as in some major cities and in France. Protesters attacked government property, tearing down Arabic-language signposts, leaving intact those in French and Tifinagh.

As noted earlier, since his election in April 1999 President Abdelaziz Bouteflika has tried to put an end to the use of language policies primarily for political objectives. But if the new president is ready to reconsider the status of French in Algeria, he remains a staunch opponent to any evolution towards a polity that is inclusive and more tolerant of linguistic diversity. During a meeting with the Kabylian civil society in Tizi Ouzou on 3 September 1999, President Bouteflika declared 'Tamazight would never be consecrated in law as an Algerian official language and if it were to be a national language, it is up to the entire Algerian people to decide by referendum' (Benrabah, 2004a: 103). In April 2001, a gendarme shot dead a young Kabylian while in custody, and a social explosion burst out with unprecedented violence. Within 10 days, around 60 protesters had been killed and 600 wounded (*Le Monde*, 2001: 1). Since April 2001, the number has gone up to 123 human casualties (Benrabah, 2004a: 104). These incidents have come to be known as 'Black Spring' (*Printemps noir*). Disturbances have prevailed ever since, reaching the point where the entire province of Kabylia 'is at risk of becoming disconnected from the rest of the country and permanently distressed' (Martín, 2003: 35). As an attentive observer of Algerian reality in general and Kabylian reality in particular, Mahé uses the term *chaos* to describe this situation (Mahé, 2001: 496–556). On 11 June 2001, the representatives of Kabylia drew up a list of 15 demands known as the *El Kseur* Platform. Fourteen out of the total claims are of a national, socio-economic, general and programmatic nature, and some are specific. But only one demand (in eighth position in the platform) deals with the Berber language and identity and reads: 'Satisfy the Amazigh claim in all its dimensions (identity, civilization, culture and language) without referendum and preconditions and recognize Tamazight as a national and official language' (Salhi, 2001: 52). Demands which used to be strictly ethnic and linguistic have become social. By putting the linguistic demand in this position, Berberists have given the *El Kseur* Platform a national impact (Addi, 2002).

Before parliamentary elections due in spring 2002, President Bouteflika tried to appease Kabylians to ensure their participation in the electoral process. He decided to reconsider Article 3 of the Constitution and to name Tamazight as the second national language. On 8 April 2002, parliamentarians voted for this amendment. From a symbolic point of view, this consecration is significant for at least two reasons. First, Tamazight has been declared a national (but not official) language without recourse to a referendum and this new status has the effect of putting an end to the improvisation of the early experience. Following its consecration as a national language, the authorities created the National Planning Centre for Tamazight (Kahlouche, 2004: 113) and the nomination, in December 2004, of a linguist (Abderrezak Dourari) as Director of the National Pedagogical and Linguistic Centre for the Teaching of Tamazight. According to the Minister of National Education, the new centre's mission was to work in collaboration with the HCA (*El Watan*, 2004c: 31). Second, this partial recognition can be considered a first step towards the establishment of a society that values its plurality. Furthermore, the latter is guaranteed by Algeria's authorities who have started to acknowledge pluralism as viable.[23] In fact, '[t]he process of reshaping and redefining the meaning of . . . Algerian identit[y] has already begun and will surely be fraught with tension and difficulty' (Maddy-Weitzman, 2001: 44). To illustrate this difficulty, the latest round of talks between

Kabylia's representatives (known by the Berber term *Archs*) and President Bouteflika's government will be addressed. In January 2005, the government spokesman declared that the two parties had agreed on a compromise to make Tamazight an official language. Following this declaration, Kabylian quarters which reject this compromise threatened to resort to street protests and violence. Islamist and Pan-Arab nationalist parties demanded a referendum and the FFS described this compromise as a 'web of deceit' that allowed the authorities to gain time and postpone the advent of a state practising real democracy (Aït Ouarabi, 2005c: 2; Hamiche, 2005: 3). During the summer 2005, however, the talks seemed more promising: the Prime Minister and Kabylia's representatives finally agreed on making Tamazight official without resorting to a referendum. The authorities also promised to create a Tamazight TV channel by 2007 and an increase of Berber-speaking TV programmes, from the present daily 15 minutes (news) to two hours a day in 2006 and six hours in the following years (Djillali, 2005: 2). Then, by the autumn of 2005, President Abdelaziz Bouteflika publicly questioned his Prime Minister's commitment to making Tamazight official (Moali, 2005: 3).

At the national level, post-October liberalisation allowed intellectuals and the public to discuss a number of issues related to language and identity that had been impossible before. One could read (or hear televised debates) on the status of French in Algeria with questions such as 'Is French an Algerian language or not?' Kachruvian ideas emerged in publications to support the indigenisation of French as a stable norm and to acknowledge the creativity of bilinguals and to reject claims that Algerian writers of French expression were 'cultural misfits' with no legitimacy in Algerian culture. In the end, these efforts at 'enlightenment' (Adegbite, 2003: 188–92) have freed a number of Algerian intellectuals of guilt. Akram Belkaïd, an Algerian journalist, writes: 'Am I less Algerian than others because I express myself in French? The French language is not merely 'war booty', to borrow Kateb Yacine's famous expression. From now on, it is a constituent part of the Algerian identity' (Belkaïd, 2005: 93). Furthermore, there are unprecedented initiatives following the so-called 'Bouteflika effect', and President Bouteflika's government's commitment to integrate Algeria into the world system. For example, in March 2003, a group of Algerians created the National Association for the Defence of Francophonia in Algeria (Benrabah, 2004a: 98). Another difference with post-independent nationalist excesses is the change of attitudes among children born of Franco-Algerian couples. In the past, they could not live with both cultures in Algeria: they could only be Arab/ Muslim and any other identification was banned. After she published her novel *Garçon manqué* in 1999, Nina Bouraoui, a young writer born of an Algerian father and a French mother, described her 'nationality' in a radio interview as follows:

> We belong to a community which represents peace between the two coun-
> tries [Algeria and France] . . . I am Franco-Algerian. I am not Algerian one
> day and French another day . . . I try to get the best of both worlds. [. . .] But I
> like this mixture. It is not a schizophrenic attitude. It is a source of wealth.

It is probably the issue of language-in-education planning that proved to be most controversial. During his brief term as Head of State (February–June 1992), President Mohamed Boudiaf broke taboos concerning educational matters

(Bensalem, 1999: 10). Before he was assassinated in June 1992, the late president declared the schooling system 'doomed ["école sinistrée"] and unworthy of the Algerian people' (Messaoudi & Schemla, 1995: 186). During his 1999 presidential campaign, and whenever talking about the Algerian school, Abdelaziz Bouteflika repeated the phrase 'doomed educational system' several times. He insisted on the urgent need to reform it. In a July 1999 public meeting, he declared:

> Standards have reached an intolerable level to the point that the Algerian degree, which used to be accepted by la Sorbonne, Harvard and Oxford up to the 1980s, is no longer recognized even by Maghreban universities. Tunisian and Moroccan students used to come to Algeria to study medicine and pharmacy. Today, the opposite is true [. . .]. I have a solemn duty towards the Algerian people to let them know about the problems facing the educational system, from basic and secondary levels to higher education. The situation is dangerous, very dangerous. If we keep on this track, we will go from one type of illiteracy to another, worse than the previous one. (Benrabah, 2004a: 99)

The implementation of an exclusively Arabic monolingual educational system in the early 1970s is considered to be at the origin of this 'failure'. No other country in the Maghreb has gone that far in imposing monolingualism.[24] A few figures will suffice to show 'the Algerian school is in bad shape' (Mostari, 2004: 34). In the first educational cycle known as 'Ecole Fondamentale' (which lasts nine years and includes Primary and Middle schools), 80% of the teaching staff have no Baccalaureate. Mathematics as a discipline is in serious jeopardy: the number of Baccalaureate candidates registered in the field of 'pure sciences' dropped sharply from 18.46% of the total number of candidates for all disciplines in 1990 to 3.84% in 1998 (*Le Matin*, 1998: 24). Out of 100 pupils entering school for the first time, just over two pass their Baccalaureate exam; i.e. 75% of the total number of schoolchildren leave the educational system before reaching secondary education (*El Watan*, 1997a: 1). During the National Conference on the Teaching of Arabic held in Algiers in April 2000, participants declared that 'after nine years in basic education, pupils still do not master Arabic properly' (*Liberté*, 2000: 24). In Higher education, more than 75% of the teaching staff are assistant-lecturers; the average rate of failure among first-year students reached 40% for all fields of study in 1989/1990; during the same period, 80% of first-year students failed in technological branches and 55% in pure sciences (Rebah, 1991: 11). At the beginning of the 21st century, only one student out of 10 manages to gain a degree. According to a medical professor, a substantial number of medical students are unable to measure blood pressure by the time they graduate (Idlhak, 1996: 7). What is more, state education does not protect anyone from fundamentalist subversion no matter how long one remains in the educational system. Indeed, it seems that the opposite is true. To illustrate this, a field study carried out between 1991 and 1995 showed that, out of 500 (fundamentalist) rebels killed by Algerian armed forces, 60% had a university level of education (*El Watan*, 1996a: 7). Hence, the educational system fuels instability by producing school-leavers incapable of meeting the social, economic and cultural needs of the country.

On 13 May 2000, Abdelaziz Bouteflika set up the National Commission for the Reform of the Educational System (known by its French initials CNRSE). In mid-March 2001, the president of the CNRSE handed in the final report. One of the recommendations was that, starting from September 2002, French ought to be introduced earlier in the school system – in Year 2 of basic education instead of Year 4 as had been the case since the early 1980s. It also recommended that, starting from September 2001, the French language be offered in (rural) areas where it had not been taught so far. Finally, the Committee recommended that scientific disciplines in secondary schools be taught in French rather than in Standard Arabic (Sebti, 2001) – a recommendation that had been supported by a survey conducted for the Algerian government, in 1999, and which revealed that 75% of the Algerian population would rather have their children study scientific disciplines in French (Djamel, 2001: 3).

However, President Bouteflika's government has been thwarted in its attempt to implement this educational reform because of strong opposition from the conservative/Islamist quarters of the Algerian social and political establishment (Belkaïd-Ellyas, 2003: 28–9). The opposition, which reflects the polarisation in Algerian society between 'Arabo-Islamists' and 'Modernists' (see Part V), came from outside but also from within the 156-member CNRSE which seemed divided on the language issue as well as on other questions, such as the teaching of civic and religious instruction (Benmesbah, 2003: 12; Grandguillaume, 2002: 160). For example, around 56 members of the CNRSE accused their colleagues who voted in favour of the reform of being 'traitors', 'agents of the French Party', 'enemies of Islam and the Arabic language' and 'supporters of forced Westernization of Algerians' (Djamel, 2001: 3). In April 2001, a former Minister of Education, Ali Ben Mohamed, declared that those who talked about the 'educational debacle' were merely ignorant journalists. In May 2001, he founded the National Coordination for the Support of the Authentic and Open School ('Coordination nationale de soutien à l'école authentique et ouverte'). He was backed by leaders of Islamist parties, some teachers' and parents' unions, religious groups and a number of politicians (Grandguillaume, 2002: 160). The polemics reached a climax when some were zealous enough to declare a *fatwa* against the reforms and their supporters (Abdelhai, 2001: 7). On 3 September 2001, the Ministry of the Interior announced the suspension of the implementation of the educational reform.

During his first term in office, President Bouteflika did not have enough legitimacy to go beyond the mere planning stage in reforming the educational system. After the 'landslide victory' of the 2004 presidential elections, he clearly had the advantage over his opponents and sufficient leeway to pursue the reforms to the end. Indeed, since September 2004, French has finally been introduced as the first mandatory foreign language in the second year with three hours a week. This innovation and the recruitment of 1500 French teachers tend to prove that the authorities are definitely engaged in educational changes (Cherfaoui, 2004: 2). Although the re-introduction of French for scientific disciplines in secondary education is not yet part of the agenda, the government has made another move against the Islamist/conservative lobby: since September 2005, the Islamic/religious courses of study in the secondary cycle and the respective exams have been discontinued (Aït Ouarabi, 2005a: 1, 3; Aït Ouarabi, 2005b: 1, 3). The reform represents a dramatic change of policy after decades of monolingualism. In linguistic terms, it became apparent that the overtly stated goals of Arabisation – create a monolingual polity and eradicate first languages and French – were not being reached, and a change was needed.

Conclusion

Language policy and planning in Algeria was initiated and controlled by government. It is thus implemented in a top-down fashion and almost no input comes from below. After a traumatic experience with French colonialism, Algeria's elite in post-colonial times 'lived at a time when it was imperative to dwell upon negative opposition and to inspire resistance' (Gordon, 1966: 130). So demands of nationalism require linguistic intervention that fulfils two roles that correspond roughly to Joshua Fishman's dichotomy *nationalism* vs. *nationism* (Fishman, 1968, 1971). During colonisation, the nationalist motive served as an instrument for colonial struggle: 'The heirs of past greatness deserve to be great again. The heirs of triumphant unity in the past must themselves be united in the present and future. The heirs of past independence cannot but be independent again' (Fishman, 1972: 45). Then after decolonisation, it seeks to reinforce political independence through socio-cultural integration based on authenticity (*Great Tradition* and glorious past) as a means to put an end to colonial alienation. The nationist intent is twofold. On the one hand, it favours efficiency that results from horizontal (geographic) integration which aggregates diverse populations with different language varieties and facilitates communication within the polity (efficient administration and rule). On the other hand, it advocates vertical (social-political) integration as a way of eliminating all intermediaries between the citizen and the centralised state: it serves as an instrument of participation and access. In other words, it sees language planning as a 'modernizing' process (Henze & Davis, 1999) that seeks to solve 'language problems' (Jernudd & Das Gupta, 1971: 211) as well as 'communication problems' (Weinstein, 1983: 37) that could rise from multilingualism. That is, in the nationist view, a single uniform language and 'high culture' supported by a fairly monolithic educational system promote nation-building (Gellner, 1983: 138). Hence, the general goal of language planning is to reduce language conflict and to contribute to the overall development of the country (Jahr, 1993: 1; Tucker, 1994: 277).

However, motives for deliberate intervention in language are 'commonly stated in altruistic terms but often not based on altruistic intents' (Kaplan, 1990: 4). Instead of serving as a tool of participation and access, the planned language may lead to expropriation and deprivation. Language planning alters existing relationships between different groups within the polity and reinforces inequalities by disallowing social groups from accessing social and political structures. Therefore, instead of reducing conflicts, LPLP 'may itself ultimately be the cause of serious problems as well as conflicts' (Jahr, 1993: 1). The cases involving the Arabised graduates and the Berber community in Algeria are good examples of conflicts that arise from interventions in language that do not meet the conditions that yield practical and lasting solutions. Halliday (1972: 5) gives two such conditions: (1) that interventions in language should go with the current, and not against it, and should follow, rather than aim to reverse, the natural course in which events are moving; (2) that interventions on language should not be over-hasty. Arabisation in Algeria goes against these conditions: it was overhasty and it did not consider any – however minimal – meaningful input into the LPLP formulation that stems from below and accounts for the plural sociolinguistic nature of the polity. Language spread has occurred within this context.

Part V: Language Spread in Algeria

The expression 'language spread' was coined by Robert Cooper to refer to the processes that allow an increase in the number of users and uses of a language (Cooper, 1982: 6). Language spread can be the outcome of military conquest, political control, economic policies, urbanisation, flourishing religious systems, neo-colonial ties, language attitudes ('openness'/'possessiveness') and so on (Wardhaugh, 1987: 6–16). Governments and central authorities adopt language policies as tools to spread (or to contract) a particular language inside (and/or outside) their country's borders (Kayambazinthu, 1999: 31). Within this tradition, planning is done at the expense of some other language or languages. Consequently, people may resist language policies which do not meet their needs: some kind of discrepancy exists between the people's desires and the state's policy (Lam, 1994: 186–7). Reactions such as these can lead to 'unplanned aspects [which] can interact with change or pervert the planned [activities]' (Baldauf, 1993/1994: 82).

Language-in-education planning

In language planning activities, status planning aims at increasing a language's use while acquisition (language-in-education) planning aims at raising the number of users (Cooper, 1989: 33). The formal educational sector plays a major role in language spread – even though it lacks 'the outreach or the available resources to impact any sector other than the schools' (Kaplan & Baldauf, 1997: 113). In Algeria, language-in-education policy has been instrumental in both planned and unplanned spread of Arabic, French and Berber. In this section, language spread in the educational system, the media and the wider context is first discussed, and then the 'unplanned' developments are described. To deal with the issue of school-acquired language(s), it is necessary to trace briefly the history of modern education in Algeria.

Post-independent language-in-education policies

After Algeria became independent, there was the intention – at least in rhetoric – to favour the national language in education: in October 1962, Ben Bella declared that Arabic was to be introduced in the educational system (Grandguillaume, 2004a: 27). During the first year of independence (1962–1963), seven out of 30 hours per week were taught in Arabic (Gallagher, 1968: 137; Gordon, 1978: 152). In the 1963–1964 school year, the teaching of Arabic became obligatory in all programmes and at all levels, and the volume for French-language teaching decreased (Bennoune, 2000: 228). In 1964–1965, the authorities arabised the first year of the primary level and increased the volume of Arabic-language teaching to 10 hours in all other levels along with the addition of religious instruction and civics (Grandguillaume, 1983: 97, 2004a: 27). At about the same time (1963–1964), a group of arabised teachers, who had graduated from Cairo's traditional Islamic institutions, exerted pressure on the authorities causing the latter to yield to their demand to integrate their centre for Islamic studies into Algiers University (Grandguillaume, 1983: 98). And the same group 'harassed' the professors in charge of the existing bilingual (Arabic/French) bachelor's degree (university *Licence*) to turn it into a unilingual Arabic-only degree based on the Levant model (Grandguillaume, 2004a: 28). In 1964, a National School of Translation was founded (Gordon, 1978: 153). As for traditional Islamic education, the Ministry of Religious Affairs opened the (first) Islamic Institute in Kabylia in September 1964, an institution completely arabised with a clearly stated religious character (Granguillaume, 1983: 97). The central authorities also helped the heirs of the Association of the Ulemas to set up a network of Islamic High Schools across the country to teach the Ulemas' ideology in Arabic. (These schools were to be integrated later within the Ministry of Education as a means to 'unify' the educational system.) In the end, the Islamic high schools acted as recruitment centres for Arabised teachers who were to demand systematic Arabisation in the 1970s and 1980s (Bennoune, 2000: 224). There were about 35 such establishments with 24,000 students by 1973–1974 (Thomas, 1999: 30).

The colonial educational system inherited by the government of independent Algeria rapidly proved inadequate for at least two important reasons: first, of a total of 27,000 educators, about 25,000 left the country when independence was declared (Assous, 1985: 105); second, student enrolment in primary schools rose from 14% to 36.37% as a result of the tremendous 'hope' generated by the liberation of the country (Bennoune, 2000: 223). In December 1962, President Ben Bella made public the following figures: 18,000 Arabic- and French-speaking teachers served in schools (including 3200 Syrians and Egyptians), 600,000 children of school age were enrolled in primary school representing 80% of the figure for the preceding year (Gordon, 1966: 196). With 48,000 students in secondary schools, there were far more registrations than in 1961. The number of students enrolled at the University of Algiers fell from 5000 to 2500. Material and personnel problems proved to be major obstacles. On 15 December 1962, the High Commission for Educational Reform made the following recommendations: progressive 'Algerianisation' of the teaching personnel, gradual Arabisation, unifying the educational system, orientation of the educational system towards science and technology, and democratisation of public instruction (Bennoune, 2000: 225).

The departure of the vast majority of French colonial teachers brought the educational system to a halt, and their replacement by Algerian nationals proved more than necessary. But, in the mean time, the authorities were confronted with a lack of well-trained teachers and literate populations from which to draw these teachers. In 1963, the total number of literate people stood at 1,300,000 (approximately 12% of the total population). Linguistic competence in Standard Arabic was relatively low (Grandguillaume, 1989: 49). Algerians who could read Literary Arabic only were estimated at 300,000 out of a population of 10 million (Gallagher, 1968: 148; Gordon, 1978: 151) while 1 million read French and 6 million spoke French (Gallagher, 1968: 134). In 1963, there were 19,908 primary school teachers: 3,452 taught in Arabic only ('Arabophones') and 16,456 in French only ('Francophones') (Bennoune, 2000: 229; Gordon, 1978: 152). Compared to Morocco and Tunisia, Algeria had by far the lowest number of teachers of Arabic:

13,000 for the former and 6000 for the latter (Gallagher, 1968: 138). The Arabisation of the teaching personnel proceeded apace and, by 1964/1965, the number of Arabophones had more than doubled (10,961).

In fact, the increase in the number of Arabic-speaking teachers generated another problem – their under-qualification: 57% lacked appropriate training (Saad, 1992: 60). In 1962/1963, the authorities hired 10,988 monitors (Assous, 1985: 106) 'whose intellectual horizons were at times only slightly less limited than their pupils' (Gallagher, 1968: 138). Teacher standards kept falling during the 1960s and beyond as a result of a large increase in the number of monitors. Their number rose from 37% in 1962/1963 to 46% in 1967/1968 while that of qualified primary school teachers fell by 22% during the same period (Bennoune, 2000: 228). In 1964, 1000 Egyptians were recruited as Arabic-language instructors; most of them turned out to be craftsmen unqualified for teaching[25] and ignorant of the social reality of Algerian people (Bouhadiba, 2004: 500; Sarter & Sefta, 1992: 111–12). 'On their return home some boasted that in their own countries they had held menial jobs whereas in Algeria they were honoured and entrusted with educating children' (Abu-Haidar, 2000: 155). And their spoken Egyptian Arabic was unintelligible to Algerians in general and Berber-speaking populations in particular (Grandguillaume, 2004a: 27–8). According to Wardhaugh (1987: 189), '[t]his experiment was a disaster: dialect differences were too great and the traditional Arabic pedagogy these teachers brought with them compounded the difficulties'. Indeed, the Egyptian teachers had been long trained in the tradition of learning by rote and class recitation. They were also accustomed to exercising strict hierarchical control over the class, and they thus demanded full obedience and respect from their students. Moreover, the majority of these teachers were members of the Muslim Brotherhood. They 'were interested more in the ideological indoctrination of the students than in teaching' (Saad, 1992: 60). According to Abu-Haidar (2000: 161) and Mostari (2004: 38), these men, as well as some women, sowed the seeds of religious fundamentalism among a population that was barely educated. Algerians were also dissatisfied with available textbooks imported from France which were sometimes culturally inappropriate (Thomas, 1999: 27).

The Algerian authorities confronted the Arabisation of the educational system with shortages of all sorts. The decline in standards derived from the lack of qualified teachers and the sheer number of pupils, which almost doubled within four years; it rose from 777,636 in 1962/1963 to 1,332,203 in 1965/1966 (Bennoune, 2000: 223). Lack of teaching personnel and classroom space led to 'double shifts': children came to school either only in the morning or in the afternoon to allow one teacher to instruct two groups of pupils in the same classroom (Saad, 1992: 61). The teaching volume went down from 30 to 24 hours per week, and, by 1965, the teacher–pupil ratio rose to 1:53 (Bennoune, 2000: 234). In the meantime, the French language remained ever present. Algeria became independent politically, but culturally, it stayed bound to France through the Evian Agreements which allowed 12,000 French teachers to return to Algeria after 1962 (Assous, 1985: 106). By the spring of 1963, their number rose to 14,872 (Gallagher, 1968: 138). Five years after independence, French educators under cooperative programmes fell to 6500 of whom 345 were in higher education (Gordon, 1978: 150). The French government maintained the *Office Universitaire et Culturel*

Français which operated between six and nine secondary schools (*lycées*) and 40 primary schools mainly for French children. These institutions provided instruction for 15,000 children of which 37% were Algerian (Assous, 1985: 107; Gordon, 1978: 150). The number of Algerian students would later rise to 13,500, most of whom came from the elite and middle class (Assous, 1985: 107). These French centres of learning maintained a high quality educational system while the national schooling system gradually and seriously declined in standards. Parents reacted in a lukewarm fashion. The Arabisation of the first grade at the primary level coupled with the lower educational quality led many parents to delay registering their children until the second year where French remained dominant (Saad, 1992: 61).

Enrolments kept rising at the primary level and doubled between 1965 and 1977: 1,332,203 in 1965–1966, 1,851,416 in 1970–1971, and 2,782,044 in 1976–1977 (Bennoune, 2000: 233). The second year was completely Arabised in 1967/1968, and 51% of the total number of teaching personnel taught in Arabic with the importation of 1,000 Syrian teachers. The number of Arabophone teachers increased substantially between 1965 and 1977. While the number of francophone teachers remained stable – from 17,897 to 19,769 – the total number of Arabophones increased by a factor of four – from 12,775 to 47,096 (Bennoune, 2000: 229, 254). In 1969–1970, the University of Algiers created an Arabised section in the Faculty of Law and a Bachelor's course in history taught in Arabic.

Systematic Arabisation and quantitative increase

The period from 1970 to 1977, which corresponds to total Arabisation, began with a cabinet reshuffle. The Ministry of Education split into three ministries: the Ministry of Primary and Secondary Education, the Ministry of Higher Education and the Ministry of Islamic Education. The year 1971 was declared the 'year of Arabisation' with the total Arabisation of the third and fourth grades at the primary level and the creation of 20 Islamic high schools by the new Ministry of Islamic Education. A Baccalaureate of Islamic education was created in 1971, officially equivalent to the Baccalaureate conferred by the National Ministry of Education. The year 1971 also saw the government adopting the 'punctual system', a method which involved the Arabisation of all subjects on a given level instead of a 'geographic' Arabisation plan (e.g. Arabising specific schools in rural and desert areas), or 'vertical' Arabisation, one with the Arabising subject by subject (Gordon, 1978: 153). In actual fact, all methods were used, thus introducing further inconsistency across the educational system: for example, authorities implemented the 'geographic' method in poor and rural areas while in Algiers the plan met with resistance (Assous, 1985: 112–13). By 1974, the whole primary educational level had been Arabised with the teaching of French as a (foreign language) subject beginning in the third year (Gordon, 1978: 153). In the following year, subjects in the humanities (geography, history and philosophy) were taught in Arabic at the secondary level, and the judicial system was also Arabised (Gordon, 1978: 158). In April 1976, a circular decreed the banning of private and religious schools: the ban openly declared the closing down of schools for the well-off (Assous, 1985: 128) but in reality the circular concerned the Islamic high schools which had become centres of fundamentalist indoctrination (Grandguillaume, 2004a: 30).

The policy of economic development adopted by the government ('industrialising industries') made it a priority for education to allow Algerians to access knowledge and its development in society. In the 1970s, the authorities adopted educational reforms that imposed three missions on schools:

(1) Enforce universal schooling through democratisation of education.
(2) Implement Arabisation as a way of expanding Algerians' competence in Literary Arabic.
(3) Promote the acquisition of science and technology so as to facilitate its transfer from industrialised polities. (Benachenhou, 1992: 210; Bennoune, 2000: 301)

To implement a school system that favours science and technology, a reform was introduced in September 1976. Before this date, the educational structure was the one inherited from the colonial period and consisted of three levels: primary school (lasting five years), middle school (four years) and secondary school (three years) with an examination at the end of the last two levels as an evaluation for access to secondary education (Sixth Form examination or *Examen de Sixième*) and to university (Baccalaureate examination) respectively. Starting from 1976, the government implemented an experimental schooling system called the Fundamental School (*Ecole Fondamentale*) which is a fusion of elementary and middle school grades with all the teaching done in Arabic – with the exception of foreign languages. The Fundamental School consists of nine consecutive years corresponding to the first educational cycle considered basic and obligatory – the first six years represent primary schooling (Assous, 1985: 132–3; Saad, 1992: 65–6).

In 1977, President Boumediene appointed Mostefa Lacheraf as Minister of Primary and Secondary Education. Lacheraf was a staunch opponent of rapid Arabisation: he favoured gradualism and bilingualism with French serving as a 'reference point, a stimulant' that will force the Arabic language 'to be on the alert' (Berri, 1973: 16). His appointment signalled a pause in the overhasty Arabisation process. Among the reasons put forward by observers to explain such a government move, there were: first the 'progressive' revolutionary image that the president wanted to project to the world tarnished by a 'reactionary' educational system (Grandguillaume, 2004a: 31), and second, the decline in school standards (Assous, 1985: 130) and alarming reports on the standards of education in general – especially a report allegedly addressed secretly to the Algerian authorities by UNESCO (Taleb Ibrahimi, 1995: 270). During 1977–1978, Lacheraf suspended the Fundamental Schools, dismissed the Arabophone personnel in his Ministry, re-instated teacher training in French and bilingualism in primary schools with scientific subjects (math, calculus, biology) taught in French. With the death of Boumediene in December 1978, Mostefa Lacheraf resigned. He was replaced by a monolingual Arabophone, a pan-Arabist Kabylian trained in Syria who 'was detested [by his fellow Kabylians] for his refusal to speak his mother tongue' (Roberts, 1980: 121). The new Minister of Primary and Secondary Education resumed the policy of total Arabisation and implemented systematically the Fundamental School where religious instruction became obligatory at all levels (Tefiani, 1984: 121–2). In the new schooling system, French was introduced in the

Fourth Grade as the first compulsory foreign language (subject) and English as the second foreign language beginning in the Eighth Grade (Middle School).

The foreign languages known as 'minority languages' (German, Italian, Russian, Spanish) were simply removed, in 1986, from Middle Schools (for students aged 12–15) thus, lengthening dole cues for teachers who were not lucky enough to be re-deployed elsewhere as teachers of French, librarians, etc. Between 1984 and 1994, deserted university departments offered 'Bachelor's degrees' for beginners in these 'minority languages' (Abi Ayad, 1998: 99; Lakhdar Barka, 2002: 8; Miliani, 2000: 18). In September 1988, the government decreed that no Algerian parents could enrol their children in the educational institutions controlled by the *Office Universitaire et Culturel Français* (Grandguillaume, 2004a: 33; Saad, 1992: 72). In fact, a 1976 ordinance had already tried to put an end to the practice that helped elites avoid sending their children to Arabised public schools (Dufour, 1978: 39). But the ban did not prevent the leadership from maintaining this practice of elite closure (Myers-Scotton, 1993: 149). They promote Arabisation as a strategy to disqualify those less fortunate and minimise competition for their own children, for whom they could assure the appropriate education needed (in French) for good careers in modern business and technology (Thomas, 1999: 26). For example, in Algiers, a small number of primary and secondary schools were unofficially maintained as bilingual schools. The most famous, the former French *Lycée Descartes* 'nationalized' and renamed *Cheikh Bouhamama*, provided instruction in French for the children of the elite (Messaoudi & Schemla, 1995: 59). While private schools were banned, the Bendali School was created on the outskirts of Algiers in November 1987. According to the founder of the school, the authorities have always helped the school 'but never officially'. As Tuquoi pointed out, several members of the political, military and educational elites 'have chosen to educate their children in this private school that the State, officially, does not recognise' (2003: 4).

Secondary education, which lasts three years, consists of a common core (Year 10) and specialisation tracks for the remaining grades (Years 11 and 12). The common core comprises three pre-specialisation tracks: Letters/Humanities, Science and Technology. In 1996–1997, enrolments for each of these tracks were as follows: Letters/Humanities: 33%, Science: 17%, Technology: 50% (Ghouali, 2002: 383). Specialisations consist of a number of tracks and sub-divisions grouped into two schooling systems. The first, general and technological, includes seven specialties with the Baccalaureate as the final evaluation for access to university. These specialties are:

- letters and humanities;
- letters and Islamic sciences;
- letters and foreign languages;
- management and economics;
- technology (with three options: mechanical engineering, electrical engineering, civil engineering);
- hard sciences; and
- experimental sciences.

Table 2 Enrolment in Fundamental and Secondary schools from 1979 to 1998

Year	Total in Fundamental School	Secondary Technical School	Secondary General School	Total Secondary School	Total
1979–1980	3,799,154	12,770	170,435	183,205	3,982,359
1983–1984	4,463,056	32,086	293,783	325,869	4,788,925
1986–1987	5,107,883	98,300	405,008	505,308	5,611,191
1989–1990	5,436,134	165,182	588,765	753,949	6,190,081
1991–1993	5,994,409	129,122	618,030	747,152	6,741,561
1995–1996	6,309,289	69,195	784,108	853,303	7,162,592
1997–1998	6,556,768	64,988	814,102	879,090	7,435,858

Bennoune (2000: 326)

The second schooling system is professional and comprises six specialties:
- building trades;
- industrial manufacturing;
- electronics;
- electro-technology;
- chemistry, and
- accountancy. (Bennoune, 2000: 318)

From a quantitative point of view, the results of 'democratisation' were impressive: the number of enrolments at the Fundamental and secondary levels increased substantially (see Table 2). In 1996–1997, the Fundamental School personnel comprised 170,956 teachers broken down into: 147,581 Arabophones, 1018 bilinguals and 22,329 Francophones. On average, there were 32 pupils per teacher for Arabic, 102 pupils per teacher for French and 60.6 pupils per teacher for English (Bennoune, 2000: 327–8). There was also a substantial development at the tertiary level both for classroom space and student enrolment. When Algeria got its independence in 1962, there was only one university (University of Algiers) and two university centres (Oran and Constantine). By 1997, students were registered in 55 tertiary establishments (including 13 universities) spread over 30 urban centres. There were only 504 Algerians in the University of Algiers in 1954, but 350,000 in 1998. The Algerian teaching personnel at the university rose from 82 in 1962 to 14,581 in 1997 (Guerid, 1998: 12–13). The Arabisation of the social sciences, economics and communication curriculum begun in 1980 was completed by 1985 (Assous, 1985: 137–8). At the college level (*Licence*), the number of Arabophone students rose substantially: 2015 in 1971/1972, 13,561 in 1978/1979, and 28,767 in 1982/1983 (Bennoune, 2000: 388; Saad, 1992: 68). The number of Arabophone students who graduated in the various disciplines also increased steadily: 529 in 1974/1975, 897 in 1975/1976, 1419 in 1976/1977, 1699 in 1977/1978 and 36,706 in 1986/1987 (Bennoune, 2000: 396, 414). The rise in post-graduate studies for Arabophones increased by 30.26% from 771 students in 1979/1980 to 1272 in 1982/1983 (Bennoune, 2000: 388; Saad, 1992: 68). By 1985, rates of Arabised students at the secondary and tertiary levels were as follows:

65% of general secondary students, 28% of secondary students in technical schools, 32.5% of undergraduate university students, and 20% of postgraduate students (Ruedy, 1992: 228). By March 1999, the rate of Arabisation in Higher Education was 46% and concerned mainly the social sciences and the humanities (Cherrad-Benchefra & Derradji, 2004: 166).

In September 1989, the 'children of the Fundamental school' – that is, Baccalaureate graduates who had gone through a completely Arabised science curriculum at the secondary school level – were registered in university departments of science and technology. Submerged, the institutions of higher education were not ready to receive them in these scientific disciplines. Students' weak proficiency in French had become a major handicap for pursuing higher studies in fields taught in French (sciences, medicine, engineering, etc.). These developments led the authorities to seriously reconsider the whole educational system. But before looking at the most recent developments in language-in-education planning and the current study plans, another instructional context needs to be mentioned briefly as well as the introduction of Berber in the educational system.

Since independence, the spread of language and literacy has been instilled through public primary (and middle) schooling. However, two other instructional contexts should be mentioned here. First, the Koranic school (*m'cid* or *jama'* in Arabic), which represents the oldest educational institution in Algeria, has not disappeared entirely and its role is not negligible. In some remote rural areas, it remains the only recourse to education when public schooling is not available (Ezzaki & Wagner, 1992: 221). By March 2005, Koranic schools in Algeria, scattered all around the country, were estimated at 3000. At the same time, the number of pupils attending these institutions stood around 500,000. They were also attended by (old) women who needed to learn Arabic (Belabes, 2005a: 3). Second, starting immediately after independence, the high rate of illiteracy among the older generation prompted the Algerian government to provide adults with programmes of non-formal instruction. Since then, government and non-government organisations have launched a series of adult literacy campaigns (Ezzaki & Wagner, 1992: 222–3). However, the emphasis put upon developing primary and secondary education led the authorities to neglect adult literacy. For example, after independence, the Algerian government planned to provide literacy programmes for 1 million workers between 1970 and 1974, a plan which was never implemented (Brahimi, 1984: 10).

On 7 October 1995, the Ministry of National Education issued Circular N° 938 allowing the creation of experimental classes for the teaching of Tamazight. The High Commission for Berber Affairs (HCA) supervised the new ministerial initiative by training teachers and introducing Tamazight as an optional subject in a number of pilot Middle and Secondary schools all located in Berberophone regions. The teaching of Berber began in October 1995 for students who were to sit for a final national exam: the final year of the Fundamental School (Grade Nine sanctioned by a certificate exam) and of the Secondary School (sanctioned by the Baccalaureate). This first experience proved to be a failure because of the optional status of Berber teaching, improvisation, educational authorities' hostility to this teaching, and the lack of planning, of students' motivation and of sufficient human, financial and pedagogical resources (Chaker, 1998: 183–4; Kahlouche, 2000: 160–2; Tigziri, 2002: 64). Then with Circular N° 887 issued on 5 September 1996, the Ministry of Education adopted a new experimental strategy for a three-year period. Berber was introduced in Grade Seven of the Fundamental School (i.e. first year in Middle School) starting from 1997–1998 – Circular N° 789 20 issued on 20 August 1997 (Kahlouche, 2000: 162).

From a quantitative standpoint, the number of Tamazight teachers decreased slightly during the last half of the 1990s: from 233 in 1995–1996, it fell to 220 in 1998–1999. The decrease was counterbalanced by the qualitative training of the personnel because the number of contract staff diminished from 99 in 1995–1996 to 43 in 1998–1999 (Tigziri, 2002: 66). However, the number of student enrolment almost doubled within five years. Nationwide, school learners of Tamazight reached 37,700 in 1995–1996, 66,611 in 1998–1999 and 69,159 in 1999–2000 (Tigziri, 2002: 65). This rise concerned mainly Kabylia while enrolment in other Berberophone areas (Shawia and Mzab, for example) remained low. In 1995–1996, 80.57% of the total number of enrolments concerned the Kabylian *wilayas* of Tizi-Ouzou, Bejaia and Bouira. The percentage rose to 89.12% in 1996–1997 then fell slightly to 85.58% in 1997–1998 (Kahlouche, 2000: 165). As far as dialects are concerned, the Ministry of Education tolerate all five major Tamazight varieties, that is, Kabyle, Mzab, Shawia, Chenoua and Tamashek. But the Kabylian variety was the most widely taught by the end of the 1990s: 88.95% of all learners chose Kabyle in 1995–1996, 92.78% in 1996–1997 and 90.09% in 1997–1998 (Kahlouche, 2000: 165). The school manuals are presented in all five dialects and three different scripts: Latin, Arabic and Tifinagh letters. Hence, the Ministry of National Education encourages the use of the three writing systems but teachers who largely use the Latin alphabet reject the use of all three scripts as anti-pedagogic (Tigziri, 2002: 68–9). In fact, the dispute over the written representation of Tamazight is mainly ideological. The Berberist Cultural Movement (MCB) has adopted quasi- unanimously the Latin writing system as an opening towards the modern Western culture while the strategy adopted by the Ministry of National Education (three scripts) aims at reversing the future tendency in favour of Arabic alphabet and of Arabo-Islamic values and culture (Kahlouche, 2000: 161, 166).

As to the most recent developments in language-in-education planning, they correspond to President Bouteflika's era. In September 2003, his government started to implement some of the recommendations made by the National Commission for the Reform of the Educational System (CNRSE). The Fundamental schooling system, considered 'as a failure' by the Minister of Education (Metaoui, 2000: 1–2), is replaced by the old structures comprising three stages: primary school which lasts five years instead of six, middle school with four years instead of three, and secondary school (three years). After graduating from middle school, students have a choice between two common cores: sciences and letters. The first year in secondary education (*Première Année Secondaire* or 1 AS) leads to specialisation tracks – *Deuxième Année Secondaire* or 2 AS and *Troisième Année Secondaire* or 3 AS. The science common core forks into two tracks: sciences and maths. The second common core also forks into two tracks: letters and languages. Moreover, with the reform, a new curriculum is also adopted with the introduction of new subjects in elementary education (scientific and technical education, music, drawing). Starting from September 2003, the teaching of English begins a year earlier in the first grade of middle school on the basis of three hours a week. As of the 2003/2004 school-year, the new curriculum is accompanied by new school manuals for both primary and middle schooling systems with a new book for French for the first year of middle school. Moreover, these manuals are no longer produced by the state establishment the (*Institut Pédagogique National*) but by private companies (Benmesbah, 2003: 12–13). Finally, in September 2003, the total number of pupils and teaching personnel for primary, middle and secondary levels were 7,805,000 student enrolments and 336,000 teachers. Furthermore, the Ministry of Education has recruited 1,500 primary school teachers for the teaching of French in Grade Two as from September 2004 (Belabes, 2004a; Kourta, 2003).

Language spread in the educational system

The above historical background shows that since the end of colonialism (1962), a shift has occurred in the language of instruction, at least in the primary and secondary levels (Belhadj Hacen, 1997: 281, 346). The change has been in favour of Standard Arabic. The languages taught through the national educational system are Standard Arabic, French and English, with 'minor' languages being taught as a third foreign language at the secondary level (German, Spanish, etc.).

Standard Arabic is the exclusive medium of instruction from Grade One onwards, as well as a subject in primary and secondary education, thus providing a total of 12 years of education. The school calendar year consists of 30 teaching weeks. It corresponds to a total of 4050 teaching hours for the primary level, 3945 hors for middle school and for secondary education; the total time-load for each one of the four disciplines amounts to 2490 hours for Letters, 2580 hours for Language, 2820 hours for Science and 2760 hours for Mathematics. In primary school, the total time-load for Standard Arabic, as a subject, is 1575 hours, which corresponds to 38.89% of the total teaching hours for the primary cycle (see Table 3). The total

Table 3 Language spread in Primary school (study plan with weekly and yearly hours)

Years / Subjects	1	2	3	4th*	5th*	Language variety used
Standard Arabic	14	12	11	8.30	7	Arabic
French	–	3	4	5	5	French
Maths	5	5	5	5	5	Arabic
Islamic Studies	1.30	1	1	1.30	1.30	Arabic
Civics	1	1	1	1	1	Arabic
Music	1	1	1	1	1	Arabic
Physical education	1.30	1	1	1.30	1.30	Arabic
Environmental studies				2	2.30	Arabic
Handicrafts/Drawing	1	1	1	1.30	1.30	Arabic
History-Geography					1	Arabic
Science-Technology	2	2	2			Arabic
Total weekly	27	27	27	27	27	
Total yearly	810	810	810	810	810	

* The 2005–2006 school year will be the last year for the Fundamental school system in the primary cycle

Table 4 Language spread in Middle school (study plan with weekly and yearly hours)

Subjects	Years 1	2	3	9th*	Language variety used
Standard Arabic	5	5	5	5	Arabic
Tamazight	3	3	3	–	Tamazight
French	5	5	5	4	French
English	3	3	3	5	English
Maths	5	5	5	5	Arabic
Biology	2	2	2	3	Arabic
Civics	1	1	1	1	Arabic
Islamic Studies	1	1	1	1	Arabic
History and Geography	2	2	2	2.30	Arabic
Drawing	1	1	1	1	Arabic
Music	1	1	1	1	Arabic
Physical education	2	2	2	2	Arabic
Physics-Technology	2	2	2	2	Arabic
Total weekly hours	33	33	33	32.30	
Total yearly hours	990	990	990	975	

* The 2005–2006 school year will be the last year for the Fundamental school system in the Middle school

time-load for Standard Arabic in middle school is 600 hours and represents 15.21% of the total teaching hours for this level (see Table 4). The total time-load for Standard Arabic and the corresponding percentages in secondary education for the four disciplines is as follows: Letters: 540 hours, corresponding to 21.69%, Language: 390 hours, corresponding to 15.12%, Science: 270 hours, corresponding to 9.57%, and Mathematics: 270 hours corresponding to 9.78% (see Table 5). In theory, all subjects – with the exception of foreign languages taught in the target language, whatever that language may be – are taught in Standard Arabic in primary, middle and secondary cycles. However, teachers and students do resort to Algerian Arabic and/or French to improve communication within the school context (management of classroom problems, technical fields, scientific jargon, etc.). Code-mixing with dialectal Arabic or French is not unique to Algeria and in fact is compatible with what has been said about other Arabic-speaking countries in the Maghreb – for Tunisia, see Daoud (2001: 14–15); for Morocco see Youssi (1991: 272–7).

French is now taught as a subject from Grade Two in primary education to the final year at the secondary cycle, totalling 11 years of instruction. The total time-load for French is as follows: 510 hours, corresponding to 12.60% of the total teaching hours for the primary level, 570 hours, corresponding to 14.45% of the total teaching hours for the middle cycle. In the secondary level and for all disciplines, 360 hours, corresponding to 14.46% of the total teaching hours for Letters, 390 hours, corresponding to 15.12% of the total teaching hours for Language, 300 hours, corresponding to 10.64% of the total teaching hours for Science, and 300

Table 5 Language spread in secondary cycle (study plan with weekly and yearly hours)

Hours per week

Years Subjects	1 AS Letters	1 AS Science	2 AS Letters	2 AS Language	2 AS Science	2 AS Maths	3 AS Letters	3 AS Language	3 AS Science	3 AS Maths	Language variety used
Arabic	5	3	6	4	3	3	7	4	3	3	Arabic
French	5	4	4	4	3	3	3	4	3	3	French
English	3	2	3	4	3	3	3	4	3	3	English
3rd foreign language	2			3				4			Spanish, German, etc
Maths	3	5	2	2	5	6	2	2	5	7	Arabic
Civics	2	2	2	2	2	2					Arabic
Biology	1	4	1	1	5	2			5	2	Arabic
Philosophy			2	2			7	5	3	3	Arabic
Physics/chemistry	1	5	1	1	5	5			5	6	Arabic
History and Geography	4	3	4	4	3	3	4	4	2	2	Arabic
Physical education	2	2	2	2	2	2	2	2	2	2	Arabic
Total weekly hours	28	30	27	29	31	29	28	29	31	31	
Total yearly hours	840	900	810	870	930	870	840	870	930	930	

hours, corresponding to 10.87% of the total teaching hours for Mathematics. With the educational reform implemented in 2003, Tamazight is now an obligatory subject taught for three hours a week in the first three years of middle school. However, the lack of teaching personnel, especially in Arabophone areas, prevents the Berber language from being offered in all schools around the country. By the end of the 2006–2007 school year, students who attend schools where Tamazight is provided will have been taught the Berber language for 270 hours, corresponding to 6.84% of the total teaching hours for the middle cycle. In addition, as mentioned earlier, the teaching of English, as the second compulsory foreign language, begins in the first year in middle school and is maintained until the Baccalaureate, totalling seven years of instruction. The total time-load for English is 420 hours, corresponding to 10.65% of the total teaching hours for the middle school. The distribution in the secondary cycle is as follows: Letters: 270 hours, corresponding to 10.84% of the total teaching hours, Language: 330 hours, corresponding to 12.79% of the total teaching hours, Science: 240 hours, corresponding to 8.51% of the total teaching hours, Mathematics: 240 hours, corresponding to 8.70% of the total teaching hours. Finally, a student who begins his secondary education in letters and then specialises in languages has to choose a third foreign language (German, Italian, Spanish, etc.) and may study it two to four hours a week for three years (see Table 5).

All in all, an Arabophone student who completes compulsory Arabic, French and English and opts for the common core where another foreign language is required can end up a quadrilingual. While a Berberophone in a similar position may be competent in five languages. In the near future, probably within five years, the five-language competence is likely to spread among Arabophones who now attend middle schools where Tamazight is offered as a subject.

Up to 1998, universities were divided into institutes each consisting of different departments. Then on 17 August 1998, Decree N° 98-253 (Article 3) introduced an organisation based on Faculties: the Faculty of Science and the Faculty of Letters and Humanities. The latter Faculty includes subjects such as the Arabic Language and Literature, Foreign Languages, Law, Economics, Social Sciences, Library Studies, Sociology, Education and Psychology. For example, the Faculty of Letters and Humanities in the University of Tizi Ouzou in Kabylia consists of the Department of Arabic Language and Literature, Department of Amazigh Language and Culture, Department of Psychology, Department of French and Department of English (Tigziri, 2002: 62). In higher education, the predominant language of instruction is French even though official circulars give time-loads

Table 6 Language spread in higher education

Hours per week		
Disciplines	*Arabic as medium of instruction*	*French as medium of instruction*
Social sciences and humanities	25	4
Exact sciences	25	4
Medicine	2	30
Veterinary medicine	4	27

Adapted from Queffélec *et al.* (2002: 76)

which are incompatible with reality (see Table 6). In all humanity disciplines, Arabic serves as the medium of instruction. At the postgraduate level, French (or Arabic-French code-switching) is common. In the Exact Science subjects, one finds Architecture, Biology, Chemistry, Civil Engineering, Computer Science, Electronics, Geography, Industrial Engineering, Mathematics, Nutrition, Physics, Technology, etc. Almost all scientific disciplines are arabised in the first year but from the second year onwards, French becomes the medium of instruction in theory, but in reality every department of science uses the pedagogical means available and the rare arabised teachers in particular specialised fields. In language departments (English, French, German, Italian, Spanish, and Russian), each language is taught in the target language concerned. With respect to language use in university classes in Algeria, no study has ever been conducted on the issue. It is most likely that the results reported for Jordan in the 1990s (Mustapha, 1995; Zughoul, 2001) are applicable to Algerian universities as well. For example, in one empirical study, seven science professors were recorded during their lectures and, out of 1409 sentences produced by these academics, 13.9% were in Arabic only, 34.8% in English only, and 51.1% in Arabic-English code-switching (Mustapha, 1995: 41). The present author's long experience as a teacher and Department Head at the University of Oran allows him to think that the results for Jordan are not far from the truth for Algeria, but with one difference: instead of English, Algerian academics would use French. In addition, in Berberophone areas, one has to account for Tamazight as another language teachers and students resort to (see Table 6).

The Arabisation of the administration and the milieu

During the colonial period, the French held the higher administrative positions and Algerians occupied lower level functions which necessitated training in French. Under the reign of General Charles de Gaulle, around 100,000 Algerian civil servants were finally integrated into the colonial administration between 1960 and 1962 (Ghouali, 2002: 260; Grandguillaume, 1983: 105). After independence, the new authorities had to start virtually from scratch since files and forms and paper work were all in French, and most of the functionaries were not sufficiently competent in written Arabic (Thomas, 1999: 25). Because of political instability, lack of trainers and motivated trainees, the first government of Ahmed Ben Bella (1962–1965) could not implement the Arabisation of the administration and merely succeeded in introducing a few symbolic acts. For example, on 12 June 1963, the National Assembly passed a motion in favour of Arabic as the working language of the Assembly / Parliament via translation. On 22 May 1964, the Higher School of Interpreting and Translating was created by decree to provide the administration with the necessary tools for gradual Arabisation. And the first *Official Journal of the Algerian Republic* was published in Arabic on 1 June 1964 (Grandguillaume, 1983: 105–6).

The government of Colonel Houari Boumediene turned out to be more assertive in Arabising Algeria in general and in the number of functionaries in particular. In April 1968, a circular required all civil servants to learn the official national language by the year 1971. On 27 June 1971, a decree was passed for the total Arabisation of the Ministry of Justice which turned out to be at the forefront of the process of Arabising the administrative sector. All courtroom proceedings as well as all written documents and judicial decisions in both civil and criminal cases were to be (translated) into Arabic. Algerian Arabic was tolerated under certain circumstances (for illiterate people) and the use of French was banned (Queffélec *et al.*, 2002: 74).

Between 1976 and 1979, the authorities arabised all civil documents (records of births, marriages, deaths, etc.), as well as all bureaucracies which directly interface with the public (the City Hall, the police, the Ministry of Information, the Ministry of Defence, the Ministry of Public Works, the Ministry of Culture, and the Ministry of Youth and Sports). By the end of December 1976, the Ministry of the Interior planned to recruit 50 arabised female police inspectors (Grandguillaume, 1983: 190). On 1 March 1976, all public signs (streets, highways, stores, administrative buildings, etc.) and car licence plates were arabised. Adequate product description and accompanying literature was to be in Arabic.[26] Furthermore, all French-named towns and cities not arabised immediately after independence were either given Arabic names or were restored to their original Arabic/Berber names: for example *Aumale* became *Sour El Ghozlane*, and *Camp du Maréchal* became *Tadmaït* (Harbi, 1984: 195; Morsly, 1985: 81). At the registry office, family names were translated into Arabic, and newly born babies were given Arabic first names; parents were forbidden to give their children Berber names (Imache, 1989: 7). Lists of names provided by the central authorities were bowdlerised of any Berber referent (Gandon, 1978: 17–19). In June 1976, the police affixed seals on the Berber publication known as *Fichier berbère* (mainly concerned with the study of the Kabylian language). The authorities described this periodical as 'regionalist and subversive' (Grandguillaume, 1983: 113; 2004a: 30). Decree N° 81-27 issued in May 1981 aimed at transcribing place names in Latin letters based on Arabic pronunciation. The task proved to be formidable because, among other things, French letters could not properly represent all Arabic phonemes. For example, planners often provided several Arabic letters for a French one: e.g. k = ك-ق, R = ر-غ, s = سل-صل, c = ص-س-ق-ك (Morsly, 1988: 169). They also ignored the sociolinguistic reality of the country, the historical evolution of these names and how people really pronounced them (Lacheraf, 1998: 165–7; Morsly, 1988: 171).

At the present time, apart from the Ministry of Justice, the Ministry of Religious Affairs and the registry offices in town halls and, to a lesser degree, the Ministry of Education where Arabisation is either totally or almost complete, all administrative texts in the other government departments are written in French and then later translated into Arabic. They are written in a highly formal French style which illustrates the linguistic competence of high-level government cadres trained mainly in European countries, France in particular.[27] At the present time, not all official documents are written exclusively in Arabic. They are often produced in French and their Arabic versions are not systematic. The *Official Journal of the Algerian Republic*, with a very high circulation, seems to be the only document first written in Arabic and then translated into French (Queffélec *et al.*, 2002: 70–2). During the meetings of the Council of Ministers, Standard Arabic is not exclusively used: the President and Ministers speak Literary Arabic and Algerian Arabic, and sometimes French (Ghouali, 2002: 261). Locally, in regions with a measure of autonomy (*wilaya, daïra* and *baladia*), Arabic-French or Tamazight-French bilingualism is the norm, with French being the preferred language for writing and Algerian

Arabic / Tamazight for oral interaction. Documents issued from the Ministry of the Interior and the Ministry of the Economy, for instance, are printed in Arabic when concerned with simple day-to-day administrative management and in French when dealing with technical matters. These texts are often sent by central government departments in French and then translated into Arabic locally. But most documents that concern the general public are either bilingual (Arabic-French) or monolingual in French. These practices affect the post-office (money orders, cheques, telephone bills, etc.), the energy sector (electricity and water bills) and the healthcare sector where French is extremely dominant. Arabic remains dominant only in courts and town halls (registry offices). According to an estimate, French is used in 70% of all written interactions between the public and local administrations. In fact, the more one moves away from interactions with the state and government departments, the more French is used. In urban centres, Algerians use Algerian Arabic (in alternation with French) when interacting orally with their local administration and Arabic or French in writing. In rural areas, it is mainly Algerian Arabic or Tamazight that dominate with French or Arabic being the language(s) for writing (Kadi, 2004: 140–2; Queffélec *et al.*, 2002: 72–4).

With post-October 1988 political liberalisation, the practice of giving Amazigh names increased; for example, since 1988, children have been named after Berber kings and historical figures: 'Amazigh', 'Massine', 'Juba', 'Jugurtha' (El Aissati, 2001: 61). At the present time, both Arabic and French are used for personal official documents (identity papers, car registration documents, etc.). Arabic remains the language of both printing and drafting while French is used for drafting to supplement information provided in Arabic allowing its certification; for example, personal names, surnames and place of birth are drafted in both languages. Papers issued by the registry office (e.g. birth, death and marriage certificates) as well as judicial documents (e.g. police records) can be issued in French on demand and bear the notation 'Valid for use overseas'. The use of three languages for passports corresponds to an international convention.

As far as faith is concerned, Islam represents the official religion, with 99% of the population being Sunni Muslims (Atlapedia, 2003; CIA, 2005). Historically speaking, the Islamic faith had a major impact on the spread of the Arabic language in Algeria; Classical Arabic remains the most important idiom for Islamic institutional practices (rites, sermon, religious education, theological debates). But since the popular uprising of October 1988 and the ensuing political liberalisation, Algerian Arabic has often been used in sermons. This is also the case for sermons in Tamazight which have been in use since the foundation of the High Commission for Berber Affairs (HCA) in May 1995 (Queffélec, 2002: 74). It should be noted that, for the first time in modern history, the Koran was translated into Tamazight. In 2003, a Moroccan scholar published his *Tarurt n wammaken n Leqran* [*Translation of the meanings of the Koran*] (Jouhadi, 2003). Roman Catholics and Jews taken together represent less than 1% of the population (Atlapedia, 2003). However, the recent conversion to Christianity, mainly in the Kabylian region, has been accompanied by the use of French in sermons (Aït-Larbi, 2005: 4).

Publishing and the media

Less than half a decade after independence, French publishers and booksellers (Hachette, in particular) still had the monopoly on the Algerian book market: they mainly distributed books published abroad. By February 1966, the authorities in Algeria founded a national publishing house called *Société Nationale d'Edition et de Diffusion* (SNED) with Arabic and French sections. The creation of an Arabic publishing sector allowed the few Arabophone writers to have their works published in Algeria instead of trying to get published in the Arab countries of the Middle East (Abu Haidar, 2000: 156; Ghouali, 2002: 263). In 1967, Ruling N° 67-191 introduced tax exemption for the publication and importation of certain books in Arabic (Kadi, 2004: 135). Between 1962 and 1973, out of a total of 1800 books on Algeria, the SNED published 555 volumes, with 287 for the Arabic section and 268 for the French one (Stora, 2001: 73). Another national publishing house was created in the 1970s known as the *Office des Presses Universitaires* (OPU). Between 1975 and 1997, the OPU published 1382 books in Arabic and 1633 in French (55%). In fact, more than half of all publication in the public and private sectors are in French (Kadi, 2004: 141).

The history of the Algerian Press goes back to the 1920s and the birth of nationalism. It was, then, a partisan-run written medium mainly sustained by the major nationalist political parties. As far as the language of publication is concerned, the circulation of the pre-revolutionary press was almost identical to the one that has been current since the independence of the country. Before the War of Algeria began in 1954 putting an end to this press, the circulation of the Francophone press was almost three times that in Arabic: 64,000 and 22,000 respectively (Queffélec *et al.*, 2002: 78).

After independence, Algerians inherited the mass media which had been under the control of the colonial authorities and the *pieds noirs*. Among these, a number of periodicals and journals soon came under government control and the FLN party and, in 1963, under the direction of *Algérie-Presse-Service* (APS). Thus, it was not a free press and served only as the authorities' official intermediary. By June 1965, the major magazines and journals with their respective circulation were as follows: *El Moudjahid* (one edition in French and one in Arabic) with 30,000 copies; *Alger Républicain* (in French) with 40,000–50,000 copies; *Révolution Africaine* with a circulation of over 12,000; *Révolution et Travail*; *Révolution à l'Université*; *Le Peuple* (circulation 100,000) and its Arabic edition *Ach-Chaab* (circulation 30,000); *La République* (circulation 50,000); La *Dépêche d'Alger* (circulation 80,000–95,000); *La Dépêche* with a circulation of around 30,000; *Atlas-Algérie*; *El-Djeich*; *Al-Djazairi*; *Révolution* (Gordon, 1966: 195–6). Most of the above publications were dull and doctrinaire, but those which were lively (for example, *Alger Républicain*) had a high circulation even though official figures on circulation are very unreliable.

Two decades later, centralised bureaucratic control over the press did not improve the situation both in terms of quantity/quality and circulation: there were only four dailies and a few magazines with low circulation for a total population of 22 million in 1984. The same year, the three major Arabophone dailies with their respective circulation were: *Ach-Chaab* (70,000), *An Nasr* and *Al Djoumhouria* (17,000 each). Their circulation represented merely half the circulation of the French-medium *El Moudjahid* which had a circulation of over 350,000 (Brahimi, 1984: 10). Created in 1978 the weekly Francophone *Algérie Actualité* managed to have some kind of freedom from the central bureaucracy. It thus doubled its circulation within four years, and it rose from 100,000 in the early 1980s to 200,000 in 1984 (Brahimi, 1984: 12). It should be noted that Algerian readers' discontent with their national press came mainly from censorship which made them prefer the foreign press when it was of good quality, be it in French or in Arabic.[28] For example, in 1984, the most common French dailies were *Le Monde* with a circulation of 15,000, *Le Matin* with a circulation of 12,000, *L'Équipe* with a circulation of 8000, and *Libération* with a circulation of 7000. Among the major Arabic weeklies, there were *El Moustaqbal* with a circulation of 45,000, *El Watan al Arabi* with a circulation of 15,000 and *Ros el Youcef* with a circulation of 5000 (Brahimi, 1984: 12).

With political liberalisation following the October 1988 unrest, an important private sector in the press came to exist side by side with the public one. Two consecutive years, 1992 and 1993 respectively, illustrate this increase in the written media and its evolution. There were, in 1992, six government-owned and two private dailies in Arabic and two public and 11 private dailies in French. The number of dailies and circulation stabilised in 1993. However, a permanent feature for circulation has not changed since the period of colonisation and the 1980s: in 1993, the circulation of French-medium dailies continued to be roughly three times that of Arabophone dailies: 220,000 and 625,000 respectively (Brahimi, 1993: 7). By the year 1994, there were over 230 press publications in Algeria (government, private, partisan, etc.) with 103 in Arabic and 134 in French. For the government-owned dailies and magazines there were four in French and 10 in Arabic; for the partisan press (political parties, organisations, etc.), there were 28 in French and 24 in Arabic, and for the private 'independent' sector (which covers 70% of the total press market in Algeria dominated by the French language) there were 102 in French and 24 in Arabic (Queffélec *et al.*, 2002: 79–80). This remained a permanent feature of the Algerian written media until the end of the 1990s (Queffélec *et al.*, 2002: 80–1). By June 2004, there were 26 dailies in French and 20 in Arabic with a total circulation of 1,600,000, with 50% for each language (Mostefaoui, 2004: 21; Vignaux, 2004: 7). The rise of Tamazight as another publishing language is a recent phenomenon developed after political liberalisation following October 1988. When the clandestine Berber political party FFS (founded in 1963) was officially recognised in 1989, it edited the first issue of a Berber newspaper called *Amaynut*. Following the creation in 1989 of the RCD, another partisan Berber newspaper was launched with the title *Asalu* (El Aissati, 1993: 100). These newspapers did not last long, soon disappearing for commercial and linguistic reasons: i. e., low circulation, language uinintelligible to the majority of Berberophones as a result of its esoteric nature due in large part to the use of many neologisms (Chaker, 1997: 95). But a less ambitious solution has been put into practice since the early 1990s: several Arabophone and Francophone national journals and magazines regularly insert a single page in Berber (Chaker, 1998: 170).

As in the rest of the Arab world, Algeria's national press has been in crisis since the end of the 20th century due mainly to the rise of satellite television (Aïta, 2003–2004: 32). After independence, the Algerian authorities also inherited the major audio-visual media that had existed during colonial times. Three radio stations were renamed:

- 'Chaîne I' for Arabophone audiences where Literary/institutional Arabic dominates,
- 'Chaîne II' a Berber radio channel which caters to the Kabylian community but which started, in the mid-1990s, to include programmes in other Berber varieties such as Shawia and Mzab (Chaker, 1997: 95), and
- 'Chaîne III' which targets Francophone listeners (Queffélec *et al.*, 2002: 82). One major innovation has been introduced on Chaine III since the 1970s against the will of the authorities: Algerian Arabic is used in parallel with French (code-switching). (Caubet, 2004: 77–8)

As a result of democratic transition, Algerian Arabic has come to be accepted even in 'Chaîne I', a doctrinaire radio station where no other language but Classical Arabic was accepted in its programmes (Caubet, 2004: 87). A similar evolution occurred in television. The single TV channel inherited from the colonial era was baptised *Radio Télévision Algérienne* (RTA) after 1962 and later named *Entreprise Nationale de Télévision* (ENTV). The total number of people who own a TV set has increased substantially after independence: 29.1% in 1970, 52% in 1980, 74% in 1992 and 83% in 2005 (*El Watan*, 2005: 31; Stora, 2001: 76). Until the end of the 1990s, the ENTV remained the sole national TV channel with Standard Arabic being the dominant idiom (Grandguillaume, 1989: 54). More recently, Algerian Arabic and code-mixing (Arabic-French) have been tolerated in programmes tailored for youth. At the present time, there are two other international television channels (*Canal Algérie* and *A3*) that address mostly Algerian nationals in the Diaspora (Mostari, 2004: 32). Since 'Act N°. 91-05 of 16 January 1991' was implemented in 1999, dubbing and subtitling has increased noticeably. However, scientific documentaries and non-Arabic speaking films are aired in French. With the spread of satellite television in the early 1990s, the dull and doctrinaire character of the Algerian national channel made Algerians turn to foreign channels and watch the ENTV only when programmes dealt with national news (Queffélec *et al.*, 2002: 82–3). Television is by far the most important medium for entertainment among youth who represent the majority of the population. In a poll published in November 2004, 73% of those aged between 10 and 35 declared watching television as their major hobby, as opposed to mainly reading the press[29] (Maïche, 2004: 1).

By the mid-1990s, one Algerian household in two possessed a satellite dish (Rossillon, 1995: 90), and French TV programmes – TF1, France 2, France 3, TV5, M6, Canal + and many other channels – were watched by 9 to 12 million Algerians in 1992 (Esprit, 1995: 159). Even TV scrambling does not seem to discourage small screen amateurs: Canal +, which is a coded channel, was decoded by Algerian hackers and, in 2002, around 600,000 households had Canal + (*El Watan*, 2002: 23). French TV scrambling companies such as Canalsatellite and TPS put an end to this hacker practice in November 2004. Some Algerians have reportedly said that this was 'treason on the part of France' arguing that 'In families, children have learned French not in school, but by watching cartoons on television. If we have to watch Arabic TV channels, they [children] won't be bilingual'[30] (Tuquoi, 2004: 1). According to Queffélec *et al.* (2002: 83), satellite TV serves as a positive learning linguistic environment for children: it has been noted that young Algerians could produce acceptable discourse in French without prior acquisition of this language in school. In the end, and on a daily basis, French TV channels are watched by 52% of Algerian households (Benmesbah, 2003: 12).

Arabic and Berber have also derived benefits from the technological revolution provided by satellite TV channels and/or radio stations and computers (the Internet). Standard Arabic has witnessed considerable spread worldwide. It is now transmitted via several satellites with C or KU bands, the major ones being: ARABSAT 2B (30.5° East), ARABSAT 2A (6° East and 26° East), EUTELSAT 2F3 (16° East), EUTELSAT 2F1 and HOT BIRD (13° East). For example, the satellites EUTELSAT 2F3 and ARABSAT 2A (6° East) provide the majority of Arabic channels (Laroussi, 2003: 251–2). Among the Middle Eastern satellite TV channels which had or still have a large following in Algeria, there are *MBC* a London-based channel founded in 1991, *Al-Jazira* based in Qatar and founded in 1996, and *Al-Arabiyya*, based in the United Arab Emirates and launched in 2003 (Gonzalez-Quijano, 2003–2004: 18–19). As for the audio-visual media in Berber, the ENTV began to diffuse two daily news bulletins in Tamazight by the end of 1991. At present, there is a daily 15 minute news bulletin. A TV channel completely devoted to Berber language and culture has been on the drawing board for quite some time (Chaker, 1997: 96). Since 2001, a Berber satellite TV station called *Berbère Télévision,* based in Paris, has been broadcasting programmes entirely in Tamazight. Such a crucial space has been enhanced in recent years by a proliferation of Internet sites and e-mail networks (Maddy-Weitzman, 2001: 42).

Arab countries lag behind technologically, especially in the field of computing. While Arabs amount to 5% of the population of the world, they represent only 0.5% of Internet users (PNUD, 2002: 82). For example, the rate of Internet connections for the entire Arab world is 24 times lower than the world average (Gonzalez-Quijano, 2003–2004: 14). Among the estimated 6 million Internet users for the Arabic language in 2003 (Maurais, 2003: 21), the number of Internet connections in Algeria was under 20,000 (Martín, 2003: 46). In the Maghreb, for example, Algeria has the lowest density of fixed and mobile telephone lines, the lowest number of computers (per 1000 inhabitants), and of Internet users (Boniface, 2005: 364, 376, 381; PNUD, 2002: 172). The lag of the Arab world is due mainly to economic constraints (poverty) coupled with educational obstacles because the use of the Internet requires minimum computer competence and, above all, competence in languages. The 'Arab Internet', started in 1999–2000 with the launching of Explorer 5 software, solved problems related to the visualisation of Arabic texts (Aïta, 2003–2004: 30). But this internet prefers to evolve in a 'multilingual environment' in order to communicate one's views of the world to the rest of the globe (Gonzalez-Quijano, 2003–2004: 12); thus, being competent in such major Western languages as English or French is viewed as a social gain. In Algeria, where the Internet is almost exclusively provided through cyberspace cafés, French is the main language used by Internet users who favour chats (Laroussi, 2003: 252; Zerrouk, 2004: 7).

All in all, Arabisation has resulted in the expansion of Standard Arabic in Algeria as a result both of the authorities' political/ideological commitment and of the substantial population increase (Sarter & Sefta, 1992: 111; Sirles, 1999: 128).

The role of politics has, in part, led to this success story, and political scientists are likely to use Algeria's case to reconcile the gap between language policy goals and outcomes (see, e.g. Sirles, 1999: 117). But when one gives primacy to language and looks at the outcome from the position of the human subjects' end, Algeria's language policy is not such a success. Arabisation has, in fact, led to unplanned development or the 'invisible planners' of an 'invisible policy' (Annamalai, 1994: 275–6; Pakir, 1994: 164–5): that is, Algeria's language policy has led to results that are different from those desired by the planners. The gap between outcomes and intents concerns conflicts, Islamisation, standards of linguistic acquisition, language shift, and so on.

Unplanned language spread

As mentioned in the introduction to this monograph, Berger (2002: 8) describes the language issue in Algeria as its 'most severe problem'. The opposition between the language of 'authenticity' (Standard/Classical Arabic) and the language of 'modernity' (French) has produced a divided society: those trained in Standard Arabic adhere to cultural norms and standards of living which are different from those shared by Algerians trained in French (Grandguillaume, 2002: 162). The polarisation of Algerian society is also visible in people's perception of the failure of Arabisation and the educational system. For the pro-Arabisation quarters, the modest success comes from the elitist nature of the Algerian leadership who have set up a language policy that excludes the masses and favours French values and Westernisation (Assous, 1985; Mansouri, 1991; Souaiaia, 1990). This is so because opponents consider Arabisation to be the major cause of the 'educational debacle' for two reasons: first, Standard Arabic is the first language of no one in Algeria; second, Arabisation and Standard Arabic in Algeria are the carrier of an outdated teaching mode which values rote learning and repetition (*hafdh* in Arabic) and attitudes not open to new ideas encouraging a retrograde interpretation of Islam (Addi, 1995; Entelis, 1981; Rouadjia, 1991). The opposition between the two groups is best illustrated by two 1990 events: on 20 April 1990, 100,000 Islamists of the FIS demonstrated in Algiers calling for the implementation of Shari'a law and the end of bilingualism; on 27 December 1990, 400,000 people joined a demonstration in Algiers in favour of democracy and against the law of total Arabisation adopted the day before by the parliament (Vermeren, 2004: 403).

According to Ennaji (1999: 390) '[Arabisation] has in a sense led to the birth and growth of the Islamic fundamentalist movement in the whole [Arab/Maghreb] region.' According to Berdouzi (2000: 21), the hasty implementation of an exclusively Arabic monolingual educational system in the early 1970s is considered to be at the origin of the spread of Islamic fundamentalism, xenophobia, chauvinism and obscurantism. The result of such polarisation in Algeria led to a 'cultural civil war' (Péroncel-Hugoz, 1994) or linguistic 'intellectual cleansing' (Vermeren, 2004: 320) whose victims were mainly secular and/or Francophone Algerians (Addi, 1995). Consequently, a large number of highly qualified intellectuals (teaching staff) left the country. According to an OECD report published in 2004, out of one million exiles for the whole Arab world, Algeria has the highest number of university-qualified expatriates: 214,000 Algerians, 202,000 Egyptians, 110,000 Lebanese and 83,000 Iraqis (Giret *et al.*, 2004: 40; PNUD, 2002: 78). According to

Vermeren, the French authorities who refuse to make the real figures official, admit unofficially that between 200,000 and 300,000 Algerian intellectuals and their families have settled in France since the beginning of the armed conflict. This brings the total number of expatriates to around 500,000 (2004: 320).

Arabisation and Islamisation

In October 1962, President Ben Bella declared: 'Arabisation is not Islamisation'. His message was meant to reassure the secular political establishment and those parts of the population that feared the institutionalisation of a theocracy (Grandguillaume, 1983: 184, 1989: 51). The Islamic 'colouring' of the Arabisation of the milieu goes back to the early days of independence when all the churches in towns and cities were turned into mosques. On 2 November 1962, the authorities opened the Katchaoua Mosque in Algiers, a structure that had been expropriated by the French military and turned into a cathedral after the conquest of Algeria in 1830 (Ghouali, 2002: 263; Grandguillaume, 1983: 110; Kahlouche, 1997: 175). Moreover, a direct consequence of the Arabisation of the Algerian legal system is its Islamisation. According to Mansouri (1991: 74), 'This [legal] system, which was not long ago an extension of French civil law, now functions in Arabic and according to Islamic (Sharia) law.' Under the pressure of the conservative quarters which felt that the equality of the sexes contravened the tenets of Islam, the National Assembly adopted, on 22 May 1984, the Family Code strongly tinged with Islamism so as to appeal to the conservative and 'macho' elements in Algerian society (Grandguillaume, 1997b: 3). According to Saadi (1991: 47) and Abu-Haidar (2000: 158), the Family Code made women's position in society inferior to that of men and instituted polygamy. Arabisation/Islamisation also means a process of de-secularisation of the educational system (mainly) through the implementation of the policy of Arabisation.

Some Maghreban authors reject Arabisation/Islamisation often on affective criteria and not on objective facts (see e.g. Miliani, 2003: 29; Moatassime, 1996: 290; Mostari, 2004: 41). For example, Mostari concludes, among other things, with the following remark: 'Algerians are well aware that Arabisation is not Islamisation, and that Arabisation's first aim is the restoration of Arabo-Islamic identity and not the re-Islamisation of the state' (2004: 41). The issue is not solely about the establishment of a theocracy at the state level: it is about how individuals come to accept obediently and uncritically xenophobic, chauvinist and obscurantist ideas. In fact, Mostari brings this home to the reader when she writes:

> Islamist intellectuals have made careers by dominating the theological and Arabic-language faculties (especially faculties of Arabic literature, Islamic studies, law, etc.), thereby gaining control of many positions, particularly among Imams in the mosques and teachers in the lycées. Thus, they have formed a strong network that ensures the recruitment of more Islamists to such positions and the inculcation of Islamist ideas among the new generations. (2004: 39)

The spread of these ideas among the new generations and the ease with which they were inculcated led several Algerian, Maghreban and non-Maghreban researchers to equate Arabisation with Islamisation (Benrabah, 1996, 1999a, 2004b; Coffman, 1992; Dourari, 1997; Ennaji, 1999; Entelis, 1981; Grandguillaume, 2004b;

Harbi, 1984, 1994; Rouadjia, 1991; Saadi-Mokrane, 2002; Vermeren, 2004). The peda-gogical practices and content of school manuals that accompanied the process of arabising the educational system and its Islamisation have been summarised else-where (Benrabah, 1996, 1999a, 2004b). However, reproduced below is a dictation presented on 1–2 June 1997 to schoolchildren who sat for the entrance examination for Sixth Form (Fundamental School). The text, a panegyric of violence, was given on the eve of the celebration of the International Day for Children.

> This country is dear to us and will remain invulnerable as long as its coura-geous combatants will defend it. This is the destiny of the sons of Algeria, as long as everyone will respond to the roll call with determination. Be a faith-ful combatant who does not fear death and who faces the enemies' bullets by offering his chest, shouting in the name of God, the Merciful, Allah Akbar. Dear children, why live in fear? Sooner or later you will die (death is inevitable). The Homeland is ours, its honour is ours.

To summarise, for the purpose of this monograph, the effects of Arabisation on new generations, attention is called to the results of a fieldwork study conducted by an Algerian historian in the early 1990s (Remaoun, 1995). He presented a closed choice questionnaire to 1629 pupils in their A levels ('Terminale'). The results for two questions are worth noting:

(1) *'In which field would you like the school to teach you more things?'*
(2) *'What are the values that you most adhere to?'*

The results in Table 7 show that Islam fares best while the Arabic language fares poorest and that the new generation values religious beliefs and Islam more than they do the Arabic language.

There are at least two factors behind the collusion of Arabisation with Islamisation in Algeria (Ennaji, 1999: 389; Grandguillaume, 1996: 45). First,

Table 7 Pupils' attitudes toward their preferred field of study and the values they adhered to

Question 1		Question 2	
Preferred field	*% out of a total of 1629 pupils*	*Values adhered to*	*% out of a total of 1629 pupils*
'Islam as religion and civilization'	20.5	Religion	16.2
'Meaning of life'	16	Family	16
'Current affairs'	15.8	Honour	15.2
'Work techniques'	15.5	Work	13.2
'History of Algeria'	10.6	Equality	8.5
		Honesty and integrity	6.7
		Nationalism	5.8
		School	4.9
		Language	4.9

Adapted from Remaoun (1995: 73–4)

immediately after independence, the lack of qualified teaching personnel caused the authorities to employ whoever was available – graduates from Koranic schools in Algeria and abroad, mainly from Egypt, who confused teaching Arabic with teaching the Koran and religion. Second, in the 1980s, the Algerian society was overwhelmed by the powerful rise of political Islamism whose partisans proved to be staunch supporters of total and complete Arabisation. Their radicalism left no breathing space for moderates, and Arabic teachers were under Islamist pressure. During an FLN-party Congress in 1986, the Minister of Education, who was the first to impose Arabisation 'at all cost' after the military coup in 1965, demanded the establishment of an Islamic republic (theocracy) in Algeria (Harbi, 1994: 204). At the beginning of the 1980s, the rise of Islamic fundamentalism urged the then Minister of Religious Affairs to repeat Ben Bella's 1962 declaration 'Arabisation is not Islamisation', but this time with a difference: the Minister meant that Arabisation as a linguistic process (Arabicisation) is not enough for the institution of a theocracy; there was a need for total Arabisation, and for him a collusion exists between Arabisation and Islamisation (Grandguillaume, 1989: 51).

Standards of language acquisition

The teaching methodology adopted since the early 1970s further impacts on the quality of children's education. In her critical analysis published in 1989, Malika Boudalia-Greffou argues that the teaching methods imposed by the Algerian Ministry of Education affect the Algerian youth's linguistic ability as well as their intellectual development. According to this Algerian pedagogue, as soon as she/he enters an Algerian school, the child undergoes a typical Pavlovian conditioning through teaching techniques and pedagogical contents that encourage ossified linguistic models at the expense of linguistic complexity. For example, the 1965 instructions sent by the Ministry of Education insist on the following:

(1) Teachers should teach 'oral Arabic', the language of dialogues and avoid language for description and narratives.
(2) Use simple linguistic structures for sentences: SVO (Subject-Verb-Object).
(3) In this 'simplified' language, only a restricted list of adjectives can be used with no more than 32 adjectives of the type 'big-small'.

One of these instructions reads as follows: 'The teacher should avoid giving a large number of meanings. He should choose the generic term "bird" instead of "swallow" and the word "red" for "ruby"' (Boudalia-Greffou, 1989: 75). These instructions insist on teaching words and expressions which refer to concrete things. Thus, the Algerian child can only deal with what she/he can see and is therefore incapable of theorising and developing abstract ideas. To illustrate the effects produced by these methods, research done by an Algerian on the production of narratives by children aged five-to-six (age when they start school) and nine are discussed. This is what she wrote about the first group's results:

> The results have proved that five- and six-year-olds were capable of producing, in a non-deviant and un-mistaken oral language, a text the length of which corresponds to the age of the child. The quantity of

sentences largely goes beyond the goals set by the school manual. (Ghettas, 1995: 324)

She also discovered that nine-year-olds who had studied in Classical Arabic for three years had their creative ability ossified. Hence, the gap widens between the child's language and Standard Arabic (Ghettas, 1998: 244; Grandguillaume, 1997: 12) or 'the Arabic of the school', as described by Algeria's youth (Tounsi, 1997: 105).

In Algeria, the general problems involved in all language teaching are compounded by the special problems involved in the teaching of diglossic languages. 'Perhaps one could define diglossia as those linguistic situations which create difficulties for teaching' (Ferguson, 1963: 176). It seems, then, that Algerian schoolchildren have difficulty when learning Literary Arabic, a state of affairs confirmed by participants in the National Conference on Teaching Arabic held in Algiers in April 2000: 'after nine years of learning in the Fundamental School, the child still does not properly master the Arabic language' (*Liberté*, 2000: 24). One of the weaknesses in the promotion of Standard Arabic as the language of literacy lies in the lack of corpus planning. Most Arabic language academies have failed to introduce innovations. For example, Hammoud (1982) has shown the obstacles created by the Arabic script for the study of science and technology. Among the shortcomings, there is the multiplicity of written forms which depend on the position and the environment for each letter (Al-Toma, 1961; Maamouri, 1983). More than 600 letter shapes make the Arabic writing system uneconomical and difficult to acquire by beginners (Ezzaki & Wagner, 1992: 220). Another weakness related to the Arabic script concerns the absence of vowels in writing – vocalic diacritic marks appear only in school books for beginners. The reader relies on the context or her/his previous knowledge and is provided with minimum visual clues. Since only consonants are represented in writing, the spelling [h-m-], for example, can have the following readings: [hamala] for 'he carried', [humila] for 'was carried', [haml] for 'carrying' or 'pregnancy', [hamalun] for 'lamb'. Educational difficulties do arise from this specific feature: 'in Arabic, one should understand in order to read correctly as if reading were to come after understanding and not the other way around' (Al-Toma, 1961: 405). Talking about the Arabisation of social sciences at the university level, an Algerian academic shows how the authorities favoured linguistic skills instead of learning (Sebaa, 1996).

As far as standards of learning are concerned, many Algerian parents worry about the levels produced by the schooling system: 'we produce generations of illiterate people who master neither Arabic nor French' (Beaugé, 2004: 17). These semi-literate generations are described as 'bilingual illiterates' because of their low language proficiency (Miliani, 2000: 20). According to Grandguillaume (1996: 41), the low standards in French among the young generations come from both the bad quality of language teaching as well as the restrictive measures adopted after independence. In fact, the evaluation of the level of competency in Arabic and French is rare. However, despite the lack of reliable standardised testing, a small number of Algerian researchers have published results of their findings. Azzouz measured the difference in linguistic performance between Grade Six pupils in 1980 and those of the same level in 1991 (the 'children' of the Fundamental School). Azzouz shows that the Fundamental School cohorts fared consistently and significantly lower than the 1980 group in the three basic disciplines: calculus, Arabic and French (1998: 52). Azzouz's results are confirmed by Coffman, who carried out a qualitative and quantitative study at the university campus in the capital city, Algiers. The American academic chose the period 1989/1990 to do his fieldwork because it coincided with the first graduation of entirely arabised students – the 'children' of the Fundamental School – being admitted to higher education. Coffman compares the linguistic competence and attitudes of the freshman group with those of older bilingual students. His results show that the freshmen 'were much weaker in French, without being competent in Arabic' (Coffman, 1992: 146–7). At the same time, Benrabah (1990; 1991) gives the results of a study conducted in Oran between June and September 1990 to probe the progress of the first fully Arabised freshman cohort to register in science and technology in institutions of higher education in Oran. The students' final results based on their access to the second year went down by 10% compared with the two preceding years. Finally, in the mid-1990s, Benaïssa studied freshmen's linguistic competence in physics by measuring their competence in the 'General Vocabulary for Sciences'. His results showed a 'dramatic drop in standards in the students' capacity for conceptualisation and abstraction': 90% of those tested confused the concepts of temperature and heat quantity, 70% confused the concepts of linear direction and orientation of a vector, 60% confused the concepts of distance and position and 50% confused the concepts of duration and event (1998: 91).

Language maintenance and spread

A series of ministerial 'Instructions on Reading, Conversation, Religious education, Koran, Writing, Arithmetic', published in 1971 by a government institution called the *Institut National Pédagogique*, clearly states that other languages or dialects have no place in the educational system. One of these instructions reads: 'Our job will be twofold. We will correct through the child the language of his family. As the child is under the influence of his family, he will influence it in turn' (Boudalia Greffou, 1989: 36). For example, this type of disassociation of child and family was also considered by one FLN party leader as a solution to eliminate another 'problem'. He forecast that in Algeria, the problem of the Berber language will be solved with the spread of Classical Arabic via the educational system and, hence, the Kabylian child would eventually be unable to understand his own parents (Saadi, 1995: 23; Saadi-Mokrane, 2002: 45).

The Arabisation process is now into its fourth decade. As far as language shift is concerned, Arabisation has not displaced other languages (or dialects) to impose Standard Arabic as the sole language of the polity. A large proportion of the Algerian population, besides having acquired the national/official language (usually for literary functions), still do speak Berber and Algerian Arabic varieties, French or some combination of various idioms. For example, as a form of resistance within the Berberophone community, parents banned the use of Arabic at home by their children (Kahlouche, 2004: 106). Joseph (2004: 23) claims:

> instances in which people are directly forced to give up their language [...] historically their usual result has been to strengthen the resolve to maintain

the language, if only in private domains (which are the essential ones where
the preservation of a language is concerned).

In truth, Literary Arabic has not really assumed an unassailable position, and
French, in particular, has been maintained. Despite a drop in standards due to
poor teaching methods or the absence of French language teaching altogether –
for example, most secondary-school students are weak in their written skills
(Miliani, 2002: 83–93) and they use a discourse style influenced by Literary
Arabic culture which cannot be found in Standard French – Algeria has become
quantitatively the second Francophone community in the world after France
(Oberlé, 2004: 9; Péroncel-Hugoz, 1994: ii–iii; Queffélec *et al.*, 2002: 118). In 1990,
there were 6,650,000 Francophones in Algeria with 150,000 L1 speakers and
6,500,000 L2 speakers (Depecker, 1990: 389). According to Rossillon (1995: 91),
the total of French-speakers in Algeria amounted to 49% in 1993 (for a population
of 27.3 million), and projections for the year 2003 were 67%. Recent polls have
confirmed this trend. In April 2000, the Abassa Institute polled 1400 households
and found that 60% understood and/or spoke French. These percentages can be
projected to represent 14 million Algerians aged 16 and over (Assia, 2000: 24).
The most recent poll conducted by the same Institute suggests that Rossillon's
projections are more or less accurate. Out of 8325 young Algerians polled in 36
wilayas in November 2004, 66% declared speaking French and 15% English
(Maïche, 2004: 32). Finally, English offered in elementary education to compete
with French was not a success. Only 3197 pupils preferred English in 1995–1996
and 834 in 1997–1998. Between 1993 – the year English was introduced in Grade
Four of the Fundamental School – and 1997, out of 2 million schoolchildren, only
60,000 chose English; that is a mere 0.33% (Miliani, 2000: 23; 2003: 24).

French as a highly valued product in the Algerian 'linguistic market' is also
symbolised in the growing number of private schools which have mushroomed
since political liberalisation in 1989. Since then, many associations of schoolchildren's parents have created these establishments which offer bilingual education
starting from nursery and extending to secondary schooling levels. Independent
education, which had existed without any legal statutes but had been tolerated
was finally legalised by Article 6 of Ruling N° 03-09 of 13 August 2003 (Nassima,
2003). Around 380 private establishments have been created with an estimated
100 Primary schools, 20 Middle schools and 10 Secondary schools (Gillet, 2004d:
1342). The total student population in Elementary, Middle and Secondary
schools was estimated at 80,000 in 2004 (Kourta, 2004: 6). As far as international
educational institutions are concerned,[31] the French *lycée* was re-opened in October 2002 (Benrabah, 2002: 7; Vermeren, 2004: 321), and Algerian and French
governments plan the creation of a Franco-Algerian university in the near future
(Belabes, 2004b: 3).

Reasons for the maintenance and spread of French in Algeria include
socio-economic, socio-political, socio-psychological and sociolinguistic factors.
One favourable condition that has led to the maintenance and spread of French is
the historical and geographical proximity: around 1 million Algerian expatriates
live in France, and French satellite TV channels are watched by 52% of Algerian
households (Benmesbah, 2003: 12). The major factors that favour the spread of
French are: the outcome of the universalisation of education discussed previ-

ously; population growth which has multiplied by a factor of three; and the structure of the population: 62.7% of Algerians are aged under 30 (Riols, 2004: 50–1): youth in general do not feel resentful about France and its heritage in Algeria (Benrabah, 2004c: 94–5). Another factor related to demography is urbanisation which has been favourable to the spread of French since 1830. The rate of urbanisation has increased steadily and substantially since Algeria was liberated – around 25% in 1962, around 60% in 2004 (Khiar, 1991: 36, 1992: 8; Rif, 2004: 6). Finally, the elite's behaviour ('elite closure') played an important role: the military and socio-political leadership resort to French *lycées* to prevent their offspring from joining schools that cater for the masses (Brahimi, 1987: 41; Grandguillaume, 1989: 50, 1996: 44; Moatassime, 1996: 288; Sarter & Sefta, 1992: 109; Tefiani, 1984: 125–6; Thomas, 1999: 26; Tounsi, 1997: 107).

The sociolinguistic factor comes from the consequences of decolonisation. As in many other former French colonies around the world, French has become an indigenised stable norm (Fishman, 1983: 15; Kachru, 1985: 11). As in South Asia, for example, the French language in Algeria has been integrated into the population's social system of values and serves at least two functions (Kachru, 1983: 41). The first one is the 'inter-personal function' performed in two ways. Firstly, it serves as a lingua franca between speakers of mutually unintelligible language varieties, for example between Berber-French bilinguals and Arabic-French bilinguals (Mimoun, 2001: 12). Second, and as shown subsequently, it is a symbol of modernisation and elitism (Derradji, 1995: 112; Queffélec *et al.*, 2002: 141). The other function concerns the 'imaginative/innovative' role of French. The end of colonialism has led to a major change in former colonised polities: phonetic, syntactic and lexical 'deviations' are more readily tolerated (Calvet, 1994: 150). This tolerance results from the absence of norm-setting institutions such as the French Academy and the loosening of standardising pressures from educational establishments (school, university, etc.) whose function is to reproduce the norm (Derradji, 1995: 118; Queffélec *et al.*, 2002: 141). Innovations in Algerian French and other languages are best illustrated by both linguistic and artistic creativity, creativity being an expression of unplanned language development (D'Souza, 1996: 247).

Creativity as unplanned development

In the following section, linguistic and/or literary/artistic creative works in the various languages of Algeria will be considered to see how each fares *vis-à-vis* the national/official language and the policy of Arabisation. French colonial policy of assimilation displaced Classical Arabic and led to its marginalisation as the language of (traditional) literary creation. This is why creative works in Arabic did not reach the scale attained in French during colonisation (Laredj, 2003: 8). This is also why contemporary Algerian literary expression differs from the rest of the Arab world: it is marked by bilingualism, literary and creative works in both Arabic and French (Daoud, 2002: 11). After independence, a small group of Arabophone authors were involved in a 'neo-classical' literary current which dealt with thematic contents of triumphalism over colonisation and the war of liberation, socialist ideology (agricultural, industrial and cultural revolutions), etc. In the 1980s and 1990s, writers of Arabic expression distanced themselves from nationalism and revolution habitually dealt with by their elders until the 1970s (Laredj, 1995 / 1996: 171). They were influenced by the movement based on prose poetry and realist literature which was born in the Middle East in the 1950s. New poets transgress the line that separates the H written code from the L spoken code and use the linguistic vitality of everyday conversational Arabic. Conservative language purists have rejected these innovations describing the literary movement as a 'plot of the West' (El Janabi, 1999: 7–24).

The policy of Arabisation has played a major role in the development of literary works in Standard Arabic. However, this literature has not caught up with that of French expression both quantitatively and qualitatively. What is notable is that since the 1970s, the thematic contents of Arabophone and Francophone literatures alike have tended to converge towards the critique of Algeria's society, its history and the regime (Laredj, 2003: 9). The major obstacle is that literary works in Arabic lack a public, especially a school public, to read it despite a substantial increase in literacy in this language (Daoud, 2002: 7). The educational authorities refrain from introducing Algerian authors of literary expression in secondary-school programmes (Abu-Haidar, 2000: 161; Laredj, 2003: 8). However, with the educational reform implemented since September 2003, there is a tendency towards a future 'Algerianisation' of secondary education programmes with the introduction of literary works by Algerian Arabophone writers (Arslan, 2005).

Algerian Francophone writers' and journalists' creative work has allowed French to be 'Algerianised' and to express Algeria's socio-cultural reality in 'un-French' contexts (Benrabah, 2004b: 100). But this practice has come a long way from the period immediately following independence. One of the major issues debated then concerned the French language – in fact, the debate, which is more political than literary, has been maintained ever since (Chaulet Achour, 2003a: 5). Was the ex-colonisers' idiom to be rejected or accepted as part of Algeria's heritage and as a working language in the country? With the demands of nationalism, ideological intransigence prevailed with a direct consequence: creative writing in French went through a period of complete apathy in the late 1960s and most of the 1970s. Writers either stopped writing or went into exile (Abu-Haidar, 2000: 156; Cherrad-Benchefra & Derradji, 2004: 165). After this period, writers of French expression felt 'free' in reaction to the policy of Arabisation and / or after they realised that French was also part of Algeria's sociolinguistic profile. This awareness is best illustrated in the words of one Francophone writer, Aziz Chouaki: 'I felt free when I discovered a simple thing: that the French language does not belong to France alone. Why this guilt complex since French is spoken all over the world, since people own it' (Caubet, 2004: 158). Creative work has been Algerianised by writers who exploit three sources: the history of the Franco-Algerian cultural conflict, the Arabo-Islamic civilisation, and the Berbero-Maghrebi cultures. The integration of these references into literature gives the French language its hybrid touch (Chaulet Achour, 2003a: 6). With the dramatic situation created by the civil war, literary creativity in French has been in a state of ferment since the 1990s (Benrabah, 1999a: 182–3; Chaulet Achour, 2003b: 104–10). Despite progress with Arabisation and the spread of Literary Arabic among new generations, the number of internationally recognised writers is higher in French than in Arabic. For example, the Algerian author

Assia Djebbar is the first Maghrebi/Arab French-speaking author ever to be elected (in June 2005) as a member of the French Academy (IMA, 2005).

Artistic and literary creativity in the first languages is particularly important in Music and theatre. In fact, from the early 1970s and following the government's repressive measures against the Berber language and culture, Kabylian protest songs provided the main impetus for the spread of the Berberist movement among the masses in Kabylia and the Diaspora (Chaker, 1998: 43, 75). This protest tradition is rich and centres primarily on the call for the freedom of speech and democratisation (Khouas, 1995/1996: 157). The role of the Diaspora in countering the negation of Berber helped the language acquire a stable written norm for the rise of a modern literature (Chaker, 1998: 82). Between the 1950s and the 1980s, tales, proverbs as well as the oral works of the great poet Si Mohand U M'Hand – who could neither read nor write – were written down. The first novel in Berber appeared in 1981 and, since 1990, several Berber literary works (poetry, plays, essays, novels) have been published (Nabti, 2003: 5). This standardising movement had been supported by the work of lexicographers in the 1970s and 1980s. They developed a bilingual (Tamazight/French) lexis called *Amawal n tmazi?t tatret* (Tilmatine, 1992: 156). The *Amawal* is part of a purification movement to stop the 'invasion' of Berber by Arabic and French lexical items (Taifi, 1997: 69–71; Tilmatine, 1992: 157). As far as creativity in Algerian Arabic is concerned, it is mainly visible in theatre and music, like Raï[32] which currently has the status of World Music (Benrabah, 1999/2000; Schade-Poulsen, 1999; Tenaille, 2002).

The struggle between Standard Arabic and Algerian Arabic as the language of dramatic works has been going on since the beginning of the modern theatre in the 1920s. For example, the first major play performed in Classical Arabic in 1923 was not a success even though the Algerian population was favourable to this language because of nationalist feelings (Bencharif-Khadda, 2003: 114). In the 1960s, there was a conflict within the Algerian theatre as an institution: advocates of socialist realism who defended Literary Arabic opposed supporters of free creativity who defended Algerian Arabic (Baffet, 1985: 24). In the end, Abderrahmane Kaki, the father of Algeria's modern theatre, decided against the use of Literary Arabic (Bencharif-Khadda, 2003: 119–20). One of the major Algerian playwrights/comedians who have succeeded in making a fusion between Standard Arabic and Algerian Arabic is Abdelkader Alloula (Chaulet Achour, 1995: 480; Médiène, 1995: 10). He has succeeded in giving Algerian spoken Arabic the status of a language of high culture even though the establishment is not ready yet to accept it (Bencharif-Khadda, 2003: 125). However,

> [o]n 10th March 1994 the playwright Abdelkader Alloula was shot in Oran. Transferred to a hospital in Paris, he died four days later. In the eyes of religious fundamentalists, Alloula was blamed for promoting theatre, an art form forbidden by Islam. He, moreover, presented his plays in Algerian Arabic, a medium of expression which fundamentalists saw as too far removed from the language of the Koran. Another victim was the Raï singer Cheb Hasni who was shot dead outside his home in Oran on 29 September 1994. Raï is totally disapproved of by the Islamists. Being the direct descendant of the political and love songs of the Oran region, Raï, strictly speaking, came into being towards the end of the 1970s and spread

during the 1980s. Because of its political and erotic thematic content, it was banned in Algeria. (Abu-Haidar, 2000: 160)

Protest musical genres such as Kabylian and Raï songs have been followed by another genre which is far more pamphleteering. By the end of the 1990s, young rap singers started using Algerian Arabic and/or French to deal with Algeria's social problems such as violence (civil war), the mediocre state of the educational system, Arabisation, illegitimate children, etc. Rap lyrics in particular are used as a political voice (Power, 2000: 23). Among Algeria's rap groups, there is the group of rappers named *Le Micro Brise le Silence* ('the Microphone Breaks silence'). In its lyrics, the group alternate Algerian Arabic and French and one of their songs, *Système primitif* ('Primitive system'), is a serious criticism of the educational system:

> The Minister of Education is fictitious/ from the primary to the university, guinea pigs/ and then it has been arabised/ they have sunk everything, those of the Fundamental School (educational system)/ People died in Bejaia and Tizi Ouzou in 1980/ We haven't studied this in school/ Tamazight for all . . . (Smail, 2000: 17)

In 1999, unexpectedly, a female rap trio named *Les Messagères* started dealing openly with taboo topics such as illegitimate children born of unmarried young girls or Algeria's civil war (Power, 2000: 23; Smail, 1999: 23).

The preceding section shows how choices made by planners for a multilingual society lead to multiple 'invisible' developments. Algeria's profusion of creativity tends to support Carter's claim when he writes 'bilingual and multilingual communities have been especially rich in the production of creative artefacts, and there is some evidence to suggest that conditions of multilingualism and multiculturalism may favour creative production' (2004: 171–2). Among these developments, the most important of which are the birth of the Berberist nationalist movement and (unofficial) language planning in the Diaspora, as well as linguistic and literary/ artistic creativity that surfaced as a reaction to the policy of Arabisation. It seems to us that the following words from D'Souza who analysed creativity in Indian and Singapore Englishes are fitting as a conclusion for the present section:

> [I]t is suggested that language policy and language planning have repercussions for creativity. These repercussions are often unforeseen by the planners/policy makers, and their reactions to them are often negative; but they are inevitable as long as policy makers base themselves on some perception of what is good for the nation and forget what is essential for the individual. (1996: 259)

Part VI: Language Maintenance and Future Prospects

Joshua Fishman (1964) coined the concept of 'language maintenance' (or 'language survival') and contrasted it with the expression 'language shift' (or 'language death'). The latter term refers to the process by which a language is gradually displaced by another within a community (Dorian, 1982: 44). Language loss occurs when community members make long-term choices and collectively accept (consciously or unconsciously) this displacement (Fasold,

1984: 213; Holmes, 1992: 65). Language maintenance denotes the survival of a language within the linguistic repertoire of a group despite the existence of a more prestigious or a more dominant (politically or numerically) language (Mesthrie, 1999: 42).

In multilingual communities, the co-existence of language groups may result in the death of one or more languages. However, any given language may survive despite the introduction of one particular language as an effort at linguacide. Language loss and language survival depend on a number of factors among which Kaplan and Baldauf (1997: 273–5) give the following:

(1) Absence/presence of intergenerational transmission (from parents to children).
(2) Maintenance/displacement of the major communication functions (or registers) of a given language because of socio-economic value attached to language(s) in society.
(3) The numerical size of the community: when contracting, it leads to language death, when stable and/or expanding the result is language survival.

Algeria is a multilingual society where the above ecological factors are already at work. They can be summarised as follows:

- Arabic diglossia has led to the maintenance of Algerian Arabic and Tamazight as home languages and languages of day-to-day interaction; thus, intergenerational transmission is accomplished exclusively in Algerian Arabic and/or Tamazight. From a numerical point of view, the two first languages have made the most of a high population growth which rose from around 10 million in 1962 to almost 33 million at the present time.
- Compared with the period immediately following independence, the number of Standard Arabic speakers has spread substantially in the country. Since 1962, this idiom has symbolised the state and those in power; currently it occupies domains (registers) such as the national system of education and parts of the administrative sector (town hall, courts of law, etc.), and certain mass media (TV and radio).
- If Standard Arabic occupies registers related to cultural power, French has sustained itself as the language of economic power. It is used in universities (mainly departments of science and technology), the industrial sector, private education, tourism, international affairs and the media. What is more, the recent educational reform favours French (Ghenimi, 2003: 109) and suggests a decline in the assertive implementation of Arabisation since 1965 (Queffélec *et al.*, 2002: 33). Consequently, the use of French has increased substantially since the beginning of the economic liberalisation of the early 2000s. For example, it is now the major – sometimes the sole – language of advertising. A few Algerian sociolinguists forecast a bright future for the 'colonial' language (Morsly, 2004: 182).
- Standard Arabic and French are in fact in complementary distribution: the former occupies functions related to cultural power and the latter to economic power. If French were to be displaced, it would not be in favour of Standard Arabic but rather of English that is, at the moment, another (less used) language of international affairs (Grandguillaume, 1997a: 13).

These trends show that the policy of Arabisation has not succeeded in displacing the two first languages and the French language. The numerical strength of these three languages has increased as a result of, among other things, the increase in population. Planners failed to allocate Standard Arabic domains occupied by French and the major obstacle was diglossia.

The future of diglossia

If the first languages of Algerians have been maintained as a result of diglossia and an increase in the numbers of their respective speakers, the geographical diversity of Arabic and Berber dialects that existed in 1962 has diminished. This is mainly due to the destabilisation of the diglossic situation in the Arab world in general and in Algeria in particular. In his groundbreaking work, Ferguson was perceptive enough to predict the outcome of diglossia and the conditions under which it could evolve. He cites three trends: (1) the democratisation of literacy, (2) a heightened sense of nationalism with the desire for an autonomous national language, and (3) broader and greater communication across social and geographical boundaries (1959: 338).

All three types of pressure forecast by Ferguson exist in Algeria. First, Part V (Language Spread in Algeria) shows how literacy in Standard Arabic has increased substantially since the liberation of the country. Moreover, the total illiterate population decreased from around 90% in 1962 to around 30 to 45% at present. Second, despite pan-Arab ideology and a common language policy (Arabisation with Standard Arabic as its carrier), decolonisation and post-independent developments in the Maghreb – liberal/capitalist system in Morocco and Tunisia and socialist/revolutionary in Algeria – have produced a national conscience that coincides with the internal linguistic unification of the respective polities (Grandguillaume, 1991: 54, 1997a: 13). One illustration of such development lies in the use of humour in relation to language use: Algerians do not find Moroccan jokes funny and vice versa because humour is deeply anchored in the social, political and linguistic contexts of each Maghrebi country (Caubet, 2002: 234, 252–3; Morsly, 1980: 134). Furthermore, the people of the Maghrebi countries tend to associate national identity not with Standard Arabic but with the form of Arabic spoken within the borders of their respective countries. The native languages in general have become symbols of the authenticity and identity of the people concerned (Ennaji, 1999: 393). In Morocco, for example, students surveyed by Marley 'do not overwhelmingly agree that it [Standard Arabic] represents their national language' (2004: 38): out of 159 students, 88.7% agreed with the following statement: 'Moroccan Arabic represents Moroccan national identity' (Marley, 2004: 37). The results for Algeria are quite similar: in the large-scale survey among Secondary school students described in Part III above, 1022 out of 1051 subjects responded as follows to the statement:

	Algerian Arabic	Standard Arabic	French	Tamazight
I feel really Algerian in	72.4%	22.4%	3%	2.2%

It is probably the third trend mentioned by Ferguson – an increase in communication across social and geographical boundaries – that seems to have the greatest impact on Arabic diglossia. In Algeria, the Arabic language has been moving towards a post-diglossic stage under the influence of two simultaneous pressures, one from the top and the other from the bottom. The former comes from elites and the latter from linguistic urbanisation and dialect levelling. When using Standard Arabic orally (media, lectures, private letters and personal communication, modern prose, dramatic dialogues, etc.), Algerian intellectuals usually resort to Algerian Arabic. This 'leaky diglossia' (Fasold, 1984: 41) produces a form of Arabic predicted by Ferguson in 1959 which he termed *al-lugha al-wusta* ('the middle language' or 'the intermediate language'). One syntactic feature used in the 'middle Arabic' of Algerians is the use of the basic and very common Algerian Arabic linguistic form, the SVO structure, instead of Standard Arabic VSO (Benali-Mohamed, 2002: 56–7).

Linguists give the new 'simplified' form of Arabic various names, the most common being Educated Spoken Arabic (ESA) or *aamiyyat al-muthaqqifiin* (Mahmoud, 1986: 246). Its emergence has two major sources: (1) the need to be intelligible to the masses, (2) the (educated) speaker's inability to master the complex rules of the H variety (Benali-Mohamed, 2002: 62). The first trend is a direct result of the recent evolution of the social and political contexts (following October 1988) which require far more democracy. For example, during the latest election campaigns (parliamentarian, presidential), politicians have usually resorted to ESA and Algerian Arabic as a way to bridge the gap between governors and governed (Grandguillaume, 2002: 163–4; Queffélec *et al.*, 2002: 33). When interviewed by the French magazine *Paris Match* (1999: 35), the current Algerian Head of State, President Bouteflika, declared: 'When I speak Arabic, Classical Arabic, some very close friends of mine call me and say: "You made a very beautiful speech. We were proud, but we understood nothing."' From the Algerian leader's discourse, one assumes that a change in attitudes towards the first languages is taking place. His words clearly show that:

(1) Diglossia is no longer simply accepted as such but is 'regarded as "a problem" by the community in which it is in force' (Ferguson, 1959: 338).
(2) It is no use to go on pretending that Classical/Standard Arabic is the first language of Algerians when it is not (Ibrahim, 1983: 514).
(3) The introduction of Low varieties in the educational system is highly required (Boudalia Greffou, 1989: 68–9; Iraqui Sinaceur, 2002: 33).
(4) The L varieties should be given official status (Benrabah, 1995; Elimam, 2004).

The disintegration of diglossia also comes from below as a result of socio-demographic developments in Algeria. By the end of the colonial period, Marçais observed the emergence of an urban Koiné resulting from the loss of linguistic differences within urban dialects and between the latter and Bedouin dialects (1960: 338). Dialect levelling has accelerated since 1962 because of the huge increase in population numbers in cities and towns – people in urban centres who represented around 25% of the total population in 1962 currently stand at around 60%. Unlike the current linguistic change in Morocco where the urban Koiné tends to be a 'ruralised' form of Arabic (Messaoudi, 2002: 232), in Algeria the tendency is towards the emergence of a compromise between the rural/Bedouin and the city varieties (Benrabah, 1992, 1994, 1999b). The rising urban Koiné also plays the role of a lingua franca for Algerians with non-Arabic backgrounds, especially for Berberophones (Benali-Mohamed, 2003: 203; Ennaji, 1999: 383). In the capital city Algiers, around half of the population is Berberophone. Yet, Berber-speaking shop owners and Berber pedestrians use Algerian Arabic with their (anonymous) customers or when asking for information respectively. Moreover, Berberophones with mutually unintelligible Tamazight dialects use Algerian Arabic to communicate with each other (Kahlouche, 1996: 38–40).

The evolution that followed political liberalisation also affected Berber. The creation of the High Commission for Berber Affairs (HCA) in May 1995 and the introduction in April 2001 of Tamazight in the Constitution as the second national language open new horizons for Tamazight as a minority language. (What is more, the demand for more autonomy for Kabylia (Chaker, 2002: 208–11) is likely to rein-force Tamazight in the region by providing it with a territory). In fact, the central authorities presently provide the necessary means for its development as a language for literacy. Furthermore, as is the case for Arabic diglossia, there is a dual movement towards standardisation and unification of the different forms of Berber. The teaching of this language in schools (both in the public and private sectors) creates the need for a type of Koiné engineered both from the top by language planners and from the bottom as a result of linguistic levelling (Chaker, 1999: 161; El Aissati, 1993: 100; Kahlouche, 1996: 43). But the process of koinezation is acccompanied by the death of a number of Berber varieties mainly as a result of urbanisation (Benali-Mohamed, 2003: 211). The spread of literacy in Standard Arabic also leads to the loss of certain forms of Tamazight, as is currently the case for Chenoua Berber, spoken west of the capital city (*El Watan*, 2004a).

The future of bilingualism and multilingualism

As for the future of individual bilingualism and societal multilingualism, Part III (The Languages of Algeria) shows that Algerians would not support or strive to have monolingual education through Standard Arabic alone. In fact, this language has not been given any real cachet in the broader political and economic context. Alternatively, the demand for education in the medium of French will continue to grow because it is a much sought-after commodity. For example, in one activity of the large-scale survey presented by this author, 1029 schoolchildren responded to the following choice.

	Algerian Arabic	Standard Arabic	French	Tamazight
My parents would be ready to invest money to allow me to learn or improve my competency in	3.3%	20.8%	74.1%	1.7%

Almost three quarters of the sample chose French. In the literature on identity and resistance through language attitudes in multilingual societies, some schol-ars argue that 'attitudes that favour bilingualism over monolingualism can support the maintenance of [devalued] languages' (Gibbons & Ramirez, 2004: 195–6). According to Bourhis *et al.* (1981) and Bourhis and Sachdev (1984), believ-ing whether or not a language will survive (language vitality) is a factor in its survival. One statement in the questionnaire was meant to measure such claims;

1042 schoolchildren made the following choices in the context of the statement 'In the future, French will disappear in Algeria':

Agree completely	4.3%
Agree	8.3%
Neither agree nor disagree	11.6%
Disagree	32.2%
Disagree completely	43.6%

In short, 75.8% believe that French will survive in Algeria in the future, while only 12.6% believe it will disappear.

Language planners and policy makers in Algeria have not come to grips with understanding one aspect of human nature: besides being loyal to one's own language for identity reasons, 'humans like butter on both sides of their bread – and if possible a little jam as well!' (D'Souza, 1996: 259). For Algerian youth, Standard Arabic does remain an important constituent part of their Arabo-Islamic culture and identity. Hence, to the statement: 'Classical Arabic represents the Algerian national identity', 1040 subjects responded as follows:

Agree completely	43.3%
Agree	37.5%
Neither agree nor disagree	8.7%
Disagree	9.6%
Disagree completely	3.0%

For Secondary school students, French and Standard Arabic represent the buttered sides of their bread. The 'little jam' aspect is best illustrated in the results obtained with one activity in the attitudinal survey. The schoolchildren were asked the question: 'Out of the following ten possibilities, what is the best choice of language(s) that could allow you to live and prosper in Algeria and elsewhere?' 1036 respondents gave the following answers for the choices provided on the questionnaire:

(1) English only	2.9%
(2) Arabic only	4.4%
(3) French only	2.8%
(4) Tamazight only	0.2%
(5) Arabic and Tamazight	0.5%
(6) Arabic and French	15.5%
(7) French and Tamazight	0.1%
(8) Arabic and English	3.9%
(9) Arabic, English and French	58.6%
(10) Arabic, English, French and Tamazight	11.1%

An interesting pattern emerged from the above responses. Answers 1 to 4 show that monolingualism is rejected despite a rather vigorous policy of Arabisation implemented in the last four decades to eradicate societal bilingualism: see Part IV (Language Policy and Planning). But the results also show that not all language combinations or bilingual choices are valued. For example, whenever one of the languages is Tamazight, the choice does not rank highly (answers 4, 5, 7 and 10). Answer 8 comes as a surprise to planners who decided to replace French by English in the mid-1990s. The most interesting pattern concerns the combination of Arabic-French bilingualism with some other language(s): note, for example, the percentages for answers 6 and 10 (15.5% and 11.1% respectively). But it is answer 9 which emerged as the most favoured choice: the majority (58.6%) valued the two local 'High' codes (Arabic and French) combined with English, a much sought-after commodity internationally.

The future of Arabic-French or Tamazight-French bilingualism in Algeria also depends on the future status of English and the struggle between the two European languages, French and English. Between the 1970s and the end of the 1990s, several Anglophone institutions and scholars predicted the replacement of French by English in the Francophone bastions of the Maghreb in general and in Algeria in particular (Battenburg, 1996, 1997; British Council, 1977, 1981; Thomas, 1999). In fact, these articles, which perhaps misrepresent the rivalry between French and English, are the consequence of the long-standing approach/practice where major imperial nations compete with one another to promote their own languages (Fettes, 2003).

In Part V (Language Spread in Algeria) the introduction, in 1993, of English in elementary education to compete with French was shown to be a failure: the total population choosing the former was insignificant (Miliani, 2000: 23; 2003: 24; Queffélec *et al.*, 2002: 37–8). What is overlooked by thinkers from major imperial nations, which have indulged in language competition for the promotion of their own languages, is that members of multilingual communities do not conceive language rivalry in terms of exclusion but in terms of addition and complementarities. To confirm this hypothesis, the survey questionnaire contained the following statement: 'When I choose English, this does not mean that I reject French'. Out of 1051 subjects, 1029 responded as follows:

Agree completely	33.4%
Agree	43%
Neither agree nor disagree	9.5%
Disagree	9.2%
Disagree completely	4.9%

These results confirm the hypothesis that languages are not perceived as being in competition (76.4% agree completely or agree). It seems that both French and English have a secure future in Algeria (Benrabah, forthcoming).

Conclusion

The language situation in Algeria is quite rich. It is rich not because of the large diversity of idioms but because of the moving nature in the allocation of domains (registers) for the several languages. Four decades ago, most Algerian planners and several observers, within and outside the country, predicted success for the policy of Arabisation, the death of the various forms of Berber and Algerian Arabic, and a definite decline in the use of French. All these predictions were incorrect: not only did the first languages (Tamazight and Algerian Arabic) survive; rather, they currently show a vigorous vitality; the maintenance of Tamazight has been accompanied by an unforeseen development, the rise of a strong Berberist movement; the high status of French has not declined. The researcher involved with Algeria's language situation cannot ignore these unplanned results, and any attention paid to future prospects must be approached with caution and care. However, a number of trends can help applied linguists have a clearer picture of language planning in Algeria so as to forecast the major future developments in this polity. In the remaining part of this monograph, the most important elements that characterised Arabisation in the past are presented; subsequently the recent developments that are likely to lead to new directions are discussed.

According to this author, the relative failure (or partial success) of Arabisation is the result of the following:

- As is often the case, the motivation behind the Algerian language policy is grounded on (almost exclusively) political/ideological objectives (Brahimi, 1987: 41) with the classical motto 'divide and rule' (Goumeziane, 1994: 256; Moatassime, 1992: 155). Since independence, the status allocated to the various languages in competition has depended on the power struggle between the various factions among the central powers (Queffélec *et al.*, 2002: 123). The result is an extremely polarised and divided society: Arabophones opposed to Francophones, Berberophones to Arabophones, etc. (Berger, 2002: 8; Cherrad-Benchefra & Derradji, 2004: 165; Grandguillaume, 2002: 161; Mostari, 2004: 40).

- Planners did not seek a solution for diglossia, and implemented the H form excluding the L forms. The latter idioms remain the first languages of socialisation, the languages of day-to-day interaction in domains related to family and affective life (feelings, religion, etc.), to economic and trade transactions, as well as to intercommunication with representatives of central and local administration (Queffélec *et al.*, 2002: 121–2). This mismatch between the status of languages that meet the real needs of modern Algerian society and their exclusion by the authorities exacerbate a general feeling of frustration, powerlessness and self-hatred (Benrabah, 1994: 36, 1995: 37, 1999a: 93–6; Cherrad-Benchefra & Derradji, 2004: 165; Dourari, 2003: 133–45; Elimam, 2004: 289–93; Grandguillaume, 1997a: 14; Manzano, 1995: 173; Saadi-Mokrane, 2002: 56). The outcome is not only language conflict but an ideological struggle that comes from two diametrically opposed social projects. One project, open to modernity and backed by Algerian Arabic (or Tamazight in Berberophone zones), is opposed to another project deeply marked by Arab-Islamic culture which values the Arab and Moslem Great Tradition and views local/national customs and languages (identities) negatively – a situation that led to the rivalry between Arabness and Algerianness (Benrabah, 1994: 36–7, 1999a: 150–3; Queffélec *et al.*, 2002: 122; Tefiani, 1984: 123–4). As Saadi-Mokrane put it: 'Arabisation is not Algerianization – far from it' (2002: 52).

- The maintenance of diglossia weakens the non-homogeneous Arabic pole (Standard Arabic versus Algerian Arabic) and, thus, reinforces the other two poles, French and Tamazight. It is probably the existence of this tripartite language context coupled with assertive authoritarian policies meant to eradicate the colonial language that allow French to survive and expand in

Algeria and Morocco where French seems in no way to be under pressure from English[33] (Manzano, 1995: 181). Arabisation also ignores the desire for openings to the outside world, particularly neighbouring Western Europe, symbolised by the French language.

- Multilingualism is viewed as a 'problem', not as an asset, and Arabisation ignored the plural nature of Algeria's landscape. Arabisation resolutely overlooked this reality and imposed instead the ideological goal of a linguistically united polity. It represents a menace to first languages and non-Arab-Islamic cultures (Grandguillaume, 1982: 56). The French assimilationist colonial model was considered the only viable policy because of the influence of French linguistic culture on Algeria's language planners (Benrabah, 1999a: 123–7; forthcoming; Chaker, 2002: 209–10; Gordon, 1985: 149; Grandguillaume, 1983: 154, 1997a: 14; Saadi-Mokrane, 2002: 44–7; Tefiani, 1984: 118). According to Saadi-Mokrane (2002: 57):

> Guilt-ridden Algerians wonder about the legitimacy of such a [multilingual] legacy. They ask themselves: Is it a feature of a thriving society or of an alienated one? Should they continue to use all their languages? Might they lose themselves, or rather, find themselves, in so doing?

The general feeling of vulnerability and powerlessness discussed previously derives, in part, from such a guilt-ridden attitude.

- The 'language plans' for Algeria overlooked or ignored the importance of methodology and a plan based on data drawn from real-life situations (Brahimi, 1987: 41; Cherrad-Benchefra & Derradji, 2004: 167; Mostari, 2004: 40; Sarter & Sefta, 1992: 116). Indeed, many Algerian politicians:

> go about language planning as if it could and should be done only on the basis of their intuitive feelings, that is, in terms of [a] language planning model [. . .] [which views] language planning [. . .] as beginning with [. . .] the policy decisions. (Kaplan & Baldauf, 1997: 118)

This is not specific to the language issue: Part II (The Economy of Algeria) showed how economic/social planning did not interest the central authorities (Hidouci, 1995: 35). Furthermore, lack of language planning seems to be a mark of all Arab polities: even when there is corpus planning, the words produced 'remain for the most part in list form, and may never even reach universities and research institutions' (Elkhafaifi, 2002: 258).

These factors that prevented Arabisation to be completely successful characterise the nationalist period. Since the end of the 1990s, Algeria's leaders have committed the country to a programme of reform to accompany a democratic transition. The post-nationalist era is marked by a decline in the policy of Arabisation and the admission of multilingualism as an asset and diglossia as a problem. The most recent developments can be considered as prior indications for the future evolution of the language situation in Algeria. The recent institutionalisation of Tamazight as a national (and possibly as an official language in the future) has created new connections between the polity's idioms and a new configuration of the linguistic market in Algeria. The transition from a socialist (nationalist) system to market economy confirms French as the language of economic power for at least the mid-term interval. The vitality of Algerian Arabic is further boosted by demands of democratisation which is likely to reinforce its status. This author believes that, in the mid-term period at least, a more open and democratic Algeria will move towards a community with different languages occupying different functions: Standard Arabic will remain the language of Arab-Islamic values, French for openings to the outside world (with the support of English for certain registers), and first languages (Algerian Arabic and Tamazight) for Algerianness and national identity.

Correspondence

Any correspondence should be directed to Professor Mohamed Benrabah, Université Stendhal Grenable III, UFR d'Etudes Anglophones, Domaine Universitaire 1180, avenue Centrale B.P. 25, 38040 Grenoble, Cedex 9, France (Mohamed.benrabah@u-grenoble3.fr).

Notes

1. The Palestinian people in the Middle East could be considered a second case even though their language, Arabic, shares official status with other languages (Spolsky & Shohamy, 1999: 116–29).
2. The whole Maghreb presents an interest for LPLP. According to (Calvet, 1999b: 241) 'the future evolution of the Maghrebi linguistic eco-systems is of great interest to those who work on the problem of language policies and on the relationship between language and nations'. See also Daoud (2001: 46).
3. When not specified, all translations from French or Arabic are the present author's.
4. One of the military generals, who handpicked Abdelaziz Bouteflika as their candidate in 1999, gives, among other things, the following reasons for their choice: 'his way of speaking and arguing and his rhetorical skills' (Nezzar, 2003: 62).
5. Article 5 reads: 'All official documents, reports and minutes of public administrations, companies and organisations are to be drafted in Arabic. The use of any foreign language in deliberations and discussions in official meetings are forbidden.'
6. There are 48 *wilayas* or provinces officially written in the Roman alphabet as follows: Adrar, Aïn Defla, Aïn Temouchent, Alger, Annaba, Batna, Bechar, Bejaia, Biskra, Blida, Bordj Bou Arreridj, Boumerdes, Chlef, Constantine, Djelfa, El Bayadh, El Oued, El Tarf, Ghardaia, Guelma, Illizi, Jijel, Khenchela, Laghouat, Mascara, Medea, Mila, Mostaganem, M'Sila, Naama, Oran, Ouargla, Oum el Bouaghi, Relizane, Saida, Setif, Sidi Bel Abbes, Skikda, Souk Ahras, Tamanrasset, Tebessa, Tiaret, Tindouf, Tipaza, Tissemsilt, Tizi Ouzou, Tlemcen (*CIA, World Factbook*, 2005; Queffélec *et al.*, 2002: 72).
7. The figure 90% is an average between the percentages given by the Algerian historian/sociologist Mostefa Lacheraf (85%), the Algerian anthropologist Mahfoud Bennoune (88%), and the American politist/sociologist A.A. Heggoy (95%) (Bennoune, 2000: 12; Heggoy, 1984: 111; Lacheraf, 1978: 313).
8. The number of workers in the agricultural sector, which represented 50% in 1967, fell to less than 30% in 1982 (Goumeziane, 1994: 58–9).
9. In 1972, the foreign debt was US$2.7 billion with a further 12% for the debt service; in 1979, it soared to US$23.4 billion with a further 25.6% for the debt service (Stora, 2001: 50).
10. Both the growth rate and the fertility rate went down in the 1980s and 1990s: 2.8% growth with 5.5 children born per woman in 1986, 2.5% growth with 4.5 children born per woman in 1990, and 2.1% with 3.85 children born per woman in 1995 (Dahmani, 1999: 243).
11. The conflict has cost US$20 billion worth of damage; Belkaïd-Ellyas, 2003: 28; *Guardian Weekly*, 2004: 7).
12. For example, the unemployment rate was estimated at 25.4–25.9% in 2004 (*CIA, World Factbook*, 2005; Giret *et al.*, 2004: 41); 7 million Algerians, representing 23% of the total

population live on less than US$1 a day (below the absolute poverty line) while a total of 14 million Algerians (43% of the total population) earn less than US$2 per day (CIA, World Factbook, 2005; Martín, 2003: 44–5).

13. Cherrad-Benchefra and Derradji (2004: 165) give 45% and Grandguillaume (2002: 161) a higher rate for the illiterate population, between 50 and 75%.

14. With a very low success rate for the Baccalaureate in 1993, 350,000 joined the cohorts of those on the dole. The situation was further complicated: in June 1996, less than 22.18% got their Baccalaureate out of which 43% were marked up (*El Watan*, 1996b: 1) and in 1997, 24.82% passed and half were marked up. In 1990, some candidates enrolled in universities with marks as low as 5 out of 20 as average for their Baccalaureate (*El Watan*, 1997b: 4).

15. An Algerian sociologist described the situation as follows: 'Algeria is like a pressure-cooker which explodes all the time. Not a week goes without the youth engage into a violent protest, for the slightest thing. It is a real epidemic.' (Riols, 2004: 50–1) In fact, these incidents are reported by the Algerian press almost on a weekly basis (Martín, 2003: 68).

16. After independence the vast majority of the Jewish community went to France and Israel and only 3500 remained in 1966, 1500 in 1969, and 500 in 1972 (Abitbol, 1999: 429).

17. For a recent expression of this theory, see Gafaïti (2002).

18. This survey data has not yet been published in a single source, although the author is currently working on preparing a report of the survey. Some of the survey data appears in three unpublished papers which are available from the author (Benrabah, 2004e, 2004f, 2005).

19. Flaitz (1988: 14) uses the term *ideology*.

20. The Prophet Muhammad is reported to have said to his followers who were not ethnically Arab: *al-'urûba laysat min an-nasab bal min al-lisân* 'Arabness does not come from blood but from language' (Grandguillaume, 1983: 164).

21. 'Ulema' means 'Muslim elder'.

22. During the War of Algeria (1954–1962), Muslim students in the University of Algiers and secondary schools went on strike in 1956 and joined the FLN.

23. This is also proof of a change in mentalities among Algeria's political elites. For example, in December 1981, the then president of the Republic, Chadli Bendjedid, told the French magazine *Paris-Match* (No. 1697) that 'You know, it is said that Berbers come from Yemen on the grounds that two thirds of words used in Berber dialects (there are dialects, and not only one) are Arabic words or have Arabic roots.' (Chaker, 1998: 134) According to this view held by Algerian Pan-Arabists, Berber does not exist as a language because it contains Arabic words (Sadi, 1991: 288–9).

24. Elsewhere in the world, a comparable situation might be that of Cambodia under Vietnamese occupation: Western languages were 'tightly controlled under the Vietnamese-oriented communist government as a means of limiting international relations' (Clayton, 2002: 5).

25. Mostepha Lacheraf reports an anecdote that is a telling comment on these teachers' skills and on the linguistic insecurity among Algeria's intellectuals who felt 'themselves to be "secondhand" in any case, condemned to have ideas and the symbols to express them passed on to them from either the Middle East or from France.' (Gallagher, 1968: 140) Ben Bella's envoy to President Nasser insisted that the Egyptian leader should send teachers to Algeria 'even if they were greengrocers' (Grandguillaume, 2004a: 28). A similar story concerning Morocco is told by Vermeren, but in this case it does not concern 'greengrocers' but rather 'panel beaters' (Vermeren, 2004: 141).

26. During one night in October 1976 and under the orders of the FLN party, a group of sanitation workers in the capital Algiers smeared all public signs in French with tar. The ensuing confusion created by this 'anarchic' campaign shocked the population, sparked off fierce debate in the media and led the authorities to put an end to these practices (Ghouali, 2002: 264; Grandguillaume, 1983: 113; Mostari, 2004: 28). The difficulties created by this rapid and unanticipated language change were still visible a year later as shown by the following practical illustration. In 1977, Robert B. Kaplan

visited Algiers on behalf of the United States Information Agency to discuss the possibility of US assistance in enhancing English language teaching. He found the city in a state of chaos because all French street signs had been replaced by Arabic signs; this caused great confusion among taxi drivers who seemed unable to find any address. Moreover, Kaplan, who speaks reasonable French but no Arabic, did not recall any difficulty in communicating with taxi drivers in Algiers (personal communication).

27. Kaplan also recalls his meetings with officers in the Ministry of Education: no Arabic was ever spoken by any of those officers; when they addressed him in a very formal French, he failed to understand them because of the extensive use of the subjunctive (personal communication). This linguistic complexity which consists of 'bookish vocabulary and exaggerated forms which make even a formal style appear 'more formal' to a speaker of [Standard French]' (Platt *et al.*, 1984: 149) seems to be typical of indigenised varieties of former colonial languages – New Englishes, New Frenches, etc..

28. In general, like people in many other parts of the world, the populations of the Arab world have always felt a deep mistrust towards the news presented by government-controlled media (Aïta, 2003/2004: 34).

29. This poll also illustrates the crisis of the written press discussed earlier: only 35% of those polled were interested in reading mainly the press as opposed to watching TV (Maïche, 2004: 32).

30. It seems that, by February 2005, Spanish hackers helped Algerians resume watching Canalsatellite (Gaïdi, 2005: 32).

31. The Saudi establishment created in 2003 for 220 pupils – the majority being Algerian – was closed a year later because 60% of the content of the curriculum was based on Wahabi ideology (Benelkadi, 2004: 3; *El Watan*, 2004b: 31).

32. Raï is a traditional musical genre born among the Bedouins in Oran region, in western Algeria (Daoudi & Miliani, (1996: 39–45). In the late 1970s, young artists modernised that music to convey their frustrations, dreams and rebellions. In Algerian Arabic, the word *raï* means 'my opinion' or 'my point of view': it values the freedom of the individual in a traditional society which dilutes it within the group. At the beginning, raï singing was a reaction against the conservatism of the society and against those who have power. This type of music which dares to deal with taboos (e.g. alcohol, sex, love, etc.) was first described as 'dirty/indecent' and singers were, thus, banned from the official media like television (Poulsen, 1993: 266). After becoming a recognised international genre (during the civil war period of the 1990s), Raï has given rise to pride in Algerian identity, hence enhancing self-esteem through an appraisal of Algerianess (Benrabah, 1999/2000: 56).

33. With an almost non-existent Berber pole and with the maintenance of Arabic-French bilingualism since independence, Tunisian language planners seem to believe in English as a viable substitute for French (Battenburg, 1996, 1997; British Council, 1981; Daoud, 2001).

References

Abdelhai, B. (2001) L'école algérienne version Ennahda [The Algerian school Ennahda style]. *El Watan* (8 April), 7.

Abi Ayad, A. (1998) L'université et l'enseignement des langues étrangères [The university and the teaching of foreign languages]. In D. Guerid (ed.) *L'Université aujourd'hui (Actes de séminaire)* (pp. 99–106). Oran: Edition CRASC.

Abitbol, M. (1999) *Le Passé d'une Discorde. Juifs et Arabes du VIIe Siècle à nos Jours [The Past of a Dissension. Jews and Arabs from the 7th Century till Today]*. Paris: Librairie Académique Perrin.

Abu-Haidar, F. (2000) Arabisation in Algeria. *International Journal of Francophone Studies* 3 (3), 151–63.

Abun-Nasr, J.M. (1975) *A History of the Maghrib* (2nd edn). Cambridge: Cambridge University Press.

Addi, L. (1994) *L'Algérie et la démocratie. Pouvoir et crise du politique dans l'Algérie contemporaine [Algeria and Democracy. Power and Political Crisis in Contemporary Algeria]*. Paris: Découverte.

Addi, L. (1995) Les intellectuels qu'on assassine [Intellectuals that are assassinated]. *Esprit* 208, 130–8.

Addi, L. (2002) La plate-forme d'El Kseur comme réponse au mal algérien [El Kseur platform as response to Algeria's problems]. On WWW at http://www.algeria-watch. de./farticle/analyse/addi_plateforme_elkseur.htm.

Adegbite, W. (2003) Enlightenment and attitudes of the Nigerian elite on the roles of languages in Nigeria. *Language, Culture and Curriculum* 16 (2), 185–96.

African Development Bank Group (ADBG) (2004) Basic indicators on African countries – Comp. On WWW at http://www.afdb.org/african_countries/information_comparison.htm.

Ageron, C.R. (1968) *Les Algériens Musulmans et la France. Tome 1* [*Moslem Algerians and France. Volume 1*]. Paris: Presses Universitaires de France.

Ageron, C.R. (1969) *Histoire de l'Algérie Contemporaine* [*A History of Contemporary Algeria*]. Paris: PUF *Que sais-je?*

Ageron, C.A. (1993) De l'Algérie antique à l'Algérie française [From ancient Algeria to French Algeria]. *Encyclopoedia Universalis* 1, 766–71.

Aggoun, L. and Rivoire, J.B. (2004) *Françalgérie, Crimes et Mensonges d'États* [*Françalgeria, Crimes and Lies Against the State*]. Paris: Découverte.

Aïssaoui, A. (2001) *Algeria: The Political Economy of Oil and Gas*. Oxford: Oxford University Press.

Aïta, S. (2003–2004) Internet en langue arabe: Espace de liberté ou fracture sociale? [Internet in Arabic: A site of freedom or social fracture?]. *Maghreb-Machrek* 178, 29–44.

Aït Ouarabi, M. (2005a) Le chef de gouvernement et la lutte contre la corruption [The head of government and the fight against corruption]. *El Watan* (10–11 June), 1, 3.

Aït Ouarabi, M. (2005b) Réunion hier du conseil des ministres. La suppression des filières islamiques confirmée [Meeting yesterday of the Council of Ministers. Suppression of Islamic fields of study confirmed]. *El Watan* (27 June), 1, 3.

Aït Ouarabi, M. (2005c) L'aile antidialogue des Archs menace: Nous allons réinvestir la rue [Menace on the part of the anti-dialogue wing of the Archs: We are going to take to the street]. *El Watan* (19 January), 2.

Aït-Larbi, A. (2005) Campagne contre les conversions chrétiennes [Campaign against Christian conversions]. *Figaro* (8–9 January), 4.

Algeria Interface (2004), Information service on Internet about Algeria. On WWW at http://www.algeria-interface.com/new/article.

Al-Toma, S.J. (1961) The Arabic writing system and proposals for its reform. *Middle East Journal* 15, 403–15.

Altoma, S.J. (1971) Language education in Arab countries and the role of the academies. *Current Trends in Linguistics* 6, 690–720.

Ambassade d'Algérie en France (2002) *Algérie. Un Guide Pratique Offert par l'Ambassade d'Algérie en France* [*Algeria. A Practical Guide Offered by the Algerian Embassy in France*]. Paris: Corporate.

Annamalai, E. (1994) English in India: Unplanned development. In T. Kandiah and J. Kwan-Terry (eds) *English and Language Planning: A Southeast Asian Contribution* (pp. 261–77). Singapore: Times Academic.

Aouad-Elmentfakh, A. (1980) Variation in the pronunciation of French loan-words in western Algerian Arabic. MPhil Thesis, London University College.

Arkoun, M. (1984) *Essai sur la Pensée Islamique* [*Essay on Islamic Thought*]. Paris: Maisonneuve-Larose.

Arslan, S. (2005) Enseignement de la langue arabe: Vers l'algérianisation des programmes [The teaching of Arabic: Towards the Algerianisation of the curriculum]. *El Watan* (19 April). On WWW at http://www.elwatan.com.

Assia, T. (2000) Sondage: l'Algérie, premier pays francophone après la France [Poll: Algeria, second francophone country after France]. *El Watan* (2 November), 24.

Assous, O. (1985) Arabization and cultural conflicts in Algeria. PhD Thesis, Northeastern University, Boston, MA.

Atlapedia (2003) Countries A to Z – Algeria. On WWW at http://www.atlapedia.com/online/countries/algeria.htm.

Azzouz, L. (1998) Problématique de la baisse de niveau scolaire [The question of slipping standards]. In M. Madi (ed.) *Réflexions. L'Ecole en Débat en Algérie* (pp. 47–57). Algiers: Casbah.

Baffet, R. (1985) *Tradition Théâtrale et Modernité en Algérie [Theatre Tradition and Modernity in Algeria]*. Paris: L'Harmattan.

Baker, C. (2002) Bilingual education. In R.B. Kaplan (ed.) *The Oxford Handbook of Applied Linguistics* (pp. 229–42). Oxford: Oxford University Press.

Baldauf, Jr., R.B. (1993/1994) 'Unplanned' language policy and planning. In W. Grabe *et al.* (eds) *Annual Review of Applied Linguistics* 14 (pp. 82–9). New York: Cambridge University Press.

Bar-Asher, M. (1992) *La Composante Hebraïque du Judéo-arabe Algérien (Communautés de Tlemcen et Aïn-Temouchent) [The Hebrew Constituent Part of Algerian Judeo-Arabic (Communities from Tlemcen and Aïn-Temouchent)]*. Jerusalem: Magnès.

Basset, H. (1921) Les influences puniques chez les Berbères [Punic influence among Berbers]. *Revue Africaine* 308–9, 340–374.

Battenburg, J.D. (1996) English in the Maghreb. *English Today* 12 (4), 3–14.

Battenburg, J.D. (1997) English versus French: Language rivalry in Tunisia. *World Englishes* 16 (2), 281–90.

Beaugé, F. (2004) Algérie, envies de vie [Algeria, aspirations for life]. *Le Monde* (7 April), 16–17.

Beblawi, H. and Luciani, G. (1987) *The Rentier State*. London: Croom Helm.

Belabes, S.E. (2004a) La rentrée scolaire prévue le 11 septembre. Moins d'élèves à l'école [School year begins on 11 September 2004. Less children in school]. *El Watan* (1 September). On WWW at http://www.elwatan.com.

Belabes, S.E. (2004b) Partenariat. Bientôt une université franco-algérienne [Partnership. Soon a Franco-Algerian university]. *El Watan* (14 October), 3.

Belabes, S.E. (2005a) Enseignement dans les écoles coraniques. L'Etat s'en mêle [Teaching in Koranic schools. The state gets involved]. *El Watan* (7 March), 1, 3.

Belabes, S.E. (2005b) Une enquête de l'Office national des statistiques: 33 millions d'Algériens en 2006 [Survey by the National Bureau for Statistics: 33 million Algerians in 2006]. *El Watan* (30 May), 1, 5.

Belhadj Hacen, A. (1997) Les Problèmes liés à l'arabisation en Algérie. Analyse et critique du système educatif [Problems related to arabisation in Algeria. Analysis and critique of the educational system]. Unpublished PhD Thesis, Université Charles de Gaulle Lille III.

Belkaïd, A. (2005) *Un Regard Calme sur l'Algérie [A Calm Look at Algeria]*. Paris: Seuil.

Belkaïd-Ellyas, A. (2003) L'Algérie meurtrie reste en panne de réformes [A wounded Algeria runs out of reforms]. *La Tribune* (30 May), 28–9.

Belkaïd, M. (1976) Le parler arabe de Ténès (Algérie) – Etude phonologique, grammaticale, et lexicale [The Arabic Dsialect of Ténès (Algeria) – phonological, grammatical and lexical study]. Unpublished PhD Thesis, University René Descartes Paris V.

Benabdi, L.C. (1980) Arabization in Algeria: Processes and problems. Unpublished PhD Thesis, Indiana University.

Benabdi, L.C. (1986) Lexical expansion in the Maghreb: The 'Functional Linguistic Corpus'. *International Journal of the Sociology of Language* 61, 65–78.

Benabou, M. (1975) *La Résistance Africaine à la Romanisation [African Resistance to Romanisation]*. Paris: François Maspéro.

Benachenhou, A. (1992) L'accès au savoir scientifique et technique [Access to scientific and technological knowledge]. In M. Lakehal (ed.) *Algérie, de l'Indépendance à l'État d'Urgence* (pp. 210–22). Paris: Larmises-L'Harmattan.

Benachenhou, M. (2000) Français, soyez moins frileux! [To the French, be less cautious!]. *Jeune Afrique-L'Intelligent* 2057 (13 –19 June), 31.

Benaïssa, M. (1998) Difficultés linguistiques à l'université et/ou mauvaise conceptualisation au lycée [Linguistic difficulties at the university and/or bad conceptualisation in secondary school]. In M. Madi (ed.) *Réflexions. L'Ecole en Débat en Algérie* (pp. 85–93). Algiers: Casbah.

Benali-Mohamed, R. (2002) On subject-verb agreement in educated spoken Arabic in Algeria. *Revue Maghrébine des Langues* 1, 55–63.

Benali-Mohamed, R. (2003) De l'utilité du berbère en licence de langue [On the usefulness of Berber for the language degree]. *Revue Maghrébine des Langues* 2, 203–15.

Benallou, L. (1992) *Dictionnaire des Hispanismes dans le Parler de l'Oranie* [*Dictionary of Hispanisms in the Dialect of the Oran Region*]. Algiers: Office des Publications Universitaires.

Benallou, L. (2002) *L'Oranie Espagnole. Approche Sociale et Linguistique* [*The Spanish Oran Region. Social and Linguistic Approach*]. Oran: Dar El Gharb.

Bencharif-Khadda, J. (2003) Le théâtre algérien [The Algerian theatre]. *Europe Revue Littéraire Mensuelle* (Special Issue on Algeria), 111–127.

Ben Cheneb, M. (1922) *Mots Turks et Persans Conservés dans la Parler Algérien* [*Turkish and Persian Words Maintained in Algerian Arabic*]. Algiers: Carbonnel.

Bencherif, M.O. (1993) Presentation of the Algerian universities ESP projects. In *Maghreb ESP Conference: Current Initiatives in ESP in the Maghreb and Future Perspectives* (pp. 12–13). London: British Council.

Benderra, O. (2003) Les réseaux au pouvoir [Networks in power]. *Confluences Méditerranée* 45, 81–94.

Benelkadi, K. (2004) Ecole saoudienne de l'intégrisme à Alger [Saudi school for fundamentalism in Algiers]. *El Watan* (5 February), 3.

Benmesbah, A. (2003) Un système éducatif en mouvement [An educational system on the move]. *Le Français dans le Monde* 330, 12–13.

Bennoune, M. (2000) *Education, Culture et Développement en Algérie. Bilan et Perspectives du Système Éducatif* [*Education, Culture and Development in Algeria. Assessment and Perspectives for the Educational System*]. Algiers: Marinoor-ENAG.

Benrabah, M. (1990) Quand le symbolique l'emporte sur la réalité – 1ère partie [When symbolism prevails over reality – 1st part]. *Le Nouvel Hebdo* 27, 10–11.

Benrabah, M. (1991) Quand le symbolique l'emporte sur la réalité – 2ème partie [When symbolism prevails over reality – 2nd part]. *Le Nouvel Hebdo* 28, 20–21.

Benrabah, M. (1992) The influence of urbanisation on one dialect group. Unpublished paper presented at Sociolinguistics Symposium 9, University of Reading, 2–4 April.

Benrabah, M. (1993) L'arabe algérien, véhicule de la modernité [Algerian Arabic, vehicle of modernity]. *Cahiers de Linguistique Sociale* 22, 33–43.

Benrabah, M. (1994) Attitudinal reactions to language change in an urban setting. In Y. Suleiman (ed.) *Issues and Perspectives in Arabic Sociolinguistics* (pp. 213–26). London: Curzon.

Benrabah, M. (1995) La langue perdue [The lost tongue]. *Esprit* 208, 35–47. Reprinted in M. Benrabah, A. Djelloul, N. Farès, G. Grandguillaume, A. Meddeb, O. Mongin, L. Provost, B. Stora, P. Thibaud and P. Vidal-Naquet (eds) (1998) *Les Violences en Algérie* (pp. 61–87). Paris: Jacob.

Benrabah, M. (1996) L'arabisation des âmes [Arabisation of the soul]. In F. Laroussi (ed.) *Linguistique et Anthropologie* (pp. 13–30). Rouen: Presses Universitaires de Rouen.

Benrabah, M. (1998) Les dénis de l'arabisation [Denials of arabisation]. *Libération*, 26 June, 4–5.

Benrabah, M. (1999a) *Langue et Pouvoir en Algérie. Histoire d'un Traumatisme Linguistique* [*Language and Power in Algeria. A History of Linguistic Trauma*]. Paris: Séguier.

Benrabah, M. (1999b) Les filles contre les mères [Daughters against mothers]. *LIDIL. Revue de linguistique et de didactique des langues* 19, 11–28.

Benrabah, M. (1999/2000) Arabisation and creativity. *Journal of Algerian Studies* 4–5, 49–58.

Benrabah, M. (2002) L'urgence d'une réforme scolaire en Algérie [Urgency for a school reform]. *Libération* (2 October), 7.

Benrabah, M. (2004a) La question linguistique [The language issue]. In Y. Belaskri and C. Chaulet-Achour (eds) *L'Epreuve d'une Décennie 1992–2002. Algérie Arts et Culture* (pp. 83–108). Paris: Paris-Méditerranée.

Benrabah, M. (2004b) Language and politics in Algeria. *Nationalism and Ethnic Politics* 10 (1), 59–78.

Benrabah, M. (2004c) Epuisement de la légitimation par la langue [The end of language legitimacy]. *Némésis. Revue d'Analyse Juridique et Politique* 5, 81–102.

Benrabah, M. (2004d) An Algerian paradox: Arabisation and the French language. In Y. Rocheron and C. Rolfe (eds) *Shifting Frontiers of France and Francophonie* (pp. 49–61). Oxford: Peter Lang.

Benrabah, M. (2004e) Le français en Algérie: État des lieux. [French in Algeria since independence]. Unpublished paper presented at the Association for French Language Studies (AFLS) Conference, Aston University, Birmingham, 3–5 September.

Benrabah, M. (2004f) Language as political choice in Algeria: State against society or official monolingualism vs. societal plurilingualism. Unpublished paper presented at the 5th Annual Conference of the International Association of Language and Intercultural Studies (IALIC): Politics, Plurilingualism and Linguistic Identity, Dublin City University, 11–14 November

Benrabah, M. (2005) To be or not to be (Arabic/French) bilingual: Recent changes in language-in-education planning in Algeria. Unpublished paper presented at the 5th International Symposium on Bilingualism, Universitat Autònoma de Barcelona, Spain, 20–23 March.

Benrabah, M. (forthcoming) Politique linguistique: Insécurité au sommet, ouvertures à la base [Language policy: Insecurity at the top, openings at the bottom]. In P. Lambert, A. Millet, M. Rispail and C. Trimaille (eds) *Publication in Honour of Jacqueline Billiez*. Paris: L'Harmattan.

Bensalem, S. (1999) Algérie: Retrouvailles en français [Algeria: Together again with French]. *Le Français dans le Monde* 307, 10–11.

Bentahila, A. (1983) *Language Attitudes among Arabic-French Bilinguals in Morocco*. Clevedon: Multilingual Matters.

Ben Yahmed, M. (2004) Les raisons d'un plébiscite [Reasons for a plebiscite]. *Jeune Afrique L'Intelligent* 2258, (18–24 April), 34–6.

Benzaghou, D. (1978) Mots turcs et persans utilisés dans le parler algérien [Turkish and Persian words used in Algerian Arabic]. *Algérie Actualité* 686, 29.

Berdouzi, M. (2000), *Rénover l'enseignement: De la charte aux actes* [*Reforming education: From the charter to implementation*]. Rabat: Renouveau.

Berger, A.E. (2002) Introduction. In A.E. Berger (ed.) *Algeria in Others' Languages* (pp. 1–16). Ithaca and London: Cornell University Press.

Berri, Y. (1973) Algérie: La révolution en arabe [Algeria: A revolution in Arabic]. *Jeune Afrique* 639, 14–18.

Bessis, J. (1978) Chekib Arslan et les mouvements nationalistes au Maghreb [Chekib Arslan and the nationalist movements in the Maghreb]. *Revue Historique* 259 (2), 467–89.

Blanc, M. (1999) Bilingualism, societal. In B. Spolsky and E. Asher (eds) *Concise Encyclopedia of Educational Linguistics* (pp. 31–7). Amsterdam: Elsevier.

Boniface, P. (2005) *L'Année Stratégique 2005* [*The Strategic Year 2005*]. Paris: IRIS/Armand Colin.

Bouamrane, A. (1986) Aspects of the sociolinguistic situation in Algeria. Unpublished PhD thesis, University of Aberdeen.

Boudalia-Greffou, M. (1989) *L'École Algérienne d'Ibn Badis à Pavlov* [*The Algerian School from Ibn Badis to Pavlov*]. Algiers: Laphomic.

Boudedja, N. (2004) 'Secteur de l'agriculture. Une croissance de 6.4% en 2004' [The agricultural sector. A 6.4% growth rate in 2004]. *El Watan* (11 October), 5.

Bouhadiba, F. (2002) Language at work: A case study. *Revue Maghrébine des Langues* 1, 13–29.

Bouhadiba, F. (2004) La question linguistique en Algérie: Quelques éléments de réflexion pour un aménagement linguistique [The language issue in Algeria: A few elements for language planning]. In J. Dakhlia (ed.) *Trames de Langues: Usages et Métissages Linguistiques dans l'Histoire du Maghreb* (pp. 499–507). Paris: Maisonneuve et Larose Institut de Recherche sur le Maghreb Contemporain.

Bounfour, A. (1994) *Le Noeud de la langue. Langue, Littérature et Société au Maghreb* [*The Language Knot. Language, Literature and Society in the Maghreb*]. Aix-en-Provence: Edisud.

Bourhis, R. and Sachdev, I. (1984) Vitality perceptions and language attitudes. Some Canadian data. *Journal of Language and Social Psychology* 3 (2), 97–125.

Bourhis, R., Giles, H. and Rosenthal, D. (1981) Notes on the construction of a 'subjective vitality questionnaire' for ethnolinguistic groups. *Journal of Multilingual and Multicultural Development* 2 (2), 145–55.

Brahimi, B. (1984) La presse d'expression française en Algérie [The French-speaking press in Algeria]. *Le Français dans le Monde* 189, 10–12.

Brahimi, B. (1987) Bienfaits et méfaits de l'arabisation [Benefits and drawbacks of arabisation]. *Diagonales* 4, 39–41.

Brahimi, B. (1993) Le champ médiatique algérien [The media scene in Algeria]. *El Watan* (3 May), 6–7.

British Council (1977) *English Language Teaching Profile: Morocco.* London: English Information Centre.

British Council (1981) *English Language Teaching Profile: Tunisia.* London: English Information Centre.

Brunschvig, R. (1940–1947) *La Berbérie Orientale sous les Hafsides des Origines à la Fin du XVe siècle* [*Eastern Berberia under the Hafsids from the Origin to the End of the XVth Century*]. Paris: Adrien-Maisonneuve.

Byrd, W. (2003) Contre performances économiques et fragilité institutionnelle [Poor economic performance and institutional fragility]. *Confluences Méditerranée* 45, 59–79.

Calvet, L.J. (1994) *Les Voix de la Ville. Introduction à la Sociolinguistique Urbaine* [*Urban Voices. Introduction to Urban Sociolinguistics*]. Paris: Payot & Rivages.

Calvet, L.J. (1999a) *La Guerre des Langues et les Politiques Linguistiques* [*War of Languages and Language Policies*]. Paris: Hachette Littératures.

Calvet, L.J. (1999b) *Pour une Écologie des Langues du Monde* [*For an Ecology of the World Languages*]. Paris: Plon.

Camps, G. (1987) *Les Berbères. Mémoire et identité* [*Berbers. Past and Identity*]. Paris: Errance.

Cantineau, J. (1960) *Cours de Phonétique Arabe* [*Course in Arabic Phonetics*]. Paris: Klincksieck.

Carré, O. (1996) *Le Nationalisme Arabe* [*Arab Nationalism*]. Paris: Payot & Rivages.

Carter, R. (2004) *Language and Creativity. The Art of Common Talk.* London and New York: Routledge.

Caubet, D. (2002) Jeux de langues: Humor and codeswitching in the Maghreb. In A. Rouchdy (ed.) *Language Contact and Language Conflict in Arabic. Variations on a Sociolinguistic Theme* (pp. 233–55). London: RoutledgeCurzon.

Caubet, D. (2004) *Les Mots du Bled* [*Words from the Maghreb*]. Paris: L'Harmattan.

Central Intelligence Agency (CIA) (2005) The World Factbook – Algeria. On WWW at http://www.cia.gov/cia/publications/factbook/geos/ag.html.

Chabane, A. (1987) La carte de la technologie [Technology map]. *Actualité de l'Emigration* 1344 (78), 5–7.

Chafik, M. (1984) Le substrat berbère de la culture maghrébine [The Berber substratum of Maghrebi culture]. On WWW at http://www.mondeberbere.com/culture/chafik/maghreb/substratberbere.PDF.

Chafik, M. (1999) *Al-Darijah al-Maghrebiyya. Majaal Tawaarud bayn al-Amazighiyya wal 'arabiyya* [*The Moroccan Dialect. Site of Interpenetration Between Tamazight and Arabic*]. Rabat: Matba'at al-Ma'aarif a-Jadiida.

Chaker, S. (1984) *Textes en Linguistique Berbère (Introduction au Domaine Berbère)* [*Texts in Berber Linguistics (Introduction to Berber Studies)*]. Paris: CNRS.

Chaker, S. (1991) *Manuel de Linguistique Berbère I* [*Manual of Berber Linguistics I*]. Algiers: Bouchène.

Chaker, S. (1997) La Kabylie: Un processus de développement linguistique autonome [Kabylia: A developing process of linguistic autonomy]. *International Journal of the Sociology of Language* 123, 81–99.

Chaker, S. (1998) *Berbères Aujourd'hui* [*Berbers Today*] (2nd edn). Paris/Montreal: L'Harmattan.

Chaker, S. (2002) Kabylie: De la revendication linguistique à l'autonomie régionale [Kabylia: From linguistic claims to regional autonomy]. In R. Bistolfi and H. Giordan (eds) *Les Langues de la Méditerranée* (pp. 203–12). Paris: L'Harmattan.

Chaulet-Achour, C. (1995) Abdelkader Alloula, 1939–1994 [Abdelkader Alloula, 1939–1994]. *Encyclopoedia Universalis – Universalia 1995*, 480.

Chaulet-Achour, C. (2003a) Introduction à la littérature algérienne [Introduction to Algerian literature]. *Page des Libraries* (November), 3–6.

Chaulet-Achour, C. (2003b) Algérie, littérature de femmes [Algeria, women's literature]. *Europe Revue Littéraire Mensuelle* (Special Issue on Algeria), 96–110.

Cherfaoui, Z. (2004) Réforme de l'école et enseignement du français. Recrutement de 2000 diplômés [School reform and the teaching of French. Recruitment of 2000 graduates]. *El Watan* (7 June), 1–2.

Cheriet, A. (1983) *Opinion sur la Politique de l'Enseignement et de l'Arabisation [Point of View on Educational Policy and Arabisation]*. Algiers: SNED.

Cherrad-Benchefra, Y. (1995) L'époque future dans le système verbo-temporel du français parlé en Algérie [The future tense in the verbo-temporal system of French spoken in Algeria]. In A. Queffélec, F. Benzakour and Y. Cherrad-Benchefra (eds) *Le Français au Maghreb* (pp. 89–106). Aix-en-Provence: Publications de l'Université de Provence.

Cherrad-Benchefra, Y. and Derradji, Y. (2004) La politique linguistique en Algérie [Language policy in Algeria]. *Revue d'Aménagement Linguistique* 107, 145–70.

Chtatou, M. (1997) The influence of the Berber language on Moroccan Arabic. *International Journal of the Sociology of Language* 123, 101–18.

Clayton, T. (2002) Language choice in a nation under transition: The struggle between English and French in Cambodia. *Language Policy* 1 (1), 3–25.

Cleveland, W.L. (1971) *The Making of an Arab Nationalist. Ottomanism and Arabism in the Life and Thought of Sati' al-Husri*. Princeton: Princeton University Press.

Coffman, J.M. (1992) Arabization and Islamisation in the Algerian University. Unpublished PhD Thesis, Stanford University.

Collot, C. and Henry, J.R. (1978) *Le Mouvement National Algérien. Textes 1912–1954 [The Algerian National Movement. Texts 1912–1954]*. Paris / Algiers: L'Harmattan et Office des Presses Universitaires.

Colonna, F. (1975) *Instituteurs Algériens: 1883–1939 [Algerian Primary-School Teachers: 1883–1939]*. Algiers: Office des Publications Universitaires.

Comrie, B., Mathews, S., and Polinsky, M. (1997) (eds) *The Atlas of Languages. The Origin and Development of Languages Throughout the World*. London: Bloomsbury.

Cooper, R.L. (1982) A framework for the study of language spread. In R.L. Cooper (ed.) *Language Spread: Studies in Diffusion and Social Change* (pp. 5–36). Bloomington: Indiana University Press.

Cooper, R.L. (1989) *Language Planning and Social Change*. Cambridge: Cambridge University Press.

Cubertafond, B. (1995) *L'Algérie Contemporaine [Contemporary Algeria]*. Paris: PUF *Que sais-je?*

Dahmani, A. (1999) *L'Algérie à l'Épreuve. Economie Politique des Réformes 1980–1997 [Algeria's Ordeal: Political Economy of Reforms 1980–1997]*. Paris: L'Harmattan.

Dalby, A. (1998) *Dictionary of Languages. The Definitive Reference to more than 400 Languages*. London: Bloomsbury.

Dallet, J.M. (1982) *Dictionnaire Kabyle-Français [Kabyle-French Dictionary]*. Paris: SELAF.

Daoud, M. (2000) LSP in North Africa: Status, problems and challenges. In W. Grabe *et al.* (eds) *Annual Review of Applied Linguistics* 20, 77–96. New York: Cambridge University Press.

Daoud, M. (2001) The language situation in Tunisia. *Current Issues in Language Planning* 2 (1), 1–52.

Daoud, M. (2002) *Le Roman Algérien de Langue Arabe. Lectures Critiques [The Algerian Novel of Arabic Expression. Critical Readings]*. Oran: Editions CRASC.

Daoudi, B. and Miliani, H. (1996) *L'Aventure du Raï: Musique et Société [The Adventure of Raï: Music and Society]*. Paris: Seuil.

Daoust, D. (1997) Language planning and language reform. In F. Coulmas (ed.) *The Handbook of Sociolinguistics* (pp. 436–52). Oxford: Blackwell.

De Haëdo, D. (1998) *Topographie et Histoire Générale d'Alger [Topography and General History of Algiers]*. Paris: Bouchène.

Déjeux, J. (1965) Décolonisation culturelle et monde moderne en Algérie [Cultural decolonization and the modern world in Algeria]. *Confluent* 47–9, 6–26.

Dekkak, B.A. (1979) An examination of Algerian French having particular regard to differences from standard French. MPhil Thesis, University of Sheffield.

Depecker, L. (1990) *Les Mots de la Francophonie [The Words of Francophonia]*. Paris: Belin.

Derradji, Y. (1995) L'emploi de la suffixation –iser, -iste, -isme, -isation dans la procédure néologique du français en Algérie [The use of suffixes –iser, -iste, -isme, -isation in the formation of neologisms in Algerian French]. In A. Queffélec, F. Benzakour and Y. Cherrad-Benchefra (eds) *Le Français au Maghreb* (pp. 111–19). Aix-en-Provence: Publications de l'Université de Provence.

Destanne de Bernis, G. (1966) Industries industrialisantes et contenu d'une politique d'intégration régionale [Industrialising industries and the content of a policy of regional integration]. *Economie Appliqué* 19 (3–4), 415–73.

Destanne de Bernis, G. (1971) Les industries industrialisantes et les options algériennes [Industrialising industries and the Algerian options]. *Revue Tiers-Monde* 12 (47), 545–63.

Dillman, B.L. (2000) *State and Private Sector in Algeria. The Politics of Rent-Seeking and Failed Development*. Boulder: Westview.

Djamel, B. (2001) Réforme de l'école, les islamo-conservateurs accusent [School reform, the accusations of Islamist-conservatives]. *Le Matin* (19 March), 3.

Djeghloul, A. (1986) *Huit Études sur l'Algérie [Eight Studies on Algeria]*. Algiers: Entreprise Nationale du Livre.

Djilali, B. (2005) Les ârouch et Ouyahia s'entendent [The Aruch and Ouyahia reach a deal]. *Quotidien d'Oran* (14 August), 2.

Djité, P.G. (1992) The arabization of Algeria: Linguistic and sociopolitical motivations. *International Journal of the Sociology of Language* 98, 15–28.

Dorian, N. (1982) Language loss and maintenance in language contact situations. In R.D. Lambert and B.F. Freed (eds) *The Loss of Language Skills* (pp. 44–59). Rowley, MA: Newbury House.

Dourari, A. (1997) Malaises linguistiques et identitaires en Algérie [Linguistic and identity malaise in Algeria]. *Anadi. Revue d'Études Amazighes* 2, 17–41.

Dourari, A. (2003) *Les Malaises de la Société Algérienne. Crise de Langues et Crise d'Identité [Malaise in Algerian Society. Language Crisis and Identity Crisis]*. Algiers: Casbah.

Duclos, J. (1992) *Dictionnaire du Français d'Algérie [Dictionary of Algerian French]*. Paris: Bonneton.

Duclos, J. (1995) Le pataouète? A force à force on oublie! [Pataouète? A force à force we forget!]. In A. Queffélec, F. Benzakour and Y. Cherrad-Benchefra (eds) *Le Français au Maghreb* (pp. 121–30). Aix-en-Provence: Publications de l'Université de Provence.

Dufour, D. (1978) L'enseignement en Algérie [Teaching in Algeria]. *Maghreb-Machrek* 80 (2), 33–46.

D'Souza, J. (1996) Creativity and language planning: The case of Indian English and Singapore English. *Language Problems and Language Planning* 20 (3), 244–62.

Economist (2004a) Freer and more peaceful: An Arab state slouches towards democracy. *The Economist* (17–23 April), 40–41.

Economist (2004b) Arab democracy. Imaginable? *The Economist* (3–9 April), 13.

Eickelman, D.F. (1985) *The Middle East: An Anthropological Approach* (2nd edn). Englewood Cliffs, NJ: Prentice Hall.

El Aissati, A. (1993) Berber in Morocco and Algeria: Revival or decay? *AILA Review* 10, 88–109.

El Aissati, A. (2001) Ethnic identity, language shift and the Amazigh voice in Morocco and Algeria. *Race, Gender and Class* 8 (3), 57–69.

El-Dash, L. and Tucker, G.R. (1976) Subjective reactions to various speech styles in Egypt. *International Journal of the Sociology of Language* 6, 33–54.

Elimam, A. (1997) *Le Maghribi, Langue Trois Fois Millénaire. Explorations en Linguistique Maghrébine* [*The Maghreban Language, an Over Three Thousand Years Old Language. Studies in Maghreban Linguistics*]. Algiers: Edition ANEP.

Elimam, A. (2003) *Le Magribi Alias Ed-darija (La Langue Consensuelle du Maghreb)* [*The Maghreban Language Alias Ed-daridja (The Consensus Language of the Maghreb)*]. Oran: Dar El Gharb.

Elimam, A. (2004) *Langues Maternelles et Citoyenneté en Algérie* [*Mother Tongues and Citizenship in Algeria*]. Oran: Editions Dar El Gharb.

El Janabi, A.K. (1999) *Le Poème Arabe moderne* [*The Modern Arabic Poem*]. Paris: Maisonneuve & Larose.

El-Kenz, A. (1994) Algérie, les deux paradigmes [Algeria, the two paradigms]. *Revue du Monde Musulman et de la Méditerranée* 68–9, 79–85.

Elkhafaifi, H.M. (2002) Arabic language planning in the age of globalization. *Language Problems and Language Planning* 26 (3), 253–269.

El Moudjahid (1990) 24 October, 5.

El Watan (1996a) 11 July, 7.

El Watan (1996b) 23 September, 1.

El Watan (1997a) 29 May, 1.

El Watan (1997b) 26 November, 4.

El Watan (1999a) 22 May. On WWW at http://www.elwatan.com.

El Watan (1999b) 3 August, 3.

El Watan (2000) 1 March, 23.

El Watan (2002) 18 November, 23.

El Watan (2004a) Tipaza – langues régionales menacées / Le crépuscule d'un dialecte [Tipaza – regional languages menaced / The dawn of a dialect]. *El Watan* (10 May). On WWW at http://www.elwatan.com.

El Watan (2004b) Benbouzid suspend l'école saoudienne [Benbouzid suspends the Saudi school]. *El Watan* (26 October), 31.

El Watan (2004c) Un nouveau directeur pour l'enseignement de tamazight [A new director for the teaching of Tamazight]. *El Watan* (28 December), 31.

El Watan (2005) Fulgurante ascension des chaînes arabes [Terrific progress of Arabic channels]. *El Watan* (27–28 May), 31.

Ennaji, M. (1999) The Arab world (Maghreb and Near East). In J.A. Fishman (ed.) *Handbook of Language & Ethnic Identity* (pp. 382–95). New York/Oxford: Oxford University Press.

Entelis, J.P. (1981) Elite political culture and socialization in Algeria: Tensions and discontinuities. *Middle East Journal* 25, 191–208.

Esprit, (1995) La politique française de coopération vis-à-vis de l'Algérie: Un quiproquo tragique [The French policy of cooperation with Algeria: A tragic misunderstanding]. *Esprit* 208, 153–61.

Ethnologue (2004) Languages of Algeria. On WWW at http://www.ethnologue.com/show.

Ezzaki, A. and Wagner, D.A. (1992) Language and literacy in the Maghreb. In W. Grabe *et al.* (eds) *Annual Review of Applied Linguistics* 12, 216–29. New York: Cambridge University Press.

Fasold, R. (1984) *Introduction to Sociolinguistics: The Sociolinguistics of Society*. Oxford: Blackwell.

Favret, J. (1973) Traditionalism through ultra-modernism. In E. Gellner and C. Micaud (eds) *Arabs and Berbers. From Tribe to Nation in North Africa* (pp. 307–24). London: Duckworth.

Ferguson, C. (1959) Diglossia. *Word* 15, 325–40.

Ferguson, C. (1963) Problems of teaching languages with diglossia. In E. Woodworth and R. Di Pietro (eds) *Report of the Thirteenth Annual Round Table Meeting on Linguistics and Language Studies* (Monograph Series on Language and Linguistics, 15) (pp. 165–77). Washington, DC: Georgetown University Press.

Ferguson, C. (1966) National sociolinguistic profile formulas. In W. Bright (ed.) *Sociolinguistics* (pp. 309–24). The Hague: Mouton.

Fettes, M. (2003) The geostrategies of interlingualism. In J. Maurais and M.A. Morris (eds) *Languages in a Globalising World* (pp. 37–46). Cambridge: Cambridge University Press.

Fishman, J.A. (1964) Language maintenance and shift as fields of inquiry. *Linguistics* 9, 32–70.

Fishman, J.A. (1968) Nationality-nationalism and nation-nationism. In J.A. Fishman, C.A. Ferguson and J. Das Gupta (eds) *Language Problems of Developing Nations* (pp. 39–51). New York: Wiley.

Fishman, J.A. (1971) The impact of nationalism on language planning. In J. Rubin and B.H. Jernudd (eds) *Can Language be Planned? Sociolinguistic Theory and Practice for Developing Nations* (pp. 3–20). Honolulu: University Press of Hawaii.

Fishman, J.A. (1972) *Language and Nationalism. Two Integrative Essays*. Rowley, MA: Newbury House Publishers.

Fishman, J.A. (1983) Sociology of English as an additional language. In B.B. Kachru (ed.) *The Other Tongue. English Across Cultures* (pp. 15–22). Oxford: Pergamon.

Flaitz, J. (1988) *The Ideology of English. French Perceptions of English as a World Language*. Berlin: Mouton de Gruyter.

Furayhah, A. (1955) *Nahwa 'arabiyya muyassara* [*Towards a simplified form of Arabic*]. Beirut: Dar al-maktab al-lubnani.

Gadant, M. (1988) *Islam et Nationalisme en Algérie d'après 'El Moudjahid' Organe Central du FLN de 1956 à 1962* [*Islam and Nationalism in Algeria According to 'El Moudjahid' Official Organ of the FLN from 1956 to 1962*]. Paris: L'Harmattan.

Gafaïti, H. (2002) The monotheism of the Other: Language and de/construction of national identity in postcolonial Algeria. In A.E. Berger (ed.) *Algeria in Others' Languages* (pp. 19–43). Ithaca and London: Cornell University Press.

Gaïdi, M.F. (2005) Après une année d'écran noir Canalsatellite décrypté [After a year of blank screen Canasatellite decoded]. *El Watan* (8 February), 32.

Gallagher, C.F. (1968) North African problems and prospects: Language and identity. In J.A. Fishman, C.A. Ferguson and J. Das Gupta (eds) *Language Problems of Developing Nations* (pp. 129–50). New York: Wiley.

Gandon, F. (1978) Arabisation et symbole collectif en Algérie [Arabisation and the collective symbol in Algeria]. *Communication et Langage* 40, 15–27.

Garçon, J. (2004) Un million de déplacés livrés à eux-mêmes en Algérie [One million displaced people left to their own devices in Algeria]. *Libération* (14 April), 9.

Garrison, G.L. (1975) Arabic as a unifying and divisive force. In B.H. Jernudd and G.L. Garrison (eds) *Language Treatment in Egypt* (pp. 2–37). Cairo: Ford Foundation.

Gellner, E. (1973) Introduction. In E. Gellner and C. Micaud (eds) *Arabs and Berbers: From Tribe to Nation* (pp. 11–21). London: Duckworth.

Gellner, E. (1983) *Nations and Nationalism*. Oxford: Blackwell.

Ghenimi, A. (2003) L'enseignement du français en Algérie: Nouvelles orientations pour répondre aux nouveaux impératifs [Teaching French in Algeria: New directions for new demands]. *Revue Maghrébine des Langues* 2, 105–14.

Ghettas, C. (1995) L'enfant algérien et l'apprentissage de la langue arabe à l'école fondamentale. Essai d'analyse des compétences narrative et textuelle de l'enfant algérien entre cinq et neuf ans [Algerian child and the learning of Arabic at the fundamental school. Analysis of narrative and text competence among Algerian children aged between five and nine years old]. PhD Thesis, University Stendhal-Grenoble III, France.

Ghettas, C. (1998) Le passage du vernaculaire à l'arabe standard à l'école chez l'enfant algérien de 5 à 7 ans [The passage from Arabic vernacular to standard Arabic among Algerian children aged between 5 and 7 years old]. In J. Billiez (ed.) *De la Didactique des Langues à la Didactique du Plurilinguisme* (pp. 241–8). Grenoble: LIDILEM-Grenoble III.

Ghouali, H. (2002) La politique d'arabisation face à la situation bilingue et diglossique de l'Algérie [The policy of Arabisation in the context of the bilingual and diglossic situation in Algeria]. Unpublished PhD Thesis, University of Paris VIII – Vincennes-Saint-Denis, France.

Gibbons, J. and Ramirez, E. (2004) *Maintaining a Minority Language. A Case Study of Hispanic Teenagers*. Clevedon: Multilingual Matters.

Gillet, N. (2004a) Macroéconomie. Etat financier excellent malgré les archaïsmes [Macroeconomics. Excellent financial state despite archaisms]. *Marchés Tropicaux* 3057 (11 June), 1320–1.

Gillet, N. (2004b) Banques. Un secteur financier archaïque [Banks. An archaic financial sector]. *Marchés Tropicaux* 3057 (11 June), 1338–9.

Gillet, N. (2004c) Les années Bouteflika. Un bilan contrasté [The years of Bouteflika. Uneven assessment]. *Marchés Tropicaux* 3057 (11 June), 1313–15.

Gillet, N. (2004d) Formation professionnelle. L'université ne répond pas aux exigences de l'entreprise [Professional training. The university does not meet the demands of business]. *Marchés Tropicaux* 3057 (11 June), 1342.

Giret, V., Mathieu, B., Neumann, B. and Olireau-Licata, D. (2004) Voyage dans une économie au bord du chaos [Journey in an economy on the verge of chaos]. *L'Expansion* 680, 38–48.

Gonzalez-Quijano, Y. (2003–2004) À la recherche d'un internet arabe [In search of an Arab Internet]. *Maghreb-Machrek* 178, 11–27.

Gordon, D.C. (1966) *The Passing of French Algeria*. London: Oxford University Press.

Gordon, D.C. (1978) *The French Language and National Identity*. The Hague: Mouton.

Gordon, D.C. (1985) The Arabic language and national identity: The cases of Algeria and of Lebanon. In W.R. Beer and J.E. Jacob (eds) *Language Policy and National Unity* (pp. 134–50). Totowa, NJ: Rowman & Allanheld.

Goumeziane, S. (1994) *Le Mal algérien. Economie Politique d'une Transition Inachevée 1962–1994* [*The Algerian Malaise. Political Economy of a Transition that Failed 1962–1994*]. Paris: Librairie Arthème Fayard.

Grandguillaume, G. (1982) Langue et communauté au Maghreb [Language and community in the Maghreb]. *Peuples Méditerranéens / Mediterranean Peoples* 18, 49–58.

Granguillaume, G. (1983) *Arabisation et Politique Linguistique au Maghreb* [*Arabisation and Language Policy in the Maghreb*]. Paris: G.-P. Maisonneuve et Larose.

Grandguillaume, G. (1989) L'Algérie, une identité à rechercher [Algeria, an identity to be sought]. *Economie et Humanisme* 309, 48–57.

Grandguillaume, G. (1990) Language and legitimacy in the Maghreb. In B. Weinstein (ed.) *Language Policy and Political Development* (pp. 150–66). Norwood, NJ: Ablex.

Grandguillaume, G. (1991) Arabisation et langues maternelles dans le contexte national au Maghreb [Arabisation and mother tongues in the national context in the Maghreb]. *International Journal of the Sociology of Language* 87, 45–54.

Grandguillaume, G. (1995) Comment a-t-on pu en arriver là? [How did it happen?]. *Esprit* 208, 12–34.

Grandguillaume, G. (1996) La confrontation par les langues [Confrontation by languages]. *Anthropologie et Sociétés* 20 (2), 37–58.

Grandguillaume, G. (1997a) L'oralité comme dévalorisation linguistique [Orality as linguistic devaluation]. *Peuples Méditerranéens / Mediterranean Peoples* 79, 9–14.

Grandguillaume, G. (1997b) Arabisation et démagogie en Algérie [Arabisation and demagogues in Algeria]. *Le Monde Diplomatique* (February), 3. English version on WWW at http://www.hartford-hwp.com/archives/32/080.html.

Grandguillaume, G. (2002) Les enjeux de la question des langues en Algérie [The issues of the language question in Algeria]. In R. Bistolfi and H. Giordan (eds) *Les Langues de la Méditerranée* (pp. 141–65). Paris: L'Harmattan.

Grandguillaume, G. (2004a) L'arabisation au Maghreb [Arabisation in the Maghreb]. *Revue d'Aménagement Linguistique* 107, 15–39.

Grandguillaume, G. (2004b) Les langues au Maghreb: Des corps en peine de voix [Languages in the Maghreb: Bodies without voice]. *Esprit* 308, 92–102.

Greffou, M. (1989) *L'Ecole Algérienne d'Ibn Badis à Pavlov* [*The Algerian School from Ibn Badis to Pavlov*]. Algiers: Laphomic.

Guardian Weekly (2004) Landslide poll win for Algerian president. 15–21 April, 12.

Guenoun, A. (1999) *Chronologie du Mouvement Berbère 1945–1990* [*Chronology of the Berber Movement 1945–1990*]. Algiers: Casbah

Guerid, D. (1998) L'université d'hier et d'aujourd'hui [The university of yesterday and today]. In D. Guerid (ed.) *L'Université Aujourd'hui (Actes de Séminaire)* (pp. 7–22). Oran: CRASC.

Haarmann, H. (1990) Language planning in the light of the general theory of language: A methodological framework. *International Journal of the Sociology of Language* 86, 103–26.

Haddadou, M.A. (1997) 'Barabrus', 'barbar', 'berbère' une stigmatisation deux fois millénaire ['Barabrus', 'Barbar', 'Berber' a stigma over two thousand years]. *Peuples Méditerranéens / Mediterranean Peoples* 79, 71–83.

Hadj-Sadok, M. (1955) Dialectes arabes et francisation linguistique de l'Algérie [Arabic dialects and linguistic Frenchification in Algeria]. *Annales de l'Institut d'Etudes Orientales* 13, 61–97.

Halliday, M.A.K. (1972) National language and language planning in a multilingual society. *East Africa Journal* 9 (8), 4–13.

Halvorsen, K.H. (1978) Colonial transformation of agrarian society in Algeria. *Journal of Peace Research* 15 (4), 323–43.

Hamdoun, M. (2004) Fishing communities in Mediterranean societies: The influence of Catalan and Spanish on the speaking of sea fishermen in Ghazaouet area (Algeria). Unpublished paper presented at the 7th Annual International Congress, Catalonia and the Mediterranean, Barcelona, Spain, 26–29 May.

Hamiche, A. (2005) Officialisation de Tamazight. La classe politique partagée [Making Tamazight official. Politicians divided]. *El Watan* (18 January), 3.

Hamman, A.G. (1979) *La Vie Quotidienne en Afrique du Nord au Temps de Saint-Augustin [Everyday Life in North Africa During Saint Augustine's Times]*. Paris: Hachette.

Hammoud, M.S.D (1982) Arabization in Morocco: A case study in language planning and language policy attitudes. Unpublished PhD Thesis, University of Texas Austin, Texas.

Haouati, Y. (1995) Trente ans d'éducation [Thirty years of education]. *Le Monde de l'Éducation* 223, 56–7.

Harbi, M. (1980) Nationalisme algérien et identité berbère [Algerian nationalism and Berber identity]. *Peuples Méditerranéens / Mediterranean Peoples* 11, 31–7.

Harbi, M. (1984) *La Guerre Commence en Algérie [The War Begins in Algeria]*. Brussels: Complexes.

Harbi, M. (1993) *Le FLN, Mirage et réalité. Des Origines à la Prise du Pouvoir (1945–1962) [The FLN, Mirage and Reality. From the Origins to Power Seizure (1945–1962)]*. Algiers: NAQD-ENAL.

Harbi, M. (1994) *L'Algérie et son Destin. Croyants ou Citoyens [Algeria and its Destiny. Believers or Citizens]*. Algiers: Médias Associés.

Harbi, M. (2002) Le poids de l'histoire: Et la violence vînt à l'Algérie [The weight of history: And then war came to Algeria]. *Le Monde Diplomatique* (July), 1, 14–15.

Hary, B. (2003) Judeo-Arabic: A diachronic reexamination. *International Journal of the Sociology of Language* 163, 61–75.

Haut Conseil de la Francophonie (HCF) (1999) Etat de la francophonie dans le monde. Données 1997–1998 et 6 études inédites [State of Francophonia in the world. Elements for 1997–1998 and 6 unpublished studies]. Nancy: Documentation Française.

Heggoy, A.A. (1984) Colonial education in Algeria: Assimilation and reaction. In P.G. Altbach and G. Kelly (eds) *Education and the Colonial Experience* (pp. 97–116). New Brunswick, NJ: Transaction.

Henze, R. and Davis, K.A. (1999) Authenticity and identity: Lessons from indigenous language education. *Anthropology and Education Quarterly* 30, 3–21.

Hetzron, R. (1987) Afroasiatic languages. In B. Comrie (ed.) *The World's Major Languages* (pp. 645–53). London & Sidney: Croom Helm.

Hidouci, G. (1995) *Algérie. La libération inachevée [Algeria. An Unfinished Liberation]*. Paris: Découverte.

Holmes, J. (1992) *Sociolinguistics. An Introduction*. London: Longmans.

Holt, M. (1994) Algeria: Language, nation and state. In Y. Suleiman (ed.) *Arabic Sociolinguistics: Issues and Perspectives* (pp. 25–41). Richmond: Curzon.

Horne, A. (1987) *A Savage War of Peace. Algeria 1954–1962*. London: Papermac.

Human Rights Watch (HRW) (2003) Time for reckoning: Enforced disappearances and abductions in Algeria. *Human Rights Watch* 15 (2), 1–98. On WWW at http://www.hrw.org/reports/2003/algeria2003/.

Ibrahim, M.H. (1983) Linguistic distance and literacy in Arabic. *Journal of Pragmatics* 7, 507–15.

Ibrahim, M.H. (1989) Communicating in Arabic: Problems and prospects. In F. Coulmas (ed.) *Language Adaptation* (pp. 39–59). Cambridge: Cambridge University Press.

Idlhak, A. (1996) L'effondrement de l'université algérienne [The collapse of the Algerian university]. *El Watan* (27 June), 7.

Imache, T. (1989) *Aït Menguellet chante . . . [Aït Menguellet Sings . . .]*. Paris: Découverte.

Institut du Monde Arabe (IMA) (2005) Communiqué de presse: Élection d'Assia Djebbar à l'Académie Française [Press communiqué: Election of Assia Djebbar to the French Academy]. On WWW at http://www.imarabe.org/perm/actualites/20050617.html/.

International Monetary Fund (IMF) (2004) *Algeria: Selected Issues and Statistical Appendix. IMF Country Report No. 04/31. February 2004*. Washington, DC: International Monetary Fund Publications. On WWW at http://www.imf.org.

Iraqui Sinaceur, Z. (2002) L'apport des langues maternelles dans le système éducatif [Contribution of mother tongues to the educational system]. *Revue Maghrébine des Langues* 1, 31–45.

Jahr, E.H. (ed.) (1993) *Language Conflict and Language Planning*. Berlin: Mouton de Gruyter.

Jaïdi, H. (2004) Appartenance sociale et usage de la langue néopunique au Maghreb à l'époque romaine [Social membership and the use of neo-Punic in the Maghreb during the Roman period]. In J. Dakhlia (ed.) *Trames de Langues: Usages et Métissages Linguistiques dans l'Histoire du Maghreb* (pp. 21–40). Paris: Maisonneuve et Larose Institut de Recherche sur le Maghreb Contemporain.

Jernudd, B.H. and Das Gupta, J. (1971) Towards a theory of language planning. In J. Rubin and B.H. Jernudd (eds) *Can Language be Planned? Sociolinguistic Theory and Practice for Developing Nations* (pp. 195–215). Honolulu: University Press of Hawaii.

Joseph, J.E. (2004) *Language and Identity. National, Ethnic, Religious*. Basingstoke and New York: Palgrave Macmillan.

Jouhadi, H. (2003) *Tarurt n Wammaken n Leqran* [*Translation of the Meanings of the Koran*]. Casablanca: An-Nadjah al-Jadida.

Julien, C.A. (1994) *Histoire de l'Afrique du Nord. Des origines à 1830* [*History of North Africa. From Origins to 1830*]. Paris: Payot & Rivages.

Kachru, B.B. (1983) Models for non-native Englishes. In B.B. Kachru (ed.) *The Other Tongue. English Across Cultures* (pp. 31–57). Oxford: Pergamon.

Kachru, B.B. (1985) Standards, codification and sociolinguistic realism: The English language in the outer circle. In R. Quirk and H.G. Widdowson (eds) *English in the World. Teaching and Learning the Language and Literatures* (pp. 11–34). Cambridge: Cambridge University Press.

Kaddache, M. (1992) *L'Algérie Médiévale* [*Medieval Algeria*]. Algiers: ENAL.

Kaddache, M. (1998) *L'Algérie Durant la Période Ottomane* [*Algeria during the Ottoman Period*]. Algiers: Office des Publications Universitaires.

Kadi, L. (1995) Les dérivés en –iste et –age: Néologismes en français écrit et oral utilisé en Algérie [Derived words in -iste and –age: Neologisms in written and spoken French in Algeria]. In A. Queffélec, F. Benzakour and Y. Cherrad-Benchefra (eds) *Le Français au Maghreb* (pp. 153–63). Aix-en-Provence: Publications de l'Université de Provence.

Kadi, L. (2004) La politique linguistique algérienne: Vers un état des lieux [Algerian language policy since independence]. *Revue d'Aménagement Linguistique* 107, 133–44.

Kahane, H., Kahane, R. and Tietze, A. (1958) *The Lingua Franca in the Levant*. Urbana: University of Illinois.

Kahlouche, R. (1991) L'influence de l'arabe et du français sur le processus de spirantisation des occlusives simples en kabyle [The influence of Arabic and French on the process of spirantisation of Kabylian simple stops]. *Awal Cahiers d'Etudes Berbères* 8, 95–105.

Kahlouche, R. (1993) Diglossie, norme et mélange de langues. Etude de comportements linguistiques de bilingues berbère (kabyle)-français [Diglossia, norm and language mixing. Study of linguistic behaviour of Berber bilinguals (Kabyle)-French]. *Cahiers de Linguistique Sociale* 22, 73–89.

Kahlouche, R. (1996) La langue berbère à Alger [Berber in Algiers]. *Plurilinguismes* 12, 31–46.

Kahlouche, R. (1997) Les enseignes à Tizi-Ouzou: Un lieu de conflit linguistique [Street signs in Tizi Ouzou: A site of linguistic conflict]. In N. Labrie (ed.) *Etudes Récentes en Linguistique de Contact* (pp. 174–83). Bonn: Dummler.

Kahlouche, R. (2000) L'enseignement d'une langue non aménagée, au statut indéfini: Le berbère en Algérie [Teaching a non-planned language, with an indefinite status: Berber in Algeria]. *Mémoires de la Société de Linguistique de Paris* 8, 157–68.

Kahlouche, R. (2004) Le berbère dans la politique linguistique algérienne [Berber in Algerian language policy]. *Revue d'Aménagement Linguistique* 107, 103–32.

Kaplan, R. (1990) Introduction: Language planning in theory and practice. In R.B. Baldauf and A. Luke (eds) *Language Planning and Education in Australasia and the South Pacific* (pp. 3–13). Clevedon: Multilingual Matters.

Kaplan, R.B. and Baldauf, Jr. R.B. (1997) *Language Planning from Practice to Theory*. Clevedon: Multilingual Matters.

Kayambazinthu, E. (1999) The language planning situation in Malawi. In R.B. Kaplan and R.B. Baldauf (eds) *Language Planning in Malawi, Mozambique and the Philippines* (pp. 15–85). Clevedon: Multilingual Matters.

Kaye, A.S. (1987) Arabic. In B. Comrie (ed.) *The World's Major Languages* (pp. 665–85). London & Sidney: Croom Helm.

Kaye, J. and Zoubir, A. (1990) *The Ambiguous Compromise. Language, Literature and National Identity in Algeria and Morocco*. London and New York: Routledge.

Kedourie, E. (1961) *Nationalism*. London: Hutchinson.

Khaldun, I. (2003) *Histoire des Berbères et des Dynasties Musulmanes de l'Afrique Septentrionale [History of Berbers and Moslem Dynasties in Northern Africa]*. Algiers: BERTI Editions.

Khalfoune, T. (2002) Langues, identité et constitution [Languages, identity and constitution]. In R. Bistolfi and H. Giordan (eds) *Les Langues de la Méditerranée* (pp. 167–85). Paris: L'Harmattan.

Khalloufi Sellam, A. (1983) A study of the teaching of English as a foreign language in Algeria, with special reference to existing language policies, teaching methods and students' attitudes. MEd Thesis, University College of Wales.

Khiar, O. (1991) Migrations dans les quatre métropoles [Migration in four metropolises]. *Revue Statistiques* 29, 34–40.

Khiar, O. (1992) Villes – hypertrophie et inégalités [Cities – overdevelopment and inequalities]. *El Watan* (21–22 February), 8.

Khouas, A. (1995/1996) Chanson kabyle et démocratie en Algérie [Kabylian song and democracy in Algeria]. *Passerelles. Revue d'Études Interculturelles* 11, 155–66.

Kloss, H. (1967) 'Abstand languages' and 'ausbau languages'. *Anthropological Linguistics* 9 (7), 29–41.

Kloss, H. (1969) *Research Possibilities on Group Bilingualism: A Report*. Quebec: International Center for Research on Bilingualism.

Knapp, W. (1977) *North West Africa: A Political and Economic Survey* (3rd edn). London: Oxford University Press.

Kourta, D. (2003) Réforme de l'école. Premiers changements [School reform. First changes]. *El Watan* (29 September). On WWW at http://www.elwatan.com.

Kourta, D. (2004) Ecoles privées. Plaidoyer pour le bilinguisme [Private schools. A plea for bilingualism]. *El Watan* (30 June), 6.

Lachachi, D.E. (2003) Réforme de l'enseignement des langues étrangères [Reform in the teaching of foreign languages]. *Revue Maghrébine des Langues* 2, 73–96.

Lacheraf, M. (1978) *L'Algérie, Nation et Société [Algeria, Nation and Society]*. Algiers: SNED.

Lacheraf, M. (1998) *Des Noms et des Lieux. Mémoires d'une Algérie Oubliée [On Nouns and Places. The Past of a Forgotten Algeria]*. Algiers: Casbah.

Laib, M. (1993) L'anglais en 4e année. La langue alibi [English in the 4th year. An alibi language]. *El Watan* (27 May), 7.

Lakhdar Barka, S.M. (2002) Les langues étrangères en Algérie: Enjeux démocratiques [Foreign languages in Algeria: A democratic issue]. On WWWat http://www.univ-paris13.fr/CRIDAF/TEXTES/LgsEtrangeres.PDF.

Lam, A.S.L. (1994) Language education in Hong Kong and Singapore: A comparative study of the role of English. In T. Kandiah and J. Kwan-Terry (eds) *English and Language Planning: A Southeast Asian Contribution* (pp. 182–96). Singapore: Times Academic.

Lancel, S. (2003) *L'Algérie Antique de Massinissa à Saint Augustin* [*Ancient Algeria from Massinissa to Saint Augustine*]. Paris: Mengès.

Lanly, A. (1970) *Le Français d'Afrique du Nord. Etude Linguistique* [*French in North Africa. A Linguistic Study*]. Paris-Montréal: Bordas.

Laredj, W. (1995/1996) Littérature(s) algérienne(s): La richesse d'une pluralité linguistique [Algerian literature(s): Wealth of linguistic pluralism]. *Passerelles. Revue d'Études Interculturelles* 11, 167–72.

Laredj, W. (2003) La littérature de langue arabe: Une difficile visibilité [Arabic-speaking literature: A difficult visibility]. *Page des Libraires* (November), 8–9.

Laroussi, F. (2003) Arabic and the new technologies. In J. Maurais and M.A. Morris (eds) *Languages in a Globalising World* (pp. 250–9). Cambridge: Cambridge University Press.

Laroussi, F. and Madray-Lesigne, F. (1998) Plurilinguisme et identités au Maghreb [Multilingualism and identities in the Maghreb]. In D. Marley, M.A. Hintze and G. Parker (eds) *Linguistic Identities and Policies in France and the French-Speaking World* (pp. 193–204). London: AFLS/CILT.

Laskier, M.M. (1994) *North African Jewry in the Twentieth Century: The Jews of Morocco, Tunisia and Algeria*. New York: NYU Press.

Le Matin (1998) 27 April, 24.

Le Matin (1999) 22 May. On WWW at http://www.lematin-dz.com.

Le Monde (1995) 4–5 June, 5.

Le Monde (2001) 2 May, 1.

Lewicki, T. (1936) Mélanges berbères-ibadites [Berber-Ibadite mixing]. *Revue des Etudes Islamiques* 3, 267–85.

Liberté (2000) Enseignement de la langue arabe. Constat désolant [The teaching of Arabic: Depressing assessment]. *Liberté*, 10 April, 24.

Llabador, F. (1948) *Nemours (Djemâa-Ghazaouât) Monographie illustrée* [*Nemours (Djemâa-Ghazaouât) illustrated monograph*]. Algiers: Typo-Litho et Jules Carbonel.

Ma'mouri, M. 'Abid, A. and al-Ghazālī, S. (1983) *Ta'thir Ta'līm al-Lughāt al-Ajnabiyya fī Ta'allum al-Lugha al-'Arabiyya* [*The Influence of Teaching Foreign Languages on the Learning of Arabic*]. Tunis: Arab League Organization.

Maamouri, M. (1983) Illiteracy in Tunisia. In P.M. Payne (ed.) *Language in Tunisia* (pp. 203–26). Tunis: Bourguiba Institute of Languages.

Maas, U. (2002) L'union linguistique maghrébine [Maghreban linguistic fusion]. In A. Youssi, F. Benjelloun, M. Dahbi, and Z. Iraqui-Sinaceur (eds) *Aspects of the Dialects of Arabic Today* (pp. 211–22). Rabat: AMAPATRIL.

Maddy-Weitzman, B. (2001) Contested identities: Berbers, 'Berberism' and the state in north Africa. *Journal of North African Studies* 6 (3), 23–47.

Maghreb Machrek (1992) Monde Arabe: Algérie [Arab world: Algeria]. *Maghreb Machrek* 135 (January–March), 107–9.

Mahé, A. (2001) *Histoire de la Grande Kabylie XIXe – XXe siècles. Anthropologie Historique du Lien Social dans les Communautés Villageoises* [*The History of Greater Kabylia 19th – 20th Centuries. Historical Anthropology of Social Relations in Village Communities*]. Paris: Bouchène.

Mahmoud, Y. (1986) Arabic after diglossia. In J.A. Fishman, A. Tabouret-Keller, M. Clyne, B. Krishnamurti and M. Abdulaziz (eds) *The Fergusonian Impact* (vol. 1) (pp. 239–51). Berlin: Mouton de Gruyter.

Maïche, Z.A. (2004) Enquête nationale sur les besoins des jeunes. La recherche d'un emploi, première préoccupation [National survey on youth's needs. Search for a job, first preoccupation]. *El Watan* (29 November), 1, 32.

Mansouri, A. (1991) Algeria between tradition and modernity: The question of language. Unpublished PhD Thesis, State University of New York at Albany.

Manzano, F. (1995) La Francophonie dans le paysage linguistique du Maghreb: Contacts, ruptures et problématique de l'identité [Francophonia in the Maghrebi linguistic landscape: Contact, ruptures and the question of identity]. In A. Queffélec, F. Benzakour and Y. Cherrad-Benchefra (eds) *Le Français au Maghreb* (pp. 173–85). Aix-en-Provence: Publications de l'Université de Provence.

Marçais, G. (1913) *Les Arabes en Berbérie du XIe au XIVe Siècle* [*Arabs in Berberia from the 11th to the 14th Centuries*]. Paris: Ernest Leroux.

Marçais, P. (1960) Les parlers arabes d'Algérie [Spoken varieties of Arabic in Algeria]. *Encyclopédie de l'Islam* 1960, 385–90.

Marçais, W. (1902) *Le Dialecte Arabe Parlé à Tlemcen* [*The Arabic Dialect Spoken in Tlemcen*]. Paris: Ernest Leroux.

Marçais, W. (1913) La langue arabe dans l'Afrique du nord [The Arabic language in north Africa]. *Revue Pédagogique* 1, 3–11.

Marçais, W. (1930) La diglossie arabe [Arabic diglossia]. *L'Enseignement Public* 97, 401–9.

Marçais, W. (1938) Comment l'Afrique du Nord a été arabisée [How north Africa was Arabised]. *Annales de l'Institut d'Etudes Orientales* 4, 1–22.

Marley, D. (2004) Language attitudes in Morocco following recent changes in language policy. *Language Policy* 3, 25–46.

Martín, I. (2003) Algeria's political economy (1999–2002): An economic solution to the crisis? *Journal of North African Studies* 8 (2), 34–74.

Martinez, L. (1998) *La Guerre Civile en Algérie* [*Civil War in Algeria*]. Paris: Karthala.

Maurais, J. (2003) Towards a new linguistic world order. In J. Maurais and M.A. Morris (eds) *Languages in a Globalising World* (pp. 13–36). Cambridge: Cambridge University Press.

McFerren, M. (1984) *Arabization in the Maghreb*. Washington, DC: Center for Applied Linguistics.

Médiène, B. (1995) Alloula et les enfants [Alloula and children]. *Les Temps modernes* 580 (January–February), 10–23.

Meouak, M. (2004) Langues, société et histoire d'Alger au XVIIIe siècle d'après les données de Venture de Paradis (1739–1799) [Languages, society and the history of Algiers in the 18th century according to elements presented by Venture de Paradis (1739–1799)]. In J. Dakhlia (ed.) *Trames de Langues: Usages et Métissages Linguistiques dans l'Histoire du Maghreb* (pp. 303–29). Paris: Maisonneuve et Larose Institut de Recherche sur le Maghreb Contemporain.

Messaoudi, K. and Schemla, E. (1995) *Une Algérienne Debout* [*A Determined Algerian Woman*]. Paris: Flammarion.

Messaoudi, L. (2002) Le parler ancien de Rabat face à l'urbanisation linguistique [Old dialect of Rabat and linguistic urbanisation]. In A. Youssi, F. Benjelloun, M. Dahbi and Z. Iraqui-Sinaceur (eds) *Aspects of the Dialects of Arabic Today* (pp. 223–33). Rabat: AMAPATRIL.

Mesthrie, R. (1999) Language loyalty. In B. Spolsky (ed.) *Concise Encyclopedia of Educational Linguistics* (pp. 42–7). Amsterdam: Elsevier.

Mesthrie, R., Swann, J., Deumert, A. and Leap, W. L. (eds) (2000) *Introducing Sociolinguistics*. Philadelphia: Benjamins.

Metaoui, F. (2000) Aboubakr Benbouzid (ministre de l'Education nationale): 'L'école fondamentale a échoué' [Aboubakr Benbouzid (Minister of National Education): 'The fundamental school has failed']. *El Watan* 4 September, 1–2.

Métaoui, F. (2002) Bouteflika rejoint la francophonie? [Bouteflika joins Francophonie?]. *El Watan* (1 October). On WWW at http://www.elwatan.com.

Meynier, G. (2002) *Histoire Intérieure du FLN 1954–1962* [*Internal History of FLN 1954–1962*]. Paris: Librairie Arthème Fayard.

Miliani, M. (2000) Teaching English in a multilingual context: The Algerian case. *Mediterranean Journal of Educational Studies* 6 (1), 13–29.

Miliani, M. (2002) Le français dans les écrits des lycéens: Langue étrangère ou Sabir? [French in the writings of secondary-school students: Foreign language or mumbo-jumbo?]. *Insaniyat. Revue Algérienne d'Anthropologie et de Sciences Sociales* 17–18, 79–95.

Miliani, M. (2003) La dualité français-arabe dans le système éducatif algérien: Entre slogans et réalité [French-Arabic duality in the Algerian educational system: Between slogans and reality]. *Education et Sociétés Plurilingues* 15 (December), 17–32.

Mimoun, M. (2001) L'Arabofrancophonie. Une réalité en devenir [Arabofrancophonia. A reality in the making]. *El Watan* (15 February), 11–12.

Moali, H. (2005) Bouteflika-Ouyahia: Jeu et enjeu [Bouteflika-Ouyahia: What is at stake]. *El Watan*, (23 November), 3.

Moattassime, A. (1992) *Arabisation et Langue Française au Maghreb* [*Arabisation and the French Language in the Maghreb*]. Paris: Presses Universitaires de France.

Moatassime, A. (1996) Islam, arabisation et francophonie [Islam, arabisation and Francophonia]. *Französisch Heute* 27 (4), 280–93.

Moatti, S. (2004) Algérie: L'économie confisquée [Algeria: An expropriated economy]. *Alternatives Economiques* 224 (April), 60–61.

Morsly, D. (1980) Bilinguisme et énonciation [Bilingualism and enunciation]. In B. Gardin, J.B. Marcellesi and GRECO (eds) *Sociolinguistique: Approches, Théories, Pratiques* (pp. 131–5). Paris: Presses Universitaires de France.

Morsly, D. (1984) La langue étrangère. Réflexion sur le statut de la langue française en Algérie [Foreign language: A reflection on the status of the French language in Algeria]. *Le Français dans le Monde* 189, (November–December), 22–6.

Morsly, D. (1985) La langue nationale: pouvoir des mots – pouvoir par les mots [National language: The power of words – power through words]. *Peuples Méditerranéens / Mediterranean Peoples* 33, 79–88.

Morsly, D. (1988) *Le Français dans la réalité algérienne* [French in Algeria's reality]. Unpublished PhD Thesis, University René Descartes, Paris.

Morsly, D. (1996) Alger plurilingue [Multilingual Algiers]. *Plurilinguismes* 12 (December), 47–80.

Morsly, D. (2004) Langue française en Algérie: Aménagement linguistique et mise en oeuvre des politiques linguistiques [The French language in Algeria: Language planning and implementation of language policies]. *Revue d'Aménagement Linguistique* 107, 171–83.

Mostari, H.A. (2004) A sociolinguistic perspective on Arabisation and language use in Algeria. *Language Problems and Language Planning* 28 (1), 25–43.

Mostefaoui, B. (2004) Quinze ans de presse privée en Algérie. 1 600 000 exemplaires par jour [Fifteen years of private press in Algeria. 1,600,000 copies per day]. *El Watan* (15 June), 21.

Mustapha, Z. (1995) Using Arabic and English in science lectures. *English Today* 11 (4), 37–43.

Myers-Scotton, C. (1993) Elite closure as a powerful language strategy: The African case. *International Journal of the Sociology of Language* 103, 149–63.

Myhill, J. (2004) *Language in Jewish Society. Towards a New Understanding*. Clevedon: Multilingual Matters.

Nabti, A. (2003) En berbère dans le texte . . . [In Berber in the text . . .]. *Page des Librairies* (November), 5.

Nassima C. (2003) L'agrément octroyé aux écoles privées [Accreditation to private schools]. *El Watan* (29 November). On WWW at http://www.elwatan.com.

Nezzar, K. (2003) *Bouteflika, l'Homme et son Bilan* [*Bouteflika, the Man and his Assessment*]. Algiers: APIC.

Nouschi, A. (1986) Réflexions sur l'évolution du maillage urbain au Maghreb (XIXe–XXe siècles) [Reflection on the evolution of urban networks in the Maghreb (19th–20th centuries)]. *Bulletin de la Société Languedocienne de Géographie* 20 (2–3), 197–210.

Oberlé, T. (2004) Algérie. Nous occupons une place croissante dans l'enseignement public. L'horizon désensablé [Algeria. We occupy an increasing position in the public educational system: Dredged up horizon]. *Le Figaro Littéraire. Spécial Francophonie* (18 March), 9.

Ollivier, M. (1992) Les choix industriels [Industrial choices]. In M. Lakehal (ed.) *Algérie, de l'Indépendance à l'État d'Urgence* (pp. 112–31). Paris: Larmises-L'Harmattan.

Ouerdane, A. (2003) *Les Berbères et l'Arabo-islamisme en Algérie* [Berbers and Arabo-Islamism in Algeria]. Québec: Éditions KMSA.

Pakir, A. (1994) Education and invisible language planning: The case of English in Singapore. In T. Kandiah and J. Kwan-Terry (eds) *English and Language Planning: A Southeast Asian Contribution* (pp. 158–81). Singapore: Times Academic.

Paris Match (1999) N° 2624 (9 September), 28–35.

Perego, P. (1960) A propos du français parlé en Algérie [On the French language spoken in Algeria]. *La Pensée* (January/February), 90–5.

Péroncel-Hugoz, J.P. (1994) Les origines d'une 'guerre civile culturelle' [The origins of a 'cultural civil war']. *Le Monde* (19 May), ii–iii.

Pervillé, G. (2003) La reconquête de la population algérienne [The reconquest of the Algerian population]. In G. Pervillé (ed.) *Atlas de la Guerre d'Algérie* (pp. 40–1). Paris: Autrement.

Petit, O. (1971) Langue, culture et participation du monde arabe contemporain [Language, culture and participation of the contemporary Arab world]. *IBLA* 128, 259–93.

Platt, J.T. (1977) A mode for polyglossia and multilingualism (with special reference to Singapore and Malaysia). *Language in Society* 6, 361–79.

Platt, J., Weber, H. and Ho, M.L. (1984) *The New Englishes*. London: Routledge and Kegan Paul.

Polk, W.R. (1970) Introduction. In J. Stetkevych (ed.) *The Modern Arabic Literary Language* (pp. xi–xix). Chicago: University of Chicago Press.

Poulsen, M. (1993) Essai d'analyse d'une chanson raï, côté hommes [Analysis of a raï song, on the part of males]. In F. Colonna and Z. Daoud (eds) *Etre Marginal au Maghreb* (pp. 259–82). Paris: CNRS.

Power, C. (2000) The new Arab woman. *Newsweek* (12 June), 22–3.

Programme des Nations Unies pour le Développement (PNUD) (2002) *Rapport Arabe sur le Développement Humain 2002* [*Arab Human Development Report 2002*]. New York: United Nations.

Queffélec, A. (1995) Le français en Afrique du Nord: 1914–1945 [French in north Africa: 1914–1945]. In G. Antoine and R. Martin (eds) *Histoire de la Langue Française* (pp. 791–822). Paris: CNRS.

Queffélec, A., Derradji, Y., Debov, V., Smaali-Dekdouk, D. and Cherrad-Benchefra, Y. (2002) *Le Français en Algérie. Lexique et Dynamique des Langues* [*French in Algeria. Lexis and Language Dynamics*]. Brussels: Duculot.

Rahal-Sidhoum, S. (2001) Sur la berbérité en Algérie [On Berberiness in Algeria]. *Sanabil* 1 (March). On WWW at http://www.maghreb-ddh.sgdg/org/sanabil.

Rakibi, A. (1975/1982) Arabiser la pensée d'abord [Arabise thought first]. In J. Déjeux (ed.) *Culture Algérienne dans les Textes* (p. 137). Algiers: OPU-Publisud.

Rebah, A. (1991) Contribution à la réflexion sur l'université [Contribution to the reflection on the university]. *El Watan* (9–10 August), 11.

Remaoun, H. (1995) Ecole, histoire et enjeux institutionnels dans l'Algérie indépendante [School, history and institutional issues in independent Algeria]. *Les Temps Modernes* 580 (January–February), 73–4.

Rif, N. (2004) 19 millions d'Algériens vivent en ville [19 million Algerians live in towns]. *El Watan* (22 December), 6.

Riols, Y.M. (2004) Le drame d'être jeune en Algérie [The drama of being young in Algeria]. *L'Expansion* 690 (October), 50–2.

Roberts, H. (1980) Towards an understanding of the Kabylian question in contemporary Algeria. *Maghreb Review* 5 (5–6), 115–24.

Rossillon, P. (1995) *Atlas de la Langue Française* [*Atlas of the French Language*]. Paris: Bordas.

Rouadjia, A. (1991) *Les Frères et la Mosquée. Enquête sur le Mouvement Islamiste en Algérie* [*The Brothers and the Mosque. Study of the Islamist Movement in Algeria*]. Algiers: Bouchène.

Rubin, J. and Jernudd, B.H. (1971) Introduction: Language planning as an element in modernization. In J. Rubin and B.H. Jernudd (eds) *Can Language be Planned? Sociolinguistic Theory and Practice for Developing Nations* (pp. xiii–xxiv). Honolulu: University Press of Hawaii.

Ruedy, J. (1992) *Modern Algeria: The Origins and Development of a Nation*. Bloomington: Indiana University Press.

Ruff, P. (1998) *La Domination Espagnole à Oran sous le Gouvernement du Comte d'Alcaudate 1534–1558* [*Spanish Domination of Oran Under the Government of Count of Alcaudate 1534–1558*]. Paris: Bouchène.

Saad, Z. (1992) Language planning and policy attitudes: A case study of arabization in Algeria. Unpublished PhD Thesis, Columbia University Teachers College.

Saadi, N. (1991) *La Femme et la Loi en Algérie* [*Women and the Law in Algeria*]. Algiers: Bouchène.

Saadi, N. (1995) FIS: Trafic de culture [FIS: Traffic in culture]. *Télérama Hors-série: Algérie, la Culture Face à la Terreur* (March), 23.

Saadi-Mokrane, D. (2002) The Algerian linguicide. In A.E. Berger (ed.) *Algeria in Others' Languages* (pp. 44–59). Ithaca and London: Cornell University Press.

Sadi, S. (1991) *L'Algérie. L'Echec Recommencé?* [*Algeria. A Renewed Failure?*]. Algiers: Parenthèses.

Sahar, L. (2004) Recettes des hydrocarbures [Hydrocarbon revenues]. *El Watan* (13 October), 4.

Saint-Prot, C. (1995) *Le Nationalisme Arabe. Alternative à l'Intégrisme* [*Arab Nationalis: An Alternative to Fundamentalism*]. Paris: Ellipses.

Salhi, C. (2001) L'Insurrection sans armes de la Kabylie [Peaceful insurrection in Kabylia]. *Inprecor* 459/460 (June–July), 49–55.

Sarter, H. and Sefta, K. (1992) La glottopolitique algérienne. Faits et discours [Algerian language policy: Facts and discourse]. *Französisch Heute* 23 (2), 107–17.

Sayad, A. (1967) Bilinguisme et éducation en Algérie [Bilingualism and education in Algeria]. In R. Castel and J.C. Passeron (eds) *Education, Développement et Démocratie* (pp. 204–22). Paris: Mouton.

Schade-Poulsen, M. (1999) *Men and Popular Music in Algeria: The Social Significance of Raï*. Austin: University of Texas Press.

Schemla, E. (2000) *Mon Journal d'Algérie. Novembre 1999 – Janvier 2000* [*My Diary of Algeria. November 1999– January 2000*]. Paris: Flammarion.

Schiffman, H.F. (1996) *Linguistic Culture and Language Policy*. London and New York: Routledge.

Sebaa, R. (1996) *Arabisation dans les Sciences Sociales: Le Cas algérien* [*Arabisation in the Social Sciences: The Algerian Case*]. Paris: L'Harmattan.

Sebti, N. (2001) Rapport de la commission. Des propositions et des échéances [Report of the commission: Propositions and schedules]. *Liberté* (20 March). On www at http://www.liberte-algerie.com.

Sekaï, Z. (1995) Berbère et politique d'arabisation [Berber and the policy of Arabisation]. *Passerelles. Revue d'études interculturelles* 11, 125–33.

Servier, J. (1994) *Les Berbères* [*Berbers*]. Paris: PUF, *Que sais-je?*

Sharabi, H. (1966) *Nationalism and Revolution in the Arab World*. Princeton, NJ: Van Nostrand.

Si Ameur, O. and Sidhoum, N. (1992) L'emploi et le chômage, de l'euphorie à la crise [Employment and unemployment, from euphoria to crisis]. In M. Lakehal (ed.) *Algérie, de l'Indépendance à l'État d'Urgence* (pp. 145–76). Paris: Larmises-L'Harmattan.

Sirles, C.A. (1999) Politics and Arabization: The evolution of postindependence North Africa. *International Journal of the Sociology of Language* 137, 115–29.

Sivan, E. (1979) Colonialism and popular culture in Algeria. *Journal of Contemporary History* 14, 21–53.

Smail, K. (1999) La parité homme-femme dans le rap [Male-female parity in rap]. *El Watan* (18 August), 23.

Smail, K. (2000) Sortie nationale du nouvel album de MBS [National release of MBS new album]. *El Watan* (7 February), 17.

Smati, M. (1999) Ibn Badis: Un projet de renouveau [Ibn Badis: A project for renewal]. In A. Kadri (ed.) *Parcours d'Intellectuels Maghrébins. Scolarité, Formation, Socialisation et Positionnements* (pp. 183–91). Paris: Karthala.

Smolicz, J.J. (1979) *Culture and Education in a Plural Society.* Canberra: Curriculum Development Center.

Souaiaia, M. (1990) Language, education and politics in the Maghreb. *Language, Culture and Curriculum* 3, 109–23.

Spolsky, B. and Shohamy, E. (1999) *The Languages of Israel. Policy, Ideology and Practice.* Clevedon: Multilingual Matters.

Stora, B. (1991) *Histoire de l'Algérie coloniale (1830–1954)* [*A History of Colonial Algeria (1830–1954)*]. Paris: La Découverte.

Stora, B. (1998) *Algérie: Formation d'une Nation* [*Algeria: The Formation of a Nation*]. Biarritz: Atlantica.

Stora, B. (2001) *Histoire de l'Algérie Depuis l'Indépendance (1962–1988)* [*A History of Algeria since Independence (1962–1988)*]. Paris: Découverte.

Stora, B. (2004) *Algérie 1954* [*Algeria 1954*]. Paris: Le Monde et Éditions de l'Aube.

Stora, B. and Daoud, Z. (1995) *Ferhat Abbas. Une Utopie Algérienne* [*Ferhat Abbas. An Algerian Utopia*]. Paris: Éditions Denoël.

Suleiman, Y. (1994) Nationalism and the Arabic language: An historical overview. In Y. Suleiman (ed.) *Arabic Sociolinguistics: Issues and Perspectives* (pp. 3–24). Richmond: Curzon.

Suleiman, Y. (1999) Language education policy – Arabic speaking countries. In B. Spolsky (ed.) *Concise Encyclopedia of Educational Linguistics* (pp. 106–16). Amsterdam: Elsevier.

Swann, J. (2000) Language choice and code-switching. In R. Mesthrie, J. Swann, A. Deumert and W.L. Leap (eds) *Introducing Sociolinguistics* (pp. 148–83). Philadelphia: Benjamins.

Tabory, E. and Tabory, M. (1987) Berber unrest in Algeria: Lessons for language policy. *International Journal of the Sociology of Language* 63, 63–79.

Taha, T.A.M. (1990) The Arabicisation of higher education: The case of Khartoum university. *Journal of Multilingual and Multicultural Development* 11 (4), 291–305.

Taifi, M. (1997) Le lexique berbère: Entre l'emprunt massif et la néologie sauvage [Berber Lexis: between massive borrowing and uncontrolled neology]. *International Journal of the Sociology of Language* 123, 61–80.

Talahite, F. (2000) Economie administrée, corruption et engrenage de la violence en Algérie [Administered economy, corruption and the spiral of violence in Algeria]. *Revue Tiers Monde* 41 (161) (January–March), 49–74.

Taleb Ibrahimi, A. (1981) *De la Décolonisation à la Révolution Culturelle (1962–1972)* [*From Decolonisation to the Cultural Revolution (1962–1972)*]. Algiers: SNED.

Taleb Ibrahimi, K. (1995) *Les Algériens et Leur(s) Langue(s). Eléments pour une Approche Sociolinguistique de la Société Slgérienne* [*Algerians and their Language(s). Elements of a Sociolinguistic Approach of Algerian Society*]. Algiers: El Hikma.

Talmoudi, F. (1984) *The Diglossic Situation in North Africa: A Study of Classical/Dialectal Arabic Diglossia with Sample Texts in 'Mixed Arabic'.* Göteberg, Sweden: Acta Universitatis Gothoburgensis.

Tefiani, M. (1984) Arabisation et fonctions linguistiques en Algérie [Arabisation and linguistic functions in Algeria]. *Französisch Heute* 15 (2), 118–28.

Tenaille, F. (2002) *Le Raï: De la Bâtardise à la Reconnaissance Internationale* [*Raï Music: From Bastardy to International Recognition*]. Arles/Paris: Actes Sud.

Thawiza (2002) Tamazight aujourd'hui [Tamazight today]. *Thawiza* 231 (28 March), 5.

Thomas, E.H. (1999) The politics of language in former colonial lands: A comparative look at North Africa and Central Asia. *Journal of North African Studies* 4 (1), 1–44.

Tibi, B. (1981) *Arab Nationalism: A Critical Enquiry.* London: Macmillan.

Tigziri, N. (2002) Enseignement de la langue amazighe: Etat des lieux [The teaching of Amazigh language: Inventory]. *Passerelles. Revue d'Études Interculturelles* 24, 61–70.

Tilmatine, M. (1992) A propos de néologie en berbère moderne [Concerning neologisms in modern Berber]. *Afrikanistische Arbeitspapiere* 30, 155–66.

Tollefson, J.W. (2002) Limitations of language policy and planning. In R.B. Kaplan (ed.) *The Oxford Handbook of Applied Linguistics* (pp. 416–25). Oxford: Oxford University Press.

Torki, R. (1984) Adhwa'a 'ala Siyaassat Ta'rib Atta'liim wa Idarah wa al-Mohiitt al-Ijtima'i fi al-Djaza'ir: Ma'rakat Atta'rib (1962–1982) [Spotlights about the policy of arabizing education, Administration and the social environment in Algeria: The battle for Arabization (1962–1982)]. *Al Mustaqbal Al Arabi* 57, 84–103.

Tounsi, L. (1997) Aspects des parlers jeunes en Algérie [Aspects of the speech of young people in Algeria]. *Langue Française* 114, 104–13.

Tucker, G.R. (1994) Language planning issues for the coming decade. In W. Grabe *et al.* (eds) *Annual Review of Applied Linguistics* 14, 277–83. New York: Cambridge University Press.

Tuquoi, J.P. (2003) L'école privée que les autorités ne connaissent pas, mais où elles scolarisent leurs enfants [The private school that the authorities do not know, but in which they educate their children]. *Le Monde* (6 March), 4.

Tuquoi, J.P. (2004) Les 'pirates' du Maghreb privés de chaînes françaises [Maghrebi 'hackers' deprived of French channels]. *Le Monde* (27 November), 1.

Turin, Y. (1983) *Affrontements Culturels dans l'Algérie Coloniale: Ecoles, Médecines, Religion, 1830–1880 [Cultural Clashes in Colonial Algeria: Schools, Medecine, Religion, 1830–1880]*. Algiers: Entreprise Nationale du Livre.

Valensi, L. (1969) *Le Maghreb avant la Prise d'Alger (1790–1830) [The Maghreb before the Takeover of Algiers (1790–1830)]*. Paris: Flammarion.

Vermeren, P. (2004) *Maghreb: La Démocratie Impossible? [Maghreb: The Impossible Democracy?]*. Paris: Arthème Fayard.

Vieille, P. (1984) Le pétrole comme rapport social [Oil as social rapport]. *Peuples Méditerranéens/Mediterranean Peoples* 26, 3–29.

Vignaux, B. (2004) Une presse libérée mais menacée [A freed but menaced press]. *Le Monde Diplomatique* (March), 7.

Vincent, B. (2004) La langue espagnole en Afrique du nord XVIe–XVIIIe siècles [The Spanish language in north Africa, 16th–18th centuries]. In J. Dakhlia (ed.) *Trames de Langues: Usages et Métissages Linguistiques dans l'Histoire du Maghreb* (pp. 105–11). Paris: Maisonneuve et Larose Institut de Recherche sur le Maghreb Contemporain.

Wardhaugh, R. (1987) *Languages in Competition*. Oxford: Blackwell.

Weber, E. (1984) *Peasants into Frenchmen*. Stanford, CA: Stanford University Press.

Weber, G. (1987) Tamashek and Tinifagh. *Language Monthly* 50, 11–12.

Weinstein, B. (1983) *The Civic Tongue. Political Consequences of Language Choices*. New York and London: Longman.

Werenfels, I. (2002) Obstacles to privatization of state-owned industries in Algeria: The political economy of a distributive conflict. *Journal of North African Studies* 7 (1), 1–28.

World Bank (2004) Algeria. On WWW at http://Inweb18.worldbank.org/mna/mena.nsf.

Yahiatene, M. (1997) L'arabisation de l'enseignement supérieur en Algérie. Etude de certains aspects didactiques et sociolinguistiques [The arabisation of higher education in Algeria. The study of some pedagogical and sociolinguistic aspects]. Unpublished PhD Thesis, University Stendhal-Grenoble III France.

Yefsah, A. (1990) *La Question du Pouvoir en Algérie [The Question of Power in Algeria]*. Algiers: EnAP Édition.

Yemloul, A. (2004) Recettes US pour le Maghreb [US Revenues in the Maghreb]. *El Watan* (14 April), 28.

Yermèche, O. (2004) L'état civil algérien: Une politique de francisation du système anthroponymique algérien? [Algerian registry office: A policy of Frenchifying the Algerian anthroponomy system?]. In J. Dakhlia (ed.) *Trames de Langues: Usages et Métissages Linguistiques dans l'Histoire du Maghreb* (pp. 489–97). Paris: Maisonneuve et Larose Institut de Recherche sur le Maghreb Contemporain.

Youssi, A. (1991) Langues et parlers: Un trilinguisme complexe [Languages and dialects: Complex trilingualism]. In C. Lacoste and Y. Lacoste (eds) *L'Etat du Maghreb* (pp. 272–7). Paris: Découverte.

Zerrouk, D. (2004) Engouement des Algérois pour internet [The general craze of Algiers inhabitants for the Internet]. *El Watan* (20–21 February), 7.

Zughoul, M.R. (2001) The language of higher education in Jordan: Conflict, challenges and innovative accommodation. In R. Sultana (ed.) *Challenge and Change in the Euro-Mediterranean Region: Case Studies in Educational Innovation* (pp. 327–42). New York: Peter Lang.

Language Planning in Côte d'Ivoire
Non scholea sed vitae discimus
We do not study for academia, but for real life

Paulin G. Djité

Chair, Division of Languages and Linguistics, Faculty of Education, The University of Western Sydney, Macarthur, PO Box 555, Campbelltown, NSW 2560, Australia

This monograph presents the language situation in Côte d'Ivoire.[1] It examines the historical and socio-political processes and the language policies and language-in-education practices of the country. It shows that the debate on language policy over the last two decades has failed to lead to the adoption of a language plan that takes into account the current language situation in the country. It also argues that, given the socio-political and economic difficulties faced by Côte d'Ivoire over the last decade, this situation is likely to remain unchanged for the foreseeable future.

Introduction

Located on the Gulf of Guinea with a landmass of 322,460 km^2 (slightly larger than the State of New Mexico), Côte d'Ivoire is bordered on the east by Ghana, on the north-east by Burkina Faso (formerly Upper Volta), on the north-west by Mali and on the west by Ghana and Liberia (see Figure 1).

The make-up of the population, the language profile of the country, language attitudes, the dynamics of the actual patterns of language use, maintenance and spread are best understood in the context of historical and present migration patterns, driven by the comparatively good state of the economy and the relative political stability in Côte d'Ivoire, especially until 1980. An examination of these matters is the subject of the present monograph.

Although little is known about the original inhabitants of Côte d'Ivoire, it is believed that they were displaced or absorbed by the ancestors of the present inhabitants who migrated to this land from the east, the north and the west, in successive waves, between the 10th and the 18th century. Before 1893, when it became a French overseas possession, the territory of present-day Côte d'Ivoire was occupied by various kingdoms: the Kingdoms of Kabadougou and Worodougou in the north-west; the Muslim empire of Kong in the north-central region, founded by the Sénufo and later conquered by the Dyula in the 18th century; the Abron Kingdom of Bondoukou (Jaman), established in the 17th century by the Kulango and also conquered by the Dyula in the 18th century; the Abron Kingdom of Indénié in the east; the Baulé Kingdom of Sakassou in the centre, established in the mid-18th century, and the Kingdom of Krinjabo in the south-east (Loucou, 1983; Niangoran Bouah, 1996).

By 1893, when the French occupied this land, Côte d'Ivoire was a melting pot of several ethnic groups the exact number of which is still a matter of debate. From 1904 to 1958, Côte d'Ivoire was part of a group of West African French colonies called the Federation of French West Africa (*Afrique Occidentale Française* – A.O.F), directly administered by France. From 1932 to 1947, following a decision by France to reorganise its colony of Upper Volta, Côte d'Ivoire

Figure 1 Geographical location of Côte d'Ivoire in West Africa

acquired part of the latter, up to Ouagadougou. This was called Upper Côte d'Ivoire. In 1947 the French decided to revert to the old administrative boundaries, and recreated Upper Volta (now Burkina Faso) as it was before 1932. Lower Côte d'Ivoire (now simply known as Côte d'Ivoire) also reverted to its old boundaries. In the 1940s and 1950s, job opportunities in the cities and in the large cocoa and coffee plantations, and the general promise of economic prosperity in Lower Côte d'Ivoire, drew yet another wave of migrants from neighbouring countries (i.e. Mali, Upper Volta, Benin, Togo, Nigeria, Niger, Guinea and Mauritania). By the time Côte d'Ivoire gained its independence from France on 7 August 1960, it was one of the most multilingual and multicultural countries in West Africa.[3] This migration process was to continue over the years.

As a result, by 1975 one out of every six persons in Côte d'Ivoire, or 21% of the total population, was an immigrant. This was, at the time, the highest proportion of foreign nationals in any country in West Africa. By 1987, 27% of the population of Côte d'Ivoire was foreign born. This proportion reached 30 to

35% of the total population in 1999 (see *Jeune Afrique* 2019: 30, 21–27 September 1999). This migrant population came mainly from Burkina Faso (1,600,000), Mali (754,000), France (over 60,000 in the 1980s), Guinea (238,000), and Lebanon and Syria (100,000 to 300,000). Other important sources of immigration are Benin, Ghana, Mauritania, Nigeria, Niger, Senegal and Togo. Most of this immigrant population consists of indentured workers. More recently, after the start of the Liberian civil war in 1990, more than 350,000 refugees fled to Côte d'Ivoire and, as of September 1998, about 85,000 still remained in the country. This continued influx of migrants, most of whom choose to take up permanent residency in the country, has contributed to the diversity of the language situation in Côte d'Ivoire and reinforced the processes of language spread and language choice.

By July 1999, the population of Côte d'Ivoire was estimated at 15,818,068 inhabitants, with an annual growth rate of 2.35% (1999 estimate) and a birth rate of 41.76 per 1000 (1999 estimate (see *CIA – The World Factbook, Côte d'Ivoire*)). Using the trends evident in these figures, the population of the country will rise to 30 million inhabitants by the year 2015. About 47% of this population was under the age of 15 in 1999 and 54.4% lived in urban centers. Fifty-seven per cent of the total population were men and 43% were women. The literate population aged 15 or over was 48.5% in 1999 (*CIA – The World Fact Book 1999, Côte d'Ivoire*).[4]

The Economy of Côte d'Ivoire

Côte d'Ivoire has the largest economy (50% of the GNP) of the West African Economic Monetary Union composed of Benin, Burkina Faso, Côte d'Ivoire, Guinea Bisau, Mali, Niger, Senegal and Togo. Its economy is largely dependent on agriculture, which engages 68% of the population and represents 50% of the GNP (with a value of US$23.9 billion in 1996), one third of the GDP and two thirds of export revenues. This reliance upon agriculture has made Côte d'Ivoire one of the world's largest producers and exporters of coffee (third largest producer in the world, after Brazil and Colombia, with 22% of total world exports), cocoa beans (largest producer in the world, with 40% of total production) and palm oil (largest producer in Africa). As a result, the industrial production, although the largest in sub-saharan francophone Africa, is mainly linked to agriculture (e.g. food processing, initial processing of rubber, sawmills, paper mills). Other major exports are rubber, timber, cotton (third largest producer in Africa after Egypt and Sudan), bananas and pineapples. This reliance on agriculture leaves the economy of the country exposed to the fluctuations in the prices of its cash crops on the international market, as well as to bad seasons affecting crop production (i.e. natural disasters, crop diseases, etc.).

In addition to its agriculture, Côte d'Ivoire has significant untapped mineral deposits of offshore oil and gas, gold, nickel, and other minerals. It is already self-sufficient in oil and has begun exporting some of its oil production to the West African sub-region. In December 1999 a Canadian company, Resources Melkior Inc., signed a contract worth US$10 million with SODEMI (the Ivorian government owned mining company) for a feasibility study for an iron ore mine at Mount Klahoyo in the west. The Mount Klahoyo deposit is estimated at 700 million tonnes of ore with a 34% iron content (*Fraternité Matin*, 10–11 December 1999: 7).

There have been three main phases in the economic development of Côte d'Ivoire, since independence from France:

(1) 1960–1980: two decades of steady growth at an annual rate of 7%. This growth was mainly attributable to the returns on cash crops such as coffee and cocoa.

(2) 1980–1993: thirteen years of economic recession and financial difficulties as the prices paid for the cash crops on the international market plummeted. The ratio of the debt service to export earnings rose from 13% to 31% between 1978 and 1983; at least five different programmes of structural adjustment were negotiated with the institutions of Bretton-Woods. In 1987, Côte d'Ivoire suspended repayments of its external debt. By the end of 1987, the Paris Club, the International Monetary Fund (IMF) and the government negotiated a new economic recovery and structural adjustment programme that granted Côte d'Ivoire a six-year grace period and rescheduled all principal due in 1987–1988 plus 80% of interest due (approximately US$500 million).

(3) From 1994: devaluation of the CFA Franc (CFA = *Communauté Financière Africaine*) by 50% on 12 January 1994, the first time in more than forty years of fixed currency parity with the French Franc and return to some form of economic health thanks to various packages of debt reduction from the World Bank and the IMF. These were accompanied by a rigorous programme of macroeconomic reform and structural adjustment. Real GDP in 1994 grew by around 1.7%, reversing the pattern of negative growth of the previous years (in 1993 the growth rate was –0.8%) and reached an average of 6.6% from 1995 to 1997, as inflation dropped to 7.7% in 1995 from 32.2% in 1994 (*The World Bank Group Countries: Côte d'Ivoire*, page 1, on www.worldbank.org).

Although some results of the structural reform programme put in place in 1994 were mixed (the structural adjustment programme had not been successfully completed by 1997), the World Bank agreed in 1998 to support a debt reduction package for Côte d'Ivoire under the Initiative for Heavily Indebted Poor Countries, and the IMF approved a new three-year Enhanced Structural Adjustment Facility, the first tranche of which was disbursed in November 1998.[5] This represented a reduction of the country's external debt burden by US$345 million in net present value terms and is estimated to translate into debt-service relief of close to US$800 million over time.

Notwithstanding these two financial packages, the budget deficit rose from 1.8% of the GNP in 1998 to 3% in 1999 (as against the 1.5% forecast) (*Fraternité Matin*, 23 November 1999: 11) due to a fall in revenue caused by the drop in the price of cash crops such as coffee, cocoa, cotton and rubber and a lack of control in the government's public expenditure.[6] In 1999 the rate of growth fell to 4.5%, far below the double-digit rate of growth predicted for the same period.

In real terms this meant that, even though the GNP per capita was US$1620, unemployment was high and over 35% of the population lived below the poverty line (i.e. with a per capita income of less than US$1 per day), leading to an outbreak of crime. Côte d'Ivoire was ranked 154 out of 174 on the Index of Human Development of the United Nations Development Program (*UNDP Human Development Report*, 1999). With the ever- increasing cost of the basic commodities of life (rice, milk, sugar, soap, gas, water, electricity, telephone, etc.), there has been a growing feeling of discontent reaching towards boiling point among the population. At the same time, unemployment and crime have been on the rise. The government has put the blame for these economic and social problems on two factors: firstly, on the greed of developed countries that have been reluctant to relieve the external debt of the country while they were buying its cash crops at bargain prices, and secondly on the unusually high percentage of foreign-born individuals living in the country.

Nevertheless, these economic difficulties have not put a stop to language contact. On the contrary, the declining national and per capita revenues, the increasing rural misery and urban unemployment, coupled with the continued immigration of nationals from even less fortunate neighbouring countries, has reinforced the already dynamic language contact situation. More than ever before, Côte d'Ivoire is at the centre of thriving language contacts.

The People of Côte d'Ivoire and Their Languages

Côte d'Ivoire has retained the French language as the sole official language of education and administration, as per Article 1 of its Constitution (see *Law* No 60–356 of 3 November 1960, last amended by *Law* No 98–387 of 2 July 1998). However, as in many former colonies, and as discussed in the introduction to this monograph, this is a multilingual country.

According to Delafosse (1904), Côte d'Ivoire had 60 languages and dialects. Later Grimes (1974) estimated the number of languages to be 58. A year later, the

Table 1 Classification of some Ivorian languages according to Lafage (1982)

Language groups	Kwa	Kru	Mandé	Gur (Voltaic)
Dominant language	Baulé	Bété	Dyula	Sénufo
Other languages	Anyi	Bakoué	Yakuba	Kulango
	Appollo	Dida	Gouro	Teen
	Attié	Godié	Kouyaka	Lobi
	Abbey	Grébo	Malinké	Other Gur
	Avikam	Guéré	Mahou	
	Alladjan	Wobé	Other Mandé	
	Aizi	Néyo		
	Abidji	Nyaboua		
	Abouré	Other Kru		
	Adjoukrou			
	Ebrié			
	Ehotilé			
	Other Kwa			

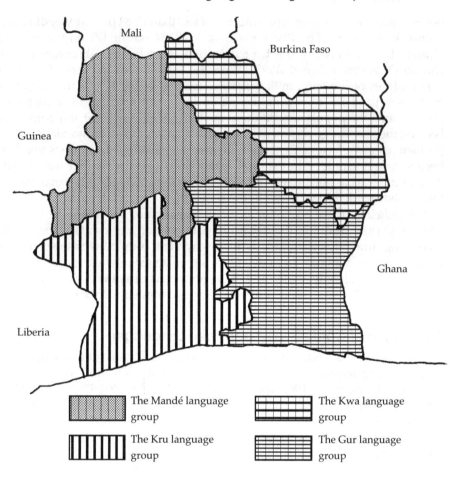

Figure 2 Geographical distribution of the language groups of Côte d'Ivoire

official Census of 1975 put this figure at 69 languages. In 1995 the Summer Institute of Linguistics (SIL) listed a total of 74 languages (73 living languages and one
extinct language). All the languages of Côte d'Ivoire (see Table 1) belong to the
Niger-Congo (Kordofanian) language family (Greenberg, 1966) and can be
subdivided into four major groups: the Kwa (estimated at 19 languages) in the
mid-eastern and south-eastern part of the country, the Kru (estimated at 16
languages) in the west and south-west, the Mandé (estimated at 18 languages) in
the north-west, and the Gur (believed to include at least 15 languages) in the
south-east (see Figure 2; also see Lafage, 1982).

Many inaccurate perceptions of the language situation in Côte d'Ivoire were
created during the colonial period, and many descriptive linguists have perpetuated the idea that the language profile of the country is one of almost unlimited
language diversity (see Delafosse, 1904; Greenberg, 1966; Grimes, 1974; Lafage,
1979, 1982; Hattiger, 1983). To this day, the exact number of languages still
remains unknown. These misconceptions were in turn picked up and spread by
the political élite of the country, some of whom go so far as to talk about

hundreds of languages (e.g. a speech delivered by Phillipe Yacé in 1976 at the United Nations, in *Fraternité Matin*, 26 April 1976: 23–4), in order to justify their inaction in the area of language policy and planning. As a result, the language profile of Côte d'Ivoire is still largely perceived as being very complex, and it is widely believed that the choice of any local language as a national and/or official language would trigger a 'tribal' war (Djité, 1991b). Hence, in the eyes of the layman, as well as those of the specialist, such a complex language profile does not lend itself to the development of a workable language plan or language-in-education plan. The only hope for peace and national unity and, above all, the only way to provide access to science and technology and to reap the benefits of modernisation is to maintain the French language.

Djité (1988a) argues that the traditional descriptions of the language situation in Côte d'Ivoire exaggerate the degree of linguistic heterogeneity within the country and give an impression of divisiveness among the population that does not actually exist. This has occurred because varieties of the same core language(s) have been presented as full-blown languages in their own right, leading to the establishment of a number of artificial language boundaries that have no social or functional reality. By way of contrast, Quirk *et al.* (1985: 13) have argued in the case of English that:

> the properties of dogness can be seen in both Terrier and Alsatian (and, we presume, equally); yet no single variety of dog embodies all the features present in all varieties of dog. In a somewhat similar way, we need to see a common core or nucleus that we call English, being realised only in the different actual varieties of the language that we hear and read.

Kachru (1982) illustrates this idea further by enumerating varieties of English – American, Australian, British, Canadian, Jamaican, New Zealand, Nigerian, Cameroonian, and so forth – each of which, in turn, has its own sub-varieties, and points out that the core of all these varieties is English. As Khubchandani (1972, 1977) has put it, a speaker may have a verbal repertoire that makes him or her a native speaker of a range of speech that is labelled with more than one name. It is in this connection that Hymes (1984: 8) suggests that 'One must ask, not about genetic relationships among languages and objective linguistic demarcation of dialects, but about communication relationships among persons and groups.' Indeed, the list of Ivorian languages in Table 1 conceals the real-life experiences of inter-ethnic communication, and native speakers of these so-called languages do not identify with many of the labels provided.

Part of the misconception about the language situation is due to the fact that national boundaries in Côte d'Ivoire, as in much of Africa, were not drawn up on linguistic and cultural criteria, but by the chance of European imperial ambitions. As a matter of fact, each of Côte d'Ivoire's large cultural/linguistic groupings has as many – and in many cases more – members outside the national territory as within. Some of the many languages shared with neighbouring countries are:

- the Kwa languages (with Ghana);
- the Kru languages (with Liberia);
- the Mandé languages (with Guinea, Mali and Burkina Faso); and

- the Gur languages (with Burkina Faso).

This was clearly demonstrated in the early 1990s, when most of the refugees fleeing from war-torn Liberia were taken in by local villagers in the west of Côte d'Ivoire. Upon repatriation of these refugees by the United Nations High Commission for Refugees (UNHCR) a few years later, some 85,000 of them elected to remain in Côte d'Ivoire. This openness and integration were mainly due to the fact that these people share the same language(s) and culture(s) (Djité, 1988b). This is in essence what King Honesty (quoted by Waddell, 1863) meant when he said: 'In my kingdom, every third village speaks another language; every tenth person on the market place speaks another language; and yet, everybody understands everybody.'

Assuming that the system of numeration is fundamental to every language, Djité (1991a: 127–9) has compared the systems of numeration for three of the four language groups listed in Table 1. Tables 2, 3 and 4 show that the systems of numeration for the Kwa, Kru and Mandé language groups are essentially the same, being much more similar than those of the Latin based languages like French, Spanish and Italian. One should also note that numeration in the Kwa language group is based on a decimal system, whilst those of the Kru and Mandé language groups are based on a bidecimal system. The comparison of these numeration systems is suggestive of some of the similarities to be found between languages and groups of languages.

Djité (1988a) has also explained some of the apparent lexical and phonological differences between some of the languages of the Kru language group and shown that, overall, they are part and parcel of the same sound system. Just as one would not argue that a Texan speaks a language different from that of a New Yorker or an inhabitant of Martha's Vineyard, one cannot say that Wobé and Guéré, for instance, are two different languages.

Moreover, a closer look at the day-to-day communication networks suggests at least two things: (1) from the point of view of their respective functions, it is possible to distinguish four types of languages in Côte d'Ivoire, and (2) the communication patterns of individuals and groups show a language repertoire that makes language demarcation an almost irrelevant exercise in this context. The four types of languages in the country are:

(1) languages of intra-ethnic communication (e.g. Anyi, Dida, Gouro, Lobi);
(2) regionally dominant languages (e.g. Baulé, Bété, Dyula);
(3) national lingua francas (e.g. Dyula); and
(4) the official language (i.e. Standard French – not shown in Table 1).

The languages of intra-ethnic communication are those languages whose domain is limited to the communicative interactions between members of the family in the home or members of the same ethnic group. The regionally dominant languages are those that are often used as media of inter-ethnic communication within a particular geographical region. A number of these regionally dominant languages (Baulé, Bété, Sénufo, etc.) are used in the media (radio and TV). The lingua francas are languages that display a dynamism that goes beyond a particular geographical and/or functional scale and cover large parts of the country or several neighbouring countries. They are usually learnt as second

Table 2 Comparison of four Kwa languages according to Djité (1991a)

Number	Baoulé	Anyi	Appollo/Nzema	Krobou
1	kùn	Kun (êkun)	êkun	(ên) kun
2	nnyn	Nnyuã	nnyuã	ê ñõ
3	nsã	Nsã	nsã	ê sã
4	nnã	Nnã	nnã	ê nnã
5	nnún	Nnun	nnun	ê nnùn
6	nsien	Nsiã	nsiã	ê nsien
7	nsô	Nsu	nsun	ê nsó
8	nmöšwé	Möšwê	møšwê	mökwê
9	ngwlã	Nguãlã	nguãlã	ngwöRã
10	blú	Bulu	bulu	bRu

Note: In the Kwa languages, 'l' and 'R' are allophones of the same phoneme.

Table 3 Comparison of six Kru languages according to Djité (1991a)

Number	Guéré	Wobé	Nyabua	Bété	Dida	Vata
1	doo	too	Doo	bhlu	bhlo	bhlö
2	'sõõ	'sõõ	'sõ	'so	'so	'so
3	tââ	tââ	tã	'ta	taa	ta
4	ñyê	ñyê	ñyê	muana	mòòna	muòna
5	mm'	mm'	muu	'bgbi	gbi	gbi
6	meo'	mêlo'	mêêlo	'ngbuplu	gbeplo	gbiflo
7	mêsõ	mêsõ	mêêsõ	ngbiso	gbòso	gbuòso
8	mêhã	mênã	mêêtã	gbuata	gbata	gbòfòta
9	mêñyê	mêñyê	mêñyê	ngbimuana	pêêna	ênu'gbienu
10	bué	pué	bué	'kugba	kogba	kugba

Note: The reader will note the similarities within the Guéré complex (Guéré/Wobé/Nyabua) and those within the Bété complex (Bété/Dida/Vata).

languages through informal language contacts and serve as languages of wider communication. In Côte d'Ivoire there are two such languages: Dyula and, to a lesser extent, Ivorian or Popular French (see the section on Language Spread).

Hence, the average Ivorian has a language repertoire consisting of at least the mother tongue (for intra-ethnic communication), the regionally dominant language and one of the national lingua francas. The educated Ivorian will have Standard French in addition to the mother tongue at least (in most cases, one of the national lingua francas is also part of his/her language repertoire). When, as in the case of the author, this person has had the opportunity to live in various parts of the country, their language repertoire often includes many more intra-ethnic and regional languages.[7] This functional perspective underscores the dynamic nature of the language situation in Côte d'Ivoire.

The history of these language choices and practices provides an interesting insight into the current language situation. Far too often, it is forgotten that

Table 4 Comparison of four Mandé Languages according to Djité (1991a)

Number	Dyula/ Malinké-Dyula	Mahou/Gyo	Yakuba	Tura
1	kélen	Kéén	do	do
2	flà	Fya	plé	piilê
3	saba	Sawa	yaaga	yàka
4	nààny	Naani	yiisié	yísè
5	looRu	LooRu	soodhu	soolu
6	wòòrò	Wòòlò	'sòado	sâado
7	wolonfla	Wòònvya	'saaplê	sâapiilê
8	ségi	Sênyin	'saaga	sâaka
9	kònõtò	Kòõdõ	'seisie	sòisê
10	tã	Tã	kõgdo	buu

Note: The reader will again note the similarities within the North Mandé complex (Dyula/ Malinké-Dyula, Mahou/Gyo) and those within the South Mandé complex (Yakuba/ Tura).

Africa was the first continent in history where literacy and schooling were implemented, in places of higher learning as diverse as Nubia, Meroe, Sudan, Timbuktu, Jenne, Gao, Kano, Katsina, Chinguetti, not to mention those of eastern and southern Africa, and the islands of the Indian Ocean. In the case of Côte d'Ivoire, history also teaches us that there were a number of large kingdoms with highly organised socio-political systems before the advent of colonialism. Clearly, these empires and kingdoms would not have existed without some mutually intelligible communicative network(s) to foster a sense of group membership and/or shared identity (Djité, 1990). It is unfortunate that, in trying to paint this part of the world as 'uncivilised' and 'backward', some 'discoverers' of new languages have failed to ask themselves how the people in these kingdoms managed to achieve such highly organised social structures.

Language choice, language use and language attitudes are all a function of a number of factors, one of which is religious practice. Often, the language (or variety and/or register of language) used in the liturgy is markedly different and can pose a major constraint on the language repertoire of speakers. The following section, while looking at the religious affiliations of Ivorians, summarises the language situation as it pertains to religious practice.

The People of Côte d'Ivoire and Their Religions

The religions of Côte d'Ivoire are as diverse as its people, and religious affiliation tends to follow ethnic lines. The results of the most recent census (1988) show that Muslims make up 25.1% of the total population, Christians 31.2% (Catholics 22.7%, Protestants 6.6%, Harrists 1.9%), practitioners of traditional religions 22.8%, and the practitioners of other religions 4%. Those who indicated no preference for any religion represented 16.9% of the total population (see, the first Annual Report on *Religious Freedom in Côte d'Ivoire* by the US State Department, quoted in *Le Jour* 1408, 14 October 1999).[8] One should note that most Christians and Muslims to some extent still follow the local native beliefs and practices.

In terms of ethnic and religious distribution, the bulk of the Muslim population speaks Dyula (see the section on Language Spread for a more detailed discussion), and lives in the north of the country and in the urban centres in the south. In 1988 the Muslims represented 47.2% of the urban population and 33.2% of the rural population, or 40.2% of the total. Most Christians live in the south, the centre and the east of the country, whilst the practitioners of traditional religions are found in the rural areas all over the country. Traditional religions vary according to ethnic group, region, village, sex, and age group or by family. Although they are not accorded the same status as the Christian and Muslim religions, most Christians and Muslims maintain certain aspects of these traditional religious practices. The members of the Harrist faith – an African Protestant denomination founded in 1913 by William Wadé Harris, a Liberian preacher – are concentrated in the south.

Several Catholic and Protestant schools were created in the 1900s during the colonial period; they played a pivotal role in the training of most of the élite of the country. Needless to say, the only language of instruction in these schools was Standard French. Although the Constitution and the Laws of the country confer no civil, political or economic advantage on any particular religion, there have been imbalances in the official approach to the Christian and Muslim religions. For instance, Christian schools received government grants and were under the direct supervision of the Ministry of Education. On the other hand, Koranic schools, until 1994, were treated as religious schools, received no government grant, and came under the supervision of the Ministry of the Interior.

In addition, whilst all Christian holidays are observed everywhere in the country, Muslim holidays were not observed until 1994. Even though the Catholic and Protestant churches set up their own radio stations in 1991 (subsequently these were officially approved in March 1999), the Muslims were not authorised to have such radio stations until 1999. Finally, from 1994 to 1999, many Muslims complained of instances of frustrating redtape on the basis of their religious and / or ethnic affiliations (e.g. control of national identity cards at the entrance of mosques, confiscation of such cards on the basis of the names sounding like those of Malians, Guineans or Burkinabè, etc., often forcing the concerned individuals to pay bribes to get their cards back). These imbalances were partly due to the continuation of the policies of the former coloniser (i.e. France) and the recent political situation in Côte d'Ivoire (1994–1999; see section on politics of ethnicity and language in Côte d'Ivoire).

Religious affiliation in Côte d'Ivoire has great social significance, for it is an undergirding factor in language spread and language choice. Just as Arabic is the language of Islam in other parts of the world, Dyula is the language of choice for Muslims in Côte d'Ivoire. It is also the language of choice of a great proportion of the foreign-born population, most of whom, incidentally, are of the Muslim faith. Christians, however, do not have a unifying language. The churches of various denominations use the language of the area where they are located, when they do not resort to Standard French. (Some parts of the liturgy are still carried out in Latin.) Ethnic and religious affiliations have become hot socio-political issues over the last few years (1994–1999), as is shown in the following section.

The Politics of Ethnicity and Language in Côte d'Ivoire

As Côte d'Ivoire faced the worst economic recession of its history in the early 1990s, the former President, Félix Houphouët-Boigny, decided to appoint a technocrat to reform the economy. Alassane Dramane Ouattara, then Governor of the Central Bank of West African States (BCEAO), became the country's first Prime Minister, on 7 November 1990, even though he was widely believed to be from Burkina Faso.[9] Félix Houphouët-Boigny was known to have made such appointments in the past. Even though he was clearly approaching the end of his reign, he had such a grip on the national politics that no one dared to question his choice.

The experience lasted three years until Félix Houphouët-Boigny died on 7 December 1993. Then, in accordance with Article 11 of the Constitution, the President of the National Assembly, Henri Konan Bédié, took over as President of the country. Alassane Dramane Ouattara joined the International Monetary Fund as Deputy Director in 1994. Henri Konan Bédié was elected President in his own right in 1995.

In the meantime, some members of the only political party, the *Parti démocratique de Côte d'Ivoire-Rassemblement démocratique africain* (PDCI-RDA), dissatisfied with the refusal of the old guard in the party to bring about change, and unhappy about the way the former Prime Minister and his followers were treated, broke ranks and created a new opposition party called the *Rassemblement des républicains* (RDR). The latter was accused by the PDCI-RDA of being a party of disgruntled Muslim members from the north (the former Prime Minister is a Muslim from the north). Soon after this, as the new party membership started to grow, the RDR made overtures to the former Prime Minister, asking him to become its president, and when he seemed to acquiesce, accusations about his nationality began to resurface.

The Constitution was amended in 1995 and again in 1998 to redefine the conditions of eligibility for the highest office in the land. Some of the relevant sections of article 10 of the Constitution now read (see *Law* No 60–356 of 3 November 1960, last amended by *Law* No 98–387 of 2 July 1998):

> . . . A candidate in the presidential election must be forty years old at least and seventy-five years old at most. He must be Ivorian by birth, and his father and mother must also be Ivorians by birth. He must have been living in Côte d'Ivoire on a regular basis for ten years before the date of the elections.
> He must never have renounced his Ivorian citizenship . . . (author translation)

Hence, a concept known as '*Ivoirité*' ['Ivorianness'] and defined as 'a symbol of modernity, a lifestyle based on republican and democratic values . . . that generates a feeling of cultural belonging …' was developed (see *Jeune Afrique* 1999: 30–31).[10] Others, finding this concept divisive, suggested a concept of '*identité ivoirienne*' (Ivorian identity) instead, meaning 'the feeling of being and thinking as an Ivorian'. Henri Konan Bédié himself went on record, in a series of interviews in France and in an autobiography (compiled in the form of a long interview) entitled *Les chemins de ma vie*, asserting that Alassane Dramane Ouattara was Burkinabè and was not eligible to run for President in Côte d'Ivoire.

Furthermore, the Commission for Social and Cultural Affairs of the Economic and Social Council (*Conseil Economique et Social*) published an alarming report on immigration in Côte d'Ivoire in October 1998. The report argued that the proportion of immigrants in the country had risen by 70% within thirteen years (from 1975 to 1988), seriously affecting the nation's religious make-up and balance. It argued for instance that the Muslim population had risen from 25% of the total population to almost 40%, and concluded that the situation was at a 'threshold of tolerance' that required radical solutions. The proportion of Muslims in the total population had in fact increased by 87.3% from 1975 to 1988 (i.e. from 33.3% of the total population in 1975 to 38.7% in 1988). Soon after the publication of this report, around 3000 fishermen from Mali (called 'Bozos') and 12,000 Burkinabè farm labourers were expelled from two localities in the east and the south-west of the country (Ayamé and Tabou) for what was generally reported as land disputes.

One should note that, as in the past, the alarmist discourse on immigration coincided with the rapid erosion of the economic gains made since the devaluation of the currency in January 1994. The IMF was openly expressing its concern about the mismanagement of public finances and warning of its plan not to renew the adjustment programme, as non-budgeted expenditure reached US$270 million, or 5% of the country's exports. At the end of 1996, outstanding internal debt was up to US$170 million, and direct and indirect embezzlements of public funds were estimated at more than US$3 billion. By the end of 1997, the economy of the country was again in the red. In September 1998, a review of the adjustment programme revealed that the problems of mismanagement still remained. An estimated US$200 million were missing from the accounts of the *Caisse de stabilisation et de soutien des prix des produits agricoles* (Caistab – a stabilisation clearing house established to guarantee the prices of cocoa and coffee paid to the farmers), while major banks were facing a cashflow crisis with over US$220 million in bad debts. In February and March 1999 the IMF concluded that negotiations for the second year of the adjustment programme put in place in 1998 could not be implemented, putting US$800 million of debt reduction for the country at risk.

The debate had reached such levels of passion on both sides that, on 24 December 1999, the army stepped in and forced Konan Bédié out of office; thus, carrying out the first coup d'état in the forty years of independence of the country and putting an end to what was known as the 'Ivorian exception'.[11] Indeed, until then, Côte d'Ivoire was the only country of the region not to have experienced a coup d'état. At the time of writing, the Constitution of the country, and all the fundamental institutions of the Republic have been suspended until further notice. All the opposition parties have been invited to contribute to a redrafting of the Constitution and a transitional government has been formed.

This situation highlights the politics of ethnicity in Côte d'Ivoire and its significance for the politics of language in the country. Dyula suffers not only from the stigma of being a language of 'Muslims', but also of 'foreigners' (43% of the total population in 1993 and 73.3% of the immigrant population), and there is an underlying fear of being overrun by people, some of whom may have only recently migrated from Burkina Faso, Mali and Guinea. The second generation of immigrants in Côte d'Ivoire, those who are legally entitled to claim Ivorian citizenship, represented 42% of all immigrants in 1988 and 49% in 1993. Article 10 of the amended Constitution disenfranchises all these individuals and also the children of any Ivorian who happens to be married to a 'foreigner'.

Thus language, in many ways, is still associated with the land in which it originated or where it is used as a first language, and not necessarily with all the people who use it. In this case, Dyula is associated with the Muslim religion, even though not all native speakers of Dyula are Muslims. Clearly the link between ethnicity, language, nationality and political leanings and/or affiliation is not that simple, but the confusion does exist and is being exploited for political ends. Although the uneasy feeling created by the debate on the nationality of political candidates and that of their parents may not directly affect the maintenance and spread of a language like Dyula, it is certain to exacerbate the suspicion that the choice of a national language has the potential to lead to social upheaval, and may be that fork in the road that forever cancels the chances for Dyula to become accepted as a national language in Côte d'Ivoire.

Needless to say, card-carrying members and sympathisers of RDR, some opposition parties, Ivorians from the north of the country, and more specifically native speakers of Dyula, and Muslims, see the amendment to the Constitution, the resorting to concepts such as 'ivoirité' and 'identité ivoirienne', and the publication of speculative reports such as the one written by the Commission for Social and Cultural Affairs of the Economic and Social Council as political manoeuvres to keep one individual, namely Alassana Dramane Ouattara, from running for President and, more generally, as exclusive and xenophobic.

Therefore, it is fair to say that the politics of ethnicity and language in Côte d'Ivoire, as it has been expressed over the last few years, owes its origins to the existing and somewhat deeply ingrained language attitudes that are partly inherited from the colonial discourse on local ethnic groups, religions and languages. Long after the country gained its independence from France the Ivorian élite, in order to strengthen and maintain its hold on power, has perpetuated the long-standing negative biases about the purported inferiority of the local languages. These have influenced the language attitudes of the average person in Côte d'Ivoire. The next section provides an overview of these language attitudes.

Language Attitudes in Côte d'Ivoire

In reply to a question on the place of African languages in African literature, Robert Cornevin (cited in Djité, 1997), a well-known French historian, recently gave the following answer: 'Literature in African languages? You've got to be joking! It can only be second rate. . . . If you teach your child in Baulé, s/he will remain in the village.' Then in response to the question: 'What you are saying is quite serious! If Baulé were the official language, why would this be a problem?' he replied: 'Aah! So you want to impose Baulé on the other ethnic groups? That will be another form of imperialism.' It is fitting to open a discussion on language attitudes with a statement such as this one, a statement that is very revealing of the attitude of many African specialists (sometimes called 'Africanists'), when they are confronted with the issue of language planning in developing countries like Côte d'Ivoire.

The rationale underlying Cornevin's argument is accepted and perpetuated by the élite, and such attitudes are deeply ingrained in the psyche of the layman. As a case in point, a study of young Baulé speakers (Marcomer, 1968), commissioned by the French Ministry of Cooperation, showed that, when asked about the language they would choose if it were absolutely necessary for all Ivorians to speak the same language, 73% indicated that they preferred Standard French and only 1 per cent preferred Dyula. A similar study of young Dida speakers (Ferrari, 1971) showed that the majority of the respondents (73.7%) said that they would choose Standard French over any local language. In a reinterpretation of this study, Duponchel (1971: 275) found that 29% of the respondents believed that 'Standard French is the language of the white man' and therefore 'the language of progress and modern life', whilst 21% said that 'French is the language of power, happiness, and socioeconomic mobility', and 2% agreed that 'French is a neutral language that does not create ethnic rivalries'. Duponchel concluded from this that:

- the spread of Standard French was on the rise geographically and socially;
- African multilingualism was on the decrease, while multilingualism in Standard French and an African language was on the rise; and
- Standard French was spreading faster than Dyula, even though it still ranked second to Dyula as a preferred lingua franca.

Duponchel also noted that the prestige of Standard French was so great that many parents were speaking Standard French to their children, in lieu of their mother tongue. According to him, all the signs were pointing to an overwhelming preference for Standard French over Dyula and all the other local languages. And this, in his view, explained why so many Ivorians were now making the French language their own, injecting into it some of their own creativity (see section on Popular French). Duponchel fails to say that some of this effect is a direct outcome of official and unofficial French efforts to promote their language in the country.

Although this statement was made in 1971, it could be argued that language attitudes have not changed significantly since then. The fact that Standard French remains the sole language of education from kindergarten onwards is a major contributing factor to these attitudes towards language. The reactions of laymen to various reports or newspaper articles on the education system in which the issue of the introduction of a mother tongue is mentioned also indicate that the general public is of the view that the élite is out to trick them into second-rate education. The more selective the education system becomes, the more determined parents are that their children should be successful within that system. Education in French is seen as the only way to move up the socio-economic ladder; put colloquially, the greater the pain, the greater the gain.

Nevertheless, many students do not achieve their goal and are left by the wayside. (See the school dropout rates in the section on the spread of Standard

French.) And even though they have a high regard for Standard French and declare that they are fluent in it, the fact of the matter is that, having failed to achieve a reasonable level of education, they resort to Dyula or Popular French for inter-ethnic communication. Whilst some speakers of Standard French can code-switch to Popular French, the reverse does not necessarily apply. Such language attitudes, formed in part by the absence of a clearly defined overt language policy, provide an indication of why there has been very little movement in the area of language policy and language-in-education planning in Côte d'Ivoire, as is shown in the following section.

Language Policy and Language-in-education Planning

Introduction

In one of the earliest definitions of language planning, Jernudd and Das Gupta (1971: 79) wrote that language planning is 'the organised pursuit of solutions to language problems, typically at the national level'. Since then, many have acknowledged the central role played by government authorities in this process. Hence Weinstein (1980: 37) suggests that language planning is 'a government authorised long term sustained and conscious effort to alter a language itself or to change a language's functions in a society for the purpose of solving communication problems'.

Kaplan (1990: 4) concurs with this definition but notes his suspicion about the motives for language planning. According to him, language planning is

> . . . an attempt by some organised body (most commonly, some level of government) to introduce systematic language change for some more or less clearly articulated purpose (commonly stated in altruistic terms but often not based on altruistic intents).

In developing countries such as Côte d'Ivoire, it is almost always the case that governments play a major role in all aspects of development. Language policy, and especially language-in-education policy and planning, is one of the key strategies available to governments to set the rules, in order to help achieve the desired objectives. However, these governments are often torn between the need to equip their citizens with a medium of communication that will help reinforce national integration and the temptation to encourage them to acquire languages that will make them members of the wider international community. Myers-Scotton (1993) has shown that governments and the élite may only be interested in what reinforces their status, thereby purposefully minimising national integration through a language policy or strategy that maintains language barriers – Myers-Scotton calls this 'élite closure'.

Theoretically, government authorities have four choices. These are to:

(1) promote the language of the former coloniser exclusively as the national and official language;
(2) give the same status (national and/or official) to both the language of the former coloniser and (a) local language(s);
(3) promote the local language(s) exclusively as (the) national and official language(s); or

Table 5 Examples of national languages in French-speaking Africa according to Calvet (1994)

Country	Approximate number of languages	National languages
1. Benin	52	19
2. Burkina Faso	70	All local languages
3. Cameroon	230	All local languages
4. Republic of Central Africa	65	1 (Standard French)
5. Congo	30	2
6. Côte d'Ivoire	65	4
7. Gabon	50	None
8. Guinea	20	8
9. Mali	12	All local languages
10. Niger	8	All local languages
11. Senegal	20	6
12. Chad	100	?
13. Togo	40	2
14. Democratic Republic of Congo (Zaïre)	250	4

(4) select a neutral language, neither indigenous nor deriving from the former colonial power (e.g. Swahili).

Whilst option 4 may be feasible in polities such as Rwanda, Burundi and the Democratic Republic of Congo (formerly Zaïre) where Swahili is quite widespread as a lingua franca, it may not be the most practical solution in the case of Côte d'Ivoire or any other West African country, for Swahili has not spread this far north. At best, it would inject some balance in the language/power nexus, as everyone would have to start learning a new language from scratch. However, from the cost-benefit point of view of language planning, it would probably be the most expensive of the four options. Option 3, would be just as short-sighted as option 1, which aims to promote only the language of the former coloniser as the national and official language. The latter option would theoretically commit most local languages to almost certain extinction, while the former would jeopardise the chance of maintaining an excellent tool of international communication.[12] This dilemma has been characterised by Fishman (1968) as 'nationalism' versus 'nationism', nationalism being 'symbolic' in nature, whilst nationism is seen as being 'pragmatic'. Forty years of imposition of the language of the former coloniser in Third World countries and other parts of the world (e.g. the forty-year long imposition of Russian in Eastern European states), suggests that while nationism may be pragmatic in the short term, it can have undesirable consequences in the long term, as the language situations in many developing countries, including Côte d'Ivoire, show.

In fact, a summary of the statistics available in the late 1970s indicated that 37 African countries were committed to using more of their national languages in the curriculum to counterbalance the dominance of the language of the former coloniser, and four others had embarked upon a study phase prior to doing so (see Poth, 1990: 51). These statistics also suggested that 41 out of 52 African states had given, or were about to give, full teaching status to national languages in their education systems. To date, the only African countries that are known to have promoted local languages to the status of official languages are Ethiopia (Amharic), Eritrea (Tigrinya), Somalia (Somali), Tanzania (Kiswahili), Burundi (Kirundi), Rwanda (Kinyarwanda) and the Republic of Central Africa (Sango). This explains why Calvet (1994: 67) suggests that a closer look at the language policies of French-speaking countries in Africa is a cruel eye-opener that reveals the absence of any planned language policy. Table 5 shows that, when most of these countries do not simply retain Standard French as the national and official language – as is the case for Gabon and the Republic of Central Africa – some go so far as to declare all local languages as national languages (as in the case of Burkina Faso and Cameroon, Mali and Niger). It remains to be seen to what extent the latter option is manageable.[13]

Language policy and language-in-education planning in Côte d'Ivoire: The art of living on borrowed tongue

The subjugation of Côte d'Ivoire by France in 1893 was not only political and economic; it was cultural and linguistic as well. The colonial discourse on the local languages and the linguistic studies of that period were generally contemptuous of all things indigenous. The purported absence of a written medium was used as proof of the inherent inferiority of these languages.[14] The imposition of Standard French was legitimised along the lines of the 'civilised' versus the 'uncivilised', and the French colonial administration had no doubt that they were conferring the greatest gift possible upon their subjects in the colony. All the necessary coercive measures were put in place to enforce the systematic use of Standard French (e.g. the decree of 1 May 1924). Even the domains of use of the local languages were carefully specified.[15]

At the Brazzaville Conference of 8 February 1944, a recommendation was made supporting French as the exclusive language for all teaching in schools, and for any pedagogical use of local languages in the classroom to be completely forbidden in both public and private schools throughout all French-speaking Africa. As one General Inspector of Education put it: 'The objective is not to protect the originality of the colonised, but to elevate them to our level' (quoted in Bokamba, 1991). Article 2 of the decree of 22 August 1945 on the reorganisation of teaching at primary school level within French Western Africa (AOF) stipulated that: 'The main objective of teaching at primary school level is to influence, direct and speed up the evolution of the African population. This teaching shall only be dispensed in the French language' (*Journal officiel de l'Afrique occidentale française*, 15 September 1945: 707) (author translation).

The consequences of this policy, at the end of the colonial period, were the total neglect of the local languages in terms of language planning and language-in-education planning. Furthermore, a number of preconceived ideas were generated about these local languages, most of which are still very much alive in the minds and language attitudes of Ivorians. These include the beliefs that:

- the local languages can not express modern scientific concepts;
- the development and choice of any of these languages as a national or official language can only lead to a 'tribal' war; and
- the language of science and development and the only language of neutrality in Côte d'Ivoire is Standard French.

When Côte d'Ivoire became independent on 7 August 1960, following an agreement with France on 12 July 1958, the change from colonial to independent status did not affect the status quo, especially insofar as the cultural and linguistic policies were concerned. It was felt that there were too many local languages with only a few native speakers each – speakers who could neither understand nor tolerate each other. In addition, none of these local languages was standardised, while Standard French, a proven medium of science and technology and a tool of international communication, was readily available, at least to the political élite. Hence the first article of the Constitution promulgated official monolingualism (and still does!) by stating that 'The official language is French'.[16]

Some in the new ruling class and élite were – and many still are – even more resistant to change than the former colonisers and have been quoted as saying that the promotion of local languages would have no value beyond a sentimental ego trip. The former President of Côte d'Ivoire described it as: 'a folklore that reminds us of the shame of the past and paralyses our economy' (cited in Person, 1981). According to the President of the National Assembly at the time, 'French .. . has been a factor of cohesion . . . in Côte d'Ivoire, where it has promoted the coexistence of more than a hundred ethnic groups' (cited in Turcotte, 1981).[17]

The choice of the French language at independence was believed to be a positive step that would discourage the rise of any ethnic or language particularities, promote the feeling of belonging together as citizens of one unified nation, and allow direct access to international communication and exchange. This approach was arguably in line with Article 6 of the Constitution that pointedly stated: 'the law will punish any particularistic propaganda of an ethnic or racial nature' (author translation). In view of this policy, some observers thought that Côte d'Ivoire was beyond the point of no return insofar as the adoption of the French language was concerned (*'le seuil de l'irréversibilité'*; see Dannaud, 1965). In other words, a bright future was being predicted for Standard French in Côte d'Ivoire.

However, at almost the same time, the idea of introducing local languages in the education system was being seriously considered. At the fourth Congress of the *Parti démocratique de Côte d'Ivoire* (PDCI) – at that time the only political party – the then Minister of National Education, reporting on the state of the Ivorian education system, acknowledged that:

> . . . the school, instead of being a factor of development, as its true vocation should be, has reached a point where it is tearing apart the fabric of our society and alienating the individual. It has become an obstacle to harmonious evolution and political equilibrium, for it does not integrate the child into the traditional environment, but gives him a means to escape it, without providing him with what s/he needs to find his/her place in the mainstream of modern society. (*Proceedings of the Fourth Congress of the*

PDCI-RDA, Maison du Congrès de Treichville, Abidjan; cited in Turcotte, 1981) (author translation)

In 1972, a National Commission was created to revise the education system in Côte d'Ivoire and adapt it to the national objectives. Among other things, a main objective of the reforms was the integration of the local languages in the education system, as a first step towards a new language policy. After several years of work, the National Assembly adopted a proposal on the Reforms of Teaching on 16 August 1976 to:

> ... ensure the provision of an education based on the national objectives of development, achieve the sociocultural integration of the citizens in the national community, as well as in the universal civilisation, and contribute in the building of the Nation through the affirmation of the Ivorian personality, the adaptation of school programs to the Ivorian and African realities. (*Law on the Teaching Reform*, p. 1, Assemblée Nationale, 16 August 1976; cited in Turcotte, 1981) (author translation)

The Institute of Applied Linguistics of Abidjan was called on to devise and implement a plan for the integration of the local languages into the education system. The Institute was asked, among other things, to 'provide the descriptions and codifications of all the languages, as well as write the grammars, lay out the lexicon, produce the teaching materials and encourage literary publications in these languages and protect their cultural character.' (Article 68 of the *Law on the Teaching Reform*, p. 13, Assemblée Nationale, 16 August 1976) (author translation). As a result, a number of research projects were carried out and descriptions of some languages were made available. Hence, Baulé, Bété and Dyula received some special attention and were taught at the *Centre de Recherche et d'Expérimentation Audiovisuel* (CERAV) of the National University for a number of years.

However, whilst the Institute of Applied Linguistics of Abidjan was advocating mother tongue education, the general approach to the language question by the Ivorian government and the main aid donors (i.e. the French government and the *Agence de Coopération Culturelle et Technique* – ACCT[18]) was more concerned about teaching methodologies and materials development in Standard French. It was not surprising therefore that, by the early 1980s, there was no more discussion of mother tongue education in Côte d'Ivoire. Instead, the pendulum had swung back and all the research carried out placed more emphasis on how best to teach Standard French, now considered an African language (Dumont, 1990) and perceived as the cornerstone of development in all the former French colonies.

Conclusion

In view of the legislative and linguistic work done to date, there is no doubt that government authorities in Côte d'Ivoire understand the centrality of language in the democratic governance and socio-economic development of the country, and that they realise that it is in everyone's interest to foster the spread of (a) widely spoken language(s), if maximum national integration is to be achieved in the long term. That is why the decision to put the emphasis back on Standard French as the official language and sole language of education in Côte d'Ivoire can only be seen as a strategy to protect the privileges of these government authorities and other élites, and to limit the effective active participation in the public domain to a select few, namely, the élite. Indeed, this decision is the source of major inequities, empowering a small group of people, while disempowering the majority and widening the socio-economic divide. Myers-Scotton (1993) has argued that the political élite are partly exercising power through the control of language, thus taking advantage of the language handicap of the masses. The active promotion of Standard French some 40 years after independence perpetuates a linguistic and cultural imbalance and can be construed as self-inflicted 'linguicism' (Phillipson, 1992: 47),[19] especially when one takes a closer look at the existing dynamics of language spread in the country. The following section provides a detailed discussion of language spread and maintenance in Côte d'Ivoire.

Language Spread

Introduction

In 1977, Heine (1977: 9) predicted that 'by the year 2000, about 60 per cent of the African population will still be ignorant of the language which is used to govern, administer, and educate them'. Over the years, many authors have shown the truth of this statement as applied to Côte d'Ivoire and other developing countries in Africa. Although Standard French is generally assumed to be the major medium of communication in Côte d'Ivoire, and despite its official status and prestige, one can safely say that it has not established itself as the dominant language of everyday communication. The discussion of language spread in this section suggests, as was argued by Djité (1988a), Hattiger (1983), and Lafage (1979), that the language situation in the country remains very fluid and dynamic and points in a direction other than the one which had been predicted all along. This raises the question of why the official language is not being learnt. Understanding language contacts and language spread in a country requires an integration and analysis of what Kaplan (1990: 10) calls 'the forces that are already in motion [or the] existing forces'. In the case of Côte d'Ivoire, the 'forces in motion' include the following extra-linguistic factors:

(1) Illiteracy in French in the general population (59.9%) and the resulting lack of knowledge of the official language has led to a language handicap for the majority of the population and a major communication gap between them and the educated élite.
(2) Internal migration (also known as rural exodus) and international immigration (mostly from neighbouring countries), and the resulting inter-linguistic communication patterns, increase the horizontal spread of the local lingua francas among the masses (e.g. Dyula).
(3) A combination of both illiteracy in French and the continued influx of migrants, who currently represent 30% of the total population and most of whom, given the make-up of their socio-economic, linguistic and religious backgrounds, assure that this population also mainly resorts to the dominant lingua francas in their inter-ethnic communication (and especially to Dyula).

(4)   Rapid urbanisation since 1950, bringing together people from different
      language and cultural backgrounds – including migrants, assures the
      continuation of the same result as in (2) and (3) above. This urban popula-
      tion grew at an average rate of 11.5% per year until 1965 and at about 8% per
      year from 1966 to 1988. In 1975, 46% of the Ivorian-born, and 75% of the
      foreign-born migrants living in the urban centres were illiterate in Standard
      French, while 58% of the total population of Abidjan (20% of the total popu-
      lation of the country) were illiterate in Standard French. In 1987, roughly
      50% of the total population lived in urban centres and were concentrated in
      the two largest cities (Abidjan and Bouaké). Hence the process of language
      spread (especially the spread of lingua francas) among the masses has
      been – and is continually being – reinforced.[20]

These 'forces in motion', in addition to the 'existing forces', have a tendency to
confine Standard French to a separate horizontal communication network that
functions primarily at the élite level and in special domains such as administration and justice.

The spread of Standard French

When the colonial administration decided to impose Standard French as the
official language in Côte d'Ivoire, it was assumed that this language would
spread quickly and, by so doing, would unify the different ethnic groups in the
country. However, the élitist education system put in place during the colonial
era, the desire of the colonial administration to keep the number of literate locals
to a strict minimum, and the selective education system adopted since independence, have all helped to undermine this original objective. Instead, the system has
fed the communication crisis by producing graduates whose talents do not fit the
economic and social needs of the polity, whilst disempowering many in the
population (i.e. women, farmers, labourers, etc.) who constitute the great majority of the workers producing goods and services. Under French colonial rule, this
type of education system produced, at best, a few hundred civil servants capable
of holding senior management positions (in some colonies such as the former
Belgian Congo – which became Zaïre and is now known as the Democratic
Republic of Congo – there were less than ten such civil servants).[21]
      These factors have been compounded by the economic crisis of the last two
decades. This, in turn, has eroded the government's ability to fund and manage
education properly and has resulted in a lack of teaching materials, the worsen-
ing of teacher/student ratios at primary, secondary and tertiary levels, record
school drop-out rates and increasing disparities in education between the rural
and urban population, girls and boys, women and men, the haves_and the
have-nots. Ki-Zerbo (1990: 78) notes that only one out of four boys and one out of
five girls, or 20% of the total population, make it beyond primary school, and
only about 20 out of 1000, or 2% out of the remaining 20%, make it beyond high
school.[22] More than 50% of this 2% quit school within the first year of higher
education and only 20% out of this 2% graduate from university. The education
system is skewed in favour of the urban centres (50% of high school students)
and sometimes the largest city alone (Abidjan), where, until recently (1990), the
entire university system was concentrated.[23] These apparent geographical ineq-

uities also result in some socio-professional or ethnic groups being more favoured than others, leading to a class system. For instance, whilst only 10% of farmers have been through the education system, and their children make up only 25% of students in the early years of high school, they constitute 70 to 80% of the population and generate 77% of the gross domestic product – and thus most of the funds available for education.

It is therefore still the case – as it has been for a long time now in Côte d'Ivoire – that access to public functions and upward socio-economic mobility are determined by one's competency in Standard French, which is proportional to the level of one's education. In spite of this reality, the suspicion remains that mother tongue education would create two unequal education systems, one for the masses and the other for the élite, thereby denying the former equal opportunity, and working in favour of the maintenance of Standard French. In this regard, it is interesting to note that the issue of the use of African languages in education in Francophone Africa was viewed with the same suspicion by the African representatives when it was brought up in the French Parliament during the colonial era. This suspicion, as well as the arguments of 'avoidance of tribal conflicts' and 'access to modernity through a language of wider communication', still plays a major role in the maintenance of the status quo in most of Francophone Africa including Côte d'Ivoire.

Unfortunately, even when they have struggled and made it through the system, school and university graduates are still confronted with large-scale unemployment. In 1985, over 230,000 graduates between the ages of 16 and 29 were unemployed. Although the ratio of medical doctors is seven per 100,000 people in the country, graduates from the Medical School can not find jobs. Moreover, even though illiteracy in French is near crisis level and schools are forced to close classrooms for lack of teachers, graduates from teachers' training colleges (primary and high school) cannot find jobs. Despite the student/teacher ratio reaching unmanageable proportions at local universities (45,000 students for 887 teaching staff at the university of Cocody alone),[24] qualified Ivorian nationals wanting to teach in higher education in Côte d'Ivoire find it very difficult to obtain positions. These problems have largely led to the academic year (October to June) being extended every year since 1990 (until September), due to several strikes by students and teaching staff alike, unhappy with their study or working conditions. In 1999, the Vice-chancellors of the three universities (Cocody, Abobo-Adjamé and Bouaké) and the two units of higher education (Korhogo and Daloa) declared the academic year null and void, the only exceptions being the Faculties of Medicine in Cocody and Bouaké, the Centre for Veterinary Sciences of Bouaké, the third year of the unit of higher education of Korhogo and students who had submitted their theses for the Master's degree. The cancellation of an academic year had only happened once in the past (1997) and that was limited to the Faculty of Medicine of the University of Cocody.

Although one cannot attribute all these problems to the imposition of Standard French, many analysts of the education system have suggested over the years that the elitist approach to the language-in-education policy that it engenders is part and parcel of the ensuing difficulties. As it is now clear that mastery of Standard French alone will not necessarily change the lives of the people, they seem to be learning the languages they feel it is in their socio-economic interest to learn (see Myers-Scotton, 1982: 85). In this case it seems that the incentive to add Standard French as a language is being weakened by the contradictions inherent in an elitist system of education and a centralised system of administration. The poorly educated are ill-prepared to add Standard French, while the educated ones who are unemployed realise that it is not likely to alleviate their current predicament in any significant way. So when all these people (presumably of different language backgrounds) come together in large urban centres such as Abidjan, and find that they cannot effectively communicate in Standard French for reasons that are beyond their control, they overwhelmingly resort to one or the other of the two dominant lingua francas: Ivorian or Popular French (henceforth Popular French) and Dyula. The less educated are regularly spoken to, and often demand to be spoken to by the educated, in one of these lingua francas in their day-to-day activities (e.g. transactions in the market place, exchanges between passengers and cab drivers/bus drivers). The educated, and especially the politicians, tend to code-switch, for their instructions and/or appeals to the less educated to be successful. But what is the nature, significance and impact of these lingua francas and what are their future prospects?

The spread of Popular French

Popular French is a local, simplified, non-élite variety of Standard French characterised by a simplified verb system, the general absence of articles, phonetic and prosodic systems heavily influenced by transfers from the local languages, and a lexicon and syntax loaded with colourful borrowings from other local languages. Some examples of Popular French are presented in Table 6.

While some expressions in Popular French (such as the ones in Table 6) are just cases of syntactic simplification (e.g. *I'veut mouiller mon pain*) or transfer from a local language (e.g. *On ne montre pas la route de son village par la main gauche*), others are much more complex, not only in structure, but in socio-linguistic and cultural terms. Such linguistic development can be seen in the two following examples:

Table 6 Some examples of Popular French

Popular French	Standard French	English
C'est versé à Abidjan	C'est chose courante à Abidjan	This is a common thing in Abidjan
On ne montre pas la route de son village par la main gauche	Il faut laver son linge sale en famille	It doesn't do to wash one's dirty linen in public
I' veut mouiller mon pain	Il veut me créer des ennuis	He wants to get me into trouble
C'est une question FRAR	C'est une question difficile	This is a difficult question
En même temps est mieux (or dès que, dès que, or demain, c'est aujourd'hui)	Il vaut mieux le faire maintenant	It is best to do it now
Tout près n'est pas loin	Maintenant	Let's do it here and now
Tu veux me faire encaisser	Tu veux me rendre jaloux	You're trying to make me feel envious

(1) *La traversée du guerrier* (meaning 'the crossing of the road by the warrior'). Whilst this expression is in perfectly good Standard French, its semantic field lies completely outside the imagination of any Francophone or French person. It refers to a sort of 'Russian roulette' played by the unemployed youth in Abidjan, whereby they blindfold themselves and cross a busy high-way during the rush hour. Hence the 'warrior' in *La traversée du guerrier* is the blindfolded young person who dares to play this game.

(2) *Bôrô d'enjaillement* (meaning literally 'bags of enjoyment' or 'lots of enjoyment'). Here, the expression, a mixture of Dyula (*Bôrô* for 'bag') and English (*enjaillement* for 'enjoyment'), refers to an equally dangerous game of 'Russian roulette' whereby the unemployed youth climb on top of a moving bus and then jump across onto another bus going in the same direction or in an opposite direction. The English word 'enjoyment' has been phonetically adapted to the sound system of Popular French.

Hence beyond its communicative role, Popular French is a means of expressing the inner soul or collective psychological state of mind of the masses, especially for the youth. In the late 1970s and early 1980s it was believed that this variety of French was spoken by 29.2% of the total population (Lafage, 1979; Hattiger, 1983). This proportion has almost certainly increased exponentially since then; unfortunately no research has been carried out in this area, and there are no data to support such a claim.

Popular French is also believed to carry the marker 'illiterate' and to be essentially limited to urban centres, where it is used mostly by labourers and construction workers. If the latter part of this assertion is near the truth, a closer look at the language creativity mentioned above suggests that there may be more to this language variety than meets the eye. The introduction of another foreign language such as English (as in *Bôrô d'enjaillement*) may be an indication of some formal education on the part of the speakers of Popular French. Furthermore, Popular French is increasingly being adopted by the general population outside the large urban centres, not just as a fashion statement, but as a necessary, useful and genuine means of communication and socialisation. Although not normally used in written form, Popular French has been used over the last twenty years as the language of various comic strips and weekly columns such as *Dago à Abidjan* (Dago in Abidjan) or *C'est moi Moussa* (It's me Moussa), albeit in a somewhat exaggerated form.

The spread of Dyula

The majority of labourers and construction workers in the urban and rural centres, mostly foreign-born, are also proficient in Dyula, a lingua franca learnt in informal contexts from friends, traders and co-workers.

Historically, Dyula is a dialect of Mandingo, a linguistic group spread over many countries in West Africa, including Burkina Faso, Côte d'Ivoire, Gambia, Ghana, Guinea, Mali, Senegal and Sierra Leone. It is mutually intelligible with Bambara and Malinké, the other two dialects of Mandingo. Most Mandé people, although they have different histories and myths of origin and different religions (Christians, Muslims and practitioners of traditional religions) speak variants of this common language, sometimes referred to as Mandé-kan (*kan* meaning language). The Malinké have adapted tenets of Islam to their native beliefs, while the Dyula are strongly Muslim; so much so that many Bambara, when they convert to Islam, refer to themselves as Dyula. Similarly, other Muslim Malinké are generally referred to as Dyula in recognition of their Islamic beliefs.

The Mandé are traders, artisans, and cultivators and have a history of itinerant preaching, teaching and trading. In their heyday they founded three large empires: the Soninké Empire of Ghana (from about the fourth to the 13th century), the Malinké Empire of Mali (between the 13th and the 15th centuries) and the Muslim Empire of Kong in the north-central region of Côte d'Ivoire (in the early 18th century). The term Dyula is used to refer to the descendants of the Bambara, Malinké and Dyula from all of these empires.

The spread of Dyula started in the Middle Ages with the Empire of Mali and the development of the commercial routes in West Africa. From north to south, the Dyula traders carried salt from Taghaza, on the northern edge of the Sahara, and brought back gold and kola nuts from south to north. Dyula was also spread south through Islam, thanks to the largely Muslim Lebanese, Syrian, Malian and Guinean migrants who control the commerce and transportation businesses, two flourishing sectors of the economy in which Dyula is the dominant language in all transactions. These migrant workers are also predominant in the areas of goods and services (e.g. hotels and restaurants) and manual labour (cocoa and coffee plantations) and through them, Dyula is the dominant language in these domains. Most of the Sénufo (Gur) and Yakuba (Mandé) of Côte d'Ivoire are also Muslims.

Often described as a simplified and neutral form of the original language called Kanjè (or Kangbè, meaning 'the real language'), Dyula is seen as an easy language to learn and an overt symbol of group membership. Being closely identified with small businesses, Islam, and indentured labourers, Dyula has not had great prestige until recently, when some members of its community have become involved in national politics (e.g. Alassane Dramane Ouattara, the first Prime Minister of Côte d'Ivoire from 1990 to 1993). More importantly, the frequent use of Dyula by the political élite and by advertising agencies on radio and television has conferred upon it a certain degree of recognition, if not prestige, as the language most accessible to the majority of the people. Dyula is now spoken in almost every major city or village in the country and almost every town and hamlet has its own 'Dyula-bugu' or Dyula neighbourhood.

Conclusion

The exclusive promotion of Standard French in Côte d'Ivoire has contributed to a number of linguistic and social distortions and inequities (e.g. élite closure, illiteracy in French, an imbalance between school and real life, high school drop-out rates, high rates of unemployment) (see Bokamba, 1991; Ki-Zerbo, 1990). These conditions have given rise to a situation that has promoted the spread of Popular French and Dyula, rather than Standard French, a language planning result that is contrary to the language policy results politicians may have planned to achieve. This may be considered an instance of 'unplanned planning' (see Baldauf, 1993/94). Instead of the development of an increasingly Standard French dominant population, a hierarchical and systematic multilingual communication network has been set in motion, starting with the mother tongue in the family domain, the regional language for inter-ethnic communication at the rural and/or regional levels, the lingua francas and/or the official language at the urban and/or national levels. These vertical communication networks form the language repertoire of the average citizen, the official language being an élite horizontal network added to this language repertoire by the educated few.

In view of this situation, the student of language always looks at what the prospects are for language spread and maintenance. The following section examines this question in the case of Côte d'Ivoire.

Prospects for Language Spread and Maintenance

Introduction

The language profile and the process of language spread in Côte d'Ivoire that have been discussed in this monograph strongly suggest that the success or failure of a language policy depends in part on how realistically and effectively the linguistic capital of the majority of the people is recognised and integrated into the language plan. For language, in this context, is not just a commodity, but a means of belonging, of managing one's socio-cultural environment and an element of intergenerational understanding. It has a day-to-day reality and use for those who speak it and serves as a major mechanism to express and construct group solidarity. When these functions are negated by a lack of policy, it is often feared that the local languages will be threatened with extinction in the long term.

In this connection, at a recent conference on Language in the Twenty-first Century at the Whitney Center for the Humanities, Yale University (6–7 June 1999), William F. Mackey recalled a Rockefeller-funded symposium at the University of Wisconsin on the fate of minority languages in America during which most linguists present concluded that, on the face of the evidence available to them, most of these languages, including French, would not survive the 20th century. We all know that the status of French in Québec has been strengthened ever since. Mackey also recalled an earlier prediction (1840s) by a British colonial administrator who had witnessed the dismemberment of the Napoleonic empire, as well as a prediction made four centuries earlier by some English academics, who had all come to the conclusion that once people were better educated in Latin and French, English would not be needed as a language of learning (Mackey, 1999: 1)!

At the moment, in the case of Côte d'Ivoire, at least for the major languages, language death does not appear to be the most likely scenario. Clearly, a number of factors are currently working in favour of the maintenance and spread of these languages. Some of these factors are: illiteracy in French, migration and urbanisation.

Illiteracy in French, migration, urbanisation and language maintenance

One can safely say that, some forty years after independence, the expectations held for the spread of Standard French in Côte d'Ivoire have not come to fruition. Despite its continued imposition as the sole language of instruction, government, administration and the courts, illiteracy in French remains very high – 59.9% of the population above the age of fifteen (34% for men and 59.7% for women). In the current socio-economic, linguistic and cultural contexts, this situation is unlikely to change.

Even the noticeable increase in inter-ethnic marriages among – but not limited to – the middle and upper classes, and the resultant tendency to use French in the home, does not imply that it is always Standard French that is spoken or passed on to the younger generation. Although inter-ethnic marriages are also increasing among the lower class, especially in the cities, in most cases it is still either the lingua franca or one of the languages of the couple, or both the lingua franca and one of the languages of the couple that tend to be spoken in the home.

It appears that a number of factors militate in favour of the maintenance and spread of the local languages, especially the lingua francas. The continued flow and the nature of immigration from neighbouring countries, as well as the rapid urbanisation of the country (54.4% of the total population lives in urban centres) reinforce the maintenance and spread of these lingua francas. This can be illustrated by the fact that, outside of the official domains, even those who speak Standard French fluently, including European or French expatriates, now tend to use Popular French or Dyula in their interactions with the general public. Djité (1988b) has discussed the reactions of those who are spoken to in Standard French, especially when their interlocutors were obviously not 'foreigners'. Taxi drivers, shopkeepers and stallholders are no longer content to refer ironically to such interlocutors as 'Mr Grammar', meaning persons who are showing off their knowledge of Standard French, and/or overcharge them for their services; they now are more likely to pointedly ask them what they are trying to achieve by speaking Standard French through expressions such as:

- *Eh, affaire-là est déjà arrivé là-bas?* (Aren't you taking this a bit too far?).
- *Eh, je ne suis pas encore arrivé là-bas.* (Sorry, I'm not prepared to take this that far!).
- *Eh, affaire-là est deveni affaire de blanc?* (Sorry, this need not be a white man's business.)

Interestingly enough, these remarks are often made in Popular French. The discourse strategy – use of question forms or negative statements – is a rhetorical one. The interlocutor refuses to follow the speaker in his/her intention to use Standard French where a local lingua franca can be used. S/he is also refusing to venture into a register where the speaker will obviously have the upper hand and is inviting him/her to code-switch. The words *'là-bas'* ('too far' or 'that far' in the examples above) means 'out of my depth', and *'affaire de blanc'* ('white man's business') means 'let's keep it between us' or 'let's speak a language we both understand'.

Therefore, in contrast to the prospects for Standard French, the chances for the maintenance of the local languages and the development of lingua francas, such as Popular French and Dyula, are better than those of Standard French, for all the reasons previously mentioned. While Dyula is readily learnt and spoken across ethnic groups, there are still some reservations about it when it is put forward as a possible national language. The argument against Dyula is not so much in terms of the difficulty of choosing one local language over the others, as the traditional view would suggest. Instead, Dyula suffers from the stigma of being a language, or a variety of a language, shared with other neighbouring countries (i.e., Burkina Faso, Guinea and Mali) and, hence, spoken by an overwhelming number of migrants. The very make-up of the bulk of the flow of immigration into Côte d'Ivoire (i.e. source countries and ethnic background) which acts as a catalyst in the development and spread of the language also works against its widespread acceptance as a national language. This problem raises the much wider issue of national identity (as was discussed above in the section on the politics of ethnicity and language). However, it is the view of this author that Dyula is on the track of languages such as Tok Pisin in Papua New Guinea and Bislama in Vanuatu (see Crowley, 2000). Over time it will overcome the stigma of being a language of foreigners, of the illiterate in French, or of people of low status, as it continues to spread, and the political élite will then have no choice but to give it an official status.

Conclusion

In light of all the foregoing, many students of the sociology of language in Côte d'Ivoire have argued that:

- most languages in Côte d'Ivoire are relatively healthy;
- it is a little premature to talk about recording the local languages for future generations to marvel at in museums for they are very much alive and healthy; and therefore,
- any suggested language planning needs to strike a balance between the pragmatic need to have access to a language of wider communication and widespread local languages (such as Popular French and Dyula), taking into account social justice and equity.

However, other linguists like Chaudenson (1989: 117, 156) disagree with this view and believe that it is 'demagogic' to talk about the introduction of African languages in the education system. Chaudenson writes (p. 95):

> As painful as this may be for a number of African intellectuals, most of them are well aware that there is no better choice and, rather than dream of some impossible idyllic Africa, it is important and urgent to plan and manage to the best of their ability the current situation, in order to make a future possible. (Author translation)

Dumont (1990: 15) concurs with this view and writes that: 'These are rearguard battles; the outcome of which has been known for a very long time' (author translation).

It is interesting to note, however, that those who hold a different view are almost always linguists from the former colonial power. And yet, after all, it makes more economic sense to ask the 10–20% of the population (the élite minority) to add another language of wider communication than to expect 80% of the population to become literate in a language divorced from their cultural and social realities. Moreover, it would seem only natural to suggest that the local languages do have a place in a language plan, if one aims to involve the majority of the people in an integrated development. As Pyles (1979: 171) put it:

> Now objecting to linguistic change is like objecting to other facts of our exis-
> tence: it doesn't get one very far along the road to understanding. [. . .] It
> does little good to protest against the law of gravity, however inconvenient
> it may prove at times; as has been pointed out by an astute commentator on
> human folly, one doesn't repeal the law by stepping off a cliff, one merely
> demonstrates it.

Even Etiemblé, a fierce defender of the French language, wrote: 'That our love for
the French language, our will to defend it, and when necessary, to attack our
enemies, [should] not lead us to lose sight of history, and especially of the history
of languages' (cited in Hagège, 1987: 75) (author translation).

Education in Third World countries is a tool for moulding the future society
and a key to socio-economic development. Together with professional training,
it is central to a development policy, for the most important resources in any
developing country are its human resources. Many developing countries equate
modernisation with education in the language of the former coloniser; yet,
education cannot be defined just in terms of economic needs. If it is true that
knowledge is power (both economic and political), then the transmission of this
knowledge cannot be the preserve of a foreign language alone, no matter how
perfect that language may be. The cultural values and spiritual aspirations of the
people have to be taken into account. In other words, the continued exclusive use
of the language of the former coloniser in such domains as education, law, or
administration, condemns the overwhelming majority of the people to second-
class citizenship and disqualifies them from taking an active part in serious
national issues. As an old African proverb goes, 'sleeping in someone else's bed
(which is tantamount to sleeping on the ground)'. That having been said, considering the economic difficulties Côte d'Ivoire has been facing over the last two
decades and is likely to be confronted with over the best part of the next decade, it
is highly unlikely that the official approach to language policy and language-
in-education policy will change significantly in the foreseeable future.

Correspondence

Any correspondence should be directed to Paulin G. Djité, Chair, Division of
Languages and Linguistics, Faculty of Education, The Uniersity of Western
Sydney, Macarthur, PO Box 555, Campbelltown, NSW 2569, Australia
(paulin.djite@uws.edu.au).

Notes

1. While the editors have a policy of translating material, including common names, into
   their English equivalent, in this instance they note that since 1984, by an international
   decree adopted at the United Nations, Côte d'Ivoire is not to be translated into any
   other language.
2. A note of caution to the reader: It is always a great challenge to examine the language
   situation in polities such as Côte d'Ivoire for, as in many developing countries, the
   research is hindered by a dearth of reliable material. What little data there is, even and
   especially when these are official figures, is often not consistent. These contradictions
   in the figures are confusing both for the analyst and the reader. Furthermore, it is
   almost an oxymoron to speak of language planning in a polity like Côte d'Ivoire, when
   compared to a number of other polities in Africa, or just West Africa for that matter, as
   no formal language planning has ever taken place in this country. Nevertheless, there

has been some considerable debate on the merits of putting a language policy in place, especially in the 1970s, and research was carried out on the topic then and in the early 1980s. Unfortunately, those involved in such research, most of whom were foreign scholars (especially French 'Technical Assistants'), had left by the mid-eighties, as a result of the policy of progressive replacement of foreign expertise by local expertise. (This was called 'Ivorianisation'.) Finally, the political uncertainty and the economic difficulties faced by Côte d'Ivoire over the last decade and a half, and the social upheavals that have ensued, have led to major disruptions at all levels, and most importantly for this study, at the level of academic research. As a result, the research output by local scholars in all areas, including socio-linguistic research, was and remains very limited. In view of the difficult work conditions at universities where academic promotions have little or no coincidence with income, most local academics are deserting their offices and neglecting their research to engage in activities (private tuition, cab driving, contracts in the private sector, etc.) likely to improve their material status.

3. The first President of Côte d'Ivoire, Félix Houphouët-Boigny, took office in 1960 and served as Head of State for 33 years. He was succeeded after his death in December 1993 by the then President of the National Assembly, Henri Konan Bédié, who was thrown out of office by a military coup d'état on 24 December 1999. This was the first coup in the country since it gained its independence from France.

4. According to the *Fact Sheet* from the *African Development Bank*, this figure was 60% in 1995; see, http://www.afdb.org/. Also see *Atlapedia Online* according to which, in 1990, the literate population aged 15 or over was 53.8% of the total population.

5. The total public debt of the country is US$18 billion, the service of which represents 52% of the annual national budget.

6. The cocoa industry is a case in point. In 1999 the price of cocoa beans fell to 42 cents per kilo, down from 90 cents a kilo in 1989. Some farmers (in the city of Bongouano and in 12 villages around the city of M'batto) have started burning part of their crop to protest at this fall in prices (see 'Cacao ça brûle encore' in *Ivoir'Soir* of 14 December 1999: 1).

7. As a child, the author followed his father – an Agronomist and public servant, who used to be posted to a different town or region every two or three years – until he went away to High School. By that time, he had picked up three languages other than Standard French and Dyula.

8. There are also wide-ranging discrepancies among the figures available for the size of different religious groups. For example, according to *CIA – The World Factbook 1999*, 60% are Muslims, 22% are Christians and 18% follow indigenous religions. According to *Atlapedia Online*, 60% of the local population follow local native tribal beliefs, while 20% are Muslims and 20% are Christians.

9. Born in Dimbokro (Côte d'Ivoire), Alassane Dramane Ouattara spent most of his early years in primary and high school in Upper Volta (now Burkina Faso) where his father (believed to be from Kong, Côte d'Ivoire) was a traditional Chief. His mother is believed to be from Gbléléban (north-west of Côte d'Ivoire). Alassane Dramane Ouattara was awarded a scholarship for undergraduate and graduate studies in the United States as a citizen of Burkina Faso and began his professional career in banking at the IMF and the BCEAO again as a citizen of Burkina Faso. He acknowledged all this in his acceptance speech as President of the *Rassemblement des républicains* (RDR) and presidential candidate of this party for the elections of the year 2000, on 1 August 1999.

10. See *Jeune Afrique* 2005, 15–21 June 1999: 30–31. 'Ivoirité' was also defined as a 'concept for unity. . . the recognition of an Ivorian specificity and an expression of our will to accept that we are different from others. . . a call to patriotism. . . etc.' (cf 'L'ivoirité est une synthèse de la diversité culturelle ivoirienne et des valeurs de société spécifiques à la Côte d'Ivoire et non une disposition du droit positif' by Faustin Kouamé in *Le Democrate*, 12 October 1999: 1–7). The concept of 'Ivorian identity' was put forward on 4 August 1999 by the Minister for Presidential Affairs, Paul Akoto Yao, in an address to the Press Attachés of Embassies and International Organisations represented in Côte d'Ivoire (see *Le Jour* 1349 5 August 1999).

11. Following a demonstration that turned violent in October 1999, the whole leadership of the RDR was arrested and thrown in jail. The President of the RDR, Alassane Dramane Ouattara, accused of having forged his national identity card and those of his parents, was forced into a three-month exile in France as a warrant was issued for his arrest.

12. It is important to stress the word 'theoretically' here, as such approaches have not necessarily led to massive language death in most developing countries. (See also Crowley, 2000.) Certainly this has not been the case in Côte d'Ivoire.

13. Recent detailed descriptions of the sociolinguistic and language policy and planning situations are available for Malawi (Kayambazinthu, 1998), Mozambique (Lopes, 1998) and Botswana (Nyati-Ramahobo, 2000).

14. See Lebeuf (1965), Niangoran-Bouah (1984) and Battestini (1997) for a contrary view. Some better known examples of more recent writing systems in local languages in Côte d'Ivoire are the Bété script devised by F. B. Bouabré in 1956 and the Gouro script invented by B. Gouré.

15. The decree read as follows: 'French must be imposed on the largest number of natives and serve as a link-language in all French-speaking West Africa. It is not acceptable that, after forty years of occupation, the Chiefs with whom we deal on a daily basis can not converse with us directly' (author translation) (Decree of May 1924, cited in Turcotte, 1981).

16. The Constitution has been amended 12 times since 1960. It was last amended in July 1998, but this article was not altered. With the advent of the coup d'état by the military junta, the Constitution is again going to be amended in the course of 2000. The author doubts that the new amendments will have any effect on the first article. As a matter of fact, in its most recent proposals for a new Constitution, the largest opposition party, the Ivorian Popular Front (or FPI) also proposes in Article 36 that 'The official language is French'. (See 'Les propositions du FPI pour refonder la Côte d'Ivoire. La Constitution: Régime semi-présidentiel' in *Notre Voie*, No. 510, 22 and 23 January 2000: 1–24.)

17. A speech delivered by Phillipe Yacé at the opening of the Conference of the International Association of French-speaking Parliamentarians at the United Nations, New York, in April 1976. *Fraternité Matin*, 26 April 1976: 23–4.

18. Now called *Organisation internationale de la francophonie* (OIF). Its new General Secretary is the former General Secretary of the United Nations, Mr Boutros Boutros-Ghali.

19. Phillipson (1992: 47) defines linguicism as 'the ideologies, structures and practices which are used to legitimate, effectuate and reproduce an unequal division of power and resources (both material and immaterial) between groups which are defined on the basis of language'.

20. As in many countries in the world, urban centres may be divided into two parts: The 'modern' centre and the 'traditional' periphery (where large numbers of migrants live in semi-permanent housing). In this periphery, the economic conditions are quite different; the residents neither participate in agriculture (as in the rural sector) nor in the sale of services (as in the urban core); indeed, there is often no 'legitimate' means of producing income. Education in these peripheral urban zones is limited or non-existent. The population tends to be ethnically and linguistically mixed to a far greater extent than in either in the rural sector (i.e. the village) or in the urban core. All of this suggests that the linguistic situation is different from the urban core or the rural sector, but this fluid language situation has not yet been investigated, for the same reasons outlined in footnote 2 above, and there is no empirical data available to provide an accurate description of this situation. This is indeed an interesting direction for future research and promises to yield a complete and much more accurate description of the language situation in the country.

21. Bolibaugh (1972: 17) is quoted in Bokamba (1991: 190) as follows: 'In 1957, the numbers (sic) of students, including Europeans, who received their baccalaureate were as follows: Guinea – 5, Côte d'Ivoire – 69, and Senegal – 172. In 1960, 31 Malians were awarded the baccalaureate. The situation has not improved much since then. In 1999, 69.83 per cent of the total candidature in Côte d'Ivoire (i.e., 70,116 students) failed the

baccalaureate. In 1998, the failure rate was 64.04 per cent for a total candidature of 71,437 students.'

22. Primary school, composed of six grades, is divided into preparatory (Years 1 and 2), elementary (Years 3 and 4) and intermediate (Years 5 and 6). Standard school-leaving exams lead to the *Certificat d'études primaires élémentaires* (Certificate of Elementary Education). Approximately 1.5 million pupils attended primary school in 1987, representing about 75% of boys and 50% of girls below age fifteen. Secondary school (*collège* or *lycée*), which lasts seven years, is divided into two cycles: the first cycle of four years is sanctioned by a *brevet d'études du premier cycle* (Certificate of Lower Cycle of Secondary Study), and the second cycle of three years at the end of which successful graduates are awarded the *baccalaureate* (Higher School Certificate) and may enter university.

23. University education was available only at the National University in Abidjan. In 1990 the National University was decentralised, with two branches in Abidjan (Cocody and Abobo-Adjamé) one in Bouaké (second largest city in the country), and two regional units of higher education, one in Korhogo (north of the country) and another in Daloa (midwest). During the early 1980s Côte d'Ivoire spent a higher share of its gross national product and of its national budget on education than any other country in the world. Nevertheless, this effort was cancelled out by the fact that salaries for expatriate teachers (called *coopérants*) accounted for a disproportionate share of current expenditures. This situation was exacerbated by the economic recession of the 1980s that saw most expatriate teachers leave the country. Soon after this, the government decided to reduce the salaries of all new teachers.

24. That is to say, there is one teaching staff member for around 51 students, or twice the ratio recommended by UNESCO (i.e. one teaching staff member for 25 students). Founded in 1959 as a Centre for Higher Education, the National University of Côte d'Ivoire (now University of Cocody) had a capacity of 8000 students in 1964. It now deals with 45,000 students, or five and a half times as many students. Teaching staff in departments start off the academic year with teaching loads of seven tutorials of 30 students each, but invariably end up with 16 tutorials of 30 students each. It is not uncommon for individual teaching staff to have to mark over 1000 final exam papers (Dr Yao Kouadio Kpli, personal communication).

References

African Development Bank (1999) *Côte d'Ivoire Fact Sheet*. http://www.afdb.org/.

Assemblée Nationale (1976) *Projet de Loi Relatif à la Réforme de l'Enseignement Présenté par le Président de la République [A Teaching Reform Bill Presented by the President of the Republic]*. (Annexe au procès-verbal de la séance du mercredi 28 juillet 1976. Deuxième session ordinaire 1976. Cinquième législature). Abidjan. Texte ronéotypé, No 17. 20 pp.

Atlapedia Online (1999) *Countries A to Z: Côte d'Ivoire*. http://www.atlapedia.com/.

Baldauf, R.B., Jr. (1993/94) 'Unplanned' language policy and planning. In W. Grabe *et al.* (eds) *Annual Review of Applied Linguistics* 14 (pp. 82–9). New York: Cambridge University Press.

Battestini, S. (1997) *Ecriture et Texte: Contribution Africaine [Writing and Text: The African Contribution]*. Québec and Ottawa: Les Presses de l'Université Laval en collaboration avec Présence Africaine.

Bokamba, E. (1991) French colonial language policies in Africa and their legacies. In D. Marshall (ed.) *Language Planning: Focusschrift in Honor of Joshua A. Fishman on the Occasion of his 65th birthday*, Vol. 3 (pp. 175–215). Amsterdam: John Benjamins.

Calvet, L-J. (1994) Les politiques de diffusion des langues en Afrique francophone [The policies of language spread in French-speaking Africa]. *International Journal of the Sociology of Language* 17, 67–76.

Central Intelligence Agency (1999) *The World Fact Book: Côte d'Ivoire*. http://www.odci.gov/cia/publications/factbook/iv.html:1-8.

Chaudenson, R. (1989) *1989: Vers une Révolution Francophone ? [1989: Towards a Francophone Revolution?]* Paris: Editions l'Harmattan.

Crowley, T. (2000) The language planning situation in Vanuatu. *Current Issues in Language Planning* 1.

Dannaud, J. (1965) Enseignement et avenir de la langue française dans les pays d'Afrique noire [The teaching and future of the French language in Black Africa]. *Communautés et Continents* 26 (6), 19–27.

Delafosse, M. (1904) *Vocabulaires Comparatifs de Plus de Soixante Langues ou Dialectes Parlés en Côte d'Ivoire et Dans les Régions Limitrophes [Comparing the Lexicon of Over Sixty Languages and Dialects Spoken in Côte d'Ivoire and the Neighbouring Regions].* Paris: Ernest Leroux.

Djité, P. (1988a) Correcting errors in language classification: Monolingual nuclei and multilingual satellites. *Language Problems and Language Planning* 12, 1–13.

Djité, P. (1988b) The spread of Dyula and popular French in Côte d'Ivoire: Implications for language policy. *Language Problems and Language Planning* 12, 213–25.

Djité, P. (1990) The French revolution and the French language: A paradox? In R. Aldrich (ed.) *France, Politics, Society, Culture and International Relations* (pp. 199–209). Sydney: Department of Economic History, The University of Sydney.

Djité, P. (1991a) Langues et développement en Afrique [Languages and development in Africa]. *Language Problems and Language Planning* 15, 121–38.

Djité, P. (1991b) Pour une linguistique du développement [The relevance of linguistics to development policies]. *Afrique 2000: Revue africaine de politique internationale* 7, October–December 1991, 105–110. Brussels: Institut Panafrican de Relations Internationales.

Djité, P. (1997) Francophonie et pluralisme linguistique [Francophonie and linguistic pluralism]. *Australian Journal of French Studies* 34 (2), 145–67.

Dumont, P. (1990) *Le Français, Langue Africaine [French, an African language].* Paris: L'Harmattan.

Duponchel, L. (1971) Réflexions sur l'enseignement du français en Côte d'Ivoire [Reflections on the teaching of French in Côte d'Ivoire]. In F. Canu, L. Duponchel and A. Lamy (eds) *Langues Négro-Africaines et Enseignement du Français: Conférences et Comptes-rendus [Negro-African Languages and the Teaching of French: Conferences and Reports]* (pp. 18–28). Abidjan: Institut de linguistique appliquée.

Fishman, J. (1968) Nationality-nationalism and nation-nationism. In J. Fishman, C. Ferguson and J. Das Gupta (eds) *Language Problems in Developing Nations* (pp. 39–51). New York: John Wiley and Sons.

Ferrari, A. (1971) *La Situation des Jeunes à Lakota. Résultats d'Enquêtes [The Situation of the Youth in Lakota. Results of Surveys].* Abidjan: Institut d'ethno-sociologie.

Fraternité Matin (1976) 26 April: 23–4, Abidjan.

Fraternité Matin (1999a) 23 November: 11, Abidjan.

Fraternité Matin (1999b) 10 –11 December: 7, Abidjan.

Greenberg, J. (1966) *Languages of Africa.* The Hague: Mouton.

Grimes, B. (ed.) (1974) *Ethnologue.* Huntingdon Beach, CA: Wycliffe Bible Translators.

Hagège, C. (1987) *Le Français et les Siècles [The French Language Through Time].* Paris: Editions Odile Jacob.

Hattiger, J-L. (1983) *Le Français Populaire d'Abidjan: Un Cas de Pidginisation [Popular French in Abidjan: A Case of Pidginisation].* Abidjan: Institut de linguistique appliquée.

Heine, B. (1977) *Vertical and Horizontal Communication in Africa.* University of Nairobi. Mimeo.

Hymes, D. (1984) Linguistic problems in defining the concept of 'tribe'. In J. Baugh and J. Sherzen (eds) *Language in Use: Readings in Sociolinguistics* (pp. 7–27). Englewood Cliffs: Prentice Hall.

Ivoir'Soir, 14 December 1999:1, Abidjan.

Jernudd, B.H. and Das Gupta, J. (1971) Towards a theory of language planning. In J. Rubin and B. H. Jernudd (eds) *Can Language Be Planned?* (pp. 195–215). Honolulu: University of Hawaii Press.

Jeune Afrique (1999a) No 2005, 15–21 June: 30–31. Paris.

Jeune Afrique 1999b) No 2019, 21–27 September: 28–30. Paris.

Journal officiel de l'Afrique occidentale française (1945) 15 September: 707. Dakar.

Kachru, B. (ed.) (1982) *The Other Tongue: English across Cultures*. Urbana: University of Illinois Press.

Kaplan, R. (1990) Introduction: Language planning in theory and practice. In R.B. Baldauf, Jr. and A. Luke (eds) *Language Planning and Education in Australasia and the South Pacific* (pp. 3–13). Clevedon: Multilingual Matters.

Kayambazinthu, E. (1998) The language planning situation in Malawi. *Journal of Multilingual and Multicultural Development* 19, 369–439.

Khubchandani, L. (1972) Fluidity in mother tongue identity. In A. Verdoodt (ed.) *Applied Sociolinguistics* Vol. 2 (pp. 81–102). Heidelberg: Julius Groos. [Proceedings of the Association Internationale de Linguistique Appliquée – Third Congress, Copenhagen]

Khubchandani, L. (1977) Language ideology and language development. *Linguistics* 193, 33–52.

Ki-Zerbo, J. (1990) *Eduquer ou Périr*. Paris: UNICEF-UNESCO.

Kouamé, F. (1999) L'ivoirité est une synthèse de la diversité culturelle ivoirienne et des valeurs de société spécifiques à la Côte d'Ivoire et non une disposition du droit positif ['Ivoirité' does not emanate from a substantive law, but is a synthesis of the Ivorian cultural diversity and of the social values specific to Côte d'Ivoire]. *Le Democrate*, 12 October:1–7. Abidjan.

Lafage, S. (1979) Rôle et place du français populaire dans le continuum français/langues africaines de Côte d'Ivoire [Role and place of Popular French in the French/African languages continuum in Côte d'Ivoire]. *Le Français Moderne: Le Français en Afrique Noire* 3, 208–19.

Lafage, S. (1982) Esquisse des rapports interlinguistiques en Côte d'Ivoire [Outline of the interlinguistic relationships in Côte d'Ivoire]. *Bulletin de l'Observatoire du Français Contemporain en Afrique Noire*. Institut national de la langue française, C.N.R.S. No 3: 9–27.

Lebeuf, J. (1965) Système du monde et écriture en Afrique Noire [World system and writing in Black Africa]. *Présence Africaine* 1er trimestre 1965: 129–31.

Le Jour (1999) 5 August: 6. Abidjan.

Lopes, A.J. (1998) The language situation in Mozambique. *Journal of Multilingual and Multicultural Development* 19, 440–86.

Loucou, J-N. (1983) Histore [History]. In Pierre Venetier (ed.) *Atlas of Côte d'Ivoire* (2nd edn) (pp. 25–55). Paris: Editions Ami.

Mackey, W. F. (1999) Forecasting the fate of languages. Paper read at the Conference on Language in the Twenty-first Century, organized by Humphrey Tonkin at the Whitney Center for the Humanities, Yale University, 6 & 7 June.

Marcomer, A. (1968) *Les Jeunes Baoulés: Besoins culturels et Développement [The Young Baulé: Cultural Needs and Development]*. 2 volumes. Paris: Secrétariat d'Etat aux Affaires étrangères. Vol. 1: October 1968, 203 pp.; Vol. 2: January 1969, 46 pp.

Myers-Scotton C.M. (1982) Learning lingua francas and socio-economic integration: Evidence from Africa. In R.L. Cooper (ed.) *Language Spread* (pp. 63–94). Indiana University Press.

Myers-Scotton C.M. (1993) Elite closure as a powerful language strategy: The African case. *International Journal of the Sociology of Language* 103, 149–63.

Niangoran-Bouah, G. (1984) *L'Univers Akan des Poids à Peser l'Or [The Akan World of Gold Weights]*. Vol. 1 and 2. Abidjan: Nouvelles Editions Africaines.

Niangoran-Bouah, G. (1996) Fondements socioculturels du concept d'ivoirité [Sociocultural foundations of the concept of 'Ivoirité']. *Proceedings of the CURDIPHE Forum* (pp. 42–55), 20–23 March. Abidjan: Nouvelles Editions Africaines.

Notre Voie (2000) No. 510, 22–23 January:1–24. Abidjan.

Nyati-Ramahobo, L. (2000) The language situation in Botswana. *Current Issues in Language Planning* 1.

Official Web Site of the Presidency of the Republic of Côte d'Ivoire: Founding Texts of Côte d'Ivoire; Constitution of Côte d'Ivoire, Act No 60–356 of 3 November 1960, last amended by Act No 98–387 of 2 July 1998; Web site address: http://www.pr.ci.

Person, Y. (1981) Colonisation et décolonisation en Côte d'Ivoire [Colonisation and decolonisation in Côte d'Ivoire]. *Le Mois en Afrique* 188–9: 15–30, August-September.

Phillipson, R. (1992) *Linguistic Imperialism*. Oxford: Oxford University Press.

Poth, J. (1990) National languages in teaching. *The Courier* 119, 51–5.

Pyles, T. (1979) *Selected Essays on English Usage*. Gainesville: Florida University Press.

Quirk, R., Greenbaum, S., Leech, G. and Svartvik, J. (1985) *A Comprehensive Grammar of the English Language*. London: Longman.

The World Bank Group Countries (1999) *Côte d'Ivoire*, http://www.worldbank.org/.

Turcotte, D. (1981) *La Politique Linguistique en Afrique Francophone: Une Étude Comparative de la Côte d'Ivoire et de Madagascar [Linguistic Policies in French-speaking Africa: A Comparative Study of Côte d'Ivoire and Madagascar]*. Québec: Presses de l'Université Laval.

United Nations Development Program (1999) *Globalization with a Human Face*. Human Development Report, 1999. New York.

United States State Department (1999) *Annual Report on Religious Freedom in Côte d'Ivoire*. *Le Jour* 1408, 14 October: 4–7.

Waddell, M. (1863) *Twenty-nine Years in the West Indies and Central Africa*. London: Nelson.

Weinstein, B. (1980) Language planning in Francophone Africa. *Language Problems and Language Planning* 4, 55–7.

The Language Situation in Côte d'Ivoire since 2000: An Update

Paulin G. Djité
University of Western Sydney, Australia

Jean-François, Y. K. Kpli
Université de Cocody, Côte d'Ivoire

Introduction

This update discusses the language situation in Côte d'Ivoire since 2000. Whilst the pidginisation and nativisation of French has further deepened since, through a variety known as Nouchi, the socio-political strife which has gripped the country since the first coup d'etat of 1999[1] may have significant effects on the potential of Dyula as a national lingua franca.

The Spread of Nouchi

Although Popular French – an Ivorian variety of Standard French – was discussed in the original monograph on the language situation in Côte d'Ivoire (*CILP* 1 (2): 11–50), little or no mention was made of Nouchi, another variety of French, closely related to Popular French, and mainly used by young people[2]. The word *Nouchi* originates from Dyula, the main lexifying language of this variety[3], and means 'nose hair' ('nou' = 'nose', and 'chi' = 'hair'), which, in the culture of this language community, is a sign of maturity. Speaking Nouchi is therefore like a rite of passage, whereby the young claim and affirm their maturity and creativity through the mastery of a code of their own. It started in the poor slums of Abidjan, the economic capital of Côte d'Ivoire, and was primarily spoken by semi-literate school dropouts. It is a cryptic language used to affirm one's membership in the group. Nouchi soon spread to university campuses in Abidjan, and other large cities with university campuses (Bouaké in the centre, Daloa in the west and Korhogo in the north of the country), in part as a fashion statement, but also because of the economic downturn and increasing political instability in the country, which caused severe overcrowding and lawlessness on many university campuses. Disruptions of all sorts have made it impossible to complete a normal academic year in the Côte d'Ivoire educational system since the mid 1980's, and this situation significantly transformed university life on campuses. The overwhelming French and Dyula substrate of Nouchi and its fashion statement aspect has also seen it spread to such countries as Burkina Faso and Mali, where Dyula is also spoken as a lingua franca. This cross-border spread (in Côte d'Ivoire, Burkina Faso and Mali) and the input into the code of various local languages make it difficult at times to trace the origins of some Nouchi words. Indeed, a number of Nouchi words and expressions are synonyms, modulated on the domain and place of interaction.

Table 1 Terms of irreverence for authority in Nouchi

1. Faut pas me *Guéi*	Do not *betray* me
2. Tu es *Gbagbo*	You *look ugly*
3. Filer des *AFP* à quelqu'un	Tell someone lies
4. Etre une *sale race*	To be *French* = to be *untrustworthy*
5. **Voir clair** dans une femme	To *make love* to a woman
6. C'est un *turbo diesel*	He *goes out with an older woman*

Table 2 Creativity in Nouchi

7. Je n'ai pas de *mago*, mais je suis avec *ma go*	I have no *money*, but I have my *honey*
8. Où y'a *gahou*, y'a bonheur	A *stupid man* makes all the girls happy
9. La fête sera *grave*	It will be a *great* event

Hence terms such as (a) 'y'a pas drap' (there is nothing) with a French substrate, (b) 'y'a likefi' (there is nothing) with a Baoulé substrate, and (c) 'y'a fohi' (there is nothing) with a Dyula substrate.

The origins of Nouchi go a long way toward explaining the irreverence for authority and crude reference to subjects that used to be taboo (e.g., sex). In the examples cited in Table 1, (1) is a direct reference to the change of heart of General Guéi who, instead of handing power over to a civilian government, tried to rig the elections, whilst (2) suggests that there is a consensus that the current President is not handsome. Examples (3) and (4) express feelings by some towards the French, since a failed coup d'etat in September 2002. Example (3) is based on the news reports of *Agence France Press* over that period. Example (4) takes this feeling of dissatisfaction much further. Examples (5) and (6) refer to sexual relations.

Nouchi has quickly become the language of the local 'rap' musicians and radio hosts (especially those broadcasting for the young public, such as *Radio Djam, Fréquence 2* and *Radio Nostalgie*), whose message is directly pitched at those of the same generation. Some of the expressions and song titles (in Table 2) reflect the creativity of the code.

But Nouchi is much more than a code of social protest; it is growing into a full-fledged variety, covering all aspects of daily life, as is shown in the random selections cited in Table 3, some of which are direct borrowings from Popular French (see examples 10, 11, 12, 13, 15, 17, 22, 23 and 24). Example 21, 'Affaire sur mollet de cafard / serpent' (much ado about nothing) refers to a matter that is all the more difficult, because it rests on the 'calf of a cockroach or snake'. Example 23, on the other hand, reduces the whole of the United States to one of its commercial (cultural?) symbols, Coca Cola. One does not just have a drink, one drinks America. Example 24 is an expansion of the French expression 'à la sueur de son front' (literally 'sweat on one's brow'); using the word 'thighs' for 'brow' here suggests that the hard work in this case is of a completely different nature. Examples 14, 16, 18, 19 and 20 are much more typical of Nouchi, in that they blend French and a local language (Dyula, Baoulé or Bété). Example 20,

Table 3 Random selection of other Nouchi terms

10. C'est dur, mais c'est pas *caillou*	It is difficult, but not *impossible*
11. Tu ne *démarres* pas	You have an *erection problem*
12. Il *a* des *feuilles*/ Il *est moyennant*	He *is rich*
13. *Afrique en danger* (pâte de farine)	*A flour meal* (heavy on the stomach)
14. Il *est poué*/ *tango tango*	He *is drunk*
15. Elle a un beau *tableau de bord*	She has nice *boobs*
16. *Taba taba de Molière*	*Standard French*
17. C'est un *woodi* de la politique	He is a *courageous* politician
18. *Aby*, c'est comment?	How are you, my *friend*?
19. Il m'a *tchèrè*	He *fooled* me
20. *Akissi/Adjoua Commissaire/Lieutenant*	*Tell tale*
21. **Affaire sur mollet de cafard/serpent**	*Difficult matter*
22. Ce qui est sûr, rien n'est sûr	Nothing is certain
23. Servez-moi *l'Amérique*	*Coca Cola*
24. Gagner sa vie *à la sueur de ses cuisses*	To be a prostitute

Table 4 Numeric system of local currency in Nouchi

25. 5 FCFA	Môrô
26. 10 FCFA	Deux môrô
27. 25 FCFA	Grô or Grôsse
28. 50 FCFA	2 Grô or Grôsse
29. 75 FCFA	Soquinze or Sogban
30. 100 FCFA	Tôgô or Mambi or Plomb
31. 125 FCFA	Tôgô grôsse
32. 150 FCFA	Tôgô cinquante
33. 175 FCFA	Tôgô Soquinze or Tôgô Sogban
34. 200 FCFA	Deux tôgô or deux mambi
35. 300 FCFA	Rabadé tout fort
36. 400 FCFA	Quatre tôgô
37. 500 FCFA	Cinq tôgô
38. 1,000 FCFA	Krika or Bar or Djalan
39. 1,500 FCFA	Krika cinq or Bar fixe
40. 2,000 FCFA	Deux Krika
41. 5,000 FCFA	Gbolon or Gbonkê
41. 10,000 FCFA	Wulé or Billet rose or Billet de tais-toi
42. 15,000 FCFA	Bar fixe wulé cinq
43. 1,000,000 FCFA	Un Kilo or Une Brique

for instance, uses one of the typical Baoulé names for women, together with the words 'Commissaire' ('Inspector') or 'Lieutenant' ('Lieutenant') of the police, to suggest the activities of officers of the law in the business of reporting suspicious activities. In this case, 'Akissi or Adjoua' is engaging in gratuitously dubbing in others.

Table 4 shows a rather complex numeric system, but interestingly applicable only to the local currency (CFA Franc).[4] While some of this terminology is somewhat transparent as in Example 41, where the French term 'billet de tais-toi' (a 'shut up' bank note) is a social comment on corruption, we are still in the process of deciphering the logic and lexical origins of many of the terms used in this system.

Nouchi even has its own abbreviations/shortenings for Short Message Services (SMSs) such as 'dev' for 'devoir' (homework), sent through mobile phones (called 'C' for the French word 'Cellulaire').

Although it sometimes doubles up with Popular French, Nouchi is indeed a code in its own right, reserved for communication between young people – a code that speakers of Popular French have to learn. Like other nativised varieties (e.g., Popular French)[5], Nouchi is still evolving, and the current political and economic instability in the country is giving its creativity a boost, as new circumstances and situations arise that need to be described and discussed.

Conclusion

After Popular French and Dyula, the spread of Nouchi confirms that a people may never be stopped from expressing their inner thoughts in the way – and in the language – they choose. Although this new variety is currently proving to be a strong identification bond for many youths, it would be interesting to see whether the strong influence of Popular French on Nouchi will result in some form of convergence, and even fusion into one code, of these two varieties in the future.

Whilst Nouchi is feeding on the current crisis in Côte d'Ivoire, Dyula, on the other hand, may be at a crossroad in terms of its status as a national lingua franca. Although there is no direct evidence to suggest a retreat in its spread and use, the failed coup d'etat of September 2002, and the ensuing political instability that has left Côte d'Ivoire split between north (mostly Dyula-speaking) and south may have irrevocably damaged the potential of Dyula as a national language. The rise of Nouchi and the possible decline of Dyula are due in part to the politics of ethnicity underlined in 'Language Planning in Côte d'Ivoire' (*CILP* 1 (2): 11–50) and the failed coup d'etat, as well as the subsequent north/south partition of the country. As one of the most reluctant countries in Africa to contemplate a language policy based on the local languages, the recent events in Côte d'Ivoire do not augur well for a change of attitude in the foreseeable future.

Endnotes

1. The coup was led by a retired General and former Chief of Staff, General Robert Guéi, against the regime of President Henri Konan Bédié.
2. See Kouadio, J. (1992) Le nouchi abidjanais: naissance d'un argot ou mode linguistique passager? [The Nouchi of Abidjan: Birth of a Slang or a Passing Linguistic Fad]

In *Centre Ivoirien de Recherche Linguistique N° 30*, Institut de Linguistique Appliquée, Abidjan: 12–27. There is now a whole web site (www.nouchi.com) dedicated to Nouchi. However, as in the case of Popular French, many of the terms on the electronic dictionary posted on the site are not attested in everyday use. On the day of 'Francophonie', in March 2006, President Laurent Gbagbo suggested that International Francophone Organisations support the evolution of Nouchi, because 'trying to stop its evolution would be tantamount to putting brakes of human inventiveness' (See 'Gbagbo justifie le nouchi' [Gbagbo supports Nouchi]. In *L'Intelligent d'Abidjan*, 21 March 2006).

3. Other lexifying languages are Agni/Baoulé, Bété, French, and even Spanish and English. Some typical words of Dyula origin are: *bramôgô* for 'friend', *kôrô* for 'big brother', *dôgô* for 'little brother', *segue* for 'tired', *blakoroya* for 'stupidity', *flôkô* for 'lies', *saya* for 'death', *faga* or *dja* for 'kill', etc. Typical words of Baoulé origin are: *likefi* as in *y'a likefi*, meaning 'there is nothing', *zinzin* meaning 'crazy', and *kodjo* for 'underwear'. A typical word from Spanish is *casa* for 'house', whilst typical words from English are 'shoes', 'all eyes on me' and 'asshole'.

4. CFA stands for 'Communauté Française Africaine' (French African Community). €1 = FCFA 655.95. The data provided here was collected from 50 informants at Université ouverte des 5 Continents in Timbuktu, 50 informants at the Université de Cocody in Abidjan, and another 50 informants across car parks in the Plateau, the central business district of Abidjan. All figures not attested by 95% of the sample have not been retained. Money in Nouchi is called *Wari*, a term of Dyula origin.

5. Although it is relatively recent, Nouchi is far from a unique phenomenon and has the features of other well-known slangs and pidgins (see for example Chaudenson, 1992; DeGraff, 2003; Rickford & Traugot, 1985).

References

Chaudenson, R. (1992) *Des Îles, des Hommes, des Langues*. [*Of Islands, Peoples and Languages*]. Paris: L'Harmattan.

DeGraff, M. (2003) Against Creole exceptionalism. *Language* 79 (2), 391–410.

Djité, P.G. (forthcoming) *The Sociolinguistics of Development in Africa*. Clevedon: Multilingual Matters.

Djité, P. G. (2000) Language planning in Côte d'Ivoire. *Current Issues in Language Planning* 1 (1), 11–46.

Kouadio, J. (1992) Le nouchi abidjanais: naissance d'un argot ou mode linguistique passager? [The Nouchi of Abidjan: Birth of a slang or a passing linguistic fad?] In *Centre Ivoirien de Recherches Linguistiques N° 30*, 12–27. Abidjan: Institut de Linguistique Appliquée.

L'Intelligent d'Abidjan (2006) Gbagbo justifie le nouchi [Gbagbo supports Nouchi], published on 21 March 2006.

Rickford, J. and Traugot, E. (1985) Symbol of powerlessness and degeneracy, or symbol of solidarity and truth? Paradoxical attitudes towards pidgins and creoles. In S. Greenbaum (ed.) *The English Language Today* (pp. 252–262). Oxford: Pergamon Institute of English.

Language Policy and Planning in Nigeria

Efurosibina Adegbija

Department of Languages and Mass Communication, Covenant University, Km. 10 Idiiroko Road, Canaanland, Ota, Ogun State, Nigeria

This monograph describes the language planning situation in Nigeria, one of the most multilingual countries in Africa. It is divided into four sections. The first section presents the language profile of Nigeria and provides a background of the general language situation in the country. The second section discusses language spread and use. It focuses particularly on language in education and the media. The core section of the monograph investigates language policy and planning, with an emphasis on the mother tongue medium (or first language) policy and the multilingual policy. The fourth discusses language maintenance and language shift in Nigeria with respect to the indigenous languages and English, the exoglossic language. It shows that in spite of the first-language and multilingual policies, English is still dominant in virtually every aspect of life and that concrete policy actions need to be taken not only to begin to break the hegemony of English but also to ensure that indigenous languages have a secure future. The final section also provides some practical insight on ways to begin to resolve some of the problems posed by Nigeria's language policies.

Keywords: language policy, language planning, language maintenance, language spread, language shift, language use, Nigeria

The Language Profile of Nigeria

Introduction

Nigeria, the most multilingual country in Africa, has well over 450 languages (see Adegbija, 2004 for a tentative list of these languages). Language policy and planning in the country are of prime importance, first because of loyalties to different languages, and second, because of the implications for other multilingual contexts all over the world. Policy is needed, as is the case for many other multilingual contexts, for official, national, educational, inter-ethnic, and international functions. Bamgbose observes that:

> as in most other African countries, language policy in Nigeria is rarely documented, but its effects can be seen in action in various domains, such as use as official language, medium of instruction in schools, language use in the media, and in the legislature. (Bamgbose, 2001: 1)

Because language issues in Nigeria are often quite explosive and conflict ridden, censuses never have items or questions on languages. Thus, reliable statistics relating to issues like number of languages, their spread, the number of speakers of each, or what percentage of the population they constitute are rarely available.

Geographically, Nigeria is divided into 36 States and a Federal Capital Territory, Abuja. Each State, for ease of administration, has been divided into Local Government Areas, the number in each State varying on the basis of population size, political clout, lobbying power of the people within the State, and the attitudes and decisions of governments both at the Federal and State levels. In all, the

190

Figure 1 Map of Nigeria showing the different States

Federal Government officially recognises 774 local governments throughout the country. This section presents the language profile of Nigeria. Figure 1 shows the 36 States in Nigeria and the Federal Capital Territory, Abuja.

Nigerian indigenous languages belong to three out of the four main language families in Africa. These are the Niger-Kordofanian phylum, to which about 70% of the languages belong; the Afro-Asiatic phylum, to which about 29.5% of the languages belong, and the Nilo-Saharan phylum, to which only about 0.5% of Nigerian languages belong. The Niger-Kordofanian phylum has as its members Kwa, Adamawa and the West Atlantic groups of languages. Most of the Niger-Kordofanian languages in Nigeria belong to the Kwa branch (Central Niger-Congo sub-branch of the Niger-Congo). Languages such as Yoruba (also spoken in such neighbouring countries as Benin and Togo), Igbo, Oko-Osanyin, Edo, Igala, Idoma, Itsekiri and Nupe belong to the Kwa branch of the Niger-Kordofanian phylum. The Benue-Congo languages such as Ibibio, Efik, Ejagham, Tiv, and the Adamawa languages such as Chamba, the Jukunoid languages, and the West Atlantic languages such as Shuwa, which is a member of the Semitic branch, are also members of the Niger-Kordofanian phylum. The majority of the Niger-Kordofanian languages are located in the southern parts of Nigeria, as well as in parts of Jigawa and Taraba States in the north. The principal representative of the Afro-Asiatic phylum in Nigeria is Hausa. Hausa is also spoken in such neighbouring countries[1] as Chad and Niger. Kanuri, Dendi and Zabarma languages are the principal representatives of the Nilo-Saharan phylum in Nigeria. All Afro-Asiatic and Nilo-Saharan languages are located in the Northern part of Nigeria. Many of Nigeria's languages share a great deal of structural similarity to each other, particularly in terms of their genetic classification (Adegbija, 2004; Agheyisi, 1984; Akinnaso, 1991; Brann, 1990; Ruhlen, 1991).

Three major types of languages are recognisable in Nigeria. These are: the indigenous or endoglossic languages; foreign or exoglossic languages; and Pidgin varieties of languages, the most dominant of which is the largely English-based Nigerian Pidgin. The major exoglossic language in evidence in Nigeria is English; others are French and Arabic. Other exoglossic languages such as German, Russian, Italian, etc have a rather minimal presence, as they are largely used in embassies and in the families of embassy employees, among a few individuals and in university classrooms. Over the years, English has metamorphosed into a second language by virtue of its functional salience, its official dominance and its role as a national lingua franca in Nigeria. English is one of Nigeria's constitutionally recognised official languages, along with three indigenous languages, namely Hausa, Yoruba and Igbo. English is the predominant language of education, the print and electronic media, the judiciary, most official transactions, and the national House of Assembly and Senate. International diplomacy is also conducted in English. The Eighth All Africa Games, at which delegates from 52 African countries were present, officially began on 4 October 2003 and ran for 15 days. Reporting of events was largely conducted in English and French. The welcome address by President Olusegun Obasanjo was delivered in English and interpreted into French. I am not aware of interpretations of any aspects of the events into any of the indigenous languages, except, perhaps brief sketches of the events during news reports. Nigeria's presidents speak English when they visit other countries and when foreign dignitaries visit Nigeria. English also plays a major role – that of uniting Nigeria's different ethnic groups. It is the principal language of both official and non-official interethnic communication and interaction. Its role is so vital that many Nigerians believe the country cannot exist, or at least its existence as one entity would be severely threatened or jeopardised, without English. Mann (1996: 104) comments on the roles and status of English in Nigeria as follows:

> It is very unlikely that there will be a significant challenge to the role of English as Nigeria's official language in the foreseeable future. The recent enhancement of the capitalist ideology – whose principal agents and actors are Anglophone or 'Anglophonising' – following the collapse of socialist systems in the Soviet Union and other East European countries, can only reinforce its status in the world stage. It would equally enjoy some fillip from contemporary tendencies to establish supranations (e.g. the European megastate), which would, necessarily, require a convergent medium of communication. Given that English remains the language of education, and, therefore, the passport to educational qualifications and upward

social mobility, these two pulls or forces, the national and the international, will continue to constitute its attraction to Nigerians. Moreover, it is unlikely that those who used it to attain an elite status will be sympathetic to a change that puts their position in jeopardy.

French, declared by official fiat as a second official language during President Abacha's era when his Government was boycotted and ostracised by America and the largely Anglophone Commonwealth, is next to English as an exoglossic language in terms of importance, though spoken by very few Nigerians. Its presence in official circles is negligible, except in interactions with French-speaking embassy employees, in translation and interpreting work (such as in the Eighth All Africa Games cited previously), in interaction with neighbours in Benin, Togo and Niger, etc. Arabic, the third major exoglossic language with some presence in Nigeria, is largely restricted in function to the Islamic religion and, occasionally, to interactions between Muslims, especially the Muslim clerics.

Three Nigerian indigenous languages, namely Hausa, Yoruba and Igbo, have been constitutionally recognised as 'major' languages among the endoglossic languages. Both Hausa and Yoruba have a population of roughly 22 million while Igbo has a population of about 18 million. Theoretically, policy makers expect the languages to be used in national functions such as national mobilisation, rallying people for national goals such as the registration of voters in an election or the registration for identity cards and in inducing unity in diversity. In practice, however, they are largely regionally based. Hausa is largely spoken in the northern States of Kano, Katsina, Adamawa, Bauchi, Gombe, Jigawa, Kaduna, Kebbi, Niger, Sokoto, Zamfara and in the Sabongari areas (enclaves settled by Hausa-speaking people) in other states in Nigeria. Yoruba is also principally a regional language, preponderantly used in the south-western States of Oyo, Ogun, Osun, Ondo, Lagos, Ekiti and partly Kwara State. Igbo is used in such south-eastern States as Enugu, Anambra, Imo, Ebonyin and Abia.

Regional compartmentalisation as well as inter-ethnic rivalries between the three major language groups has severely curtailed the potential national utility, functions and impact of Hausa, Yoruba and Igbo. Compared to other indigenous languages, each of these three languages has received significant governmental attention manifested by language development, assignment of official functions, and frequency of use in national media, especially in electronic media (radio and TV). The development of a meta-language for use in technical functions, and the encouragement of literary productions in the indigenous languages, further illustrate such attention. Languages such as Fulfulde, Efik, Kanuri, Tiv, Ijo, Edo, Nupe, Igala, Idoma, Ebira, Ibibio, which closely follow Hausa, Yoruba and Igbo in terms of numerical importance, have more than 1 million speakers each. Fifty other languages are spoken by about 100,000 people each. The remaining languages are small group or minority languages 'with varying functions, extent of use in formal education, and degree of official recognition, acceptance, as well as levels of development' (Adegbija, 2004: 71; also see Akinnaso, 1991; Brann, 1990; Jibril, 1990).

In each State, languages most predominant in population, status and function serve as major State languages and as 'unofficial official' languages. In Adamawa

State, for instance, the Fulfulde language is very dominant, and so functions as an 'unofficial official' language, just as:

- Ibibio and Efik do in Akwa Ibom;
- Tiv and Idoma in Benue State;
- Igala and Ebira in Kogi State;
- Efik in Cross River State;
- Urhobo and Itshekiri in Delta State;
- Edo in Edo State;
- Mada, Rindre and Eggon in Nassarawa;
- Ikwerre, Ijaw and Kalabari in Rivers State; and
- Jukun in Taraba State.

Dominant languages at the local government levels also function unofficially as official languages at local government levels. In Kogi State, for instance, Oko functions *de facto* in the Ogori-Magongo Local Government Area as the unofficial official language and the predominant language of interaction even in official settings where interactions are limited to the indigenous people of the local government area. Interactions involving non-indigenous people of a particular local government would occur in English, the official language.

It is worthy of note that most indigenous languages in Nigeria have dialects, most of which are not mutually intelligible. Thus, for instance, whereas Yoruba is the major language in Ekiti State, it has as dialects Ekiti and Owo, among others. Also in Ogun State, Yoruba is the major language. Its dialects include Egba, Owu, Egbado (spoken in Yelwa North Local Government Area), Ijebu, Remo and Awori. Pawpaw, for instance, is called *ibepe* in mainstream Yoruba. However, the Egbas call it *sigu*; Cassava is *Paki* in the Egba dialect but *Ege* in mainstream Yoruba. Dog meat, a delicacy known as *lokili* in Ondo State, is known as *eran aja* in mainstream Yoruba. Virtually every State in which Yoruba is predominantly spoken – Ekiti, Ondo, Kwara, Oyo, Ogun, Oshun, Lagos – has several dialects, not necessarily mutually intelligible to Yoruba speakers in other States.

Overall, then, indigenous Nigerian languages function in a naturally graded hierarchical structure at the national, state or regional, and local government levels as lingua francas or link languages, as unofficial, quasi-official languages, and as languages of informal interaction.

English is officially used in all State Houses of Assembly, including those where the majority of people speak one dominant or major indigenous language. For example, in the Ogun State House of Assembly, English is the language of legislative discussions. It is also the language used for recording such discussions. Yoruba, the indigenous language in the State, is used mainly when members of the House want to sound philosophical or to provide solutions from folk wisdom to thorny problems. At such moments, recourse is made to proverbial usage in the Yoruba language. The same point may be made about other State Houses of Assembly.

Igbo is one of the three constitutionally designated 'major' Nigerian languages. Some of its speakers now complain that their language is endangered and its speakers marginalised as an ethnic group (Ohiri-Aniche, 2001). Like Hausa and Yoruba, it has witnessed considerable language development attention. The

Church Missionary Society (CMS) opened its first station in Igbo land in 1857 and showed a particular interest in its development from the very beginning. Missionaries were motivated to study African languages by the desire to communicate Christianity to Africans, not only through spoken language but also through the production of Bible translations and catechisms. By 1915, the missionaries, in an attempt to create a universally acceptable Igbo dialect, produced translations in at least six different dialects: the Isuama dialect, the Onitsha dialect, the Bonny Igbo dialect, the Unwana Igbo (by the Church of Scotland Mission), the Union Ibo and the Onitsha Adapted Union Ibo (a brand peculiar to the Onitsha area). While the Catholic mission did most teaching in English, the CMS missionaries believed in vernacular education and used Igbo in schools. Initially, the Colonial Government did not consider the Igbo language a priority either in education or in administration. Consequently, colonial administration was conducted in English and colonial officers did not communicate in Igbo. They relied on Igbo clerks and messengers who exploited their positions as intermediaries. Igbo was not an essential part of the curriculum. Moreover, the Nigerians were themselves more interested in education in English than in Igbo (van den Bersselar, 2000: 125).

Diversity in the language profile

Language profile varies from State to State. Most States, like the entire nation, are characterised by dense multilingualism, the dominance of English in official contexts, the official neglect of indigenous languages, and the functional predominance of indigenous languages in informal contexts. Most of Nigeria's languages, except for the three major languages, the major State languages and a few others such as the languages spoken in Rivers State, have not been studied, have no orthographies, are not used in print or in the electronic media, and have not been assigned any significant national, State, or even local government roles. Since it is virtually impossible to discuss the 450 or so Nigerian languages individually here, the language profile of only a few States is provided to illustrate and pinpoint the complexity and diversity of the language profile of Nigeria.

Abia State

Igbo is the predominant language spoken in Abia State. Abia is one of the main one-language States, in the sense that most of the indigenous people speak Igbo as a first language. Bilingualism in Igbo and English is also quite common, much more so than bilingualism in Igbo and another indigenous language. Visitors or foreigners to the State speak English and other indigenous languages, depending on their place of origin. Federal government workers from other States living in Abia State communicate largely in English. Igbo in Abia State has several dialects including the following: Arochukwu, Ohofia, Alayi, Igbere, Ntigha, Ngwa, Akwuete, Abam, Nkporo, Uzuakoli, Ohuhu, Ezeleke. Pidgin is largely used in informal settings.

Cross River State

Cross River State is a good illustration of the complex and intriguing language situation in Nigeria. It has a land area of about 30,000 square kilometers, a population of roughly three million persons and a linguistic inventory of about 67 indigenous languages (see Adegbija, 2004). The major languages of Cross River

State are Annang, Bokyi, Bekwara, Effik, Ejagham, and Ibibio. The 78 languages used in the State are:

> Abini, Adim, Agoi, Agwagwune, Akama, Alege, Annang, Abanyom, Bakpinka, Bokyi, Bekwara, Biase, Bembe, Bette, Doko-Uyanga, Eja, Effik, Eket, Ekajuk, Ejagham, Etung, Ehom, Gham, Ibibio, Ishibori, Ibeno, Iyala (Yala), Icheve, Ikom-Olulumo, Iyoniyong, Igede, Isi-Ezaa, Ikwo-Mgbo, Kohumono, Korop, Kukule (Ukele), Lokae, Legbo (Agbo), Leyigha, Lenyima, Loko (Yakurr), Lokoli, Lubila, Lokobi, Levigha (Yigha), Lenyima, Mbube, Mbembe, Adun, Apiapum, Akama, Ekuma, Ofombonga, Okom, Osophong, Nkari, Nkem, Nde, Nselle, Nta (Atam), Nnam, Obudu, Ogoni, Oron, Ochukwayam, Ofutop, QUAS, Sankula, Tiv, Ukpet-Ehom (Ubetena, Ukpet), Ubaghara, (Biakpan, Etono, Utama), Umon, Utukwana, Ugep, Wori, Yahe, Yache. (Essien, 1982: 120)

In this State, Ejagham speakers (whose language is similar to Efik) feel threatened because of the dominance of the Efik language. Pidgin is commonly used in informal settings such as in marketplaces and interpersonal interactions. The University of Calabar teaches the Efik language, and this has served to promote the language further. The Iboto cultural group promotes the Efik language and culture.

Delta State

The major languages in Delta State include:

- Urhobo, spoken mainly in Ugheli, Agbaro and Oghara;
- Isoko, spoken mainly in Oleh and Emevo towns;
- Itshekiri, spoken in Warri, Koko, Ugborodo;
- Ijaw, predominantly spoken in Bomali, Forcados, Patani and Ukuani, sometimes referred to as Kwale, spoken largely in Ubiaruku town.

Other languages spoken in the State are Ika, spoken in Agbor, Igbo (sometimes referred to as Bendel Igbo, now Delta Igbo) and Effurun, spoken in Warri town. Okpe is spoken mainly in Sapele and Orerokpe towns. The Okpe people live among the Urhobos as a minority group. Its speakers have refused to have their identity diffused into that of the larger Urhobo ethnic group. Instead, they have maintained a distinct cultural and linguistic identity.

Pidgin English is more commonly heard in day-to-day interactions in this State than in most other States in the Federation. Some people in this State even claim to speak Nigerian Pidgin English as their first language. It is used in homes, in the markets and in other types of commercial transactions, in banks, in public places and in the electronic media. The Itshekiris and Urhobo-speaking ethnic groups have constantly been at each other's throats. Frequent inter-ethnic/ linguistic clashes among them have often resulted in death and have disrupted the smooth flow of oil, the mainstay of Nigeria's economy. The problem between these two linguistic groups is at once political (desire for different local governments and for recognition), linguistic (quest for dominance) and economic (the desire for a larger share of the oil produced on their land).

Edo State

Edo is a major language in Edo State, spoken by the Bini people. It is spoken mainly in the Oro Edo Local Government Area. Ishan, with Uwesan as a dialect, is another major language in Edo State, spoken in Edo North, especially in Ekpoma, Uromi, Ubiaja and Irrua towns. Afemai is spoken in Auchi in the Akoko Edo Local Government Area. It has Oza as a dialect. Agbede is spoken in the Agbede Local Government Area. Its speakers have the reputation for being extremely culturally homogeneous. They also take great pride in the Agbede language. Other languages in the State include Ora, Igarra, Ison (Ijaw), Okpella, Ososo, Ekpedo, Emai. Most of these languages are not taught or used in schools, and no daily newspapers are published in any of them. Church services in Edo are common in Benin City, with English also spoken sometimes by the same preacher. Pidgin is another very common language in the State, especially in informal interactions, which are differentiated between Pidgin and the indigenous languages.

Ekiti State

Yoruba is the sole language of a majority of the Ekiti people. It has Ekiti and Owo as dialects. Yoruba is used in most informal interactions and in several formal ones such as in churches, banks, post offices, etc. Interpreting from Yoruba into English or English into Yoruba are common in some church functions, depending on the nature of the audience. English is used in the State House of Assembly and in official functions such as broadcasts by the State Governor, and in advertisements. Most of these are usually translated into Yoruba.

Gombe State

The languages of this State are (in alphabetical order): Awak, Bangwinji, Bole, Burak, Dadiya, Dijim-Bwilim, Fulfulde, Hausa, Jara, Kamo, Kughi, Kutto, Kwaami, Loo, Ngamo, Tangale, Tera, Tso, Tula, and Waja. The predominant language of Gombe State is Hausa. Fulfulde is a minority language in the State and intermarriages of its speakers with other Gombe indigenous people decrease the chances of its survival. Other minor languages within the State are Tera, Bolewa and Tangale. Arabic is also in evidence, especially in mosques and in Islamic education. The language is known only by a few clerical people, although portions of the Qur'an have also been memorised by laypeople of the Muslim faith.

Kogi State

The dominant languages in Kogi State are Igala, Ebira and Okun, with its many dialects such as Owe and Yagba. Other languages in the State include Bassange, Bassankwomo, Oko-Osanyin (Ogori-Magongo), Nupe, Kakanda, Etuno, Tapa, and Koto. These languages are all largely restricted to their traditional domains. Ebira, for instance, is largely restricted to Ebira land. It is spoken in towns such as Okene, Obehira, Ogaminana, Ogboroke, Osara, Ikuehi, Agassa and Ogevba. Igala is also largely spoken in Igala areas and towns such as Idah and Ankpa. The Okun language, along with its numerous dialects, is spoken in places such as Kabba, Egbe, Aiyetoro-Gbedde, Ponyan and Ekinrin-Ade and other parts of Okun land. There is constant inter-ethnic rivalry among the three major language groups (i.e. Igala, Ebira and Okun) within the State. The rivalry is motivated largely by a perceived dominance of the Igala language and people over other people in the State. In the Nigerian context, numerical dominance is almost always accompanied by linguistic, political and economic dominance. Other ethno-linguistic groups normally protest against being dominated. Pidgin is used largely in informal contexts. It is widely spoken in Lokoja as a language of inter-ethnic communication.

Ondo State

Ondo is one of the States with a predominance of Yoruba as the language common to over 90% of the indigenous people. Dialects of Yoruba in Ondo include: Akure, Ondo, Ikale, Owo, Ilaje, Ikare, Ile-Oluji, Ijare, Oke-Igbo (Idanre), Efon Alaye, Igbo bini, Ayetoro, Ido Ani, Ore, Ilara-Mokin, Igbara Oke (Odo), Akoko, Oka, Ajowa, Arigidi, Ifura, Ogbaji, and Isua. Virtually every village has its own dialect of the Yoruba language. A second language with a notable presence in Ondo State is Ijo, largely spoken in the riverrine areas of the State. Apoi and Arogbo are also used in coastal areas. Pidgin is used mainly in interactions with non-indigenous people of the State. As in most other States, English is used in most official functions.

River State

The 33 languages in River State are: Abuan (Abua), Abuloma, Akaha, Akita, Baan, Biseni, Dekafa, Degema, Echie, Egbema, Ekpeye, Eleme, Engenni, Epie (Atisa), Gokana, Ibani, Igbo, Ikwere, Ison (Ijo), Kalabari, Kana, Kolo, Kirike, Ndoni, Nembe, Nkoro, Obolo, Odual, Ogbah (Egnih), Ogbia, Ogbogolo, Ogbronuagum, and Tugbeni. The four major languages are Ikwere, Ison (Ijo), Kalabari and Kana. Linguistically, this is the most developed State in Nigeria, thanks to the work of Professor Kay Williamson and her team at the University of Port Harcourt. Orthographies and primers have been prepared for all the languages of this State and they are all, to some extent, used in education. Twenty of these languages have had, or still have, some form of radio coverage. Only five – Ikwere, Ison, Kalabari, Kana and Ogbia – are used on television. Sixteen of them have one reader (i.e. person reading on radio) each; two, Abua and Obolo, have two readers; while one, namely Egbema, has three readers. The remaining 14 languages have no readers. The languages in the State belong to six language groups, namely: central Delta, Ijo, Igboid, Lower Cross, Ogoni (Kegboid), and Delta Edoid. One of the languages, Obolo, is notable for having an active language committee (Williamson, 1976, 1979, 1990, 1992).

Taraba

At least 73 languages have been identified as spoken as a first language in this State alone. These are:

Abon, Akum, Anca, Batu, Bete, Bitare, Bukwen, Buru, Como Karim, Dadiya, Dirim, Dong, Dza, Dzodinka, Etkywan, Etulo, Fali of Baissa, Fam, Fulfulde, Fum, Gbaya, Jibu, Jiru, Jukun Takum, Kam, Kapya, Kholok, Kona, Kpan, Kpati, Kulung, Kutep, Kwak, Kyak, Laka, Lamnso, Leelau, Limbum, Loo, Lufu, Maghdi, Mak, Mambila, Mashi, Mbembe (Tigon), Mbongno, Moo, Mumuye, Mvamp, Nde Gbite, Ndoola, Ndunda, Nshi, Nyam, Pangseng, Piya-kwona, Rang, Samba Daka, Samba Leko, Shoo-Minda-Nye, Somyewe, Tha, Tita, Tiv, Viti, Vute, Waja, Waka, Wannu, Wapan, Yamba, Yendang, Yukuben. (Dr Ume Seibert, Department of

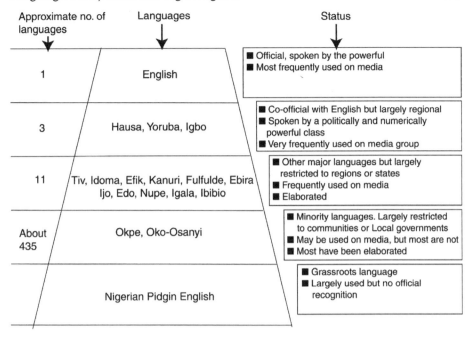

Figure 2 Approximate hierarchical representation of languages in Nigeria

Languages and Linguistics, University of Jos <www.viowa.edu/intlinet/ unijos/nig>)

The major ones are Etkywan (Ken), Fulfulde, Jukun, Kpan, Mumuye, Samba Daka, Samba Leko, Tiv, and Yendang. Kpati is extinct, while Bete and Fali of Baissa are seriously threatened. Jukun is a language of informal interaction and literacy in this State. Hausa, on the other hand, is a language of inter-ethnic communication and constitutes a serious threat to minor languages in the State. Taraba, obviously, has the largest number of languages in Nigeria, most of them endangered due to the strong influence of Hausa and Fulfulde. Figure 2 illustrates the hierarchical nature of language use, status and functions in Nigeria.

Minority languages in Nigeria

The world today has about 210 nations and 5000 languages (Ruhlen, 1991). Five per cent of the approximately five billion inhabitants of the world speak about 4500 languages, widely distributed all over the world. Africa, with well over 1000 languages, has many linguistic minority groups. In Nigeria, where there are over 450 languages, ethnolinguistic minorities speak well over 90% of these languages. In fact, the Nigerian Constitution, as noted earlier, recognises only Hausa, Yoruba and Igbo as 'majority languages'. By implication, all other languages are minority languages. However, all constitutionally implied minority languages are not equal. Thus, whereas languages like Tiv, Idoma and Ebira have up to 1 million speakers, others like Oko-Osanyin of Kogi State have only about 50,000 speakers. Yankam, a language in Plateau State, was reported to

have a population of only 7500 speakers in the 1963 census (Jibril, 1990: 16), and
the population of its speakers was reported to have been declining in favour of
Hausa. Notions about minority languages also vary from country to country.
Thus, whereas Oko-Osanyin, with its 50,000 speakers is a minority language in
Nigeria, languages like Enga and Toaripi in Papua New Guinea, with about the
same number of speakers, are regarded as major languages. A minor language in
one multilingual context can thus be a major language in another. In the Nigerian
context, as in many other multilingual African contexts, the following attributes,
identified in Adegbija (1997a: 9–11), characterise minority languages:

- comparative or absolute smallness in population size;
- low language development status;
- membership in the endangered or threatened languages list;
- absence of political or economic power;
- susceptibility of the language and its speakers to discrimination;
- restricted functional scope, especially at the national and regional levels;
  and
- neglect at the national or regional levels.

'Low language development status' and 'restricted usage' are two key phrases
that describe the plight of minority languages in Nigeria. Most of these
languages, such as Yankam, Wurkum, Yeskwa, Tal and Youm of Plateau State,
and Kiballo, Kitimi, Hyam and Kadara of Kaduna State, have no orthography,
and, consequently, no written literature. Most of them are also not used in formal
education, except sometimes orally in the first three years of primary education.
A majority of them are also not used in the media. A few are used in the electronic
media. Emenanjo (1990: 91) observes that only 44 of the Nigerian indigenous
languages have standard orthographies: '14 of these were published by the
Language Development Centre; 28 of the Rivers State languages under the
auspices of the Rivers Readers Project; four of the Niger State languages and 14 of
the Edo and Delta (former Bendel State) State languages.' A few individual and
communal efforts like the Oko-Osanyin Orthography Project (Adegbija, 1993)
have also resulted in the production of orthographies in small-group languages.
The Language Development Centre has produced orthographies for 33 Nigerian
languages in six manuals. In all, therefore, about 65 out of the 450 languages in
Nigeria now have orthographies in one form or another.

Without orthographies, other aspects of language engineering or modernisation – materials production, metalanguage, etc – which are crucial for the
language planning process, are virtually not feasible. Put bluntly, the development of small languages has been largely neglected. In such an atmosphere of
neglect, only community and individual efforts can provide a ray of hope for the
survival of small languages. The present language policy recognises only Hausa,
Yoruba and Igbo as 'major' languages, and so does not give equal rights to all
languages. Assimilation to lingua francas has been the plight of many minority
languages. For instance, in Taraba State, the Bete and Fali of Baissa are seriously
endangered due to the strong influence of Hausa. Another language in the same
State, Kpati, has already become extinct. Small-group languages in Nigeria, as in
many other multilingual contexts all over the world, suffer neglect because of

extremely limited numbers of speakers, their restricted roles, limited human and material resources at the disposal of their speakers and their not being considered a priority due to other issues being considered more pressing. It is also felt that developing small-group languages would cut the speakers off from mainstream life. Thus, their neglect and assimilation to major languages is seen as giving their speakers a window on the world.

Nigerian Pidgin English

Nigerian Pidgin English is another language with a notable presence in the Nigerian linguistic landscape. It coexists with English and the indigenous languages. Mann (1996) refers to it as 'Anglo-Nigerian Pidgin', and observes that it is an endogenous, Atlantic Pidgin, which originated from contacts between the natives of the coastal areas of present-day Nigeria and, initially, with Portuguese sailors in the 15th century, giving rise to Negro Portuguese. In the 18th century, contacts with British traders, missionaries and colonisers led to a process of re- and adlexification from English. It is variously called 'Nigerian Pidgin English', 'Nigerian Pidgin', 'Broken English', 'Broken', or Anglo-Nigerian Pidgin'. It is today commonly heard in urban communication in Nigeria. Its stronghold is in the multilingual Delta Region, particularly in Warri, Sapele and Effurun, where some speak it as a first language. Indeed, Elugbe and Omamor (1991, cited in Mann, 1996) claim that it has been 'nativised' in the Delta, after undergoing a process of creolisation, that is, structural complication, elaboration and extension in use (Mann, 1996: 94). It is commonly used at present in the media for news broadcasts, drama sketches, discussion and programmes in which songs preferred by people are played on radio (known as request programmes). More particularly, it is used in advertising and in radio and TV presentations. Advertisements in Nigerian Pidgin English are quite popular and publicly appealing. Ken Saro-Wiwa (now deceased) and Tunde Fatunde also commonly use it in the writing of literature. It is also used in mass mobilisation. These attempts have contributed towards its graphicisation. At present, however, it still has no standard orthography. It also serves largely as an inter-ethnic lingua franca, particularly among those who are not Western educated. These expanded functions of Nigerian Pidgin English have somewhat enhanced its prestige, but not to the extent of its being highly respected or accorded a high status commensurate to that given to indigenous languages.

Nigerian Pidgin English plays a major role in the country even though it is not officially recognised, because it is socially perceived as a stigmatised language. It has very low social prestige. It is, in the main, a grassroots language used principally among people of low social status. The marketplace is one major domain of Nigerian Pidgin English usage in Nigeria. Thus, in many Nigerian markets, especially in the southern part of the country, Nigerian Pidgin English can be heard as the major language of inter-ethnic interaction. It is also the principal language of inter-ethnic communication in military barracks and in related functions, and on college and university campuses, particularly in the Federal Government Unity schools, which have students from different States of the Nigerian Federation.

Language in religion

The religious factor is a dynamic in inter-ethnic communication in Nigeria.

Religion also appears to unite people, in the sense that people of different languages tend to flock together when they belong to the same religion.

Three main religions can be recognised in Nigeria: Christianity, Islam and traditional African religion. Arabic is the principal language of Islam, at least officially. However, most Muslims cannot speak the language. So, the Muslim clerics study the Qur'an and interpret it to the Muslim worshippers. Typically, the cleric speaks in Arabic and an interpreter relays his message to the worshippers in the predominant indigenous language of the area. Some clerics speak partly in Arabic and partly in the indigenous language. Arabic is a dynamic language of solidarity among the Muslims of Nigeria, even though most of them do not speak it. They are attached to it as the language of their religion and of the Qur'an. The Arabic language and Islam work in tandem to unite Nigerian Muslims, no matter their geographical origin. A concurrent translation of messages from Arabic into the indigenous language of the area in which a mosque is located is commonplace all over Nigeria. Arabic in Nigeria is inseparable from the Islamic religion. Except in school contexts, it has very little life outside Islam. Erudition of Nigerian Muslims is measured by their competence in the Arabic language and their ability to recite extended portions of the Qur'an. While the Arabic language unites Muslims, Christians interpret competence in Arabic as evidence that one is a Muslim fanatic or a potential troublemaker. This emphasises the intricacy of the unifying and separatist function of the Arabic language in the religious domain in Nigeria.

Nigerian indigenous languages are the sole media of African traditional religions. Indeed, it would be taboo for English to be used in them, except in scholarly settings when some aspects of the traditional religions are being discussed or studied. The African traditional religion is seen as a deep display of the complexity of the various indigenous languages and as a repository of indigenous lore, languages, mores, and cultures. Traditional religion is often secret and esoteric. Worshippers need to be specifically initiated into its patterns, language, liturgy, songs, rituals and ceremonies before they can be considered faithful worshippers. Adherents often operate in a deep invisible supernatural realm both from the point of view of language and of the practice of their religion. The language of the traditional religions is sometimes coded so that non-initiates cannot participate in the messages being passed across to the initiated.

The language situation and usage in Christianity is somewhat more complex. This is so because language usage in the Christian religions and worship in churches is dictated largely by the denomination, the educational status and language background of the majority of members of the congregation, the geographical location of the church, and, sometimes, the language background of the pastor in charge of the congregation. In some churches, for example, the Faith Tabernacle in Ota, Ogun State, believed to have the largest church building in the world, the Bishop in charge ministers only in English. This is understandable because he has a diverse and multilingual mixture of worshippers numbering about 50,000 from different ethno-linguistic groups in Nigeria. Sermons, prayers, testimonies, songs, choruses, and meetings are all conducted in English. Interpretation into a few indigenous languages such as Yoruba and Igbo is presented in separate corners within the church, in such a manner that only a very attentive listener will be aware that such interpreting is going on. In some other congregations, the indigenous languages or Nigerian Pidgin English are used for all activities. Some other churches function multilingually.

In effect, communication occurs in the principal language of an area, for instance, Yoruba, while simultaneous interpretations or consecutive translations are presented in the languages of members of the congregation with a noticeable numerical presence in the church. This kind of language scenario typically occurs in the Deeper Life Bible Church, especially during the Easter and Christmas Retreats. At the United Missionary Chapel, Ilorin, Kwara State, opposite Matchco, services are conducted mainly in English but Sunday school classes are conducted both in English and Yoruba, the predominant language of Ilorin. The United Missionary Church of Africa (UMCA) denomination, however, also has branches of churches within the metropolitan Ilorin area that function exclusively in such Nigerian indigenous languages as Igala, Nupe, Hausa and Yoruba. These services are intended to cater for speakers of these languages resident in Ilorin town. Branches of the church in different parts of Nigeria typically function in the predominant language of the geographical area in which they are located. This is characteristic, too, of branches of other churches. For instance, UMCA churches located in Okene, Ogaminana and Ikuehi function exclusively in the Ebira language because this is the predominant language of Ebira land.

English is viewed as a tool of Christianity, especially in the Nigerian Muslim north. The English language certainly plays a more dominant role and has a greater perceptual salience in Christianity in Nigeria than it does in Islam or Traditional religions. English is most common among Pentecostals and Independent Ministries, though indigenous languages are used as well, but largely in interpreting. Indigenous languages are more prominent among traditional Christians such as the Protestants, Anglicans, Methodists and Catholics. Evangelicals, as in the Evangelical churches of West Africa and in Spiritualist churches, such as the Aladura and Celestial churches, typically function in indigenous languages, though they use English as well. In religious worship, multilingual competence is highly esteemed and envied, perhaps because of the ability to reach the various members of an audience directly. Thus, any preacher able to use many languages, or to spice a message with proverbs, riddles, jokes, etc from indigenous languages like Yoruba, Hausa, Edo or Nupe (depending on the location of the religious institution) tends to win great esteem and accolade. Adegbija (2004: 69) comments as follows on the functions of language in religion:

> Generally, then, in the religious domain in Nigeria, language could function as a potent weapon for cementing a spiritual bond, for identifying the faithful (in the case of Arabic and traditional religionists in particular, especially as far as the reciting of incantations is concerned), and for enlisting a moral army, dedicated to a spiritual course and to goodness in this world and in the world beyond. In performing these functions, any of the three main types of languages (exoglossic, endoglossic, or endoexoglossic) in the country could be employed, the final choice being largely dependent, to a large extent, on the sociolinguistic composition of a majority of the religious congregation and the geographical location of their place of worship. On the whole, the functions of language in the religious domain, an impor-

tant factor in Nigeria's total cultural make-up, must be seen as a crucial dimension in the understanding of the multiglossic sociolinguistic situation.

Languages of literacy

Literacy is the backbone of national development. All over the world, there are about 862 million illiterate people, two-thirds of whom are women. In Nigeria, over 60 million people are illiterate; about 10.3 million adults are illiterate. Nigeria has been ranked as third from the bottom of the list of countries in the world in achieving literacy for all (*NTA News*, 9 pm, 18 September 2003). UNESCO now aims at Basic Education for all by the year 2015 based on the argument that neither good governance nor democracy can thrive in illiteracy. In Nigeria, agencies like the National Commission for Mass Literacy, the Universal Basic Education Board, UNESCO and UNICEF are all collaborating to ensure that such a goal is achieved.

Literacy programmes in Nigeria are characterised by diversity in the language used from one State to another. Several aspects of the sociolinguistic profile of Nigeria closely impinge on literacy in the country. The country is characterised not only by dense multilingualism, but also by dense multidialectalism in virtually every State. Another aspect of the sociolinguistic profile that impinges on literacy is the haphazard distribution of indigenous languages throughout the 36 States and Abuja, the Federal Capital Territory. Although the multilingual language policy stipulated by the *National Policy on Education* (*NPE*, 1981) has assisted the spread of Hausa, Yoruba and Igbo, and the Mother Tongue[2] Medium Policy in the primary school has assisted the status of some of the indigenous languages, there is still no Nigerian language that is spoken as a first language by more than 50% of the entire population. And even though English is recognised as the official language, it is still largely a minority language because it is spoken by less than 20% of the Nigerian population. These facts have important implications for the planning of literacy programmes in Nigeria.

Basic literacy programmes in Nigeria are essentially concerned with reading, writing and numeracy. They also emphasise moral and civic education and functional education for adults. Many of the agencies for Adult and Non-formal Education are also involved in rural and continuing education, whose principal goal is inculcating functional skills, assisting adults to enhance their knowledge of their social and physical environment and assisting them to improve their modes of living as well as organising workshops, seminars, and other courses for semi-literates to ensure that they do not revert to illiteracy. (See, for instance, the Ondo State Agency for Adult and Non-formal Education Annual Report, 1991). Sections in literacy programmes include those of basic literacy, functional literacy, vocational literacy (e.g. motor mechanics, carpentry and vulcanising skills), and post-literacy continuing education, including planning, research and statistics, finance and supplies and personnel development. A women's education programme has been added to the literacy programmes in some States due to the different self-improvement programmes championed by the wives of some past presidents – for instance, during Sani Abacha's presidency, the 'Better Life for Rural Women' programme. President Babangida's wife modified this and renamed it the 'Family Support Program'. Such initiatives have resulted in a women's education programme being added to the literacy programmes in some states, for example, Benue State. The core principle of such programmes is that illiterate and unskilled women are taught literacy through practical activities such as cooking, bakery skills, sewing, knitting, laundry, childcare, house management and care. The overall effect is to prepare otherwise illiterate and unskilled women for improved standards of living and self-employment (Ministry of Education, Benue State, personal communication).

The language usage practices in literacy programmes in each State are characterised by diversity and variety. So is the practice in teacher recruitment for literacy programmes. The general policy pattern, however, is to use the main language in each State in basic literacy. The minority languages are neglected completely or their speakers are made to acquire literacy through the medium of the main language of the State. Rivers State is the only exception to this. This is so because, thanks to the Rivers Readers Project, virtually all the languages of the State are used in literacy programmes.

In many of the States, post-literacy programmes are conducted in English. Tiv and Idoma are used in Benue State and many northern States such as Sokoto, Katsina, Kaduna, Kano, and Kebbi use Hausa as the main language of literacy. In States such as Ogun, Ondo, Oyo, Osun and Lagos States, Yoruba is the language of literacy.

Most States employ serving teachers, particularly Grade Two or National Certificate of Education retired teachers or holders of the General Certificate of Education and the West African School Leaving Certificate on a part-time basis as literacy teachers. These teachers do not receive full salaries but are normally paid honoraria. Some States use referred Grade Two teachers who are briefly retrained as literacy instructors.

The venues for literacy programmes include primary school buildings, churches, mosques, and palaces of chiefs, markets and town/community halls. The syllabi employed in the post-literacy programmes are generally a modification of primary school classes 3–6 syllabuses. Contact hours also vary from about six hours a week for as long as nine months, as is the practice in Ondo State or for one year or two years, as is the practice in Ogun State. Candidates who successfully complete the two-year post-literacy programme are awarded a certificate equivalent to the First School Leaving Certificate. In many small villages and among speakers of small languages in various parts of the country, there are simply no adult literacy programmes at all. Whereas all States have adopted the UNESCO declaration aimed at reducing the level of illiteracy or achieving literacy for all by the year 2000, none has achieved this goal. Some also have adopted the philosophy of 'each one teach one, or fund the teaching of one' as a strategy for ensuring that the 2000 goal was realised. Such a philosophy is weak, however, since it assumes that everyone qualifies to be a teacher in literacy programmes.

Past evaluations of mass literacy programmes in Nigeria have not been positive. The 1982–83 mass literacy campaign showed that the average enrolment rate was only 2.8% of the illiterate population. The number of literacy classes was also found to have decreased in comparison with previous years. The illiteracy rate in the entire country was conservatively put at 70% of the population. Although many illiterates enrolled for the basic literacy classes that ran for nine months, only a few continued in post-literacy classes, which ran for a further one or two years. Consequently, many neoliterates very easily reverted to illiteracy, before reaching a permanent literacy level. Drop-outs from the primary school system are also constantly increasing the number of illiterates within the country. In spite of the launching of the International Literacy Year and the establishment in Nigeria of the National Commission for Mass Literacy, Adult and Non-formal Education in June 1990, as well as the proclaimed desire of the Federal Government to achieve literacy for all by the year 2000, this picture has changed only a little with the Universal Basic Education Program of the Obasanjo administration in 1999 (Adegbija, 1992a, 1997b; Okedara & Okedara, 1992).

In summary, the following observations may be made about the language profile of Nigeria:

- It is characterised by dense multilingualism and dense multidialectalism. Language and dialect loyalties are deep and widespread (see Adegbija, 2004 for details).
- No single language is predominant throughout the entire country. Instead, there are regionally and locally dominant languages. No single language is spoken as a first language by more than 50% of the population. This unevenness in the distribution of languages is a major challenge for language policy and planning. While languages like Hausa, Yoruba, Igbo, Tiv, Fulfulde, Gwari, and Nupe are spoken across many States, some others such as Edo and most of the small-group languages are virtually limited to one State. Jibril (1990: 116) gives examples of the Ganawuri and Yankam languages as examples of 'one-village languages'.
- More than 85% of the languages within the country have not been linguistically developed, elaborated or harnessed for formal use, for instance, in education. Only about 15% (or 67 Nigerian languages) have *standardised* orthographies. Williamson (1990) indicates that 118 Nigerian languages have one form of writing or another, though the orthographies may not be standardised. This means that at least 62% or about 280 languages used in Nigeria have no written form at all. This severely restricts their use in very crucial official domains.
- Many of the languages are threatened or endangered, because of their limited functional roles or restricted usage.
- English is a dominant minority language spoken by about 20% of the population. It is constitutionally recognised as an official language. It is used as a medium of instruction in schools, as a subject in the curriculum, in the mass media, in the judiciary, in governance, banking and commerce. Its specialised use has resulted in the development of a power-brokering educated elite distinguished largely by the mastery of the English language and separated from the non-Western educated populace that cannot function in the English language.
- Hausa, Yoruba and Igbo are the three demographically dominant languages. Theoretically, they have official recognition for legislative matters and as subjects of instruction in the school curriculum at the secondary school level. In practice, however, they are hardly used in legislative houses. They are also largely regionally restricted.

- A hierarchical relationship exists between the languages in Nigeria. Akinnaso (1991: 32) proposes a simple three-tier hierarchy as follows: national, regional and local. Languages like English, Hausa, Yoruba and Igbo are used at the national level. Others like Efik, Ijaw, Ibibio, etc, are used at the regional level and yet others like Uwu and Oko-Osanyin are used at the local government level. A finer-grained five-tier hierarchical system may be proposed as follows (see Figure 2):
  - English as the official language;
  - Hausa, Yoruba and Igbo as the three main Nigerian languages;
  - network languages used in different regions such as Edo, Efik, and Fulfulde;
  - other major Nigerian languages such as Nupe, Igala, Ebira; and finally,
  - minority languages of which there are about 390 (cf. Agheyisi, 1984: 244).
- The languages of smaller groups, such as Efik, Ijaw and Urhobo are used as medium of instruction and learnt as subjects at the primary school levels in their roles as first languages or languages of the immediate community.
- Several minority languages are limited to local usage. Many minority languages are seriously threatened due to competition from major languages. This is particularly true in the northern part of the country, where many speakers are shifting to Hausa, perceived to have more functional utility and a greater future in the national scheme of things.
- Although Nigerian Pidgin is widely used at the grassroots level, it has no official recognition and is assigned no role, particularly in educational establishments. Its role is largely informal.
- Arabic is seen as the language of Islam, the indigenous languages as the languages of traditional African religions. In the northern part of the country, English is also largely perceived as the language of Christianity.

The next section examines language spread in the Nigerian multilingual context.

Language Spread

Introduction

This section discusses language use and spread in education and the media. With respect to education, it focuses on language use at the pre-primary, primary, secondary and tertiary levels. Cooper (1982: 6) defines language spread, which he considered as 'a more active notion of language shift' as 'an increase over time, in the proportions of a communicative network that adopts a given language or language variety for a given communicative function'. He also proposes that acquisition planning is a formal mechanism for language spread and language maintenance. It is, therefore, interesting to examine the languages used in education and the media, two very powerful, diverse and mutually reinforcing agencies in language spread and maintenance in Nigeria. A common observation is that of shift towards the dominant indigenous languages that are found to be of more utilitarian value. There is also a significant shift, particularly in the educational domain, towards English, perceived to be the language of a promising educational and economic future. Kaplan and Baldauf (1997: 285) observe that language shift may be caused by, among others, the following factors:

- proximity to a 'larger' language;
- changes in social attitudes towards other language communities without reference to proximity;
- permeable borders between languages in such a way that borders become unidentifiable;
- availability of resources in one language not found in another.

Language shift may also be the result of a changing popular attitude towards the external language.

The focus on language use in the media will be its use in television, on radio and in the print media. A principal point of note in both education and the media is the remarkable dominance of English. This has been so since colonial times and continues to be so even at the present time.

Language spread through education

The language-spread policies in Nigeria are evidently displayed in the educational domain. The slant in spread policies, however, favours English more than it does the indigenous languages. This accounts very easily for the reason why English has become heavily entrenched in Nigeria's body politic, while the indigenous languages largely suffer neglect and are mostly restricted to their domains or regions of use.

The first primary schools in Nigeria were established in 1842 during the missionary era, specifically through the activities of the Church Missionary society, the Wesleyan Methodists, the Baptists and the Roman Catholics. Later on, other missionary bodies such as the Evangelical Churches of West Africa also established schools. At present, many newer denominations such as the Living Faith Church, the Redeemed Christian Church of God, etc. have not only introduced primary and secondary schools, but also universities, such as Babcock University, owned by the Seventh Day Adventists and Covenant University, established by the World Mission Agency.

Language is both a medium and a subject in the school curriculum. Education is the chief medium of the official spread of the different languages, particularly English. This is so because using a language as its medium or as a subject both directly and indirectly spreads and entrenches it. Education itself is imparted through language.

Pre-primary education

The *National Policy on Education* stipulates that the first language should be the medium of education at the pre-primary level of education. It is the neatest bridge between the home and the school and the least emotionally stressful. First-language usage in education at this level also prepares the child for language use at the primary level of education. A wide gulf does exist, however, between theory and practice. First, a majority of children, especially in rural areas, never go to pre-primary schools. They simply begin their education at the primary school level. Children who go to pre-primary schools, mainly children of the wealthy and of the elite, begin with an early immersion in English. More than 90% of the pre-primary schools in Nigeria do not follow the prescription of the *National Policy on Education* to the effect that the first languages should be the medium in early education. Consequently, right from the first contact with school, children are given their first dose of English. This fulfils the desires of the proprietors of the schools and of elitist parents (Omojuwa, 1983). Incidentally, in many homes of the elites and the wealthy, English is also frequently used, perhaps in an attempt to start preparing the child for pre-primary education. The early start with English is also seen as an attempt to give the child a window on the world right from the outset. Thus, the English begun at home is reinforced right from the pre-primary school level, contrary to the dictates of the *National Policy on Education*. Since most pre-primary schools are privately owned, the Government has only had a very marginal impact, if any, on language use at this level, nor has it been able to enforce the first-language medium policy. Therefore, a language-related problem is created for the child right from the beginning – education is begun through the medium of English. At the beginning of primary education, English is also largely the medium in most schools, contrary to policy dictates. Most pre-primary schools have continued the policy of the early entrenchment of English by also beginning a primary level of education. Thus, it is very common to hear of such 'nursery and primary schools' named Kingdom Heritage Nursery and Primary School (in Canaaland, Ota, Ogun State) or Tenderfoot Nursery and Primary School (in Fate, Ilorin, Kwara State). In cases where English is much spoken in homes, the pre-primary school reinforces English at school and the home also reinforces the school language. This contributes greatly to the entrenchment of English in the psyche of the child right from the early stages of life.

Language spread at the primary school level

To understand fully language spread at the primary school level in Nigeria at the present time, a background of what transpired during the colonial era may be useful. The colonial period began when the British took over all trade in 1821.They introduced British-style law and order. In 1861, Lagos was annexed to Britain. Soon after, governing aristocrats began to arrive in Nigeria to settle. Indigenous languages (today fondly called 'heritage languages' in the West) were considered inadequate to bear the weight of the importation of modern skills and knowledge. Thus, Metcalf Sunter, the first inspector of schools in English-speaking West Africa, insisted that the natives must learn English because it is 'the language of commerce and the only language worth a moment's consideration' (quoted in Wise, 1956: 22). Soon after Sunter's observation, an Educational Ordinance, which made English the language of instruction in schools, was passed. Another Education Ordinance followed in 1926. This historical legacy, which has not been rooted out, has been the foundation on which contemporary policy makers have built.

The language policy relating to primary school education in Nigeria stipulates that the first language is to be used in the early stages of education and English at a later stage. It is, however, vague on when this 'later stage' should occur. Consequently, most primary school teachers oscillate from the first languages to English. Understandably, this is sometimes done out of the desire to be understood. However, this policy of using the first language at the early stages, and then later to shift to English, inhibits the objective of the acquisition of permanent numeracy and literacy. The unwritten assumption is that the first languages are not sophisticated enough to cope with the demands of education beyond the first three years of primary education. This policy decision has been the undoing of indigenous languages as it has denied them the kind of spread and growth that would have resulted had the languages been used to express modern scientific concepts early in the educational domain.

While the language policy was intended to assist the spread of the first languages, it has, due to the failure to implement policy, been more beneficial for the spread and the entrenchment of English. First, English is the language that is officially, and is in practice, continued in the curriculum after the first few years of primary education. Second, it is also taught as a subject. This provides added impetus for its spread. The first languages are not recognised as subjects in the curriculum. The new Federal Government Universal Basic Education policy, which aims at providing primary education, has not done anything tangible to redress this situation.

A principal challenge to first-language medium of education policy relates to its implementation in cosmopolitan areas like Lagos, Ibadan, Port Harcourt, Kaduna and Abuja, cities in which people from many diverse ethnic groups live. Akindele and Adegbite (1999: 115) note, however, that there is no reason why the first-language medium policy cannot succeed in such cosmopolitan areas because the majority of children are normally from a particular language group. Thus, such children could be taught in their first languages while special schools could be established for children not catered for in the first-language medium policy, where other languages, both foreign and indigenous, could serve as media of instruction.

Language spread at the secondary school level

Undoubtedly, the secondary school level is the *most effective and widespread organ* for formal language spread, particularly the spread of English.

- A larger number of students attend secondary school than attend the universities. Many children drop out of schooling at secondary level.
- Proficiency in, for instance, English, for most Nigerians, seems to crystallise at this level, except for those who go on to tertiary institutions.
- Students from many parts of Nigeria study indigenous languages like Hausa, Yoruba, Igbo and Efik as subjects at the secondary school certificate level.

These factors have contributed significantly to the spread of these languages. However, the largest numbers of schools that offer them as subjects at the secondary school certificate level are often located in the regions in which these languages are spoken. The spread of Hausa, Yoruba and Igbo has been some-what partially boosted by the language policy that stipulates that, at this level of education, each child should learn either Hausa, Yoruba or Igbo as a subject in the curriculum. Although this policy has been only haphazardly implemented, when implemented at all, it has given some impetus to the spread of these languages, at least theoretically, in states in which they are not native. The prob-lem of teachers, materials and resources has made the implementation of this policy difficult in the states that would have been happy to implement it. However, Federal Government or Unity schools in all the States of the Federation mandatorily implement the policy, and this has aided the spread of the three major languages.

A similar observation cannot be made about other such indigenous languages as Tiv, Idoma, Ebira and Kanuri, which are largely restricted to their locality. An exception occurs when a large number of speakers have migrated to another language area because of trade, farming, other occupations, or some unfavourable condition that may make migration to another area mandatory. There may also be a factor in the host community, such as availability of land for farming, that is attracting speakers of other languages. This kind of migration has often assisted the spread of such a language. The Tiv language, for instance, is spoken largely in Plateau and Benue states. However, because of farming, many speakers have migrated to parts of Oyo and Kwara States. Thus, one hears Tiv being spoken in settlements in Jamparta in the Igbeti area of Oyo State and Pampo Ogele, as well as in Pampo Obada in Kwara State. Residency in such areas is sometimes temporary, and this does not permit effective and intensive spread of such languages to the host community.

Different indigenous languages have been spread in different parts of Nigeria among host communities through the creation of language enclaves. A language enclave develops when speakers of a particular language settle in an area of a community to which the language is not native. In Nigeria, the most notable of these are the Sabongari and Sabo areas in which the Hausa-speaking people have settled. Thus, in many predominantly Yoruba towns like Ilorin, Ogbomosho, Oyo, Sagamu and Ibadan, there are Sabongari and Sabo enclaves occupied largely by Hausa-speaking people. (Sometimes, an area in northern Nigeria, in which non-Hausa-speaking people have settled, is also referred to as Sabo.) In such linguistic enclaves, the settlers even appoint their own chiefs, perpetuate their culture and ensure the intergenerational transmission and spread of their language through informal education, cultural initiation and celebrations, and conscious oral language tutoring within families.

Although statistics are not available, the impact of internal immigration on language distribution is remarkable. Reference has already been made to Sabongari enclaves in different parts of Nigeria, to which Hausa people have migrated and settled, thereby spreading the Hausa language. At Sagamu in Ogun State, for instance, there is a heavy presence of the Hausa language and culture. While a few indigenous people of the host communities do pick up a few words and expressions of the language of the incoming immigrants, the impact of such language enclaves on the entire host community appears to be rather minimal, because language is a very sensitive affair and each community jealously guards its identity and maintains its language, protecting the community from encroachment. In spite of such an attitude of language loyalty, intermarriages and the natural course of interaction when two languages coexist results in a greater appreciation of the diversity in language and culture. Some Hausas have naturally learned to speak Yoruba just as some Yorubas have learned the language of their guests – all these interactions occur in spite of the generally perceived mutual antipathy between the two dominant groups in Nigeria, especially since the assumption of the presidency by Olusegun Obasanjo, when

Hausa people have complained of being marginalised by the Obasanjo administration. In effect, meaningful interactions naturally occur between speakers of
the host language and those of the migrating language.

The language policy at the secondary school level mandates the use of English
both as the medium of instruction and as a core subject in the curriculum. This
policy has enhanced the spread and entrenchment of English in the Nigerian
community. Although the National Policy on Education does not categorically
state the medium of education in secondary education, it is clear, and the practice
shows, that English is expected to be the medium, particularly since a changeover was supposed to have occurred in the later stages of primary education.

Language spread at the tertiary level of education

The tertiary level of education – the colleges, polytechnics and universities in
particular – constitutes the *predominant organ* for the entrenchment and spread of
English in Nigeria. The importance of tertiary institutions for career goals, life
achievements and upward social mobility emphasises the importance of
English. In fact, students cannot be accepted into most of these institutions without a credit pass in English. Students with a deficiency, if they are admitted at all,
have to make up for such a deficiency in one way or another before graduation.
English for Academic Purposes is also a general course undertaken as a subject
by students in such institutions. This general course is referred to as the 'Use of
English' course in most universities and colleges. In most universities, it is
usually a four-credit (60 hour) course, which must be passed by students before
they graduate. Such a policy assists the spread and entrenchment of English not
only in the Nigerian educational system but also in the psyche of Nigerian
youth. Given the fact that graduates of such institutions spread out around
Nigeria after graduation, occupy positions of authority, prominence and
power and become policy makers and power brokers in different walks of life,
the impact of this level of education in the spread of English in Nigeria can be
easily understood. No indigenous language, *de jure*, enjoys this kind of privilege and patronage. This practice, naturally, gives the spread of English an
undue advantage, particularly in formal settings. In fact, indigenous languages
are stigmatised in this domain in most African countries. The following observations by Kamwangamalu about indigenous languages in South Africa are very
true of Nigeria as well:

> It does not take long for the language consumer to realise that education in
> an African language does not ensure one social mobility and better
> socio-economic life; that those who can afford it, among them policy
> makers themselves, send their children to English-medium schools; and
> that when all is told, only education in English opens up doors to the
> outside world as well as to high-paying jobs. In this regard Carol Eastman
> (1990) is right when she says that people would not want to be educated in
> their indigenous language if that language has no cachet in the broader
> social, political and economic context. The difficulty of marketing African
> languages has helped former colonial languages, in this case English, and
> to some extent Afrikaans, to remain central to administrative, educational,
> business and technical domains. (1997a: 245)

Examinations, also very crucial for the destiny and future of graduates of tertiary institutions, are also largely conducted in English. Over 98% of library books stocked in Nigeria are written in English. Official interaction within the university is predominantly in English. Memos, notices and other types of information and correspondence are written in English. Textbooks are written in English. The Internet is accessed in English. Tertiary education in Nigeria is, therefore, like a grand master plan for promoting the spread and entrenchment of English in the country. This dominance of English has constituted an obstacle to the spread of indigenous languages in the educational domain. Graduates of this kind of English-dominant education determine the country's future and policy. It can, therefore, be easily understood where their sympathies will lie. It is also understandable why English will remain the language of power in Nigeria. The restriction of most of Nigeria's indigenous languages to their local areas and their endangerment in those situations partially accounts, too, for the regression or the stagnation of these languages.

Language spread in the media

The media are a potent and dynamic agent of language spread in Nigeria. Media language use has a multiplying and reinforcing effect through the senses of sight and hearing. Normally, the larger the number of newspapers, radio or TV programmes in a particular language, the greater is the potential spread and dissemination of the impact, prestige and esteem of that language. Particularly, the print media reinforce literacy and thereby succeed in widening the communicative network in which a particular language is used. In doing this, they further entrench the spread of the language being used.

Incontrovertibly, the dominant and the supreme media language in Nigeria is English. Over 90% of newspapers and magazines in Nigeria are published in English. The majority of programmes on radio and TV, perhaps over 60%, are also in English. Virtually every one of the 36 States in Nigeria has an English newspaper published daily or weekly. However, very few indigenous newspapers are published regularly, perhaps not more than five in the whole country.

Folarin and Mohammed (1996: 101) have classified the establishment and appearance of indigenous Nigerian newspapers into what they have called five 'waves'. They propose that *Iwe Irohin*, a Yoruba newspaper, is in a class of its own in the first wave (1859–1867). This certainly contributed to the stature and significant literary spread of the Yoruba language among Nigerian indigenous languages. The second wave covers the period 1885–92, and features two Efik papers, *Unwana Efik* and *Obukpon Efik* as well as a Yoruba paper *Iwe Irohin Eko*. The third wave started with the founding in Yoruba of *Eko Akete* in 1922, and ended with the second and final death of the paper in 1937. The fourth wave began with the publication of *Gaskiya Tafi Kwabo* (1937/38) and continued until Nigeria's independence and republican status in the 1960s. The fifth wave includes the rest of the development of indigenous newspapers up to the present time. Unfortunately, of all the newspapers from the first to the fourth wave, only *Irohin Yoruba* and *Gaskiya Tafi Kwabo* still exist today.

As far as publishing in the indigenous languages is concerned, the Yoruba language has been particularly vibrant. It can boast three newspapers that have lasted for some time in the recent past. These are *Iroyin Yoruba, Gbohungbohun*

and *Isokan*. *Iwe Irohin Fun Awon Ara Egba Ati Yoruba*, established by Reverend
Henry Townsend, a Church Missionary Society (CMS) missionary, was the first
Yoruba newspaper and the first indigenous language newspaper in Africa. It
was first published on 3 December 1859 but publication came to an abrupt end on
13 October 1867. An aspect of the paper that made it appealing and potent in
spreading the Yoruba language in Nigeria was that it focused on a range of issues
then considered as very topical, namely, births, deaths, movements of religious
ministers, parish activities, baptism and confirmation, politics, particularly those
relating to Abeokuta and its environs, and economic matters such as trade
reports – cotton statistics and produce prices. News about the colonial administration, some foreign news, advertisements and public announcements were
also included. Other Yoruba newspapers, all now defunct, emerged later, including *The Yoruba News*, *Eko Akete*, *Eleti Ofe* and *Eko Igbehin*. On 4 June 1945, the late
Chief Obafemi Awolowo, who had great faith in the Yoruba people and
language, established *Iroyin Yoruba* (still published today by the African Newspapers of Nigeria Plc., which also publishes the *Nigerian Tribune*, an English
daily). The regular features of *Iroyin Yoruba* include news, particularly the weird
and the sensational, as well as the religious (traditional, Christian and Islamic),
the staking of pools,[3] market days in Yoruba land, socials, poetry, fictional and
true to life stories, humour, etc. A 1990 issue of the *United Nations Handbook* put
the circulation figure at about 20,000 copies, but Salawu (2003: 96) claims that a
source from the publishers put the number of copies sold per week at between
8000 and 10,000. The newspaper is read by people of all ages, education, voca-
tions and values, and it is highly sought after. This fact assists the spread and
maintenance of the Yoruba language. It is seen as educative, informative and
entertaining. Salawu (2003: 96) observes that, 'The newspaper appeals to Yoruba
audience in its entirety ranging from the young, to the aged and the scholars.'

Gbohungbohun, another Yoruba newspaper, also a weekly, first appeared on 29
October 1970. The Sketch Press Limited, a subsidiary of the O'odua Group of
Companies, published it. The paper aimed at providing information for the
people and receiving their feedback. According to Salawu, it was perceived as an
opportunity 'to give the semi-illiterates an opportunity to read'. This role assists
the spread and entrenchment of the Yoruba language. The *United Nations Handbook* put the circulation figure in 1990 at about 23,000. Due to the high cost of
newsprint in Nigeria, circulation had fallen to 10,000 by 1993.The paper is now
defunct.

Isokan, another Yoruba newspaper published by the Concord Press of Nigeria,
first appeared on 15 July 1980. Just like the other indigenous newspapers, this
one aimed at reaching the grassroots. The *World Media Handbook* put the circulation figure at 25,000. It is also now defunct. The Concord Press also published
Amana in Hausa from 1980, and *Udoka* in Igbo, from 1981. With the demise of the
Concord Press, these indigenous papers have become defunct.

Alaroye is a more recent Yoruba newspaper/magazine. Its publication started
in 1996. For now at least, the paper appears regularly on newsstands. Other
newspapers like *Alaye*, *Ajoro* and *Kowee* have been irregularly published
(Salawu, 2003: 90).

Gaskiya Taqfi Kwabo (Truth is Worth More than a Penny), published in Hausa,
has also appeared fairly regularly and over a very long period of time (since

1937/1938). The paper, established by the Gaskiya Corporation, had as its main objective the promotion of literature in northern Nigeria. Given that objective, it has also effectively been the chief promoting agent for the spread of the Hausa language. Its circulation has spread literacy in Hausa to many parts of northern Nigeria. At various times, the Gaskiya corporation had been renamed the Northern Literature Bureau and the Northern Literature Agency (NORLA) to accommodate the gradual expansion of the enterprise. The corporation had published other periodicals in the different languages of the region, e.g. *Ardo* in the Fulfulde language for the Adamawa state, *Gamzaki* in Hausa for Bauchi, *Mwanger U Tiv* (1948) for the Tiv language, *Okaki Idoma* in the Idoma language for Benue State, and *Albashir* (1951) in Kanuri for Borno. The Gaskiya Corporation has thus functioned as a major and dynamic agent for the spread of many of Nigeria's indigenous languages, especially in the northern part of the country. Unfortunately, such vibrant indigenous language promotion and spread by the Gaskiya media organisation is not being vigorously pursued at the present time, largely for financial reasons.

The Tiv language is another Nigerian indigenous language that has benefited from some media advantage. Information provided in Tsumba (2002) indicates that between 1911 and 1980, first language education was planned, organised and implemented in the Tiv language by the Dutch Reformed Church Mission (DRCM) and later by the Church of Christ, known among the Tiv as the *Nongo U Kristu Hen Sudan Hen Tiv* (*NKST*). This first language education provided impetus for the spread of the Tiv language. As from 1940, some newspapers and magazines began publishing in the Tiv language, edited by journalists with Tiv as their first language. Table 1 gives examples of such papers. Tsumba observes that, in spite of the exclusive use of Tiv language in the DRCM/NKST school, the first graduate ever produced in Tiv land, a 1964 chemistry graduate of the University of Ibadan, was a product of the school. The first Tiv lawyer was also from that school. Education in Tiv, for these and other graduates trained through the medium of the language, would certainly have enhanced their positive attitude towards the language, its spread and maintenance.

Most other Nigerian indigenous languages simply have no dailies or weeklies published. This absence of newspapers or magazines in those languages has denied them the kind of vibrancy that a language acquires naturally through its use in a print medium. A far larger number of Nigerian languages are used on radio and in television[4] than in the print media. Languages like Idoma, Tiv, Ebira, Ibibio, Ejagham, etc are used on radio and in television for news and special programmes. Such use has definitely helped to enhance their spread and maintenance at least as oral media of communication.

Most minority languages are almost totally neglected in the print media, except perhaps in the occasional publication of local magazines or pamphlets

Table 1 Examples of Tiv newspapers

Newspaper	Date	Editor
Mwanger u Tiv (monthly)	1940s	Akigasai
Icha regh (weekly)	1950s	Isaac Kpum
Mkaanem (monthly)	1950s	Pastor S. Saai

such as *Asekee (The Trumpeter* – now defunct) by the Ogori Students Association and similar papers, which are normally short-lived. Many minority
languages are briefly used on radio and occasionally in television for particular
programmes. This encourages their spread, boosts their image and encourages a
sense of identity in them.

Language Policy and Planning in Nigeria

Introduction

Kaplan and Baldauf describe language planning as

> . . . a body of ideas, laws, and regulations (language policy), change rules,
> beliefs, and practices intended to achieve a planned change (or to stop
> change from happening) in the language use in one or more communities.
> To put it differently, language planning involves *deliberate*, although not
> always overt, *future oriented* change in systems of language code and/or
> speaking in a societal context. (1997: 3)

They propose an 'eco-system' model (see p. 311). Similarly, Mühlhäusler
(2000: 303) argues for ecological thinking in language planning. He sees it as
an approach which considers 'not just system-internal factors but wider environmental considerations emphasising the interlinked sub-systems in an
overall ecology of the language'. He argues that languages are not isolated
systems but have interactions with other systems outside what is strictly
considered to be linguistics. Such systems include culture, politics and environment. Any language planning system which treats one part of the system
has an impact, even if not intended, on other parts. According to Mühlhäusler,
an ecological approach to language planning shows an awareness of the dangers
of monoculturalism and extols the benefits of linguistic diversity. Thus, any
attempt to streamline ecolinguistic diversity would be counterproductive.

Haugen (1972) identifies four stages in language planning: norm selection,
codification, implementation and evaluation. Bamgbose (1983a) refers to these
stages as fact-finding, policy decision, implementation and evaluation. Bamgbose
also sees this as 'the canonical model of language planning', and suggests that it
needs to be revised to reflect the reality of language development activities in
many developing countries where 'planning' sometimes takes place without real
planning. Adegbija (1989) proposes five somewhat similar stages in language
planning. First, there is the spadework and preparation stage (during which
fact-finding is done and policy formulated). Second, there is the mass mobilisation and enlightenment stage, during which the plan is advertised, the citizenry
is educated about it and familiarised with it. Third, there is the implementation
stage, which handles the details of the language policy. Fourth, there is the evaluation stage, a continuous process for monitoring the effectiveness, problems and
prospects of the policy from the perspectives of the set objectives. Finally, there is
the review stage, also seen as a continuous process in which changes, informed
by findings in the evaluation stage, are effected from time to time as the situation
demands. He identifies the following contexts as pertinent to managers of
language resources: the language context, the socio-political context, the psychological context, the administrative/governmental context, the educational

context, the historical context and the resource context. This array of contextual features again emphasises the ecolinguistic perspective for language policy and planning proposed by Kaplan and Baldauf as well as by Mühlhäusler and is based on the awareness that languages are not isolated systems but are part of an ecolinguistic structure impinged upon by other elements within the structure. Adegbija argues that, in multilingual environments, at least the following aspects of public life and domains of language use deserve special language planning attention: the national languages, the languages of nationism or official languages, the languages of intercultural or interethnic communication, the languages of international communication, and, most importantly the languages of education (Adegbija, 1989: 2003). In the Nigerian context, it is language planning for education that has received most attention, perhaps because this domain also affects other domains for which language planning is required. For instance, it impinges on language planning for official language use or nationism, a role which English has played in Nigeria since colonial times. Attempts have also been made to cultivate Hausa, Yoruba and Igbo into national languages through language planning, but those attempts lag in implementation and have not enhanced the success of the policy. As far as planning for international purposes is concerned, the policy has not overtly stated so, but English has naturally played and still plays this role. Language policy in Nigeria has not also overtly indicated planning for inter-ethnic communication, but major community languages have served in such a capacity in most States.

Colonial language policy

The Colonial Government, due to a general re-evaluation of colonial language policy in education, took the decision to encourage vernacular education in 1926. The Government continued to depend on African clerks and messengers who were fluent in English. However, the administration or commercial firms could not employ all school leavers who had some knowledge of English. The Colonial Government, therefore, became concerned that education in English was creating expectations of employment and status that could not be realised. This line of thinking governed the decision to develop vernacular education. Education in Igbo thus became official policy. The Government initiated and supported Igbo language research by European scholars. The Colonial Government decided to recognise and promote only four vernaculars or indigenous languages – Hausa, Yoruba, Efik and Igbo – based on practical considerations relating to efficient administration and financial constraints. Professional linguists were hired to advise the Government on choice of languages. The Government also funded a translation bureau to produce textbooks. The status of the chosen languages was instantly affected by the new colonial language policy. By the 1920s, Efik, Igbo and Yoruba each had its own orthography, though the results were inconsistent, thus hampering the production of textbooks. This situation resulted in an invitation to Professor Westermann, a leading German scholar on African linguistics, to visit Nigeria to make recommendations. After touring Nigeria in 1929, he advised the adoption of a new orthography (which could also become the standard orthography for African languages), for both Efik and Igbo. This new proposal was resisted by the missionaries, especially those in the Anglican and Catholic missions, who had already been publishing their own Igbo orthographies and who thus saw no reason to invest in a new orthography. They also argued that the new orthography would not be understood by those already literate in Igbo (van den Bersselar, 2000).

There was a debate over which Igbo dialect to use as a standard. Protestant missionaries preferred their own Union Ibo dialect as standard, while the Government preferred a dialect from the Owerri area, called 'central Igbo', proposed by Dr Ida Ward. Onitsha clerks preferred the Onitsha dialect, rather than 'Union Ibo' or Central Igbo, which they considered Owerri dialects and which they were not ready to endorse. Most Igbo parents still preferred literacy in English and wanted their children taught in English. Although the CMS missionaries and the colonial administration forced some vernacular literacy on the people, there was considerable interest in Igbo, which was used to publish a leaflet popularly referred to as 'Onitsha Market Literature' (see van den Bersselar, 2000).

Since the time of the British colonial administration, constitutional provisions have been made for languages. In 1945, Richards, one of the British government officials, had argued that there was disunity in Nigeria and that the 1922 Constitution did nothing to address this problem. In 1947, the Richards Constitution made English the official language in southern Nigeria and Hausa in the north. This action was the foundation of a language-based north–south dichotomy in Nigeria, with Hausa in the north and English in the south. The 1951 Constitution confirmed the status quo, but the 1954 Constitution refined it. Article 114 of the 1954 Constitution provided the foundation for a functional hierarchical use of language in Nigeria by recognising two levels of official language usage in Nigeria – national and regional. English was to be used at the national level, while at the regional level English was to be used in the south (west and east) and Hausa and English in the North. This was so because Hausa was already seen as a unifying lingua franca in the north. It was also the language of the Hausa Fulani elite and of trade. Additionally, many northern ethnic groups had accepted Islam and its Arabic culture and would not accept English, which was perceived to be closely linked with Christianity. On the other hand, in the south, where contact with the English language was greater due to a heavy presence of missionaries, especially in the schools, there was no common language that could be used in regional administration. The Richards Constitution stipulated that English would be the acceptable language of documentation whenever there were disputes between English and Hausa in writing parliamentary bills. The Constitutions of 1960 and 1963 simply confirmed the 1954 declarations, especially with regard to the role of English. The practice of using indigenous languages in the first three years of primary education and changing over to English in the fourth year also had its foundation laid during British colonial rule. In terms of the fate of the indigenous languages, article 51 of the 1979 Constitution, which stipulates that the first language or the language of the immediate community should be used in initial education, was the beginning of the official recognition in language policy provisions.

Overall, the colonial British language education practice may be summarised as follows:

- An educated elite being groomed to assist the British in administration was taught good English in model institutions like King's College, Lagos.
- British examinations and certificates were available to reward the efforts of English learners.
- The English language was a requirement for entry into some cadres of the civil and public service.
- English was the language of instruction and was taught as a subject at the secondary school level.
- First language education was encouraged in many primary schools along-side the learning of English.

Many schools used the first language as a medium for the first three years and taught it as a subject thereafter. The number of first languages taught was, however, limited to those with a writing system, i.e. Yoruba, Hausa, Igbo and Efik. In many other primary schools, particularly in urban centres, it was a 'straight for English' policy. For a long time after independence, this colonial language policy was largely maintained (Akinnaso, 1991: 39; Dada, 1985: 286).

Language policy and implementation currently in place

In present-day Nigeria, there is no document that may be referred to as a 'language planning legislation document' per se. However, the *National Policy on Education* (*NPE*) contains very important provisions, which may be regarded as the most comprehensive provisions available anywhere on language policy and planning in Nigeria. It is, therefore, the *National Policy on Education* that most Nigerian scholars, and anyone who has to deal with language policy or language planning legislation in Nigeria, would refer to as the basic document on language planning in Nigeria. This *National Policy on Education* begins with what it calls the five main national objectives of Nigeria as stated in the Second National Development Plan, endorsed as the necessary foundation for the *National Policy on Education*. They are the building of: (1) a free and democratic society; (2) a just and egalitarian society; (3) a united, strong and self-reliant nation; (4) a great and dynamic economy; (5) a land of bright and full opportunities for all citizens (*NPE*, 1985: 7).

Certainly, to achieve these noble goals successfully for the nation, language and communication in general must play a pivotal and comprehensive role. To some extent, at least in policy if not in implementation, the language provisions of the *National Policy on Education* have taken cognisance of the fact that Nigeria is a multilingual society. Consequently, two broad language policies have been stipulated. Nigerian scholars refer to these as the 'mother tongue medium policy' (MTM) and the 'multilingual policy' (as per Bamgbose, 1991). Ecolinguistic diversity has been implicitly extolled in these two policies.

The *National Policy on Education* was prepared by the Nigerian Federal Government. It was first published in 1977 and revised in 1981 and 1985. It is the first major response to the calls for the formulation of a language policy for Nigeria, especially with respect to the domain of education. Following from this, sections 51 and 91 of the 1979 Constitution of the Federal Republic of Nigeria stipulate or imply:

- The use of English as an official language in Nigeria. Although the policy does not explicitly say so, it is taken for granted that this will also be the first language of international collaboration.

- The cultivation of Hausa, Yoruba and Igbo as co-official languages with English. They are also to be used in the National Assembly. Their widespread use could eventually result in their functioning as national lingua francas.
- The use of indigenous languages in initial education, and English thereafter.
- The promotion of select indigenous languages in each State to be co-official languages with English. These could then be used as State lingua francas. Even though the policy does not explicitly say so, this seems to be the unwritten agenda.

Constitutions after 1985, as well as revised versions of the *National Policy on Education* produced to date, have retained the above provisions that may be seen as the core elements of Nigeria's language and literacy policy. The *National Policy on Education* discusses key elements of education from the nursery school level to the university level.

The language provisions in the *NPE* are as follows:

Section 1: 8

In addition to appreciating the importance of language in the educational process, and as a means of preserving the people's culture, the Government considers it to be in the interest of national unity that each child should be encouraged to learn one of the three major languages other than his mother tongue. In this connection, the Government considers the three major languages in Nigeria to be Hausa, Ibo and Yoruba. (*NPE*, 1985: 9)

Section 2:11(3)

Government will ensure that the medium of instruction will be principally the mother tongue or the language of the immediate community, and to this end will: (a) develop the orthography for many more Nigerian languages, and (b) produce textbooks in Nigerian languages.

Some of these developments are already being pursued in the university Departments of Linguistics and under the auspices of some State Ministries of Education. The Federal Government has also set up a Language Centre as part of the educational services complex under the Federal Ministry of Education. This Language Centre will be expanded so as to have a wider scope (*NPE*, 1985: 10).

Section 3:15(4)

Government will see to it that the medium of instruction in the primary school is initially the mother tongue or the language of the immediate community and, at a later stage, English. (*NPE*, 1985: 13)

Section 4 of the document deals with secondary education. No direct policy pronouncement is made on language. However, the outlined curriculum indicates what the policy is intended to be.

Section 4:4

The junior secondary school will be both pre-vocational and academic; it will be as free as soon as possible, and will teach all the basic subjects which will enable pupils to acquire further knowledge and develop skills. The curriculum should be structured as follows:

Core Subjects	*Pre-Vocational Subjects*	*Non-Vocational Electives*
Mathematics	Woodwork	Arabic Studies
English	Metal Work	French
Nigerian Languages (2)	Electronics	
Science	Mechanics	
Social Studies	Local Crafts	
Art and Music	Home Economics	
Practical Agriculture	Business Studies	
Religious and Moral Instruction		
Physical Education		
Pre-Vocational Subjects (2)		

In selecting two Nigerian languages students should study the language of their own area in addition to any of the three main Nigerian languages, Hausa, Ibo and Yoruba subject to availability of teachers. (*NPE*, 1985: 17)

Section 4:6 focuses on the senior secondary school curriculum and has aspects that relate to English and one indigenous language. It stipulates that:

The senior secondary school will be for those able and willing to have a complete six-year secondary education. It will be comprehensive but will have a core curriculum designed to broaden pupils' knowledge and outlook. The core-curriculum is the group of subjects, which every pupil must take in addition to his specialties.

A. Core Subjects

1. English Language.
2. One Nigerian Language.
3. Mathematics.
4. One of the following alternative subjects – Physics, Chemistry and Biology. One of the following: Literature in English, History and Geography.
5. Agricultural Science or a Vocational Subject. (p. 17)

Section 7:52(6)
A new nation-wide emphasis will be placed on the study of Nigerian Arts and Culture. The National Commission will work out the overall strategy for the inclusion of Nigerian Arts, Culture and Languages in Adult Education programmes.

The policy also mentions language as a part of the General Studies component in the Teacher Training programme.

Sections 51 and 91 of the 1979 Constitution of the Federal Republic of Nigeria relate to the use of language in the National and States Houses of Assembly:

Section 51
The business of the National Assembly shall be conducted in English, Hausa, Ibo and Yoruba, when adequate arrangements have been made therefore.

Section 91
The business of the House of Assembly shall be conducted in English but
the House may in addition to English conduct the business in one or more
languages spoken in the state as the House may by resolution approve.

Many members of the Constitution drafting committee were bitterly opposed to
the use of any Nigerian language in any official manner. Acrimonious debates
over the provisions ensued. Consequently, they were deleted from the draft
Constitution. The Supreme Military Council, however, reviewed and amended
the draft Constitution. It included the deleted provision relating to the language
of official business in the National Assembly by decree and provided the following nationalistic rationale:

> At this point in our development as a nation, it is unacceptable to make
> English the only language of business of our national Assembly and to
> proceed even further to enshrine it permanently in our Constitution.
> Section 51 of the Constitution has therefore been amended to ensure that
> Hausa, Igbo and Yoruba shall be additional languages of business to the
> National Assembly and shall be so when appropriate arrangements can be
> made for their use. (*New Nigerian*, 22 September 1979, p. 13)

These provisions in the *National Policy on Education* and the 1979 Constitution are
the core provisions that most scholars usually refer to as Nigeria's language
policy document. There is no other government document that has come out
more clearly than these two on language policy, nor is there any document that is
specifically devoted to language policy and language planning.

Nigeria, as indicated earlier, is characterised by multilingualism,
multidialectalism, statism, ethnicism, rural–urban divide, poor communication
systems, a high level of illiteracy[5] and a low level of formal language development. These factors all have a bearing on language policy implementation and
constitute part of the ecology of the language planning and implementation
context in Nigeria. To neglect them is to imperil the language planning and
implementation processes or to look at the processes naively. It is against such a
background that the previously outlined language policy provisions have to be
implemented. State governments play a crucial part in taking initiatives in implementing the language policy provisions of the Constitution and the *National
Policy on Education*. There is natural hostility to any policy perceived as discrimi-
nating against some language groups. Thus, the provision which stipulates that
Hausa, Yoruba and Igbo be learned has been frowned upon by many Nigerians
from minority language backgrounds who have often complained of being
marginalised in the national scheme of things both politically and socioeconomi-
cally. Bamgbose (2001) observes that the rural–urban divide is related to uneven
development and affects language policy with regard to implementation in
which, due to the lack of infrastructure support in rural areas, agreed policies are
subject to distortion. He observes:

> it is well known that in rural areas the English-medium policy in upper
> primary classes is often a misnomer, as the level of competence of teachers
> is grossly inadequate and there is lack of reinforcement outside the class-

room. Language policy, particularly at its implementation stage, therefore has to take into consideration the considerable difference between rural and urban areas. (Bamgbose, 2001)

Political instability has been a principal impediment to the implementation of language policy in Nigeria. Previously agreed policies are often abandoned by new regimes and implementation is truncated. There is policy fluctuation, reinterpretation and misinterpretation and ad hoc and arbitrary policy initiatives. For instance, due to frequent military incursions into Nigeria's governance, plans made for implementing the use of Nigerian languages at the National and State Houses of Assembly (i.e. the training of interpreters and translators, language elaboration, vocabulary expansion) had to be shelved and have not been revived even with the restoration of civilian rule. Instability also results in a constant turnover of policy makers and implementers, thus resulting in a lack of continuity in policy making and implementation (Bamgbose, 2001). President Abacha, for instance, suddenly introduced French as a second official language in Nigeria when the Anglophone world boycotted and ostracised him due to his draconian policies and appalling record on human rights.

To meet the challenge of effective national communication, Nigeria has continued with the colonial policy of using English as an official language, even though only about 20% of Nigerians are proficient in the language. English is thus largely a minority language monopolised by the elite, and the policy of its use as Nigeria's official language has resulted in the exclusion of the masses from participation in national affairs. A major challenge for language policy is thus to make it possible for the masses to participate in the national scheme of things without proficiency in English.

Bamgbose (2001) observes that language policy in Nigeria, as in most African countries, is rarely documented, but its effect can be seen in action in various domains such as official language, medium of instruction in schools, language use in the media and in the legislature. He cites an incident in the Lagos State House of Assembly on 9 December 1999 in which there was a debate about the desirability of using Yoruba, (the dominant language of the state) as the language of discussion in the House in line with the provisions of the Constitution, which empowers each State to decide whether or not to adopt such a language in addition to English. Yoruba, the dominant Nigerian indigenous language, was rejected by the House on the grounds that:

> Yoruba language is not appropriate for the conduct of business of the House of Assembly since Lagos is a cosmopolitan city. Besides, its use is capable of demeaning and reducing the intellectual capacity of the legislators. (*Guardian*, 10 December 1999)

This incident, according to Bamgbose (2001), illustrates vividly the problems of language policy making in Nigeria, among which are:

- negative attitudes to Nigerian languages;
- overwhelming bias in favour of English;
- reliance on sentiment rather than on objective data (e.g. statistics of language use);

- elite domination of policy making;
- equation of elite interest with public interest;
- plain ignorance about language (as shown in the false claim that the use of one's language will reduce one's intellectual capacity).

The educational system is one major avenue for pursuing the above language-policy provision objectives in national life. The 'mother tongue medium policy' has been practised since the early colonial period. Three distinct senses of the word 'medium' in the concept of the 'mother tongue medium policy' have been identified:

- the use of language for oral presentation only;
- the use of language for initial literacy (reading and writing) only; and
- the use of language for teaching all subjects except English.

In the first sense, virtually all Nigerian indigenous languages may be regarded as a medium of instruction in all schools except private schools and some schools in urban centres with students from different language backgrounds. The use of language for teaching all subjects other than English, including written exercises, 'is medium of instruction par excellence and it is this kind of situation that is least encountered in Nigerian primary schools' (Bamgbose, 1977: 20).

Actual implementation of the mother tongue medium (MTM) policy in Nigerian schools reflects considerable variation ranging from zero in special English-medium schools (mostly private and fee-paying schools and many schools in urban centres) to six years, as in the Ife Six Year Primary Project, where Yoruba was used throughout the primary school. The commonest practice, between these two extremes, is that in which the first language medium is used for the first three years of primary school and a changeover to English occurs in the fourth year. This policy was inherited from colonial times and continues to the present in most Nigerian schools.

To implement the provisions of the *NPE* and use Nigerian first languages as a medium of instruction even in basic literacy, there is a clear need for the elaboration and codification of Nigerian indigenous languages. Such elaboration would entail:

- the linguistic analysis of the sound system and the grammar of the language;
- the devising of a practical orthography based on the linguistic analysis or the adaptation of an existing orthography;
- the preparation and testing of primers and readers, as well as supplementary readers;
- the preparation and introduction of teachers' notes and manuals to guide teachers in the use of such primers and readers, and to explain the principles of the orthography.

In situations where other subjects have to be taught through the language, the following additional requirements are desirable: preparation of textbooks in the school subjects concerned; preparation of a dictionary and a practical grammar of the language and encouragement of written literature in the language. Work on textbooks will require extensive corpus planning or language development. Appropriate terminology would have to be developed for elementary mathematics, science, social studies, etc. Some curriculum development would also have to be carried out (Bamgbose, 1977: 21; Ntinsedi & Adejare, 1992: 38; see also Adegbija, 2004).

A close look at the official provisions indicates, among others, the following.

(1) The Government recognises the importance of language in the nation.
(2) The importance of a child's first language is accepted; this explains the MTM policy.
(3) The dynamics of language ecology in a multilingual context is somewhat recognised by that aspect of the policy that stipulates that one of Hausa, Yoruba and Igbo be learned apart from the first language of the child.
(4) The domain of education is considered crucial in language policy making and planning; consequently the *NPE* document makes provisions on all crucial aspects of education from the nursery school level to the university level.
(5) As Bamgbose (1977: 20) rightly observes, the policy rests on two cardinal planks: the use of the first language as a medium of instruction in early formal education (the MTM policy), and the requirement that every Nigerian child learn one of the three constitutionally recognised languages in addition to his or her own language and English (the multilingual policy).
(6) The statement of the desire to develop orthography for many more Nigerian languages and produce textbooks in Nigerian languages is indicative of a seriousness of purpose to pursue the policy. It constitutes also a recognition of possible obstacles that could thwart the successful implementation of the policy and is indicative of the intention to confront such obstacles head on.
(7) The English language and one Nigerian language are listed as 'core subjects' (*NPE*, 1985: 17), indicating the importance the policy attaches to them.
(8) The policy seems to assume that English will be used as a medium of instruction after the secondary school level. It generally gives English first place as a medium of instruction. This obviously has implications for enhancing the prestige of English in the educational system.
(9) Hausa, Yoruba and Ibo, designated as the three major Nigerian languages by the policy, are being groomed to be co-official with the English language. Such an evolution seems to be taken for granted, or at least implied, in the policy on Nigeria's official language, particularly with regard to the role assigned to English in the National and State Houses of Assembly. Recognition of the fact that indigenous languages need cultivation to national status is indicated both by their initial inclusion by the Constitution drafting committee, and by their re-inclusion by the Supreme Military Council after the provision relating to them was deleted.

As noted previously, the changeover to English in most schools normally takes place in the fourth class of primary school, and one of the major Nigerian languages continues as a subject in the school curriculum up to the secondary school level. Often, the incompetence of pupils in the use of English in practical classroom situations necessitates the use of one of the major Nigerian languages to levels beyond which the language policy has given them legitimacy as medium of instruction. In most States, the reality of implementation is that the first language of most pupils is never used. Rather, the dominant first language of an area in which a school is located is used in initial literacy no matter what the different first languages represented may be. Most elites send their children to private nursery schools, which defy the policy because of the early immersion of children in English. These elites believe that children so immersed in English right from early education have a greater opportunity for upward social mobility and a brighter educational future than children who learn in the first language. Moreover, such private schools are normally better staffed and have better facilities for the provision of education than the government schools. The results of the performance of pupils in public examinations like the Common Entrance Examination and the Federal Government College Examinations also show that children in such private nursery and primary schools perform far better than do children in government schools.

In an address delivered on 10 December 1991, a one-time Oyo State Commissioner for Education, Youth and Sports provided the general rationale behind the first language medium education:

> The idea of using the mother tongue as a medium of instruction in primary schools is mooted on the premise that the children learn better when they can use previous knowledge to solve new problems. The school age child has acquired such knowledge through the mother tongue, which is his first language. He would therefore feel more at home with the school, if the language he has already acquired could be used to advantage at least for the first few years of his school life. (see Commissioner's Address, 1991)

Moreover, it is believed that the first languages have many natural resources including natural artefacts, a rich and predominantly oral culture, that can be tapped to ensure maximum understanding in the school environment. The child is already familiar with such natural artefacts and so reference to them in the classroom can facilitate teaching and learning.

Bold attempts at the MTM policy implementation

Attempts to implement the MTM policy in Nigeria must be viewed from the perspective of over 450 indigenous first languages. As indicated earlier, most of these have no orthographies; indeed, more than half of them have no written form whatsoever. The policy context is also one in which three Nigerian languages, namely Hausa, Yoruba and Igbo, have been constitutionally proclaimed as 'the three major Nigerian languages'.

Some outstanding projects in first language education in Nigeria are practical demonstrations of the attempt to implement the MTM policy, and it is instructive to study them briefly. These are the Primary Education Improvement Project, the Six Year Primary Project and the Rivers Readers Project.

The Primary Education Improvement Project (PEIP)

Although language development was not the basic goal of the PEIP when it began, its implementation resulted in considerable language development effort. The project, when it began in January 1971, in the primary schools in what were then Nigeria's six northern States, aimed at the production of new instructional materials, the revision, updating and standardising of existing ones, and an effective use of materials, which carried with it the responsibility of training teachers. The ultimate goal was to improve the low educational attainment standards that had been caused by poor teaching, inadequate materials, lack of professional supervision and guidance of classroom teachers, ineffective use of languages used as media of instruction in the educational process, and the limited nature of the contents of the primary school curriculum. In the former Kwara and Benue-Plateau States, the language of instruction was English at all stages of primary education. Hausa was officially the medium in all other northern States in the first two or three years. Thereafter, English became the medium of instruction, but generally, educational attainment was poor (e.g. Omolewa, 1978: 365).

The project created subject panels including those in languages – English and Hausa – empowered to develop a new curriculum with existing or new materials. Teams of mobile teacher trainers, who were in the schools every day, were also introduced. They assisted with in-service courses for classroom teachers.

In the implementation of the project, language planning was the first major task. The language planning consisted of two options, either:

(1) (a) Hausa as a medium in the first three years and thereafter as a subject of instruction from the beginning to the end of primary education.
  (b) English as a subject for the first three years and thereafter as a medium of instruction.
  (c) Arabic as an optional subject from the first to the sixth year;

or

(2) (a) English as a medium of instruction from the beginning to the end of primary education.
  (b) A Nigerian language as a subject where possible.
  (c) Arabic as an optional subject. (Omolewa, 1978: 365)

Option (1) was adopted in Kano, Sokoto, Kaduna (Katsina Province), and Bauchi States with some measure of language homogeneity, while option (2) was mainly adopted in Kwara, Benue and Plateau where there is language heterogeneity.

A major problem encountered involved getting Hausa specialists to produce instructional materials in the language as a medium of instruction – a task they were not accustomed to performing. The Institute of Education embarked on its own programme of training Hausa specialists to fulfil this task. Omolewa observes:

> There was hardly any IM [instructional material] to be used with Hausa as a language of instruction. We had to start from scratch to write materials in all the subjects introduced into the primary curriculum in both English and Hausa. (1978: 367)

Another problem encountered in implementation related to the utilisation of the materials produced. Classroom teachers found the project classes more demanding and rigorous than non-project classes, and yet they received no extra material rewards or incentives. One strategy adopted for solving this problem was a coveted, image-boosting one-year diploma course that focused on methodology, the teaching of Hausa at primary level, the teaching of Arabic at primary level, and educational planning and administration.

The acceptance of the project, even though it broke no new ground, lay in its modification and improvement of the existing infrastructure. It succeeded in making the curriculum more relevant to the Nigerian context and in strengthening the primary school curriculum. Language planning, which affects all aspects of a school curriculum, turned out to be a major component of this apparent innovation, and herein lies its chief strength:

> Elementary science, cultural activities, and social studies were introduced for the lower classes, irrespective of the medium language [*sic*], English or Hausa. Language medium [*sic*] resources were thoroughly exploited for educational purposes in a manner quite unknown in the traditional system. (Omolewa, 1978: 368)

The feedback from and evaluation of the project indicated that the integrated approach to learning and the informal setting in groups were highly valuable. This is so because the pupils, compared to those in control classes:

(a) were more confident in talking about their experiences to both the teacher and to one another;
(b) were more fluent users of both English and Hausa;
(c) were more aware of the events and phenomena in their immediate environment;
(d) were more aware of the elementary laws of nature (scientific concepts);
(e) achieved literacy faster in English, Hausa and Arabic as from their second year at school;
(f) achieved numeracy and mathematical concepts faster. (Omolewa, 1978: 368–9)

Commenting on the positive values of the project, Omolewa observed:

> Quite apart from its direct effects on learners, the project has been of value in some other aspects. First, it brought home to the initiators at the outset the various types of inadequacies which had escaped attention and without which education via the medium of a national language cannot be undertaken. These include lack of specialists to write Hausa IM as well as those to teach it and also a lack of IM on which the burden of Hausa as a language of education is to be rested. (1978: 369)

This awareness led the Institute to create a number of courses for the training of Hausa specialists at various levels of education.

Additionally, the Project has proved that, in order to be used as a vehicle for national education, an indigenous language has to be developed up to the point where it can effectively perform this function. Thus, against a complete vacuum when the project began, there is now a wide variety of instructional materials in Hausa intended to establish literacy in Hausa and focusing on the following areas: (1) physical and health education, (2) cultural studies, (3) modern mathematics, and (4) elementary science. These are in addition to those instructional materials specifically written in English for the English-medium classes.

The Six Year Primary Project (SYPP)

The SYPP started in Ile-Ife, Nigeria, in 1970, at the former University of Ife, now Obafemi Awolowo University. Before the project began, it was discovered that primary education in English all over Nigeria left pupils, after six years, virtually ignorant and functionally illiterate. The problems identified in the Primary Education Improvement Program – large classes, untrained teachers, scarcity of instructional materials, poor supervision of teachers, outmoded curriculum – are also in evidence in this programme, since the two projects are both operated in the Nigerian context.

The SYPP aimed at developing a better curriculum, better materials and appropriate methodology; to teach English effectively as L2 through specialist teachers, and, most importantly, to use the Yoruba language as the medium of instruction in all subjects, except English, throughout the six-year duration of primary education. Experimental and control groups were created. Metalanguage for the teaching of mathematics, English, science, Yoruba, social and cultural studies in Yoruba was developed and specialist English teachers were trained. Regular and very elaborate evaluations of the project were undertaken.

The results, overall, indicated that the experimental groups did significantly better than the control groups, even when given the same treatment, except for the language variable (see Afolayan, 1976; Fafunwa *et al.*, 1989; Ojerinde, 1979; 1983; Ojerinde & Cziko, 1977, 1978 for further details).

Even though the evaluations also indicate better performance in English by the experimental groups compared with the control classes, observations and isolated instances of self-reports point to the possibility that the students encountered initial difficulty in adjusting to the use of English as a medium of instruction at the secondary school level and sometimes even up to the university level. This problem associated with the project implies either the need to develop Yoruba for use beyond the primary school level, or the need to conduct more follow-up studies on project participants to investigate whether the beneficial effects recorded in the use of the first language in initial literacy are indeed sustained on a longer term basis.

Interestingly, the project went beyond being merely experimental. Post-project activities relating to the adoption of the findings of the SYPP by some State Governments in Nigeria include the following:

(1) It provided a strong input into the *National Policy on Education*, particularly as it relates to its language policy provisions. It also gave a special impetus to many corpus and status planning programmes of Nigerian indigenous languages. A special National Institute for the Training of Teachers of Nigerian Languages as MTs and Second Languages has been established. Also, the Federal Ministry of Education has published the Vocabulary of Primary Science and Mathematics, produced in nine Nigerian languages, in three volumes (Vol. I: Fulfulde, Izon, and Yoruba; Vol. II: Edo, Igbo and Kanuri; Vol. III: Efik, Hausa and Tiv) (Afolayan, 1992: personal communication).

(2) The Oyo State Government has, since 1985, embarked on a pilot implementation of the project as it relates to paragraph 15(4) of the *NPE* (see section 9.2), utilising the results of the SYPP and working in close collaboration with a team under the chairmanship of the consulting linguist and acting chair-

man of the Executive Committee of the SYPP. This pilot scheme has the blessing of the National Implementation Committee of the Federal Ministry of Education. In Oyo State, since 1986, 131 schools were teaching in the mother tongue and using materials prepared in Yoruba (Commissioner's Address, 1991).

(3)   The Oyo and Osun States decided to adopt the results of the project in implementing the relevant provisions of the *NPE* systematically during the 1991–92 school year. All class one pupils used books published by the project, with the adoption of the project's books continuing progressively. In December 1991, an induction workshop was provided for teachers in the use of the first language as a medium of instruction in primary schools in Kwara, Lagos, Ogun, Ondo, Osun and Oyo States. SYPP books in the five subject areas of English, Yoruba, mathematics, science, and social studies number altogether over 100 volumes, and work was in progress for the production of Hausa and Igbo editions of the books (Afolayan, 1992: personal communication).

(4)   A Consultative Committee of all Yorub teaching States in Nigeria was established in 1991 to stimulate the effective joint efforts of all the States in the implementation of the *NPE*.

However, political developments (i.e. the creation of new States and the preparations by the military to hand over authority to a civilian government) sometimes created situations that either drew attention away from, delayed, or totally hindered the implementation of decisions – illustrating that the political life of a nation can impinge on the implementation of language planning and literacy decisions.

The two projects discussed thus far relate to the planning and management of major languages, both indigenous and exogenous, in Nigeria. Most of the small-group languages have not received the kind of developmental attention described for Hausa and Yoruba. However, one notable exception is the Rivers Readers Project, from which other multilingual contexts can learn many useful lessons about the treatment of small-group or minority languages.

The Rivers Readers' Project (RRP)

Rivers State, the home base of the RRP, has a population of 3,983,857 (1991 census) speaking about 34 languages/dialects, most of which are small. The traditional response to literacy teaching in such a multilingual situation would be to provide literacy in Igbo, a major Nigerian language and a lingua franca, in spite of the different language backgrounds of the pupils. However, the project did not have its hands tied by tradition. Instead, RRP planners aimed, in principle, at introducing initial literacy in all of the small languages in the State, which ranged in size from 42,800 pupils for the Ikwere language to 1200 pupils for Degema. The small languages were used as media for all subjects, except English, in the first two years of primary education (Williamson, 1976).

Undoubtedly, the project set itself a formidable task with many problems, including at least the following, which could be of interest in all densely multilingual contexts:

(1)   How does one cope, in the educational domain, with a multilingual and

multicultural society with small-group languages, many of which are not even graphised?

(2) How can limited resources be managed to cater for a situation in which many languages demand basic developmental attention involving graphisation, improvement of old orthographies, production of Readers, etc?

Of necessity, the implementation of the project involved:

- language analysis;
- creation of alphabets;
- the improvement of some alphabets which had been created by linguistically naïve missionaries;
- the harmonisation of orthographies in different languages and dialects;
- the writing of primers, supplementary texts, teachers' notes, etc.

A significant innovation of the project, responsible for considerable cost cutting, was the strategy of using identical formats and illustrations for the readers in different languages. However, several cultural aspects and details in the readers were adjusted when a new language was being dealt with and when the context demanded it.

Cheap production technology methods – e.g. neat typing, printing by offset – were adopted in order to cater for most of the languages and to avoid the problems of printers who did not have access to the required typefaces (see Williamson, 1976, 1990). By 1990, 61 publications were available in 21 small languages under the Rivers Readers Project (Emenanjo, 1990: 94). These included primers, supplementary readers, teachers' notes, orthography booklets, and dictionaries. Bamgbose comments:

> The difficulty of using smaller languages in education should not be exaggerated. We now have the example of the Rivers Readers Project, which has so far succeeded in developing initial literacy materials for twenty languages/dialects ...This project shows that where there is the will to do it and determined leadership, the MTM policy is possible, even for the so-called smaller languages. (1977: 23)

Undoubtedly, the project has contributed immensely to general language planning in education, especially for small languages. Many other Nigerian small language groups are beginning to copy the laudable examples set by the project. RRP's main strengths, noted earlier, are worth restating for emphasis. It is community based. Every draft orthography and draft reader is normally worked out by, or in conjunction with, a local committee representative of responsible and home-based educated people. The project follows a common pattern with necessary built-in diversity to reflect particular contexts or past experiences. It is simple and based on easily accessible technology. This is responsible for the considerable cost cutting referred to earlier. It is run by a small and informal committee that can take decisions easily without being hindered by the elaborate machinery of bureaucracy.

However, in spite of its numerous merits, a project of this nature cannot but have some weaknesses from which other multilingual contexts can draw useful lessons. Some of the basic weaknesses of the project include:

- the lack of full-time trained and committed persons whose primary responsibility is the project;
- the lack of professional input from the education side in developing methodology for the teaching of local languages and in doing a professional assessment of what has been done; and
- the lack of a proper distribution network for readers that have been produced (Williamson, 1992: personal communication);
- the absence of a systematic evaluation of the programme, as was the case with the SYPP.

Bamgbose points out that one major lesson to be learned from the SYPP is that 'the hitherto unquestioned transition from a mother tongue to English at the beginning of the fourth year of primary education may not be the right policy after all' (1992: 10). Moreover, the assumption of the present system of education that every primary school teacher 'is automatically a good model of English' is another lesson to draw from the use of specialist teachers in the SYPP. The PEIP points to the need for greater attention to a curriculum that is more relevant to the needs of pupils, while RRP, as well as the SYPP, demonstrates that even for speakers of small languages, education is possible in the first languages, at least up to the primary school level, if there is the will.

The multilingual policy

The multilingual language policy is the second major plank of language policy in Nigeria. In the interest of national unity, it is believed that each child should be encouraged to learn one of the three major Nigerian languages – Hausa, Igbo or Yoruba – apart from his or her first language. Garcia (1997: 409) proposes the following advantages for a proper biliterate and multilingual/multiliterate language education policy:

- increased cognitive advantages such as more divergent or creative thinking;
- greater metalinguistic awareness and cognitive control of processes as well as increased communicative sensitivity.

Bilingualism and multilingualism, according to Garcia, can also promote 'a greater understanding among groups and increased knowledge of each other' (Garcia, 1997: 409). Language minorities who lack self-esteem and ethnolinguistic vitality can be reassured that their languages are valued and accepted when a bilingual and multilingual policy is adopted. A multilingual policy, therefore, serves as a kind of 'empowerment pedagogy' (Garcia, 1997: 409).

Obviously, the hidden and unspoken agenda of the Nigerian multilingual policy as it is formulated is that one of the three major Nigerian languages being studied should be cultivated into national prominence and thus ultimately should become the national language. Unfortunately, the policy cannot be said to have become active and successful in any of the States even up to the present time (May, 2004). Fakuade in fact, suggests that the policy cannot succeed because 'languages in Nigeria are tribe-bound' (1989: 540). Problems that need to be solved before the policy can be fully implemented, and problems being encountered by States that have attempted implementation of the policy, include the following:

- poor national coordination;
- lack of teachers for the three languages in all the States;
- absence of suitable L2 materials in the three languages; and
- lack of textbooks (Akinnaso, 1991: 48).

Other problems include:

- threats felt resulting from the political implications of the possibility of one of the languages becoming entrenched as the result of the policy (Jibril, 1990);
- lack of resources;
- varying interpretations of the provision – is one language to be taught in each State, or must each State school teach all three?

The question regarding what is to be done when a pupil already speaks a major language in addition to the first language has not been answered by the policy as currently stated and so is open to different interpretations. For instance, while Awobuluyi (1979: 19) suggests that, in a situation in which the language of the immediate community is one of the three major languages, children should be required to learn another language. Bamgbose (1977: 23), on the other hand, observes that children who already speak a major language in addition to their first language (e.g. Itshekiri-speaking children who already speak Yoruba, or Duka-speaking children who already speak Hausa) should merely continue their study of the major language. He notes, however, that those who already speak a major language will be advantaged in the sense that they will then speak two major languages, while others will speak only one major language and their first language.

While the 1977 version of the *NPE* does not indicate the level of formal education in which the MTM policy is to be implemented, and has been criticised for this by scholars like Awobuluyi (1979), the secondary school edition of the 1985 version of the *NPE* (Section 4: 19(6A)) indicates that 'One Nigerian Language' should be one of the core subjects at the secondary school level. Nigerians, depending on whether they belong to majority language groups or minority language groups, have perceived the MTM policy differently. While the majority language groups have tended to be favourably disposed towards the MTM, the members of minority language groups have generally viewed it with disdain and antagonism. Essien (1990), for instance, has observed that the MTM policy tends towards artificial forced assimilation. He notes that it is an unfair demand, and that speakers of major languages in Nigeria should also be required to learn a minority language, in order for the intended unity, which the policy makers claim they want to maintain in Nigeria, to be reciprocal rather than unidirectional. Bamgbose (1992: 7) partly shares this view and suggests that, to prevent a feeling of superiority on the part of speakers of major languages, and a corresponding feeling of inferiority on the part of speakers of other languages, the policy should require speakers of major languages to learn a language other than their own.

The proliferation of implementing agencies has been observed to be a major problem confronting both aspects of the Nigerian national language policy. Among officially recognised implementing agencies – specifically mentioned in the *NPE* as implementing agencies – are University Departments of Linguistics, State Ministries of Education, a National Committee, Teachers' Resource Centres, Federal and State Governments, the Educational Research Council, the National Book Development Council, Mass Literacy Boards, and Language Centres. While it may be argued that each implementing agency could be involved in a different aspect of the policy (e.g. the Book Development Agency in the production of books for implementing the policy), such proliferation has inadvertently left the implementation to no agency. Moreover, the *NPE* does not assign specific and tangible roles to each agency, gives no indication of the relationship between the different agencies, and does not stipulate how the different agencies will be coordinated to ensure a harmonious implementation of the policy. It is, therefore, not surprising that the multilingual policy has not been implemented at all in most Nigerian States. Consequently, each State has done as it has found convenient, and different discordant tunes are sung as far as the implementation of the MTM and multilingual policy is concerned.

Many professional language-related associations and societies have complemented the activities of educational institutions such as universities in different ways and so are sociolinguistically significant in language promotion in Nigeria. There are, for instance, the Yoruba Studies Association, the Society for the Promotion of Igbo Language and Culture, the English Studies Association, and the Linguistic Society of Nigeria. The Linguistic Society of Nigeria has been particularly influential in promoting research and in publishing books on different aspects of language in Nigeria. Occasionally, these various associations have served as linguistic lobbying groups in pressuring the Government to focus attention on a particular language issue in the country. Somewhat related to these are community development associations – like the Ogori Descendants Union, and the Ebira Descendants Union/Association – which, though basically political in orientation, also promote the development of the languages and cultures of the communities they represent.

As far as English is concerned, the British Council has been very influential in ensuring the promotion of English in Nigeria; so have also the United States Information Agency, CNN, BBC and the Voice of America. The absence of coordination among these various language promotion agencies, and the consequence of the lack of coordination in the Nigerian context, should serve as a warning for other multilingual contexts, as far as the implementation of language policies is concerned. The reorganisation of the National Educational Research Council and the Language Development Centre, Abuja, offered some ray of hope for the implementation of Nigeria's language policy provisions. Unfortunately, not much has been heard from these government agencies with respect to the implementation of Nigeria's language policy. The vicissitudes of the agencies change when the directors change, and this often has serious consequences for the implementation of language policy provisions. Changes in government have also resulted in changes in the interest to implement or not to implement language policies. During the Abacha era, for instance, rejection by the Anglophone countries resulted in him being forced to seek friendship with Francophone countries, whereupon he suddenly declared that French would be a second foreign language in Nigeria. Since his demise and the beginning of the Obasanjo regime, the kind of vigour, which the Abacha regime wanted to inject in the pursuit of French as an additional second language in Nigeria, seems to have waned.

A point worth noting as far as the implementation of language policy in Nigeria and the agencies of implementation are concerned, is the role played by individual agencies or groups that are not directly sponsored or inspired by government. For instance, Omamor studied and prepared the orthography of the Okpe language. This study has given the language a little more prominence than it would otherwise have had. Efforts to develop the Oko language in Kogi State, Nigeria, have also been due largely to the Ogori Descendants Union, the political and development organ of the Ogori community. This union has been keenly interested in the development of the Oko language and culture. Consequently, it has initiated and encouraged the codification of the language and its ultimate graphicisation, which is a very important step in the direction of the implementation of the MTM policy in Nigeria. Different members of the community carried out the harmonisation of earlier orthographies, devised respectively in 1982, 1987 and 1989. Adegbija (1993) prepared a standard orthography for the Oko language. Such harmonisation was aligned on current linguistic insights on the development of an orthography. The involvement of ODU has helped to avoid the kind of incidents which, in some languages like Igbo in Nigeria and Occitan in France (Coulmas, 1983: 12), resulted in two independent orthographies being used concurrently when different interest groups become enthusiastic about cultivating the languages into literacy tools (Adegbija, 2003: 308).

Nigerian Pidgin

One language in Nigeria that has continued to serve a vital and increasing role, has creolised and is continuing to spread in many parts of Nigeria, especially in the south, is Nigerian Pidgin. As Mühlhäusler (1995) observes, Pidgins are symptomatic of a disturbance in the linguistic ecology as a result of linguistic imperialism, but have developed to become crucial repositories of indigenous cultures. However, in spite of the important role that Nigerian Pidgin plays, it has not been mentioned in any of the policy provisions made for the functioning of languages in Nigeria. Scholars such as Mann (1991) and Oladejo (1991) have observed that it plays a very crucial role in the promotion of horizontal communication at the grassroots level within the country. *De facto*, Nigerian Pidgin serves, at least the following functions in Nigeria:

(1) It has creolised as the first language of quite a large number of Nigerians in the Delta region.
(2) It is a solidarity and intimacy language at the grassroots level. It creates a common bonding and connectedness at the grassroots level.
(3) It is the most effective language of national mobilisation and motivation at the grassroots level. President Babangida and President Obasanjo have occasionally used it when they wanted to be close to Nigerians. During one of his visits to South Africa, for instance, President Obasanjo used it in his interactions with Nigerians in that country.
(4) It is perhaps the most successful language for popular and grassroots litera-

ture. As already mentioned, authors like Ken Saro Wiwa and Tunde Fatunde have used Nigerian Pidgin in some of their literary productions.

(5) It is the lingua franca in many Nigerian army barracks, colleges, and universities in most forms of informal interpersonal interactions.

(6) It is the trade language in most Nigerian markets, especially in the southern part of the country.

(7) Its function has extended into the media – both the print and electronic media.

(8) It is a popular and extremely successful language of entertainment in films, plays, soap operas, motion pictures, etc.

(9) It is used in many informal and even formal education literacy programmes within the country.

The functions and roles of Nigerian Pidgin seem to be continuously expanding to accommodate greater communicative demands, and its future seems to be even brighter. Given such widespread and far-ranging functions in the nation, Nigerian Pidgin deserves mention in Nigeria's language policy provisions.

Four ideologies

Overall, Nigeria's language policy implementation discussed thus far reflects the numerous tensions normally experienced in the management of multilingual resources. The language policies discussed simultaneously reflect the four different types of ideologies which Akinnaso (1991: 41) says are present in developing nations: linguistic pluralism; linguistic assimilation; vernacularisation and internalisation. Akinnaso observes:

> The four ideologies are based on two basic sets of opposition: multilingualism vs monolingualism and indigenous vs exogenous languages. Linguistic pluralism accords official recognition to more than one language while linguistic assimilation is the belief that everyone, regardless of linguistic background, should learn the dominant language in the society. Elaboration or restoration of an indigenous language and its adoption as an official language are the goals of vernacularisation, while internalisation emphasises the adoption of an exogenous language of wider communication either as an official language or for such specific purposes as education, bureaucracy, trade, or world politics. The orientation of each language policy tends to stem directly from whichever of these ideologies is adopted. None of these ideologies has been adopted by Nigeria in toto. Rather, elements of each are adopted in the policy and this makes Nigeria's language policy 'inherently ambiguous'. (Akinnaso, 1991: 42)

While linguistic pluralism appears to be encouraged by the cultivation of Hausa, Yoruba and Igbo to official status alongside English, the requirement that every Nigerian child learn at least one of these smacks of linguistic assimilation. Elements of vernacularisation are evident in the attempt to elaborate and restore Nigerian languages, even though this has not been vigorously pursued. Internalisation is partly implied in the emphasis placed on the dominance of English in virtually all aspects of life in Nigeria, especially in official circles. As Akinnaso observes, however, the different ideologies are not necessarily mutually exclusive even though emphasis on one or the other varies from nation to nation.

This discussion demonstrates that Nigeria has attempted to grapple with crucial language policy issues in a multilingual context. Such issues come into greater prominence particularly in the domain of education. They include the following:

(1) The choice of the most appropriate language to use in education in a linguistically heterogeneous society. This is the *what* question of language education that policy has to stipulate.

(2) There is also the crucial question of *when* to introduce a language that is not the first language of the learners, particularly in situations where the first language cannot be used at every level of education. Many multilingual contexts all over the world have considered it prudent to adopt an exoglossic language. Policy provisions also have to answer the question of the nature of the use of the language – as a medium of education or as a subject in the curriculum, or as both. Many multilingual contexts have to make policy provisions to address these questions or at least confront them in reality. These are the *when* and *how* language policy questions in a multilingual setting.

(3) Also very crucial is the attitudinal question; that is, the attitudes of learners relating to the language being used as a medium of instruction. This attitudinal question deserves attention in every multilingual context because insensitivity to language attitudes that affect language policies can mar the entire language policy implementation process in a multilingual context. A case in point is the declaration of Hindi as a national language in India and the ruckus it caused. Resistance to Afrikaans in South Africa by Black South Africans is also a good instance of how insensitivity to attitudes could destroy language policy making (see Adegbija, 1994a; Kamwangamalu, 2001; Pattanayak, 1981). On the other hand, the Rivers Readers Project in Nigeria is a case in point about how sensitivity to the linguistic ecology of a community and ecological language planning can nurture positive feelings and enhance pride to speakers of small languages, because they are not discriminated against in the policy provisions and implementation of language planning. Involvement of the community in which language is being planned almost always results in a positive attitude towards the language planning process. Conversely, attempting to impose language policies on a community tends to lead to resistance (see Adegbija, 1994a for further details on language attitudes and language policy and planning).

(4) The need to formulate ecologically sensitive pragmatic language policies that take cognisance of the *what, when,* and *how* and of attitudinal perspectives towards language in a multilingual context is another major aspect of education language planning in a multilingual context that should be of concern to language planners. This is the *policy aspect*. The quality of policy determines the success of language planning efforts.

(5) Finally, another crucial issue in ecologically sensitive language planning relates to the provision of the linguistic and pragmatic context in a multilingual and multicultural context in which the educational skills learned can be

nurtured, stimulated and perpetuated. This is the *linguo-pragmatic* dimension of language policy in education in multilingual contexts. It is this dimension that ensures that a literate environment that guarantees the perpetuation of the success of effective language policy implementation is created and sustained. (Adegbija, 2003)

Obviously, each of the above issues poses a serious challenge to language policy planners and implementers in a multilingual context. Sensitivity to the dangers of monoculturalism and the benefits of linguistic and cultural diversity are vital strategies for ensuring harmony in the ecolinguistic system in a multilingual context. Emphasis has to be placed on

> . . . wider environmental considerations emphasising the interlinked sub-systems in an overall ecology . . . [There must also be recognition of the fact that] languages are not just isolated systems but have interactions with other systems outside what is usually considered strictly to be linguistics, including culture, politics and environment. (Liddicoat & Bryant, 2000: 303)

Generally, in Nigeria, policy attention seems to focus on the English language and on major languages. A great deal of corpus planning still needs to be done before many of the minority languages can have any presence at all in language policy implementation, even where policy provisions seem to have been made for the preservation of ecolinguistic diversity. Insufficient attention to corpus planning, especially for minority languages, poses a great danger for language loss or language death for many of these languages. Many of the minority languages are being lost because of the assimilative influences of major languages, particularly of Hausa in the northern part of Nigeria. National coordinated attention is desirable to harness all of Nigeria's linguistic resources for the national good. Such an effort must accept ecolinguistic diversity as a fact of life. As Liddicoat and Bryant put it: 'structural diversity of ways of speaking rather than monolingualism is the natural state of affairs and . . . any attempts to streamline ecolinguistic diversity are misguided' (Liddicoat & Bryant, 2000: 303). As Adegbija observes:

> Attempts should be made to manage language resources in multilingual settings in such a way that communication is enhanced, each language group feels valued, the target country is not torn to pieces, and maximal and optimal participation in national affairs for the citizenry is made possible. To achieve these goals . . . there has to be a basic recognition and acceptance of the integrity and right to existence of all languages. Artificially robbing Peter to pay Paul, deliberately planning some languages for death, or to be displaced by others, cannot bring this about. Instead, such goals can be achieved through a kind of equitable treatment in which language policy is utilized 'on behalf of fostering a stabilised coexistence between the weak and the strong, between the lambs and the wolves' (Fishman, 1988: 4), to provide succor for the weak languages, encouragement for the strong, and a loving accommodation between all languages and their speakers, no matter their numbers. In spite of such an atmosphere of language planning, it is still very likely that the different languages in a multilingual context

will grow and develop differently owing to natural sociolinguistic ecological forces. However, language planners and managers will at least be able to wash their hands with a clear conscience from different language developmental or growth rates not due to inadequate planning, management inertia, default, and covert or overt attempts at linguistic genocide. (2004: 184)

Literacy planning is an important aspect of language policy in any country, particularly because it is very crucial for the mobilisation of the citizenry in totality. Literacy policy will be briefly examined specifically in the Nigerian context.

Literacy planning or legislation currently in place

Kaplan and Baldauf (1997: 288) observe that, in many contemporary societies, social and economic mobility is dependent on literacy. They also note that literacy is not a *state* or a *condition*, but that it is a flexible continuum. Thus, according to them, considerations of literacy – to what degree and in what languages – are central to any language policy development effort. Omolewa (2003: Internet source), writing on 'the language of literacy', argues that three broad issues have dominated the debate on literacy promotion and practice during the last century. These are: (1) the notion that literacy is a means to an end or an end to a means; (2) issues relating to the economic limitations of literacy, namely that it cannot put food on the table; and (3) the choice of the language of literacy. The issue of the choice of the language of literacy, he argues, has been governed mainly by two main lines of reactions. There is the emotional perspective, which argues that language is a gift of nature and a people's language is a cultural factor that helps in the preservation of the identity of a people and therefore learning must be founded on the indigenous language. On the other hand, there is the rational perspective. The main thrust of this perspective is that realistic and practical considerations should guide language choice in literacy. In Nigeria, for instance, where there are over 450 languages, this rational stance argues that language is merely an instrument for literacy and that, consequently, it would be wasteful and rather unrealistic to promote several languages. The policy in Nigeria has been that of using the major languages of a community. It is argued that education promotes unity, and language choice should be deliberately aimed at promoting this goal. The Federal Government, in collaboration with the European Community, supported a project to prepare literacy primers in eight of the indigenous languages of two of the States in Nigeria. The response from the people was quite enthusiastic, and adult learners who would otherwise have eschewed literacy began to enrol and to remain in the classes. As Omolewa puts it, the literacy programme gives them the opportunity to 'join in the process of rewriting their history and in documenting songs, idioms and proverbs in the area' (2003: Internet source).

The *National Policy on Education* provides fairly detailed information germane to literacy planning in section 7 under the title 'Adult and Non-formal Education'. It begins by explaining that:

51. Adult and Non-formal Education consists of functional literacy, remedial, continuing, vocational, aesthetic, cultural and civic education for youths and adults outside the formal school system. (p. 32)

The document states that the objectives of adult and continuing education should be:

- to provide functional literacy education for adults, who have never had the advantage of any formal education;
- to provide functional and remedial education for those young people who prematurely dropped out of the formal school system;
- to provide further education for different categories of those who complete the formal education system in order to improve their basic knowledge and skills;
- to give the adult citizens of the country necessary aesthetic, cultural and civic education for public enlightenment.

The *National Policy on Education* further states that 'in order to eliminate mass illiteracy within the shortest possible time, an intensive nation-wide mass literacy campaign will be launched as a matter of priority and as a new all-out effort on adult literacy programmes throughout the country'. The following definite policies on mass literacy are also included in the document:

> **Section 7: 2**
> In order to encourage individuals to see literacy as a means of self-improvement, the government will draw up a list of occupations which require literacy for their efficient performance and arrange facilities to make it possible for illiterate workers in those jobs to attain, through functional literacy programmes, the minimum qualification of literacy necessary for improved performance in their jobs.

> **Section 7: 3**
> In character and content all mass literacy programmes will be adapted in each case to local cultural and sociological conditions and each will also contain basic civics instruction aimed at generating qualities of good citizenship and active involvement by all in the national development process. The Mass Literacy Boards, working in close cooperation with the Ministries of Education, the National Commission for the Development of Adult Education and the Universities' Adult/Continuing Education Departments will implement this.

The Government has indeed gone a long way in the pursuit of its literacy programme. A national Commission for the Development of Adult Education has been directed to explore ways and means of getting institutions to grant admission to products of Adult Education. Adult Education is pursued at the local, state and national levels. A National Commission for Adult Education has been vigorously involved in coordinating the activities of the various adult education/mass literacy programmes. Mass literacy committees are based in the States, and they work in collaboration with the State Ministries of Education to ensure effective literacy. The *National Policy on Education* states that Adult and Non-formal Education should continue to be under the Ministries of Education and that

> Literacy, post-literacy and adult education provided by the universities should not be exempted from the coordination arrangements of the State Ministries of Education. Local Adult Education Committees also exist.

> They are responsible for the day-to-day control and administration of local adult education programmes; recruitment of teachers and learners for functional literacy and post-literacy; and the provision of feedback to the state and Federal Ministries with regard to curriculum and materials development, techniques of teaching, evaluation of procedures, and the collection of data. (*NPE*, 1985: 35)

The language used in carrying out mass literacy campaigns varies from State to State and local government to local government. In most States, the major languages of the State are normally employed.

The Nigerian Government has continued to adopt several strategies to promote literacy. In 1999, President Olusegun Obasanjo announced the Universal Basic Education policy that aims at providing high quality basic education to all school-age children. This programme has had a remarkable impact in the enhancement of the overall rate of literacy in Nigeria. To help in fulfilling the objectives of the policy, in July 2001, USAID launched the Literacy Enhancement Assistance Programme (LEAP). The goal of LEAP is to help all Nigerian students attain literacy and numeracy by the end of Grade Six. One of the innovative strategies adopted in LEAP is the use of a new technology in literacy in the Nigerian environment – interactive radio. This has generated interest in the project, which has already begun to make a significant contribution to the enhancement of literacy in Nigeria. USAID aims at sustaining the effort at least until February 2004.

The Education Development Centre (EDC) and its partners, the Research Triangle Institute (RTI) and World Education, are implementing educational reform in three of Nigeria's 36 States, namely, Kano in the north, Nassarawa in the centre, and Lagos in the south. There is also a plan to include the numerous Qur'anic schools throughout Kano in the programme. The intention is that, if LEAP ultimately succeeds, it will be replicated in other Nigerian States, with lessons learned on how literacy can be further enhanced within the country.

LEAP adopts, in the main, a three-part strategy that targets teachers in the classroom, parents in the community, and government administrators. EDC conducts in- service for teachers with a focus on a proven methodology referred to as student-centred teaching (SCT), which utilises strategies such as cooperative learning, modelling, multi-sensory learning, continuous assessment, and student self-assessment. EDC has also been developing literacy and numeracy instructional materials for Grades 3, 4, 5 and 6, including interactive radio instruction (IRI) programmes. IRI uses radio broadcasts that summon the participation of groups of listening students while onsite teachers facilitate their activities.

World Education is also working with parents and other community members to organise Parent Teacher Associations (PTAs) and community-based organisations that mobilise and support schools and generally increase civic participation in education. RTI is also assisting the Federal and State Ministries of Education in the improvement of the administration and funding allocation methods to ensure, among other things, that teachers are adequately paid. RTI also helps the Government in school data collection and data transfer processes, in order to ensure that sound education management and policy decisions are made.

Another aspect of LEAP is an incentive grants programme, which offers fund-ing to schools, PTAs or other community group applicants to initiate projects that improve the quality of local education and literacy. This programme has been largely successful. Teacher training seminars have been conducted, much needed school buildings have been constructed and whole school library book collections have been purchased. State governments in Kano and Nassarawa, which have awarded funding to PTAs for school enhancement projects, have copied the grants programme. Such efforts that target government, communities and teachers are succeeding in bringing the Universal Basic Education mandate to fruition and could make progress in bringing numeracy and literacy to a large proportion of Nigeria's illiterate youths (National Universities Commission, 2003).

Literacy is sometimes carried out through individual efforts. For instance, Stella Cattini-Muller, a primary school teacher, developed a curriculum for enhancing English literacy in a remote area of north-eastern Nigeria centred around Dzgo, a mountain village in the Gwoza Hills (Mandara Mountains). This area is only accessible by foot. Hundreds of children in this area have no access to primary education. The Dzgo Learning Support was founded by Stella Cattini-Muller in 1998 and began with only 40 children. Enrolment has increased to 300. Neither the State nor the NGOS are active in the Gwoza Hills. Cattini-Muller raises her funds from London and from her colleagues.

Overall, except for individual and community efforts at language planning, current official language policies in Nigeria are largely rooted in policies formu-lated since colonial times. However, there is often a substantial gap between what policy stipulates and what actually happens in practice. This implementa-tion lag has been the bane of otherwise potentially progressive and far-sighted language policies in Nigeria.

The next section investigates language maintenance and language policy prospects in Nigeria.

Language Maintenance in Nigeria

According to Kaplan and Baldauf (1997: 77), language maintenance (LM) is a superordinate category which subsumes areas such as language revival, language reform, language shift, language standardisation and terminological modernisation. They observe that it occurs in two contexts: 'community LM' and 'dominant LM'. Community languages that are threatened require language maintenance. At the same time, dominant languages require some measure of maintenance to ensure that there is no drift away from the standard model. Language maintenance is therefore intended to slow the rate of drift and to narrow the gap. Fishman (1972: 76) sees language maintenance in terms of the relationship between change or stability in language usage patterns on the one hand, and ongoing psychological, social and cultural processes on the other in populations that use more than one speech variety for intra-group or intergroup purposes. He also sees language shift in the sense of speech communities whose native languages are threatened 'because their intergenerational continuity is proceeding negatively, with fewer and fewer users (speakers, readers, writers

and even understanders) or uses every generation' (1991: 1). Language maintenance is the opposite of language shift.

A discussion of language maintenance and language shift in the Nigerian
context will necessarily centre on the status of indigenous languages and English
starting by examining maintenance and shift with regard to indigenous
languages.

Language maintenance and shift: Indigenous languages

One crucial and dynamic factor in the maintenance or shift of indigenous
languages is negative or positive language attitudes. While a positive attitude
towards a particular language tends to enhance maintenance, a negative attitude
generally contributes towards shift from one language to another. Attitudes
towards languages are motivated by several factors including their perceived
socioeconomic value, their status-raising potential, their perceived instrumental
value, their perceived esteem, their perceived functions or roles in the nation,
their numerical strength, the perceived political and economic power of its
speakers, their use in official domains, their educational value, etc. Generally,
positive attitudes, covert or overt, are developed towards a language that is
perceived to have value in all these different areas. In essence, positive attitudes
develop towards a language in proportion to its enhanced function and use.
Conversely, negative attitudes, overt or covert, develop towards a language in
proportion to its lack of function or narrowing of its distribution in registers.

Major indigenous languages have very similar factors contributing to their
maintenance or shift. In many parts of northern Nigeria, for instance, many
speakers of minority languages have a positive attitude towards Hausa. There
are several reasons for this: its speakers are seen as politically powerful. The
language is seen as having some measure of influence at the national level. Ability to speak it raises one's ego and links one with many powerful people. Hausa is
also seen to be the language of a politically, linguistically and economically
dominant group, a traditional power-brokering elite-ruling oligarchy whose
voice counts. Therefore, many speakers of small languages (e.g. Gure-kahugu,
Gwandara, Gbayi, Amo Kata, Kamuku Kitimi, etc.) in Kaduna State, or minority
languages (e.g. Angas, Barke, Barawa, Boboli, Gera, Gewzawa, Kayung, Jeraina,
etc.) in Bauchi state struggle to learn the Hausa language. Another reason why
they desire to learn Hausa is that it has a strong appeal as a lingua franca. It is
perceived to be socially and economically more powerful than the minority
languages. Consequently, there is transitional bilingualism in Hausa and the
minority language until, in many cases, the minority language is given up. These
factors contribute to the maintenance and hegemony of the Hausa language in
northern Nigeria. Hausa is also graphised and has an enviable stock of literature
compared to the minority languages. A Hausa newspaper, *Gaskiya Tafi Kwobo*, is
published on a weekly basis. Hausa is frequently used on radio and on TV. These
factors make it perceptually salient and make speakers of minority languages
feel that it is a language with power.

Lack of intergenerational transmission is another major factor that has
contributed to the maintenance or shift of the indigenous languages. While a
language used by parents and transmitted to their children tends to be maintained, one that is not transmitted from parents to children tends to gradually

lose its value. Such a language may eventually atrophy and its speakers may eventually shift to a major language in the community or to English, the school language. In most of the rural areas in particular, parents speak indigenous languages to their children. This, however, is not always the case in urban centres, which constitute the principal locus of language shift. For instance, many children of speakers of some languages (e.g. Baatonu, Barutin and even Nupe) raised in an urban area such as Ilorin grow up not able to speak their indigenous language. Instead, they gain greater facility in Yoruba, the dominant language of the Ilorin community. This is so, because Yoruba is the most salient language in the community. Additionally, the children have greater environmental support for Yoruba than for their own first languages. Furthermore, many of their parents do not speak their first languages to the children in the home context. Instead, they prefer to speak English as a strategy for giving their children a head start in the language for the future. It is not unusual, for instance, to find English being spoken in the homes of many people in urban centres in Nigeria, instead of Nigerian indigenous languages. The lack of home support for indigenous languages is, therefore, a principal cause of shift from minority languages to either English or major indigenous languages. To make matters worse, many nursery and primary schools to which elites in urban centres prefer to send their children are English-medium schools. A shift towards English is thus gradually taking place among many people of the younger generation. Most cannot speak their own first languages. In informal interviews with students at Covenant University, for instance, it was discovered that a large proportion of them have never visited their parents' home towns as they were born in Lagos and have lived there all their lives. Some do not even know the names of their villages! Such youths, from different parts of Nigeria, whose parents have settled in Lagos, have shifted to Yoruba, the community language, and to English, the school language. In essence, contact with a powerful and socially utilitarian language in urban centres seems to make the transmission of the indigenous language to children unnecessary. Commenting on this phenomenon, Ohiri-Aniche (1997: 75) notes that small Nigerian languages are dying because of the trend to bring up children as monolingual speakers of English. This is

> Exerting a heavy affective price in that such children now hold our language[s] in disdain and feel ashamed to be associated with them. The situation is now such that in many urban schools even those children who understand local languages will pretend not to. Otherwise, they speak such languages at the peril of being mocked and jeered at by their peers . . . We need to pay attention to the damage being done to the psyche of Nigerian children who are neither wholly 'European' nor Nigerian while also giving thought to the social malaise that this confusion of identities is engineering. (Ohiri-Aniche, 1997: 75)

She adds that the great danger inherent in this phenomenon is that:

> When this generation of children becomes parents, they will not be able to pass on these languages to their own children. The result is that in a few generations, as the old people who know these languages die off, the languages also decline and eventually become extinct. This is the fate that

has befallen many formerly flourishing languages of the world, the best examples being the native Indian languages of North and South America. (p. 75)

When this kind of phenomenon happens on a large scale, and there is a mass exodus of youths from the villages into urban centres in search of jobs and the benefits of modernisation, language loss or language death is the inevitable consequence.

The educational system in Nigeria is a major factor for language maintenance and language shift. Learning a language as a subject in the school curriculum naturally maintains the language; lack of presence in the school environment results in regression in the use of the language, at least in the formal context. Nigerian indigenous languages like Hausa, Yoruba, Igbo and Efik, learnt up to the West African School Certificate level, receive a boost as far as maintenance is concerned. Other major indigenous languages such as Ebira, Tiv, Gwari, Idoma, Fulfulde, etc. orally used in school environments because of the MTM policy, also receive a maintenance boost.

Usage in the media, or lack of it, is another dynamic factor of language maintenance or language shift in Nigeria. Generally, languages used as media languages – in print and electronic form, radio, TV, newspapers and magazines – have their maintenance prospects highly enhanced, while indigenous languages, with no presence whatsoever in the media, are the ones that speakers tend to shift away from. Media usage inherently boosts the prestige of a language, while lack of it subtly lowers its esteem. It is not surprising, therefore, that languages used in the media in Nigeria, generally, are more salient nationally and regionally than languages not so used.

Indigenous languages with larger numbers of speakers also have a greater tendency towards natural maintenance ability than those with smaller numbers. Thus, languages such as Hausa and Yoruba, with over 22 million speakers each, stand a greater chance of being maintained than a language such as Oko-Osanyin, a minority language in Kogi State with only a little above 50,000 speakers. In essence, numerical strength boosts language maintenance, while numerical weakness tends to lead towards language shift.

Language development and elaboration is an aid to the maintenance of indigenous languages. Languages that have been developed stand a better chance of being maintained than languages that have no orthography. More than half of Nigeria's languages still have no orthography. Most speakers of such languages, therefore, cannot write in their languages. They have already shifted to English in the official domain. Major languages such as Hausa, Yoruba and Igbo, and others such as Fulfulde, Tiv, Idoma, Ebira, etc, which have some form of printed literature, such as the Holy Bible, are naturally being maintained among speakers. The graphisation of a language is, in and of itself, a maintenance mechanism and strategy. A graphised language gains in importance, esteem and prestige. Its speakers use it more often, both orally and in writing; usage enhances maintenance, disuse causes a language to atrophy and encourages language shift. It is not surprising, therefore, that language shift among Nigerian indigenous languages is more common among languages without orthography than it is among languages that are already used as a written medium.

Vibrant language activism promotes the maintenance of a language, especially a minority indigenous language. Activism gives a language a voice that
raises the awareness of the speakers to the fact that they need to have a stake in
the growth, development and survival of their language. Okpe (in Delta State)
and Oko-Osanyin (in Kogi State), though minority languages, have enjoyed an
activism that has resulted in orthographies being written for them. This has
contributed positively to their maintenance. A number of minority indigenous
languages in Nigeria are sustained and maintained due to community or individual language activism and promotion efforts. Language maintenance among
minority languages in Nigeria sometimes takes the form of cultural revival; for
example, deliberate linguistic strategies such as giving names that are rooted in
the minority language to children who are born in the community (Adegbija,
2001a).

Language maintenance and shift: The case of English in Nigeria

Indisputably, English is a powerful minority elite language in Nigeria. Since
the colonial masters introduced it in the 19th century it has grown stronger and
stronger in Nigeria. Its functions in governance have increased. The number of
its speakers has increased. Its functions within Nigeria – in the media, in the judiciary, in international functions, etc. – have increased phenomenally over the
years. Education has been the key agent for the maintenance of English in Nigeria. At present, the Internet and other communication functions are competing
hard with the educational domain in ensuring the maintenance of English in the
country. The Nigerian is constantly bombarded with news from the BBC, VOA,
CNN, etc. Owning a satellite dish or cable television has become a status symbol,
and Nigerian elites struggle not to be left out. Listening to the news from CNN is
considered more rewarding and more informative than listening to the news
from the Nigerian Television Authority. This perception contributes towards the
maintenance of the dominance of English in Nigeria. The Nigerian mass media
contribute daily to the hegemony of English in Nigeria. English is also gradually
invading informal interactions in many families, especially in the homes of children of the younger generation born in urban centres.

Economic and technological developments encourage the maintenance of
English. Joint venture companies (the Nigerian Government encourages foreign
investment) almost always operate in English. Legal documents of joint
ventures, memoranda of understanding, as well as international legal agreements are all in English. Many new companies in international trade involving
export and import create a need for back-office workers and sales and marketing
staff with skills in English. Technology transfer is closely associated with the
maintenance of English. Technology transfer extends to associated infrastructure expansion, for example, airports, railways, telecommunications, etc. The
new Global System for Mobile Communications operates largely in English. The
big four – MTN, Econet, Global and MTEL – have spread their operations and
activities to most parts of Nigeria, including villages, using the medium of
English. Their advertisements, as well as the advertisements of many other
companies, are presented almost exclusively in English.

A recent addition to English maintenance agencies in Nigeria is the Internet.
Today, Nigerian youths take pride in visiting a cyber café. Their activities at the

cafés are carried out almost entirely in English. This is naturally so, since English is the dominant language of the Internet. Thus, the Internet has become a subtle language maintenance agency *par excellence* in the Nigerian context. The youth are interested in it and spend a lot of their time with it. Their thoughts are concentrated on it, and for a large percentage, their lives are directed, controlled and governed by it. Graddol remarks: 'Many regard the Internet as the flagship of global English. A frequently quoted statistic is that English is the medium for 80% of the information stored in the world's computer' (1997: 50).

With the impact of the Internet, an English-medium educational system with English textbooks, English as a core subject, English as a medium of examinations, English as a medium of communication, sometimes officially so legislated within schools in the sense that students are instructed to speak English only within the school premises, the maintenance of English and shift to English and away from the indigenous languages by many Nigerians can be better understood. This process of the entrenchment of English is strengthened by governmental institutional support through policies; for example, the policy that makes English mandatory for admission to universities. Government employment in Nigeria is virtually impossible without English proficiency. There is unfortunately no similar support for the maintenance of most of the indigenous languages. The policy support that makes Hausa, Yoruba and Igbo the three major languages has certainly contributed to their maintenance on the national scale. The three languages have soared in prestige and esteem. They are much talked about. They are heard on TV and radio and in many government functions. However, English still dominates, because of the many additional factors in its favour. One such factor is its international esteem. English has developed into the world's global international language *par excellence*. All over the world, it is used in international diplomacy. English fills the control towers in the world's airports. It dominates world banking and finance from the activities of the IMF to the World Bank. Worldwide, English is predominant in the entertainment industry from the language of Hollywood actors to the language used in many Indian films. The world's technology is dominated by English from the label on the small stabiliser to the complicated instructions in aeroplanes. Educational conferences all over the world are predominantly conducted in English, whether they are held in Belgium or in Nigeria. English is the language of the Internet, of modern communications, of international commerce, of popular culture. The modern Nigerian youth cannot eat or drink or wear clothes or sleep without items with a bearing on English in one form or another. This pull of and towards English seems likely to continue and will constitute a maintenance mechanism not only in the psyche of Nigerian youth but also in their day-to-day existence.

These factors will almost certainly continue to generate a positive attitude to English from one generation of Nigerian youth to another. In a nutshell, the maintenance factors in support of the hegemony of English in Nigeria ensure that the future of English in the country is secure. The very presence and prestige of English in Nigeria and the functions it performs create not only a lack of interest in the indigenous languages among many youths, but also a perceived lack of need for the indigenous languages for those youths in urban areas who boldly claim that English is their first language. The inferiority complex associated with a majority of the Nigerian indigenous languages, and their neglect in governmental policies and practice, compounds this situation. Commenting on this, Adegbija points out: 'Indigenous languages are officially considered unworthy of being used in official contexts because of their low development status. Their perceived unworthiness increases year by year as frontiers of knowledge continue to expand' (2001b: 285).

In conclusion, the aggregate effect of the picture painted thus far with respect to language maintenance is that, while English continues to grow stronger in virtually every sphere of life in Nigeria, the indigenous languages continue to diminish in esteem compared to English. It is not surprising that, among the youths in particular, there is a shift away from the indigenous languages to the English language. This scenario is, however, by no means limited to the young. Even among adults between 40–60 years of age in Nigeria, such a shift has already occurred, especially in the official domain. A significant proportion of such adults, though they can speak their first languages, cannot write them. Some cannot read their first languages fluently. In official contexts, they are unable even to communicate orally in their first languages. In effect, for them, in the official domain, a shift has already occurred from the indigenous language to English. Many such elites speak English to their children at home. This ensures a shift away from the indigenous languages to English among the younger generation, both in the official and non-official domains. English thus continues to thrive and gain in hegemony. The scenario described here is by no means limited to Nigeria. Writing on Zaire, Kamwangamalu (1997b) calls for a 'revalorisation' of Ciluba, Lingala, Kikongo and Swahili, the country's four national languages (virtually neglected in planning as a result of the emphasis on French), through status replanning and a cohabitation policy whereby both French and indigenous languages would function, not one at the expense of the other, but one in addition to the others.

Overall, then, in the absence of any bold language policy change in favour of the indigenous languages, the English language will continue to spread in influence and have dynamic maintenance prospects in the educational domain, the media, technology and science, the Internet, literature, the judiciary and other domains, while the indigenous languages may continue to dwindle functionally. In fact, in many communities, absence of maintenance support for the indigenous languages will translate into large scale shift from the indigenous languages to English, particularly among people of the younger generation who are, at present, constantly being lured to English by the status, functional power and intrinsic value of the English language, both within Nigeria and globally.

Conclusion

Language policy and planning in Nigeria has been such that English has been given great prominence, particularly in education and officialdom, while the indigenous languages play rather insignificant roles. Indigenous languages can be said to be powerless. This is a carry over from the colonial legacy (see Kamwangamalu, 1997b). When compared with English, this observation is true even of the so-called three major Nigerian languages. For example, while English looms large in the mass media, in education, in the judiciary and in nation-building in general, the indigenous languages have very few functions as far as these domains and the domain of officialdom in general are concerned. This scenario has an unfortunate consequence for the future of indigenous languages. Given the pervasive impact of the Internet and its potential to increase the functions and prestige of the English language, the impact of the English language will continue to become wider and wider in the future. This trend is already quite noticeable in view of the fact that, for instance, in a university such as Covenant University in Ota, Ogun State, attended mainly by children of the elite, many of the students do not even know the names of their ancestral towns, not to mention not being able to speak the languages of their parents. Most of these children have been brought up in Lagos and have not visited their parents' homes. English has been their home language right from birth. This obviously poses a big threat to the intergenerational transmission of the indigenous languages.

In order to reverse this trend of language shift, from the indigenous languages to English from one generation to another, bold and concrete policy decisions need to be taken to 'revalorise' the indigenous languages (see Webb, 1994) and to achieve the kind of 'status replanning' and 'cohabitation policy' where English and indigenous languages can function side by side and not one at the expense of each other (see, e.g. Kamwangamalu, 1997b: 71 with reference to Zaire). Such revalorisation, according to Webb, will give the languages a higher functional/instrumental value and a more positive social value. It can be achieved through statutory and government measures for indigenous languages, such as their use for political debate, supporting their use in the media and in publications, or training translators and interpreters in the use of these languages. Indigenous languages could also be revalorised through language laws and policy formulations that eventually result in positive attitudes towards them. For instance, a policy that requires a credit pass in one Nigerian indigenous language before admission to the university would certainly succeed in boosting the prestige of indigenous languages. Also, Nigerian presidents could decide, as a status planning measure, to speak their own indigenous languages when foreign dignitaries visit the country and have someone else translate what is being said into the foreign visitor's language. This can be a deliberate status planning strategy for indigenous languages.

The economic values of the indigenous languages can be enhanced if they are used as a medium of instruction in primary and secondary schools, offered as school subjects if teaching materials and textbooks are prepared for them and if effective literacy and adult training programmes are available in them. The sociocultural meaning of the indigenous languages can be enhanced if the leading social groups in the country learn other languages apart from theirs, the languages become symbols of cultural identity and symbolise people's link with a glorious past. Deliberate corpus planning strategies also need to be adopted. Concrete steps need to be taken to standardise indigenous languages that are not standardised, to codify them by the production of grammars, dictionaries and word lists, to provide technical terminology, to promote technical registers and styles of speaking, to disseminate relevant information via newspapers, radio and television, schools and language agencies, to develop the indigenous languages for media use, and to promote the general use of new terms in the indigenous languages in various communities (see Adegbija, 2000; Webb, 1994 for details). Indigenous languages need to be institutionalised in the public domains so that they can gain acceptance and respectability for official functions. By the time such practical steps begin to be taken, the prestige of indigenous languages is bound to be influenced positively.

This monograph on language policy and planning in Nigeria demonstrates that the language situation in Nigeria is a complex and intriguing one. It is complex because of the large number of languages that have to be planned for, and intriguing because of the many non-linguistic factors such as ethnicity, politics, number of speakers, the economy, etc, that impinge on language policy and planning. Nevertheless, multilingualism should be seen as a national resource and a stimulation and privilege for cultural development, enrichment and pluralism in a context in which different languages positively impact on one another in an atmosphere of mutual coexistence, rather than as a distraction, a problem or an evil to be expunged from the nation. Sensitivity to this ecology of language planning is a necessity for effective language policy and language planning in the many domains of language functionality. As long as policies remain as they have been since colonial times, English will continue to retain its pre-eminence in Nigeria. Given the complex situation of ethnicity in Nigeria and its accompanying multiplicity of languages, it is very unlikely that any indigenous language will displace English. In fact, because the policy in favour of the maintenance of indigenous languages exists mainly in principle, but not in practice, the hegemony of English in the Nigerian context will continue to increase.

The present global status of English, which continues to gain in momentum by virtue of the dominance of English on the Internet, in technology, communications, world diplomacy, popular culture, and international commerce, will continue to strengthen and to ensure the maintenance of English in Nigeria. As long as present language policies in Nigeria remain, the current position and status of English will most likely remain unassailable, and its future will be solidly secure, while the statuses of the indigenous languages will remain threatened and their position jeopardised.

The insecurity in the status of a large number of indigenous languages is certainly not healthy for Nigeria. It has grave implications for the indigenous languages being able to make the necessary contribution to Nigeria's national development. Urgent action therefore needs to be taken to ensure their security. First, policies need to be formulated that can raise the status and prestige of those languages. Second, they need to be institutionalised for use in official circles. Third, they should be deliberately assigned high functions in national life. Fourth, they have to be introduced into the educational system both as media and as subjects in the curriculum. This should be done not only in primary education but also in tertiary education. Usage at the lower levels only confines the indigenous languages to lower functions and gives the erroneous impression that they cannot function at higher levels of education and for expressing concepts involved in the educational domain, in science and in technology. As the indigenous languages begin to be used at the higher levels of education, areas in which more elaborate registers are required will emerge and more complex registers will be developed for them to express new concepts. This will definitely increase the confidence of speakers in the potential of the indigenous languages for being used in official contexts. Systematic and concrete steps should therefore be taken to intellectualise and technologise them (see Adegbija, 1994b for details and more strategies for enhancing attitudes towards the indigenous languages and for raising their prestige). Until such steps are taken, the future of Nigeria's indigenous languages may remain bleak, and they will also not be able to make the necessary contribution towards Nigeria's development. Moreover, the natural ecological symbiotic relationships between English and the indigenous languages may be difficult to achieve.

I should like to conclude this monograph with the following words of Banjo:

> The dominance of the English language at this stage of modernisation is inevitable, but the situation is evolving rather than static. In that process of evolution, all the languages have a part to play, and if Nigeria is to make a distinctive contribution to human civilisation, it will have to be as a result of the symbiotic relationship between English and the indigenous languages, a pooling of the resources of all the languages without foreclosing the contributions that any of them can make. (Banjo, 1995: 187)

Notes

1. Hausa and Yoruba are spoken in neighbouring countries, e.g. Hausa in Chad and Yoruba in Benin, but the cross-border ecological impacts of these languages have not received much scholarly attention (but see Omoniyi, 2004, in press). Furthermore, when language policy and planning are being done, very little cognisance is taken of these cross-border interactions.
2. While one can debate the accuracy of using 'mother tongue' as a linguistic descriptor, 'mother tongue' and 'first language' are used synonymously in Nigeria (and in many other parts of the world), in many programme titles and documents.
3. 'Pools' are a type of game played on a billiard or pool table. It usually involves betting with money. It is the Nigerian equivalent of gambling.
4. With regard to the use of indigenous languages on radio and television, their use can be said to be still largely restricted when compared to the use of English. Moreover, it is mainly the major languages within a particular State that are used. Languages used are mainly employed to relay news, present soap operas and drama sketches, translate special broadcasts by the state governor or the President of the nation, provide information about preventing AIDS, etc. On national television and radio, Hausa, Yoruba and Igbo, the three major languages, may be heard. On State radio and television, the major languages of the State are used, in addition to English, to relay news.
5. Literacy is used here in the sense of functional literacy, that is, the kind of literacy that equips a person to read and write and to be able to apply what is read to his or her personal good on a day-to-day basis. For instance, literacy is considered functional for a farmer if the farmer can read instructions relating to pesticides, seasons of planting, improved crops, etc, that is, to be able to apply them to benefit his farming activities. A literate person is also expected to acquire basic information in the language of literacy that will keep him or her abreast of the basic happenings within the country, for instance, as they relate to politics, the economy or social life. By contrast, a functionally illiterate person cannot read and write or cannot make meaning out of what is read or written. Such a person cannot derive any practical benefit or value from written or read materials.

References

Adegbija, E. (1989) The implications of the language of instruction for nationhood: An illustration with Nigeria. *ITL Review of Applied Linguistics* 85&86, 25–50.

Adegbija, E. (1992) Language attitudes in Kwara state (Nigeria): The bottom-line attitudinal determining factors. *Multilingua: Journal of Cross-cultural and Interlanguage Communication* 13 (3), 253–84.

Adegbija, E. (1993) The graphicisation of a small-group language: A case study of Oko. *International Journal of the Sociology of Language* 102, 152–73.

Adegbija, E. (1994a) *Language Attitudes in Sub-Saharan Africa: A Sociolinguistic Overview.* Clevedon: Multilingual Matters.

Adegbija, E. (1994b) The context of language planning in Africa: An illustration with Nigeria. In M. Pütz (ed.) *Language Contact and Language Conflict* (pp. 139–63). Amsterdam/Philadelphia: John Benjamins.

Adegbija, E. (1997a) The identity, survival and promotion of minority languages in Nigeria. *International Journal of the Sociology of Language* 125, 5–27.

Adegbija, E. (1997b) The language factor in the achievement of better results in literacy programs in Nigeria: Some general considerations. In B. Smeija and M. Tasch (eds) *Human Contact Through Language and Linguistics* (pp. 221–42). Berlin: Peter Lang.

Adegbija, E. (2000) Language attitudes in West Africa. *International Journal of the Sociology of Language* 141, 75–100.

Adegbija, E. (2001a) Survival strategies for minority languages: The case of Oko. *ITL Review of Applied Linguistics* 103&104, 19–38.

Adegbija, E. (2001b) Saving threatened languages in Africa: A case study of Oko. In J. Fishman (ed.) *Can Threatened Languages Be Saved?* (pp. 284–308). Clevedon: Multilingual Matters.

Adegbija, E. (2003) Central language issues in literacy and basic education; three mother tongue education experiments in Nigeria. In A. Ouane (ed.) *Towards a Multilingual Culture of Education* (pp. 299–332). Hamburg: UNESCO Institute for Education.

Adegbija, E. (2004) *Multilingualism: A Nigerian Case Study.* Lawrenceville, NJ: Africa World/Red Sea.

Afolayan, A. (1976) The six year primary project in Nigeria. In A. Bamgbose (ed.) *Mother Tongue Education: The West African Experience* (pp. 113–34). London and Paris: Hodder and Stoughton Educational and UNESCO.

Agheyisi, R.N. (1984) Minor languages in the Nigerian context: Prospects and problems. *Word* 35 (3), 235–53.

Akindele, F. and Adegbite, W. (1999) *The Sociology and Politics of English in Nigeria: An Introduction.* Ile Ife: Obafemi Awolowo.

Akinnaso, N.F. (1991) Toward the development of a multilingual language policy in Nigeria. *Applied Linguistics* 12 (1), 29–61.

Awobuluyi, O. (1979) *The New National Policy on Education in Linguistic Perspective.* Ilorin Lecture Series. Ilorin: University of Ilorin.

Bamgbose, A. (1977) Towards an implementation of Nigeria's language policy in education. In *Language in Education in Nigeria.* Proceedings of the Kaduna Language Symposium. Lagos: National Language Centre.

Bamgbose, A. (1983a) When is language planning not planning? In S. Hattori and I. Kazuko (eds) *Proceedings of the 13th International Congress of Linguists* (pp. 1156–9). Tokyo: Proceedings Committee.

Bamgbose, A. (1991) *Language and the Nation: The Language Question in Sub-Saharan Africa.* Edinburgh: Edinburgh University Press for the International African Institute.

Bamgbose, A. (1992) *Speaking in Tongues: Implications of Multilingualism for Language Policy in Nigeria.* National Merit Award Winner's Lecture. Kaduna.

Bamgbose, A. (2001) Language policy in Nigeria: Challenges, opportunities and constraints. A paper presented at the Nigerian Millennium Sociolinguistic Conference, University of Lagos, 16–18 August.

Banjo, A. (1995) A historical view of the English language in Nigeria. *Ibadan* 28, 63–8.

Brann, C.M.B. (1990) The role and function of languages in government: Language policy issues in Nigeria. *Sociolinguistics* 19 (1–2), 1–19.

Commissioner's Address (1991) An address by the Oyo State Commissioner for Education, Youths and Sports to the inaugural consultative committee of the ministries of education of states in which Yoruba language can serve as a medium of primary education in accordance with the national policy on education.

Cooper, R.L. (1982) A framework for the study of language spread. In R.L. Cooper (ed.)

Language Spread: Studies in Diffusion and Social Change (pp. 5–36). Bloomington: Indiana University Press, and Washington, DC: Center for Applied Linguistics.

Coulmas, F. (ed.) (1983) *Linguistic Minorities and Literacy*. Berlin: Mouton.

Dada, A. (1985) The new language policy in Nigeria: Its problems and its chances of success. In J.A. Fishman (ed.) *Language of Inequality* (pp. 285–93). Berlin: Mouton.

Emenanjo, E.N. (ed.) (1990) *Multilingualism, Minority Languages and Language Policy in Nigeria*. Agbor: Central Books in Collaboration with the Linguistic Society of Nigeria.

Essien, O.E. (1982) Languages of the cross river state. *Journal of the Linguistics Association of Nigeria* 1, 117–26.

Essien, O.E. (1990) The future of minority languages. In N.E. Emenanjo (ed.) *Multilingualism, Minority Languages and Language Policy in Nigeria* (pp. 155–68). Agbor: Central Books in Collaboration with the Linguistic Society of Nigeria.

Fafunwa, B.A, Macauley, J. and Sokoya, J.A.F. (1989) *Education in Mother Tongue. The Ife Primary Education Research Project (1970–1978)*. Ibadan: University Press.

Fakuade, G. (1989) A three-language formula for Nigeria: Problems of implementation. *Language Problems and Language Planning* 13 (1), 54–9.

Federal Republic of Nigeria (1979) *The Constitution of the Federal Republic of Nigeria 1979*. Lagos: Government Printer.

Federal Republic of Nigeria. (1989) *The Constitution of the Federal Republic of Nigeria 1989*. Lagos: Government Printer.

Fishman, J.A. (1972) *Language and Nationalism: Two Integrative Essays*. Rowley, MA: Newbury House.

Fishman, J.A. (1988) Language spread and language policy for endangered languages. In P.H. Lowenberg (ed.) *Language Spread and Language Policy: Issues, Implications, and Case Studies* (pp. 1–15). Washington, DC: Georgetown University Press.

Fishman, J.A. (1991) Three dilemmas of organised efforts to reverse language shift. In U. Ammon and M. Hellinger (eds) *Status Change of Languages* (pp. 285–93). Berlin: Walter de Gruyter.

Folarin, B. and Mohammed, J.B. (1996) The indigenous language press in Nigeria. In O. Dare and A. Uyo (eds) *Journalism in Nigeria*. Lagos: NUJ, Lagos Council.

Garcia, O. (1997) Bilingual education. In F. Coulmas (ed.) *The Handbook of Sociolinguistics* (pp. 405–20). London: Blackwell.

Graddol, D. (1997) *The Future of English?* London: British Council.

Haugen, E. (1972) *The Ecology of Language. Essays by Einar Haugen*. (Edited by A.S. Dill). Stanford, CA: Stanford University Press.

Jibril, M. (1990) Minority languages and lingua francas in Nigerian education. In E.N. Emenanjo (ed.) *Multilingualism, Minority Languages and Language Policy in Nigeria* (pp. 109–17). Agbor: Central Books in Collaboration with the Linguistic Society of Nigeria.

Kamwangamalu, N.M. (1997a) Multilingualism and educational policy in post apartheid South Africa. *Language Problems and Language Planning* 21 (3), 234–53.

Kamwangamalu, N.M. (1997b) The colonial legacy and language planning in Sub-Saharan Africa: The case of Zaire. *Applied Linguistics* 18 (1), 69–85.

Kamwangamalu, N.M. (2001) The language planning situation in South Africa. *Current Issues in Language Planning* 2 (4), 361–445.

Kaplan, R.B. and Baldauf, R.B. Jr (1997) *Language Planning from Practice to Theory*. Clevedon: Multilingual Matters.

Liddicoat, A.J. and Bryant, P. (eds) (2000) *Current Issues in Language Planning* 1 (3). [*Language Planning and Language Ecology*.]

Mann, C.C. (1991) Choosing an indigenous official language for Nigeria. In P. Meara and A. Meara (eds) *Language and Nation* (pp. 91–103). British Studies in Applied Linguistics 6. British Association of Applied Linguistics.

Mann, C.C. (1996) Anglo-Nigerian pidgin in Nigerian education: A survey of policy, practice and attitudes. In T. Hickey and J. Williams (eds) *Language, Education and Society in a Changing World* (pp. 93–106). Clevedon: Multilingual Matters.

Mühlhäusler, P. (1995) The interdependence of linguistic and biological diversity. In D. Myers (ed.) *The Politics of Multiculturalism in the Asia-Pacific* (pp. 154–61). Darwin: University of the Northern Territory.

Mühlhäusler, P. (2000) Kommunikations probleme der anglikanischen Mission in Melanesien und deren Losungen [Communication Problems of the Anglican Mission in Melanesia and their Solutions]. Paper presented at the Hagen Conference, Interdisziplinares Kiolloquium Kommunication an Kulturellen Grenzen Akteure, Formen, Folgen, 11–12 January.

National Policy on Education (1977) Lagos: Federal Government Press.

National Policy on Education (revised) (1981) Lagos: Federal Government Press.

National Policy on Education (revised) (1985) Lagos: Federal Government Press.

National Universities Commission (2003) Virtual Institute for Higher Education Pedagogy (VIHEP), Lesson 7: Interactive radio and computer-assisted learning, NUCVIHEP Course, Module 3, 20 November. Abuja: National Universities Commission.

Ntinsedi L. and Adejare, R.A. (1992) Language education and applied linguistics in Nigeria. *Newsletter of the British Association for Applied Linguistics* 41 (Spring), 36–42.

Ohiri-Aniche, C. (1997) Nigerian languages die. *Quarterly Review of Politics, Economics and Society* 1 (2), 73–9.

Ohiri-Aniche, C. (2001) Language endangerment among a majority group: The case of Igbo. Paper presented at the Millennium Sociolinguistic Conference, University of Lagos, Akoka, Lagos, August.

Ojerinde, A. (1979) *The Effects of a Mother Tongue, Yoruba, on the Academic Achievement of Primary Five Pupils of the Six Year Yoruba Primary Project: June 1978 Evaluation.* Ife: University of Ife Institute of Education.

Ojerinde, A. (1983) *Six Year Primary Project – 1979 Primary Six Evaluation.* Ife: University of Ife Institute of Education.

Ojerinde, A. and Cziko, G.A. (1977) *Yoruba Six Year Primary Project – June 1976 Evaluation.* Ife: University of Ife Institute of Education.

Ojerinde, A. and Cziko, G.A. (1978) *Yoruba Six Year Primary Project – June 1977 Evaluation.* Ife: University of Ife Institute of Education.

Okedara, J.T. and Okedara, C.A. (1992) Mother tongue literacy in Nigeria. *ANNALS, AAPS* 520, 91–102.

Oladejo, J. (1991) The national language question in Nigeria: Is there an answer? *Language Problems and Language Planning* 15 (3), 255–67.

Omolewa, M. (1978) The ascendancy of English in Nigerian schools 1882–1960. *West African Journal of Modern Languages* 3, 86–97.

Omolewa, M. (2003) The language factor in literacy. On WWW at http:L//www.iis-dvv.de/englisch/publikationen/Ewb._ausgaben/55_2001/eng_Omolewa.html.

Omoniyi, T. (2004) *The Sociolinguistics of Borderlands: Two Nations, One Community.* Trenton, NJ: Africa World.

Omojuwa, R. (1983) A literary policy for the Nigerian educational system. In S.O. Unoh, R.A. Omojuwa and S.K.M. Crom (eds) *Literacy and Reading in Nigeria* (vol. 1) (pp. 33–48). Zaria: Institute of Education, Ahmadu Bello University, Zaria. Proceedings of the 1st National Seminar on Reading held in Zaria, 9–13 August 1982.

Pattanayak, D.P. (1981) *Multilingualism and Mother Tongue Education.* Delhi: Oxford University Press.

Richards, A. (1945) *Proposals for the Development of the Constitution of Nigeria, as Presented by the Secretary of State for the Colonies to Parliament by Command of His Majesty.* London: Government Printer.

Ruhlen, M. (1991) *A Guide to the World's Languages. Volume 1: Classification.* London: Edward Arnold.

Salawu, A. (2003) A study of Yoruba newspapers. *UNILAG Communication Review* 4 (1), 90–101.

Tsumba, Y.I. (2002) Literacy in indigenous languages in Nigeria: The Tiv experience. *Literacy and Reading in Nigeria* 9 (2), 211–24.

van den Bersselar, D. (2000) The language of Igbo ethnic nationalism. *Language Problems and Language Planning* 24 (2), 123–47.

Webb, V. (1994) Revalorising the authochthonous languages of Africa. In M. Pütz (ed.) *Language Contact and Language Conflict* (pp. 181–203). Amsterdam/Philadelphia: John Benjamins.

Williamson, K. (1976) The rivers readers project in Nigeria. In A. Bamgbose (ed.) *Mother Tongue Education: The West African Experience* (pp. 135–53). London and Paris: Hodder and Stoughton Educational and UNESCO.

Williamson, K. (1979) Small languages in primary education: The rivers readers project as a case history. *African Languages* 5 (2), 95–105.

Williamson, K. (1990) Development of minority languages: Publishing problems and prospects. In E.N. Emenanjo (ed.) *Multilingualism, Minority Languages and Language Policy in Nigeria* (pp. 118–44). Agbor: Central Books in Collaboration with the Linguistic Society of Nigeria.

Williamson, K. (1992) *Reading and Writing Egnih (Ogbah). Rivers Readers Project*. Port Harcourt: Faculty of Humanities, University of Port Harcourt and the Rivers State Ministry of Education.

Wise, C.G. (1956) *A History of Education in Tropical West Africa*. London: Longman.

The Language Situation in Tunisia

Mohamed Daoud
Professor of Applied Linguistics and Director of The ESP Resource Center, Institut Supérieur des Langues de Tunis, Université 7 Novembre à Carthage, Tunis, Tunisia

This monograph describes the current language situation in Tunisia while maintaining a historical perspective that is helpful in understanding how language-related changes have come about, and a prospective view which may illuminate future developments. Even though Tunisia is an Arab country where Arabic is the official language, the current language situation is complex and dynamic. Over the last 100 years or so, and particularly since independence from France in 1956, different generations of Tunisians have had different experiences with the languages used in the social and work environment, the educational system, government, and the media. Such experiences have produced discontinuities with respect to language and literacy and helped to shape different attitudes towards these languages. Language policy and planning in Tunisia have been both instrumental in shaping such experiences and attitudes and subject to their influence.

Introduction

Tunisia is located in North Africa. Bordered by Algeria on the west, Libya on the south-east, and the Mediterranean Sea on the north and east, it covers an area of 163.6 thousand km^2 (slightly larger than the state of Georgia, see Figure 1). With a population of 9.6 million (62% urban) and a per capita income of US$2100 (GDP purchasing power parity of $5500, according to the CIA, *The World Factbook*, 2000), Tunisia is considered a middle-income country that is doing better than many countries with comparable resources.[1] It was ranked 102 out of 174 on the Human Development Index of the United Nations Development Program (UNDP, 1999) and is very likely to improve this ranking given the sustained growth it has experienced in recent years. According to the *Africa Competitiveness Report* (World Economic Forum, 2001), Tunisia had the most competitive economy in the continent in 2000.

Lacking in natural resources such as oil, minerals, and water (due to irregular rainfall), Tunisia has traditionally given priority to developing its human capital, generally devoting more than 30% of its budget to education and vocational training and encouraging the diversification and liberalisation of its economy. Such policies have led to (1) one of the highest educational levels in the region, with one scientist or technician per 2000 inhabitants –comparable to the rate in Malaysia – and the highest rate of vocational training in Africa (cf. *Middle East Magazine*, 1999; Price Waterhouse, 1998); and (2) a steady annual GDP growth from 3.5% in 1979–89 to 6.2% in 1999, with an average estimate of 5.8% for 1999–2003 (World Bank, 2000).

Tunisia is often called by Arabs from more arid regions 'Tunisia the Green' (*Tunis al-khadhra*) for its cereal fields in the north-west, orange groves and vineyards in the north-east, olive groves along the eastern regions stretching far into the central and southern parts of the country, and date-producing oases in the south. While this still leaves nearly half the land as desert (the south and

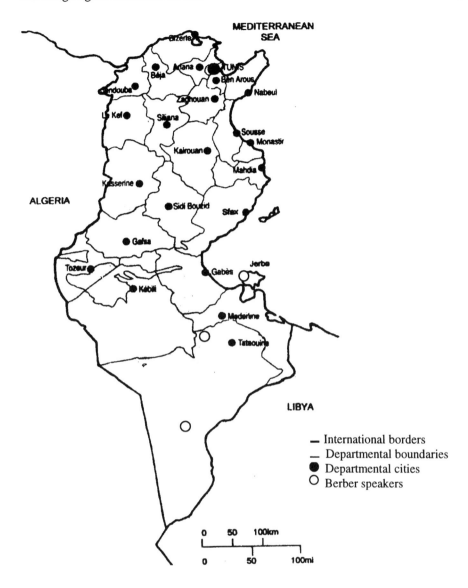

Figure 1 Map of Tunisia

south-west), Tunisia is virtually self-sufficient in agricultural products, and in some cases a net exporter (olive oil, dates, oranges, and dairy and fishery products).

Even so, the country has moved away from a traditional reliance on agriculture to a more diversified and liberalised economy, spurred in particular by the signing of a trade partnership agreement with the European Union in 1995 (the first such agreement with a Mediterranean country, due to take effect in 2008). From 1979 to 1999, agriculture contributed only 13% to the GDP, while industry and services contributed 28% and 59%, respectively

(World Bank, 2000). The manufacturing/industrial sector now contributes over 50% of the country's exports, which include textiles and footwear, mechanical goods, phosphates and chemicals, agricultural products, and hydrocarbons. As for services, they comprise tourism and related activities as well as thriving computer software production and consultancy sectors (Price Waterhouse, 1998).

Tunisia's location on the Mediterranean – close to Europe, the country's main trade partner, as well as to the Arab Gulf region and the Middle East – made it a crossroads of civilisations in the past, and a hub of economic activity and investment today. Since 1989, Tunisia has undertaken structural reform in order to improve economic competitiveness and meet the requirements of the partnership accord with the European Union, which includes provisions for a free trade zone. While gross domestic investment has grown steadily from minus 2.5% in 1979–89 to 4.3% in 1989–99, then to 11.6% in 1999, foreign direct investment reached US$800 million in 1998, and the country's external debt decreased to a moderate level estimated at US$10.8 billion at the end of 1999, which corresponds to about 52% of GDP, down from 60% in the early 1990s (World Bank, 2000). IMF records show a further decrease of the external debt to 49% in 2000 and 44% in 2001 (*Jeune Afrique L'intelligent*, 2001: 18).

The *Middle East Magazine* (1999) finds that thanks to this structural reform 'the work culture has undergone a revolution, and gains in productivity over the last five years [1995–99] have added a very impressive 30 per cent to GNP (sic). The target is to increase this figure to 40% by the end of the current development plan in 2001.' The World Bank finds that '[a]ll this adds up to a very robust economy, ideally positioned, both in terms of capacity and geographical situation, to confidently enter the Euro zone in the first decade of the new millennium' (World Bank, 2000).

Making the case for the Tunisian government, Chaabane (1999: 33–44) draws the profile of an emerging country based on its position in several ratings:

(1) First in North Africa in terms of real GNP growth, with a consistent positive trend from 1972 to 1996.
(2) Seventeenth among thirty countries with the highest economic growth rate between 1965 and 1996, according to the World Bank.
(3) Twenty-third among forty countries whose economies are considered 'emerging', according to the *World Future Society*.
(4) Strong creditworthiness and investment grade ratings, including France's Export Credit Agency (COFACE) as well as Moodys and Standard and Poors.
(5) A low poverty rate of 7% (World Bank 1995 estimate, down from 40% in the 1960s).
(6) A higher proportion of scientists and technicians than South Africa, Turkey or Thailand, and greater investment in telecommunications than South Africa, Poland, or Thailand (adapted, author translation).

The *World Bank Country Brief* (World Bank, 2000: 3) draws a positive profile of Tunisia, noting that '[a]t the end of March 2000 the Bank portfolio in Tunisia comprised 20 ongoing projects, amounting to US$1.4 billion'. The document adds that:

a distinct shift has been made in recent years towards fewer traditional projects and more sector investment loans so as to incorporate sector policy reform with modernization investments (...). As another aspect of the program, the Bank's non-lending services have been increased to Tunisia in response to the desire of government officials to assess how other countries have handled different problems of designing, sequencing and implementing policy and institutional reforms.

However, the major challenge to the government's development programme remains high unemployment, which hovers around 16%.[2] According to the 1999 population-employment count of the official census bureau (*Institut National de la Statistique, INS*, 2001), Tunisia has a labour force of 3.1 million people aged 15 to 59 (24% women) which is distributed as follows: services 43%, agriculture 33% and industry 24%. Given the relative youth of the population (37% under 18 in 1999), this labour force grows by nearly 3% annually.

The choices that the government has made to integrate the country into the global economy have had a positive impact on social development. Available data indicate a life expectancy of 72 years (70 for males and 74 for females), which is higher than the average of 68 years for the Middle East and North Africa (MENA), and an infant mortality rate of 26 per thousand (against 48/1000 for MENA; see World Bank, 2000). The population is growing by only 1.12% thanks to a comprehensive family planning programme implemented since independence, with a target of 0.9% by 2025. Adult literacy is around 67% (79% for men and 55% for women), although government figures show a higher rate of 73% (INS, 2001), with primary school enrolment of six to 15 year-olds reaching 96% (*Neuvième Plan de Développement*, NPD, 1997–2001).

These choices have had obvious repercussions on language policy and planning, particularly in the educational and vocational training sectors, the main purveyors of a skilled workforce that would guarantee the competitiveness of the Tunisian economy. Reflecting the government's agenda for comprehensive development, Chaabane (1999), Ismail (1992) and Zaitouni (1995), who respectively deal with future perspectives on the Tunisian economy and society, basic education, and the reform of the administration, underscore the importance of human resource development (HRD) through a system of life-long learning ('*l'apprentissage durant toute la vie*', Chaabane, 1999: 107).[3] Thus, the political discourse and subsequent policy and planning decisions have targeted the following language and literacy objectives, with the goal of developing autonomous learning:

(1) reinforcing functional literacy in Arabic (the national language);
(2) improving functional competence in foreign languages, particularly French and English; and
(3) generalising computer literacy.

These objectives were reflected in the Tunisian president's decisions announced on the 13th anniversary of The Change (*al-taghyeer* or *al-taHawwul*, a reference to the transfer of power from former President Bourguiba to President Ben Ali on 7 November 1987 and to the subsequent structural reform programme). These decisions included:

(1) the design of operational curricula for establishing *l'Ecole de Demain* (the School of the Future), based on the introduction of new communication technologies;

(2) further reinforcement of competence in foreign languages and modern science; and

(3) rationalising the relationship between education and training for the workplace (Ben Ali, 2000) (author translation).

These language policy and planning issues are best understood in the context of the current language profile of Tunisia.

The Language Profile of Tunisia

Historical perspective

The language situation in Tunisia has a long history stretching over three millennia that shows both its complexity and dynamism. This history has never been systematically studied. It has been documented only occasionally (and rather tangentially) by geographers, historians (with the exception of the notable, well-documented *History of Ibn Khaldoun*, written in the 14th century, see Ibn Khaldoun, 1988), and a few contemporary linguists. A very brief account of this history, which will be reviewed below, is offered by Baccouche (1994, in press, based on an earlier report by Baccouche and Skik, 1978).

The oldest language spoken by the indigenous people, who were called Berber (i.e. barbarous) by the Romans, was Libyc. With the arrival of the Phoenecians from Tyre (Lebanon) and the founding of the Carthagenian Empire (814–146 BCE), bilingualism began to develop, as indicated by Libyc-Punic coin inscriptions dating back to 139 BCE (Fantar (2000) documents archeological Libyc-Punic plaques that date back as far the 3rd century BCE). Subsequently, bilingualism evolved into Libyc-Latin with the Roman domination of the region (146 BC–349 CE); however, Punic survived more than six centuries after the destruction of Carthage before giving way to Latin as the official language. After the Vandal/Germanic period (439–533 CE), the Byzantine Empire (533–647) revived Roman culture, which was heavily influenced by Hellenism, thus allowing the Greek language to take hold and leave traces till the present time.

Arabic was introduced with the spread of Islam to North Africa in 647, and Arab Muslims took another 50 years to wrest control of Carthage from the Byzantine-backed Berber leader Al-Kahina. The linguistic landscape was then multilingual, with substrates of the various languages (Berber, Punic, Latin, and Greek) that are still reflected today in the dialectal vocabulary and in the names of many cities and villages all over Tunisia. Coins from the Muslim period as well as writings by Arab geographers and historians attest to the fact that Latin remained in use by the Muslim administration at least until the end of the 11th century. When the Banu Hilal tribes were sent to Tunisia by the Fatimid King of Egypt in successive waves in 1050–1052 to punish the rebellious Berbers, Arabic-Berber bilingualism was spreading. The near total conversion of Berbers to Islam and the Banu Hilal invasion accelerated the predominance of Arabic. Ibn Khaldoun describes in detail how Arabic spread at that time at the expense of Berber which was gradually confined to isolated locations. Berber is now considered a dying language in Tunisia. It is estimated to be spoken by less than 0.5% of Tunisians on the island of Jerba and in a few southern villages in the departments of Mednine and Tataouine (see Baccouche, 1998; Battenburg, 1999; Pencheon, 1968).

Since the 11th century, Arabic has grown to become the dominant and eventually official language of Tunisia in its literary / religious (Qur'anic) variety, while the spoken varieties of the Arab tribes that settled in the country since the seventh century continued to evolve into mutually intelligible regional dialects. These literary and spoken varieties, while absorbing the anterior influences of Punic, Berber, Latin and Greek, form the basis for the current diglossic situation. However, Arabic still has had to bear the influence of several other languages of subsequent invaders and neighbours of Tunisia.

Spanish language influence was mainly due to the exodus of Arab-Berber Moors when Spain reclaimed its territory from them from the 11th to the 14th centuries. Spanish nomenclature is still found in names of families, towns (especially coastal ones in the north-east that had been occupied by Spanish forces or ones that served as settlements for the Moors a little further inland), some vegetables and fruits, crafts and card/board games.

For nearly three centuries, rivalry over the domination of the Mediterranean basin placed Christians (mainly Spanish) and Muslims (mainly Turkish) in opposition until the Turks secured their authority over Tunisia from the end of the 14th to the 19th centuries. Throughout this time, conflicts and trade caused the movement of populations and regular contact between speakers of the various languages around the basin. The Turkish language predominated in the administration and army, leaving a substantial number of words that are still used in literary and spoken Arabic in these sectors as well as in the musical, clothing and culinary lexicons.

In the 19th century, it was the turn of other European languages, particularly Italian and French, to leave their mark on Tunisian Arabic. The Italian community living in Tunisia reached 90,000 by the first quarter of the 20th century, thus outnumbering the French community of about 70,000 settlers. Italian is particularly noticeable now in the lexicon of the following sectors: industry and crafts, building, agriculture, marine activity and the arts. Along with Italian, there was much interference between Arabic and Maltese – itself a blend of Tunisian Arabic and a Sicilian dialect of Italian – with the settlement of several thousand islanders in Tunis, Sfax and Sousse. The intense trade activity in the Mediterranean basin, with Tunis as the southern hub, helped consolidate a pidgin called *Lingua Franca* (sic, with a French matrix and embedded Spanish, Moorish, Italian, Corsican, Maltese, Berber, Arabic and Turkish expressions) which had been in the making since the 14th century and probably served as a two-way bridge for loan words. This pidgin was widely spoken by merchants and seamen, in particular, and occasionally served as the written code of legal documents (e.g. commercial contracts) as well as the language of diplomacy (see Bannour, 2000).

French influence began systematically with the protectorate regime in 1881, in the wake of Italian-French colonialist rivalry over the North African territories. The French, who had already made inroads into Tunisia through settlements and trade, soon turned the protectorate regime into a colonial one, making French the official language for administration and in the public schools. By the time Tunisia gained independence in 1956, French had a firm foothold in the country's administrative and educational systems as well as in general everyday use to the extent that it is currently difficult for academics (Baccouche, in press; Battenburg, 1996, 1997; Daoud, 1991a; Garmadi, 1968; Maamouri, 1973; Salhi, 1984, 2000; Walters, 2000) as well as journalists (Jourchi, 2001; Kefi, 2000) clearly to distinguish its status as a second or foreign language.

This issue will be developed further in the following sections, but it is important to note that French has greatly influenced both literary and spoken Arabic in Tunisia at the level of vocabulary, structure and even discourse. Concerning spoken Arabic, Baccouche (in press: 3) states:

> French currently holds the leading position among the languages that have influenced Tunisian [i.e. spoken] Arabic with several hundred more or less integrated borrowings in all domains. Its influence continues at present to mark the linguistic situation in Tunisia after forty years of independence. (author translation)

The influence on literary Arabic can be clearly seen in the lexicon, syntax and, I would argue, in the rhetoric of Arabic in literary works and in the written media, in particular. This influence distinguishes literary Arabic from the Arabic used in publications from other Arab countries that have had little or no contact with French.

Thus, the current language situation in Tunisia may be characterised as both diglossic and bilingual. Diglossia concerns the uses of Arabic along a written-spoken continuum, while bilingualism has to do with the ongoing interaction between Arabic and French. The dynamism and complexity of this situation is further enhanced by the promotion of several foreign languages, especially English as the modern language of science and technology, international trade and electronic communication.

Diglossia

Tunisian Arabic (TA) is the language of communication in everyday life, particularly in the family, but it is also widely used in the media (radio and television programmes) and in the theatre and cinema, where productions very rarely use Literary Arabic. TA is a spoken form with a variety of mutually intelligible regional dialects, including a countrywide urban/rural distinction signalled most clearly by the allophonic unvoiced/voiced velar stop [q/g]. Over the years, a substantial record of written TA has been accumulated, including popular tales (e.g. Al-Eroui, 1989), songs, poetry of Bedouin origin (*malhun*), proverb collections, the recent publication of a daily newspaper (*Al-Sareeh*) and the first novel ever (a 1997 translation of *Le Petit Prince* of Antoine de Saint-Exupéry, by Hédi Balegh, a vocal advocate of TA). Written Arabic (WA) is the official language of Tunisia. It is the language of religion, government, the law, the media and education (arts and human and social sciences).

However, the distinction between TA and WA is far from being clear cut. WA itself, which has evolved out of Classical Arabic (CA, the language of the Qur'an), now represents a gradient of varieties. It extends from CA, embodied in religious and legal texts and classical works of literature that are still read today, to Modern Standard Arabic (MSA) which is the language of modern literature (hence Literary Arabic), school manuals, official documents, the written media,

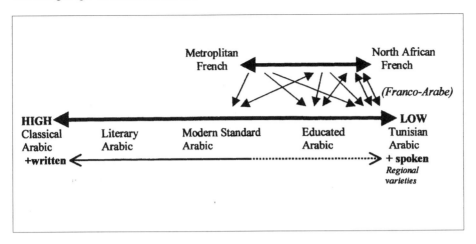

Figure 2 Arabic diglossia and Arabic-French bilingualism in Tunisia

and some political speeches and radio/TV programmes. The extent to which the language of these sources tends towards 'pure' CA or 'low' MSA depends very much on the educational background and language mastery level of the writer or speaker, his/her cultural affiliation and attitude towards the language as well as the audience and the topic at hand (see Daoud, 1991a).

Likewise, TA is spoken along a similar gradient, overlapping to some extent with MSA at the high end, and extending to the most popular regional vernacular at the low end. Here again, the variety used depends on the interlocutors, the situation, and the topic involved. There is so much overlap and flexibility among the gradients in WA and TA that together they form a continuum, which explains the general perception that WA and TA are simply the high and low forms of the same language. Some have attempted to categorise these varieties and describe them, thus producing more labels such as Median or Intermediate Arabic (Garmadi, 1968) and Educated Arabic (EA) (Maamouri, 1983), all referring to a spoken form of WA, or MSA, that is characterised by less formality, more syntactic and morphological flexibility and lexical borrowing from TA. This continuum may be represented as in Figure 2, bearing in mind that MSA and EA are understood across the Arab World, notwithstanding country/regional variation. This is why the label TA is reserved for the low end of the continuum to designate the Tunisian dialect with its regional varieties.[4]

Bilingualism, biculturalism and literacy

Grafted onto the Arabic continuum is French, which is often mixed in with the spoken varieties of Arabic (TA) in everyday conversation (*Franco-Arabe*), or used by itself in the media (at least three daily newspapers, several weekly publications and a radio channel), secondary and tertiary education (in the sciences and economics disciplines) as well as social, work and professional settings. Mixing TA and French ranges from simple code-switching involving the use of French words in Arabic discourse to extensive code-mixing where speech may become predominantly French. French interacts with MSA and EA in more subtle ways, thus influencing MSA syntax and word choice, mostly through a process of translation, and going as far as rhetorical organisation (see Daoud, 1991b).

French is so rooted in the socioeconomic fabric of Tunisia that it is considered necessary for having the simplest office job or running a neighbourhood grocery store. A small-scale survey[5] conducted for the purposes of this monograph revealed that in the grocery trade, as presumably in many others, while daily interaction is conducted in the vernacular or in *Franco-Arabe*, and all official documents have in recent years been switched to MSA (licenses, taxes, etc.), wholesale invoices and price lists are in French and are not likely to change soon given the greater reliance on computers, which use French software. This has led many, usually older, retail grocers who could not read French to post illegal higher prices, incurring heavy fines that eventually force them to leave the trade.

The survey also asked a sample of students and teachers from secondary school and university the question: 'Can you live and prosper in Tunisia being literate in the following languages?' The answers were as follows:

(1) Arabic only?   Maybe (several said: No).
(2) French only?   Yes.
(3) Arabic and French?   Yes.
(4) English only?   No.
(5) Arabic, French and English?   Yes, (most added: the best).

Although the sample may not be representative of all Tunisians, the first and second answers are indicative of the extent to which French literacy is valued as a means of having a good education and making a good living in this Arab country. The general perception is that literacy in Arabic alone is not sufficient to secure a prosperous future, in spite of a rather vigorous Arabisation campaign that started in the mid-1970s (see the Policy and Planning section that follows). The fifth answer is also interesting because it reflects the public perception that, all other things being equal, a third language (namely, English) can give one an edge in finding employment or succeeding in business, accessing information and being a citizen of the world.

The 1994 census (INS, 1996) generally confirms the language profile described thus far. In the section devoted to the 'educational characteristics' of the population, the census asked whether a person 'can read and write' in the following categories: 'Illiterate'; 'Arabic'; 'Arabic, French'; 'Arabic, French, English'; 'Arabic and other'; 'Other, not Arabic'; and 'Undeclared'. Although respondents may have overestimated their competence in these languages, one can safely draw the following conclusions about language and literacy based on the data collected in 1994 and in the 1998–99 population-employment surveys (*INS*, 2000; see Table 1).

(1) A very high number of Tunisians are literate in MSA, with nearly universal literacy among the younger generations born after 1979. This speaks for the progress of Arabisation, particularly in view of the fact that only four decades ago only 30% were literate.

(2) Similarly, literacy in French is very high, with a peak of 82% among 15 to 25 year-old Tunisians, indicating the value of French as a language of social and economic promotion. It is interesting to note, though, that while literacy in this language has gone up, always being 10 to 20% behind Arabic, it

Table 1 Evolution of illiteracy rates (INS, 2000)[7]

Population age 10 plus						
Sex	*1966*	*1975*	*1984*	*1989*	*1994*	*1999*
Both	67.9	54.9	46.2	37.2	31.7	27.0
Male	53.9	42.3	34.6	26.4	21.2	17.7
Female	82.4	67.9	58.1	48.3	42.3	36.3
Population age 10–29						
Sex	*1966*	*1975*	*1984*	*1989*	*1994*	*1999*
Both	51.2	33.0	24.8	16.0	12.8	9.1
Male	33.3	18.9	13.6	7.0	6.0	4.7
Female	69.3	47.2	36.5	25.2	19.7	13.6

has apparently started to decline with the generation born in 1980 and thereafter.

(3) Illiteracy in rural areas has always been higher than in urban areas, particularly in the north-west and central-west where it ranged from 54% to 58% in 1994. However, the effort to ensure universal schooling has reduced these rates among the younger generations, as indicated in Table 1, and a recently reinvigorated 1993 campaign to 'eradicate or erase illiteracy'[6] is expected to help the older generations and women, in particular.

(4) The 1994 census revealed higher literacy levels among males, who maintained an advantage of 5 to 10% over females in the generation born after 1979. Even so, the female literacy rate is considered a major achievement, bearing in mind that women lagged behind by about 23% in Arabic and French in 1965 (11 years after independence) and about 30% 10 years earlier than that (1955). This gap may be closed in the near future as indicated by the fact that, for the first time, the female university student population surpassed the male population in 1999–2000 (50.4% out of a total of 180,044, see *Ministère de l'Enseignement Supérieur*, 1999/2000).

It appears that the *normative range of literacy* (Kaplan & Palmer, 1992: 194) for Tunisia has changed. Until the middle of the 1980s, there did not seem to be any real change taking place in the country's economy, the general work environment, the educational and training sectors and society at large. However, the change of leadership in 1987, which coincided with international transformations in the economic, technological and communication domains, spurred action at every level. Above and beyond the government's programmes to reform education and improve adult literacy in order to secure employability and economic competitiveness, there has been strong public motivation to learn in order to prosper. If one stood in the city centre of any major town at the end of a working day, one would not think that many people were going home to have dinner; almost everyone seems to be taking evening classes in foreign languages (particularly English), computer skills, management, etc. There is a real public feeling that basic literacy skills in Arabic and French are not any longer sufficient. In addition to higher proficiency in these languages, Tunisians feel they have to have additional competencies and are willing to invest time and money to develop them.

Language Spread

The spread of Arabic and French, and to a lesser extent English, is a fact in Tunisia even though the level of mastery of these languages remains an issue for lack of reliable standardised testing. This section describes language spread in the educational system,[8] the media and the wider context. Issues related to language-in-education as well as literacy policy and planning will be covered in the next section.

Languages in the educational system

When Arab Muslims came to North Africa in the seventh century, they soon established the *Zaituna Mosque* in Tunis, around 670 CE. This mosque became the first university in the Muslim World and was devoted to Qur'anic studies, Islamic law, reading and writing classical Arabic and some science teaching. It also encouraged a country-wide network of *kuttab* (classes held in the mosques) that taught young boys the Qur'an and basic literacy skills in Arabic. The *kuttab* system has survived to this day and is sometimes chosen by parents as an alternative to the secular preschool (*école maternelle*).

Secular, bilingual education started in 1875, six years before the French protectorate, with the founding of *al-Madrassa al-Sadiqiyya*, an Arabic-French bilingual school that introduced a 'modern' (European) curriculum and was the purveyor of education for the children of the social elite then, including some of the future nationalist leaders of Tunisia. French-medium schools which were established during the colonial period (1881–1956) reinforced secular education and led to the adoption of French curricula in Tunisian bilingual schools, a practice that continued well into the 1970s. In fact, the French educational system continues to influence contemporary Tunisian education in subtle and not so subtle ways. These are discussed here and in the next two sections of this monograph.

After independence, educational reform began with the Educational Reform Law of 1958 that laid out a ten-year plan to:

- unify Tunisia's various school systems (*kuttab*, French and bilingual schools) into a bilingual system under the control of the Ministry of National Education;
- establish a new organisational structure, including a six-year primary school cycle, a six-year secondary school cycle sanctioned by the French-style *baccalauréat*, and a three- to five-year university programme;
- nationalise the curricula and restore the primacy of Arabic as the medium of instruction;
- make education public and free at all levels; and
- increase enrolment, especially of rural and female youth, at all levels.

The latest educational reform of basic and secondary education (1987–1997/ 98) follows on from the structural reform programme just discussed. Spurred by The World Bank and the European Union, it brought about a new, business-oriented approach (based on cost-benefit analysis and market demand for knowledge and skills) to tackle Tunisia's educational problems (high dropout rates as early as the sixth grade, which stem in large part from the irrelevance of the curriculum to the student's career opportunities, the inadequacy of learning materials, poor teacher preparation and questionable assessment tools). It was obvious to everyone that youngsters who dropped out of school at age 12 or 13 lacked the necessary literacy/numeracy skills to contribute effectively to economic growth, and were consequently going to be a burden on society.

The objectives of this reform, as implemented in the official programmes signed into law on 29 March 1993, included:

- adapting education to the requirements of the changing socioeconomic order;
- establishing the *Ecole de Base* (Basic School), thus making education compulsory to the ninth, instead of the sixth year;
- developing basic vocational skills in the seventh to ninth years to allow the weaker students who could not reach secondary school to secure a job;
- providing a more thorough, comprehensive education in secondary school (years 10 to 13);
- improving the curriculum by incorporating new technologies, teaching more foreign languages and generalising computer literacy; and
- increasing the range of specialisation tracks leading to the *baccalauréat* and then to university.

This reform has been paralleled since 1990 by an overhaul of the vocational training sector to make a highly skilled labour force out of the students who dropped out of secondary school or early university studies. Lastly, the reform of the university initiated in 1993 has just entered its final stage, with the highest priority being given to 'employability' in the global economy (see *Al-Sabah*, 2000; Chraiet, 2001). The Minister of Higher Education was reported as saying in a news conference that 'the ministry will avoid in the future the specialties that offer no job prospects' (*Al-Shuruuq*, 2000: 28, author translation).

The curriculum in the primary cycle (years 1 to 6) of basic education has been completely Arabised. As shown in Table 2, it includes teaching MSA (reading, writing, oral expression, and grammar) to children whose native language is TA and most of whom would have developed some knowledge of MSA (the alphabet, from preschool, as well as some oral comprehension ability from children's TV programmes). Proficiency in MSA among these children varies depending on the child's family situation (as determined by the parents' level of education, in particular), but it is presumed to develop rather quickly so that the child can study the other school subjects that are taught in MSA. French is introduced as a foreign language in the third grade, but at the intensive rate of nine to 11.5 hours a week, almost as many as for MSA (the decrease in MSA from the fifth year is compensated by its use in other subjects).

In the second cycle (years 7–9) – which is really the beginning of secondary education, since classes are taught in secondary schools by subject-specialist teachers – competence in MSA is reinforced through direct language instruction and reading/writing skills development as well as the teaching of other subjects. French is taught at the substantial rate of 4.5 hours a week, but only as a foreign

Table 2 Language spread in basic school

Hours per week										
Years Subjects	1	2	3	4	5	6	7	8	9	Language variety used
MSA	11.5	11.5	10.0	10.0	7.0	7.0	5.0	5.0	5.0	MSA
French			9.0	9.5	11.5	11.0	4.5	4.5	5.0	French
English							2.0	2.0	2.0	English
Humanities	3.0	3.0	3.5	3.0	4.0	4.5	5.0	5.0	5.0	MSA/EA/TA
Maths & science	5.5	5.5	5.5	5.5	5.5	5.5	5.5	5.5	5.5	MSA/EA/TA
Other	2.5	2.5	2.0	2.0	2.0	2.0	6.0	6.0	6.0	MSA/EA/TA/ French
Total	22.5	22.5	30.0	30.0	30.0	30.0	28.0	28.0	28.5	

Note: 'Other' includes music, art and technological and physical education. In the right-hand column, the language listed first for each subject is the mandated language of instruction and examination.

language. As for English, it was introduced in the eighth and ninth years at first in 1996/97, then in the seventh year in 2000–2001. Prior to 1996, it was taught only from the tenth year of the 13-year school system.

To be admitted to secondary school, children have to have the *diplôme de fin d'études de l'enseignement de base* (diploma of completion of basic education). This requires passing a regional, state-run examination that gives a heavy weighting to language ability in Arabic and French (reading, writing and grammar) as well as to maths and science. Once admitted, students study for two years in a common-core cycle (10th–11th year), then another two (12th–13th year) in one of five specialties (experimental sciences, technology, mathematics, letters, and economics and management). Students who successfully complete the entire four-year programme take the national French-style *baccalauréat* examination, which is a requirement for university admission. Examination questions are in the languages in which the respective subjects are taught, which are listed first in the right-hand column in Tables 2 and 3.

Instruction in secondary education is in MSA in the humanities and the arts, but in French in the hard and experimental sciences, mathematics and economics. In addition, French is taught as a subject 2–4 hours/week. English is also taught 3–4 hours/week to all students. The study load varies from 27 to 34 hours per week, but in years 11–13, new subjects are introduced, some being obligatory, others optional (e.g. philosophy, a third foreign language, computer skills). A student must take two out of the three optional subjects, and if he chooses a third foreign language (German, Italian or Spanish) he may study it two hours a week for three years (see Table 3). Thus, a student who completes compulsory Arabic, French and English and opts for another language (though s/he has other options) can end up a quadralingual.

It may seem from this discussion that the Arabisation campaign – initiated since independence, and implemented more vigorously since 1976 – has run its course in basic and secondary education, and that French is highly unlikely to be phased out as the medium of instruction for mathematics, science and economics

Table 3 Language spread in secondary school

Hours per week								
	Common core		Specialisation tracks Years 12–13					
Subjects	Year 10	Year 11	Letters	E&M	Maths	Exp. Sc.	Tech.	Language variety used
MSA	4.5	4.5	5–4	3–0	3–0	3–0	3–0	MSA
French	3.5	3.5	4–3	3–2	3–2	3–2	3–2	French
English	3.0	3.0	4–3	4–3	3–3	3–3	3–3	English
3rd foreign lang.	(2)	(2)	(2)	(2)	(2)	(2)	(2)	Foreign lang.
Humanities	5.5	5.5	7.5–11 (1.5)	4.5–7	3.5–4 (3)	3.5–4 (3)	3.5–4 (3)	MSA/EA
Maths & science	8.5	8.5	4.5– (4.5)	4–5 (3)	13.5	14	10 (1.5)	French/TA
Econ. & Mngt				9–9				French/TA
Technology							8–8	French/TA
Other	4	4(2)	2(2)	2(2)	2(2)	2(2)	2(2)	MSA, French or FL/EA/TA
Total	29	33	31–27	32–32	32–29	32–29	34–33	

Note: 'Other' includes music, art, computing and technological and physical education, with a choice of two out of three to eight optional subjects (shown in parentheses), one of which may be a third foreign language (German, Italian or Spanish).

in the 10th to 13th years and later at university. However, it is difficult to predict what will happen. Two observations are worth making at this point; first, about the language varieties that are actually spoken by students and teachers in the classroom, even though the textbooks are in MSA, and second, about the switch from Arabic to French that the students have to make to study mathematics, science, technology and economics and management subjects starting from the 10th year. The first issue has not been investigated in any direct way by researchers interested in the language situation in Tunisia, except some 25 years ago by Skik (1976), relative to bilingualism in primary school, or more recently by Brahim (1994), with a special focus on the deviance of university students' French syntax from the standard. As for the second issue, it has yet to surface as a matter of academic investigation or public debate since the 1993 reform was initiated and in spite of the national consultation over *l'Ecole de Demain* (the School of the Future) launched in October 2000 (*La Presse*, 2000).

It is important to qualify the use of the languages shown in Tables 2 and 3 in the classroom. In the case of language teaching proper, it has always been the norm in Tunisia that language teaching be conducted in the target language itself, whatever that language. Teachers may resort to the vernacular or to translation only to deal with learners in the early stages of instruction or to resolve classroom management problems. An interview with a small sample of students from grades 7–13 indicated that their MSA and French teachers consistently use the target language, rarely do any code-switching (to French or Arabic), or make mistakes, although some complained about the poor accent of their French and English teachers. However, students in the lower grades in basic school reported less than spontaneous use of MSA and French by the respective teachers and a prevalence of TA in explaining or giving instructions and managing the classroom.

As for the Arabised subjects in the humanities and sciences, while teaching materials and examinations are in MSA, the language spoken by teachers and students in the classroom reflects very much the diglossic continuum discussed earlier, and may involve a variable degree of code-switching and code mixing, depending on the subject taught and the individual teacher. Overall, teacher talk in the humanities is predominantly in MSA during lectures, but it shifts towards EA and TA during question and answer and discussion periods. Students report that their overall participation in class is very limited to begin with, and that they use TA exclusively, except for the better students (about 30% per group) whose patterns of language use approach that of the teachers. The students interviewed agree that the majority of their peers are unable to improvise in MSA.

In Arabised mathematics and science classes (up to the ninth year), teacher talk involves more EA and some degree of MSA-French code-switching because the teachers have been educated in their subjects in French. For instance, a 7th grader reported that her biology teacher uses MSA/EA together with French jargon for which she admits she does not know the Arabic equivalent. Teacher and students then spend some time using TA and trying to identify what she is talking about. Students also reported that teachers make basic language errors such as (1) the incorrect use of the genitive case marking the dual, as in *Inna al-mustaqimayni mutawaaziayni* (verily the two lines are parallel), where the accusative form *mutawaaziaani* is required; or (2) improper vocabulary, as in: *tash3uru tunis bi-l-i3tizaazi* (Tunisia feels proud), where the Arabic verb *tash3uru* (feels) collocates only with a human subject.

The school subjects included under 'Other' involve a great deal of TA and/or French, particularly art and physical education where most of the jargon is in French. Furthermore, several courses as well as other school-related procedures and documents are usually referred to in French, such as m*aths* instead of *Hsaab* in TA or *riadhiyyaat* in MSA, *science naturelles* instead of *3uluum tabi3iyya*, *Monsieur* or *Madame* (to call the teacher) instead of *sidi* (TA) or *sayyidati* (MSA), *billet* (written permission to enter the classroom when a student is late) instead of *ithn bid-dukhuul* or *bitaaqat dukhuul*, etc.

Along with all this, there has been a noticeable drop in the level of French that the students themselves acknowledge. Seventh to ninth graders report a very low level in this language, illustrating that with the fact that very few students can answer the French teacher's questions or participate in class at all. In the words of a seventh grader, 'students would start answering in French, then they are blocked and revert to TA' (author translation). This is confirmed by a group of 13th year students who are preparing for the *baccalauréat* examination and who have, in fact, studied mathematics and science in French before Arabisation spread to years 7–9. They report that only their mathematics and physics teachers use French consistently; however, their biology teacher sometimes translates technical terms to TA, but not to MSA. These students estimate that the majority of their peers (at least 70%) have very poor French and are much more likely to ask for clarifications, etc., in TA, with French technical terms mixed in. They all recognise that they have a problem expressing themselves in examinations, where they have to write in French. Interestingly enough, they add that Tunisian students lack spontaneity while speaking in MSA as well.

Even without a systematic survey of language use in Tunisian classrooms having been carried out to date, it seems reasonable to argue that the situation just described bears within it the seeds of a serious language-related dilemma that Tunisian educational policy makers will have to face sooner or later as more and more of the younger students who are educated in Arabic reach the tenth year. This dilemma concerns whether to continue teaching the mathematics, science and economics subjects in French and risk serious breakdowns in communication and poor overall achievement, or to Arabise these subjects, and if so, how far to push Arabisation in the university tracks. Furthermore, if Arabisation is chosen, will the teachers be adequately trained to teach their courses, and will the teaching resources (textbooks, etc.) be available in Arabic to fulfil the objectives of the educational programmes? The 13th graders interviewed report that in the philosophy course, a subject that was Arabised at the start of the campaign in 1976, their teacher uses French words in his EA discourse, since according to them, the references he uses to prepare the course are in French.

An insider at the Ministry of Education said that a *de facto* separation has taken place between teachers of mathematics and science in years 7–9 and 10–13, speculating that teachers at the lower levels have overcome the difficulty of switching from French to Arabic, since the Arabisation of these grades was completed in 1996/97. This informant felt that these teachers would no longer be willing to teach grades 10–13, just as the higher level teachers would be unwilling to make the linguistic shift necessary to teach grades 7–9 in Arabic.[9]

In the vocational training sector, French is the medium of instruction, at least in the teaching/training materials. Also, because this sector benefits from the active collaboration of French-Canadian funding and expertise in the context of the PRICAT project,[10] all curricula are in French. Having coordinated the English for Occupational Purposes (EOP) curriculum and textbook design for this sector and visited many vocational training centres around the country, I personally witnessed the fact that classes and workshop training sessions involve a high degree of French-TA code-switching and code mixing. EOP and French classes are now compulsory subjects in vocational training at the rate of two hours a week each, but not MSA. This language situation also prevails in the *instituts supérieurs d'études technologiques* (ISET, higher institutes of technological studies), which are higher education counterparts of the vocational training centres.

In higher education, in general, the predominant language of instruction is French, which has been added as a required subject at the rate of two hours per week for two years in all the disciplines since 1998. Arabic serves as the medium of instruction in the Arabic language departments as well as in a number of disciplines or individual courses related to Islamic studies, civil and criminal law and the like, which draw on a rich store of traditional religious and legal texts and an abundant locally produced literature. Foreign language and literature majors (English, Italian, Spanish, German, Russian and Chinese) are each taught in the target language in question.

Teaching English for Specific Purposes (ESP) has been part of the university programmes since the national university system was founded in 1958, but it has witnessed a significant growth since the early 1980s that culminated in the generalisation of ESP to all higher education majors without exception in 1996–97. Outside the academic teaching areas, there has been an unprecedented demand for English by business companies and the general public, which has prompted many private institutions to teach it, along with the British Council, AMIDEAST, the Tunisian American Chamber of Commerce, and the *Institut Bourguiba des Langues Vivantes (IBLV)*, a government adult school which, until 1999 according to its director, had 27 branches across the country and a fee-paying student population of about 8000 (A. Labadi, personal communication; also see Daoud, 1996, 2000, in press b, and Shili, 1997). In addition, several private and public-sector companies and governmental institutions have their own ESP programmes (e.g. oil and gas companies, the national airline company Tunis-Air, the Central Bank, etc.). These programmes employ one or more Tunisian EFL teachers on a full- or part-time basis and involve little or no coordination with a professional EFL/ESP agency, such as a university English department or ESP Resource Centre.

No one has investigated language use in university classes to see the extent to which there is any code-switching or code mixing similar to what has been described above in relation to basic and secondary education. One expects university instructors in the various disciplines taught in French to be more proficient in this language for obvious reasons (longer education history, involvement in research and more international contacts); however, language ability and use always remain an individual matter. There is really no reason to exclude instances of code-switching, code mixing and mistakes from occurring in the classroom and in other formal contexts; I have witnessed similar instances in the staff meetings and interdisciplinary functions that I have attended over the years.

As for the university students' use of the languages in question, my own experience with students, even at the graduate level, leads me to confirm the trends indicated in the feedback from the secondary school sample interviewed for this monograph. Tunisian students lack spontaneity in MSA and French, the two languages of literacy. They learn them at school, but do not develop native-speaker mastery or awareness of either language. Their situation is compounded by the fact that educational decisions about language choice have been inconsistent, thus depriving students of the opportunity to be taught in one language, which would provide authentic contexts for learning that language and consolidating it. A civil engineering instructor interviewed for this study reports that his students cannot produce complete and clear questions in French in class and, most importantly, write so badly that their examination results are greatly affected by the poor level of French.

Languages of the media

Another area which contributes to language spread and reflects language change over time is the area of the print and audiovisual media, particularly if one gauges the preference of the public for one language or another. In 1989, Daoud (1991a) found that the Tunisian print media (newspapers and magazines) were evenly distributed so that on any day of the week readers could find an equal number of publications in Arabic and French. However, with the addition

Table 4 News publications in Tunisia

Arabic	French	Bilin-gual(A-F)	English
Newspapers			
Al-Hurriyya (d,g,o,*) Al-Sabah (d,*) Al-Shuruuq (d,*) Al-Sahafa (d,o,*) Al-Akhbar (d) Al-Sada (2/w,*) Al-Bayan (w,*) Al-Anwar (w,*) Sabah al-khayr (w,*) Al-Sabah al-usbu3i (w) Al-Sha3b (w) Al-Musawwir (w) Al-Adhoua' (w) Al-Hadath (w) Al-Jumhuriyya (w) (25,000) Al-Shabab (w) Al-Usbu3 al–3arabi (w) Donia al-mala3ib (w) Al-Sareeh (w, TA)	Le Renouveau (d,g,o,*) La Presse (d,o,*) (50,000) Le temps (d,o,*) Tunis-Hebdo (2/w,*) Promosport (w)	Al-I3laan (w,*)	Tunisia News (w) (2,500–3,000)
Magazines (g)			
	Réalités (w,o,*) Tunisie Economique (m,o) L'Economiste Maghrébin (m,o)		
Websites (g)			
www.radiotunis.com/ www.tunisiatv.com/		www.tunisieinfo. com/	www.tunisiaonline.com/ www.tunisieinfo..com/
News bulletins online (g)			
Akhbar Tunes	Nouvelles de Tunisie Economie et finance La semaine en Tunisie La page sportive		Tunisia online news Business and finance

Note: d = daily, 2/w = twice a week, w = weekly, m = monthly, g = government publication, o = online version, TA = Tunisian Arabic, figures in parentheses = circulation, * = available in 1989 (cf. Daoud, 1991a).

of foreign publications which were abundant and more varied or specialised (politics, economy, fashion, hobbies, etc.), the balance clearly tipped in favour of French. At the news stand, Tunisians seemed to prefer French-medium publications, particularly foreign ones, because they were deemed more informative and more credible.

Today the situation is somewhat different. There are now 19 daily and weekly[11] newspapers in Arabic, instead of 11 in 1989, while the number of local French-medium newspapers has remained the same, with a few old titles dropping out and new ones coming onto the list (see Table 4). In addition, the readership has apparently changed; according to some news vendors I interviewed, only the older generation (40 or older) tend to buy the French papers and magazines. This would be the last generation that had been schooled mostly in French before the Arabisation campaign became more systematic in 1976. This indicates that the younger generations, who have been educated mostly in MSA, seem to be more comfortable reading Arabic rather than French.

Note, however, that the preference for French-medium foreign publications remains stronger in urban areas, particularly among the better educated who can afford to pay the much higher prices of these publications. The better educated are also the most likely to read the local French-medium magazines and to have access to the greater number of online publications[12] which are almost exclusively in French and English (*Akbar Tunis* is the only news site in Arabic, but note the availability of the French and English versions: *Nouvelles de Tunisie* and *Tunisia Online News*).

With respect to the audiovisual media, Tunisia has three national radio channels (two in Arabic and one in French, *Radio Tunis Chaine Internationale, RTCI*) and several regional Arabic radio stations that can be heard over most of the country given its small size. For the same reason, it is possible to pick up broadcasts from neighbouring Arab countries in their vernacular or MSA as well as from nearby European countries, particularly Italy and France. Local radio and television broadcasts are mostly in TA (sitcoms, drama and call-in game and talk shows), and sometimes in EA (issue-related programmes that have a more educational tone). The news is read in MSA, except for one noon-time newscast in TA on national radio and a late-night one in French on national television. One Sunday afternoon newscast in MSA incorporates a translation in Arabic sign language.

France 2, of *France-Télévision*, used to broadcast live on Tunisian national television, having greater air time than Tunisian programming, but it was shut down (together with several newspapers and magazines which were censured) in the wake of criticism by the metropolitan French media of the presidential and parliamentary election campaign and results in October 1999. However, many Tunisians were already circumventing that censorship by watching French satellite channels and/or subscribing to the French-Tunisian cable company *Canal Horizons*. In addition, Tunisians can watch the most recent movie releases in French at the local cinema or rent the video version at the local video store. Many Tunisians also watch Arabic-medium satellite channels broadcasting from different Arab countries and from Europe.

In the absence of surveys of who is watching what and in what language, claims about the contribution of the audiovisual media to language spread can only be speculative. Overall, there is a clear preference for the non-Tunisian media channels for the simple reason that people are looking for better entertainment and more credible news. The effect of exposure to international satellite TV on the language profile of Tunisia would be to reinforce mutual intelligibility among the various Arabic regional dialects and strengthen MSA and EA as pan-Arab language varieties. As for French, it would also be strengthened, particularly among members of the urban upper and middle classes who watch French channels (the daily programmes of these channels are routinely published in Tunisian newspapers along with local programming).

English seems to be gaining little ground in the local media, with a daily one-hour programme on *RTCI*, two thirds of which is devoted to songs and the rest to a news brief and occasional interviews with visiting native speakers (note that the French programmes on RTCI also play many English songs). The radio show hosts are Tunisians whose English can hardly be called a good model for the young listeners to emulate. There is a local weekly newspaper (*Tunisia News*) which is circulated mostly through subscriptions to foreign agencies and companies in the country and Tunisian embassies abroad. I doubt that many Tunisians read it on a regular basis because it generally abstracts the news of the week that would be stale by the time the paper is delivered.

There is another monthly magazine, *English Digest*, but it is an irregular publication that seems to target the English-learning population with newsy texts and English idioms (with the French equivalent). Then, there is the growing number of web sites and electronic news media. The English used in the local media is not always native-like in terms of accent (when spoken, of course), correctness of grammar, register and style; it often sounds translated from French, but rarely from MSA. Exposure to English is also facilitated by satellite access to the ubiquitous CNN and frequent English/American movies and sitcoms on some Arab satellite channels.

Other foreign languages, particularly German, Italian and Spanish, are spreading, but much more slowly than English. There are no local publications in these languages, but given the large and varied tourist population that visits Tunisia, a considerable number of international magazines in the major European languages are on sale at most news stands in major cities and hotels. *RTCI* broadcasts a one-hour daily programme in these three languages, as it does in English. Access to these languages is also easy for those interested through satellite channels and the Internet.

Language spread in the wider context

Over the last two decades, Arabic has become more widespread in Tunisia. It is now required and used in government documents (forms, permits, certificates, correspondence and notices addressed to Tunisians). It is also more prominent in shop signs and on billboards (although its use is often a transliteration of French, and more recently, of American English brand names). Its spread in basic and secondary education has clearly made it the predominant language, particularly among the younger generation of Tunisians born in 1980 and thereafter. (See the previous discussion of the 1994 census.) Although this gain has been at the expense of French, the latter, which more and more Tunisians no longer seem to associate with the colonial past, is still widely used in the ambient environment.

All banking, insurance and medical documents are in French, regardless of whether one is dealing with a private or a public agency or service provider. Most Tunisians write their cheques in French and everyone gets their medical prescriptions and laboratory reports in French as well. Wholesale and retail shops issue invoices and receipts in French, even when they are written by hand, and they are rubber stamped in French even though it is just as easy to have Arabic stamps made (in fact, stamping is itself a relic of the French administration). Many company names are apparently conceived first in French, then translated into Arabic, often literally and awkwardly, and their French acronyms are then transliterated into Arabic and used in advertising. This is also the case of many institutions and programmes in the administration and the educational system. For instance, all Tunisians refer to the national water, power and tele-communications companies by their French acronyms or labels (*SONEDE, STEG* and *Tunisie Télécom*, respectively). Although these companies have recently switched their bills to Arabic, the rest of their documents (contracts, invoices, etc.) which involve contact with the public are in French or in both languages. *Tunisie Télécom* has recently introduced an electronic payment system on its web site using e-Dinars (the Dinar is the local currency), but the whole web site and the receipts it issues are in French. If the water and power companies adopt the same electronic strategy, which according to insiders is now being considered, it will bode well for the longevity of French in Tunisia.

In the educational system, MA-level studies are called DEA studies, from the French *Diplôme d'Etudes Approfondies*, and secondary school teacher certification is called CAPES, from the French *Certificat d'Aptitude au Professorat de l'Enseignement Secondaire*. In both of these cases, it is not only the label that is borrowed from France, but the whole concept. (See Daoud, in press b, for more of these labels throughout the educational system.) Furthermore, the government itself, which has recently mandated the exclusive use of Arabic in any correspondence addressed to Tunisians (*Premier Ministère*, 1999), continues to issue annual income and tax reports and pay slips in French and uses it exclusively on its official web site.

In the minds of most Tunisians, Arabic (with its varieties) and French are still assigned to particular domains and uses, as summarised by a Tunisian writer and poet cited by Kefi (2000: 32):

> With my own [family], I use Tunisian spoken Arabic, which is my real native language; that is to say, that Arabic language mixed with French words, often arabised, especially in the technical domain, but also Italian, and sometimes even Spanish, words. Literary Arabic, [which is] learnt at school, brings with it its wisdom, richness, beauty, and its Qur'anic heritage.

Kefi (p. 31) completes the frame by stating that French is

> without a doubt more present today than in the colonial period, when it was the attribute of an educated elite. In any case, it is mastered by a majority of Tunisians. It is the language of the economy, of the technocracy, and to a lesser extent, of intellectual production. (author translation)

As a matter of fact, a considerable number of original Tunisian publications are written in French, including academic journals and textbooks in scientific and literary domains, novels and poetry (not to mention the government's own official journal, *Le Journal Officiel de la République Tunisienne*, where the new laws are published in both Arabic and French). The country brief of the *Organisation Internationale de la Francophonie* on Tunisia notes that 'the rise of the new Tunisian literature in the French language starts in the 1970s' (Francophonie, 2001: 4), citing at least 15 titles of novels, in addition to numerous essays and poems. In a 1993–94 survey of Arabisation in the Arab World, Ammar and Al-Khury (1996: 53) report that in Tunisia 203 books were authored in a foreign language (French), against 538 in Arabic. Also Tunisia awards an annual prize for literature in Arabic and French called *le COMAR d'Or* (the Golden COMAR), with the fifth awards ceremony to be held in 2001.

Besides these written manifestations, French is used by Tunisians in academic and professional conferences, not only in the scientific and economic domains, but in the social sciences and humanities, particularly when the latter involve international participation. French is also the preferred and dominant written and oral mode of communication of NGOs, of which there are about 600 in the country. This may be explained by the fact that the members of these organisations are highly educated professionals who were mostly schooled in French in Tunisia and / or in France.

In everyday conversation, French is used extensively by the middle and upper classes in urban areas, and by women in particular, as it still confers upon its users a high degree of sophistication and prestige. Among educated Tunisians in general, it is not unusual to hear a complete conversation in French between friends, or while conducting business, although this no longer seems to be the case among the younger generation educated predominantly in Arabic, whose French is weaker and who are more likely to code-switch.

What we have so far is an unclear, but changing situation; however, it does seem that French is slowly losing ground to Arabic despite the interview responses reported in the previous section about French being more important than Arabic for one to live and prosper in Tunisia. Young Tunisians who aspire to have a good education, a good job and a productive life, know that they cannot achieve these goals without French. They also believe they could do even better if they learnt English as well. It is ironic that the mastery of one language can only happen at the expense of another, for as we will see in the last section of this monograph, the rivalry between Arabic, French and English is real. Let us assume for the time being that French is being challenged by English. I am using the word 'assume' advisedly because it remains to be seen whether English can challenge French in any significant way in this profoundly Frenchified country (see Battenburg, 1997; Daoud, 1991a, Garmadi, 1968; Salhi, 2000; Walters, 1999).

The 1994 census data revealed the onset of a rise in literacy in Arabic, French and English combined, as claimed by respondents born in 1970 and thereafter, with a high of 27.4% among men and 30.8% among women (see *INS*, 1996; Walters, 1999). The introduction of English in the years 7–9 of basic education and its generalisation in vocational training (1.5 to 2 years) and in higher education (2.5 to 5 or 6 years) since 1996, is bound to accelerate the spread of English. We must remember, however, that it all depends on the quality of instruction and on a number of other factors involved in the implementation of the policy to promote this language (see Daoud *et al.*, 1999; Daoud, 2000). But we will leave these policy and planning issues for the next section and focus now on the spread of English in the general environment.

Since the early 1990s, there has been an unprecedented demand for English in the business sector, stemming primarily from the structural economic reform initiated in 1989. This demand is illustrated by the surge in ESP courses, described above, and the use of English to advertise for jobs in Tunisian newspapers (see Labassi, in press; Daoud & Labassi, 1996). The companies that do this are clearly using English to screen job applicants at the outset; in other words, they are saying 'If you cannot read this ad, don't even apply.' This strategy seems to be based on the assumption that there are enough Tunisians with the work skills and language proficiency required to warrant the investment in full or half-page advertisements.

Walters (1999: 38) describes the spread of English in the general environment where it is used more frequently by various service providers in the tourist trade to address foreigners, whereas in the 1970s and 1980s French was used exclusively for this purpose. It is also found on billboards, shop signs and casual clothing, where it 'seems to be more cited than used (...) like French in upscale advertisements in Britain and the United States (...) more for its snob value than for communicative purposes'. Walters cites several examples to show that English is used more and more for marketing purposes, often incorrectly or inappropriately. The following are two examples that I have seen recently.

(1) A new interior design company in my home town displays its name, 'Well Design', in a huge neon sign using Disney fonts and colours. (Note the partial homophony between Well Design and Walt Disney, which probably led me to read Wall Design for a while before I realised the difference. What the author probably means is 'Good Design'.)

(2) A computer company van that displays the name, *Tunisie Informatique Services*, which uses the English word order, but keeps the French spelling. (The correct phrase in French would be *Services Informatiques de Tunisie*.)

In such cases, the advertisers are clearly assuming some shared knowledge of American culture in addition to a degree of competence in the English language, of course. However, it is more interesting to note that they are using such English glosses, very much as in the rest of the world, to claim integration in the global economy, as if to say that their product or service meets international standards in terms of quality, workmanship, etc. Perhaps the extreme illustration of this phenomenon is on school uniforms and bags/backpacks, which apparently have to have some English on them, even if it is sometimes improper for school (e.g. 'I am a Barbie girl').

Another phenomenon which is noted in other parts of the world as well (see Kaplan & Baldauf, 1997: 233–5) concerns the occurrence of English, specifically American English, on T-shirts, which are bought mostly in the flea market and worn by the young and not so young, and in songs played on the national French-medium radio channel *RTCI*. This kind of English is best described as occurring, rather than being used, because it is largely misunderstood by the wearers of these garments and the radio audience. Evidence for this claim is found in cases such as the middle-aged man who was wearing a T-shirt with the inscription 'Lite Beer' on it during Friday prayers which were actually broadcast on national television, or the obscene lyrics of some pop songs which would certainly be banned should the authorities discover their meaning.

Thus, in spite of the spread of English, particularly in the educational and business sectors, Walters (1999: 58) concludes that,

> It seems safest to think of English as a veneer. Like a veneer, English in Tunisia has been applied to an already existing surface, in this case an especially complex linguistic situation characterized by a post-diglossic Arabic continuum and post-colonial bilingualism (...). As with a veneer, the

already existing surface shines through as French and Arabic influence the nature of the English found here. Just as a veneer adds beauty, durability, and value to the object to which it is applied, English will make Tunisia a more attractive place for English-speaking tourists to visit, for anglophone corporations to transact business, and for English-speaking Tunisians seeking to keep abreast of international developments in many domains. Finally, much as a veneer does not generally penetrate deeply, and where it does, it does so unevenly, (…) English has not penetrated the Tunisian society or the linguistic situation here at an especially deep level (…) and in cases where it has penetrated to some degree, it has done so unevenly.

There is a great deal of truth in this assessment as illustrated by the few cases of deeper penetration where English is used a little more often for genuine communicative purposes, for instance, in the newspaper advertisements mentioned above, in the banking sector where some banks offer a choice between French, Arabic and English on their telephone answering service, and more significantly in the academic domain where a few local and/or international conferences are held exclusively in English or allow presenters to choose one of the three languages. In the case of scientific conferences, though, the choice is limited to French and English. In addition, most Tunisian academics, particularly in the science and business sectors, recognise the importance of English in their disciplines and report that they have to read in this language in order to update their knowledge and prepare their course materials. More and more of them also try to publish in English, acknowledging that publications in this language receive greater recognition than those in French (Daoud, in press a; Labassi, 1996).

Language Policy and Planning

Language policy and planning in Tunisia have been applied to three domains: arabisation,[13] or the promotion of MSA as the language of education, the administration and wider communication; the maintenance of French to achieve modernisation and economic development; and more recently, the promotion of English as a means of access to science and technology and global trade. This activity has been led by the government in the context of language-in-education policy and planning, but other actors, such as foreign agencies, international organisations and the local business community have influenced the process. It is important to note that this process has been a highly charged one, as it has been in other polities which gained political independence and are now trying to achieve socioeconomic development under a centralised system of government (e.g. Crowley, 2000; Djité, 1992, 2000; Lopez, 1998). There are three main reasons for this which will be developed in this section in view of the current situation in Tunisia:

(1) Arabic, the official language, was used along with religion and ethnicity, as the major force to rally the people behind the nationalist elite in the struggle for independence, and continues to serve this nationist/nationalist agenda (Fishman, 1968) by denoting the acceptance or rejection of foreign (particularly French) interference in internal affairs.

(2)   The promotion of Arabic, French and other languages has often been
      encouraged or discouraged as a means to pursue and maintain power and
      socioeconomic influence in the face of competing elites.
(3)   The promotion of these languages has been, and continues to be, used as a
      means to achieve socioeconomic development in ways that bring out diver-
      gent views about how best to do this.

The rivalry between Arabic and French

As shown in Table 5, Arabic and French have been subject to a tug of war since
the first educational reform, initiated in 1958, and particularly since Arabisation
began to be implemented systematically in 1976. There was a time (1986–1989/
90) when doubt resurfaced about the extent to which the government was
committed to spreading Arabic in education, particularly after establishing five
pilot schools that used French as the medium of instruction of mathematics and
science from the seventh year. One of these, the Ariana Pilot School, was the first
Tunisian school ever to use English as the medium of instruction. When it
switched back to French in 1989, it was thought that the piloting was going to
lead to the generalisation of French in the years 7–9, but that did not happen.
Instead, these pilot schools were aligned with the current four-year secondary
school system (years 10–13).

At the start of the 1958 educational reform, former President Bourguiba
declared:

> Education in the secondary schools will be oriented towards Arabisation
> and the use of Arabic so that it can serve to teach all the subjects, unless
> necessity and circumstances force us, for a limited period, to use French to
> take advantage of the possibilities that are available to us until teacher
> training schools provide us with the necessary staff who will ensure the
> teaching of all subjects in Arabic. (*L'Action*, 1958: 1) (author translation)

However, this nationalist objective had not been achieved by the time the presidency changed hands 29 years later, nor had there been any evidence in the
concurrent educational, cultural and economic policies that it was truly desired.
In his speech in the first francophonie summit (see *L'Action*, 1986: 1, 3), former
Prime Minister Mohamed Mzali, a graduate of *Al-Sadiqiyya* bilingual school and
the Sorbonne and a long-time proponent of Arabisation and Tunisification,[14]
hailed 'the Tunisian president's action of promoting French as that of a pioneer of
francophonie'. He maintained that 'Tunisia has retrieved its Arab-Muslim identity, successfully promoted Arabic as its national language', and was using
French as 'an adjuvant language' to gain access to modernity and scientific and
technological progress and to broaden the cultural horizon of its people. He
highlighted 'the common cultural affinities, which form strong ties between the
francophone countries' and called for establishing an economic organisation,
which he considered 'a civilisational contract' (author translation).

This speech faithfully reflected, as did several statements by the former president, the Tunisian elite's strong attachment to the French language and cultural
value system and provided evidence, 30 years after independence, that this elite
was inconsistent in promoting Arabisation; instead, it made a consistent effort to
promote bilingualism and biculturalism. Garmadi (1968) saw a paradox in that

Table 5 Chronology of decisions concerning Arabisation in Tunisian schools
(Updated from Daoud, 1991a; Grandguillaume, 1983)

Dates	Decisions/declarations
25 June 1958	First reform of the educational system • Closing of the Qur'anic schools and laicization of education • Arabisation of 1st and 2nd years of elementary school (i.e. all subjects taught in Arabic), French also dropped as subject of instruction • Creation of Section A, a high school track in which all subjects were taught in Arabic (abandoned in 1964)
September 1969	Reintroduction of French as a subject in 1st and 2nd years
March 1970	Mzali, Minister of National Education, declares the government is considering dropping French in 1st year
October 1971	French dropped in 1st year
October 1976	• French dropped in 2nd year • Arabisation of history and geography in secondary school • Arabisation of philosophy in final year of secondary school (13th year)
October 1977	• Arabisation of 3rd year of elementary school • Mzali declares he is in favor of maintaining French as a subject in years 4–6
September 1979	• Arabisation of 4th year • French maintained as a subject, taught 3 hours/week
September 1980	Arabisation of 5th grade, French maintained as in 4th year
September 1981	• Arabisation of 6th (final) year of elementary school, French maintained as in 4th and 5th years • Arabisation of 1st year of secondary school (7th year), French maintained as a subject, taught 5 hours/week • French also maintained as medium of instruction of mathematics and science subjects
September 1982	Arabisation of 8th and 9th years, French maintained as in 7th year
September 1983	• Establishing the English-medium Ariana Pilot High School (cf. Table 6) • Establishing the French-medium Tunis Pilot High School
June 1986	Then President Bourguiba declares that poor achievement in mathematics in elementary and secondary school is due to lack of proficiency in French
September 1986	• Reintroduction of French as a subject in 2nd and 3rd years of elementary school, taught 5 hours/week • Increase in French instruction from 3 to 5 hours/week in years 4–6
September 1988	French dropped from 2nd year
September 1989	• French reintroduced in 2nd year • Creation of 5 pilot secondary schools in Tunis, Ariana, Sfax, Le Kef and Gafsa where French is the medium of instruction of mathematics, science and technology
September 1993	French dropped from 2nd year
September 1997	• Arabisation of mathematics, sciences and technical education in years 7–9 • Pilot schools no longer accept students from 7th year, but from 10th.

the elite, which was greatly influenced by the French language and system of values, was the one that had to implement Arabisation, and at a time when Muslim fundamentalism represented a challenge to the new leadership which came to power in 1987, Daoud (1991a) concluded that French was going to be maintained, not only as a means of access to modern science and technology, but also as a symbol of modernity and openness, as opposed to Arabic, which was viewed as closely tied to traditionalism, backwardness and obscurantism. Note in Table 5 the indecision regarding Arabisation and the reinforcement of French in basic education from 1986 to 1993.

It would be misleading and unfair to explain these language-related decisions only by the political challenges at that time. There were educational reasons as well, such as the high failure rate registered in the sixth year (*Sixième*) and *baccalauréat* examinations in June 1986, which was ascribed by the former President to the poor level of French. The President was understood to be saying that Arabisation had been pushed too fast, and perhaps too far. In addition, the influence of the French government clearly had a role in reasserting the prominence of French in the context of the growing rivalry between French and English (see below).

The discourse and policy of the current leadership, which came to power in 1987, indicate a stronger commitment to Arabisation and a greater sense of independence vis-à-vis the former colonial power which seemed to depoliticise the issue, thus placating internal competing elites and deflecting external French influence. To placate internal competition, Arabisation has been implemented in education as far as the ninth year (see Table 5) and mandated in the administration and in particular areas in the general environment.

The following excerpt from the National Pact (*Pacte National*, 1988), a document cosigned by the various political parties and prominent national organisations, stresses the national character of Arabic, but unlike the 1958 statement by Bourguiba (cited previously), it situates the language and its rehabilitation through Arabisation in a global, humanistic context. Note the plural reference to 'other civilisations and languages', which denotes independence from, though not exclusion of, French civilisational and linguistic influence.

> The national community is called upon to reinforce the Arabic language so that it becomes the language of wider communication, the administration and education. It is certainly necessary to be open to other civilisations and languages, namely the languages of science and technology, but it is obvious that the national culture can only develop in, and by means of, the national language, and we must strive, in this regard, to avoid the split between the elite and the popular masses, for this might render the elite sterile and isolate the masses from modernity.
>
> Arabisation is a pressing civilisational requirement. It is one of the best guaranties to transform modernity into a popular asset and to make it part of the general consensus. It is necessary to help upgrade the national language so that it becomes a language of science and technology, encompasses contemporary thought, be it an innovation or a creation, and contributes in its own right to human civilisation. (author translation)

The document implies that Arabisation will be pursued in the educational sector; however, as noted in the previous section on language spread, the country is already facing a dilemma related to whether to continue this process, and if so, how far to go into secondary and higher education, or to stop at the ninth year of basic school and leave students to face the drastic switch to French in the scientific disciplines in the tenth year. It is not difficult to gauge the short- and long-term implications of either option on the quality of instruction and the resulting qualifications of the students. For instance, one senses some indecisiveness in the Arabised version of the mathematics courses in years 7 to 9. In an apparent attempt to prepare the students for the language switch, the textbooks present the equations from left to right, following French directionality, while the rest of the text (presentation, explanation, problem, etc.) is in MSA, written from right to left. Furthermore, the terms of the equations are in French, while the teacher and students are required to read the signs (+, =) in Arabic. For example, the equation $a + b = c$ is verbalised as *a m3a b yussaawi c* ((French /a/) (Arabic for 'plus') (French /b/) (Arabic for 'equals') (French /c/)). Similarly, geometrical figures are labelled in one language and named in another (e.g. line A_____B is printed as such and read in Arabic as *khatt AB*). It is very difficult to understand how such a manoeuvre would prepare the students for the switch to French in secondary education. (See Tsao, 1999 for a similar discussion of the problem of mixing directions of text flow in Mandarin (vertical, right to left) and its Romanised version (horizontal, left to right) in Taiwan.)

Several other problems remain unresolved at the level of planning and implementation, primarily because there is no planning agency in charge of Arabisation, as there is for literacy, for example. Thus, there is no systematic follow-up and evaluation of the policy, its implementation and impact. Teachers are not properly retrained to teach with the Arabised textbooks, which not only causes breakdowns in communication, but results in inconsistency among classes and, eventually, inadequate competencies which are carried over to the higher levels.

The will to Arabise the administration has recently been reasserted in unequivocal terms, compared to the situation described in Daoud (1991a), thanks to a circular issued by the Prime Minister (45/29-10-99). In keeping with a 1993 law (64/5-7-93) which made the Arabic version of any legal or organisational text the only legal reference, the circular addressed to national and local officials stipulates the following regulations:

(1) It is forbidden to use any foreign language in correspondence addressed to Tunisians.
(2) It is forbidden to use any foreign language in all internal documents that regulate the work of the administration and other public agencies, including circulars, decrees, notices, reports and correspondence between these parties as of 1 January, 2000; however files may include attachments in other languages.
(3) The Arabisation of all administrative forms must be completed before 31 December 2000, but if necessary, such forms may be in one or more foreign languages in addition to Arabic.

(4) French forms may be used until the stock is used up, provided that this does not extend beyond 31 December 2000. It is forbidden to reproduce such forms except for use with foreign parties.

(5) The Arabisation of software and databases in the administration and public agencies must be completed before 31 December 2000.

(6) Work on the dictionaries necessary for providing an Arabic lexicon in all areas of knowledge must be completed before the end of December 2001.

(7) It is not permitted to use any forms and software that are not in Arabic after 31 December 2000, except by permission from the Prime Minister.

(8) A report on the implementation of this circular must be submitted to the Prime Minister, mentioning the problems, if any, and making recommendations to overcome them before 31 December 2000. (author translation)

The reader should note that this is the first time in Tunisia that texts have been issued to mandate the use of Arabic in the administration and regulate it, despite the stipulation in the Tunisian constitution that the official language is Arabic. The only text available previous to these is Article 1 of a decree dated 8 September 1955, a year before independence, which relates to the publication of the various legal and regulatory texts in the *Journal Officiel* in two languages, namely Arabic and French (see Hamzaoui, 1970).

The Prime Minister's circular uses strong language to indicate the commitment of the government to Arabisation; however, it sets requirements and deadlines which most Tunisians find unrealistic. Recall the examples given in the previous section, such as the fact that French is still being used exclusively in pay slips and tax forms issued by the government itself. But what people find most unrealistic is the requirement in Article 6, relating to the preparation of dictionaries to facilitate Arabisation 'in all areas of knowledge' before December 2001. It is true that a number of committees have been set up to develop an Arabic lexicon for various fields of knowledge (see Ammar & Al-Khury, 1996), but their work has not progressed satisfactorily, particularly in the science and technology disciplines. More importantly, there has been no structured effort to train people in the various domains to use this lexicon, even if we assume that all that is needed for communication in Arabic is a lexicon. It is difficult to see how the state hospitals, for instance, could switch to Arabic even five years past the deadline of December 2001. In one of the least problematic areas, school administration, Arabising documents has been left to the local secretaries (most of whom have barely finished high school) and their superiors. There has been no formal training given to anyone.

It is apparently for these reasons that a follow-up circular (46/20–11–00) issued by the Prime Minister in November 2000 restated only Articles 1, 2 and 5, above, and required the various agencies to submit quarterly reports on the progress of implementation, including mention of any problems as well as suggestions for solving them. This is an indication that the government is serious about the matter and willing to tackle the problems that may arise, taking into account the suggestions of administrators in the field. The government is following the approach that it has followed in the whole structural reform process, moving from a top-down policy decision to a bottom-up consultative process of implementation and evaluation. The only problem is that the process of

Arabisation is tied to an unrealistic deadline. However, most Tunisians would accept the argument that, without this deadline, even if it is broken, nothing would be accomplished. As for the criticism that there is no agency that is specifically in charge of Arabisation, officials make the point that the Prime Ministry itself is taking charge of the matter, which puts an end to the argument.

Thus, one may argue that the ruling elite has shown enough determination to be able to depoliticise Arabisation in order to placate the competing elites which may challenge it or simply to dissipate the passion that this issue generates in the general public. However, the issue does not seem to want to go away. One often reads calls from the popular masses in the media, as the *National Pact* calls them, for the reinforcement and speeding up of Arabisation, such as Bakir (2000) who warns against the threat of globalisation to the purity of the Arabic language as used by the media; or Fellah (2000: 10) who wonders why we continue to think that Arabic is unfit for use in the scientific and technological domains, adding that 'it is time to relieve our children of the burden of bilingualism in speech and writing' (author translation); or the more challenging and persistent nationalist argument, as formulated by Jourchi (2001: 3) relative to the Maghreb region:

> So the issue of Arabisation in the Arab Maghreb continues to be raised with intensity in political and cultural circles, so much so that a Tunisian magazine called it 'the mother of battles'. It is not simply a language issue, but a political, cultural and economic one that has strategic implications related to the balance of power and local and regional equilibrium. (author translation)

On the pro-French front, many still see French as a means to access information, modernity and a better education, and to avoid censorship and 'deadwood discourse' (Kefi, 2000: 32, author translation). The views of scholars and journalists, together with the feedback gathered for this monograph from students and teachers, converge on the fact that French is still widely used and continues to be valued for the educational and economic advantages it represents and the prestige it confers on the people who use it. Francophiles, including some officials, are quick to argue that French has ceased to be viewed as the language of the coloniser, a symbol of domination and cultural alienation – as if to close the nationist/nationalist argument – and the above excerpt from the *National Pact* even denies it the status of 'a privileged foreign language'.[15]

In spite of what the *National Pact* said in 1988, the strong Arabisation drive in 1999 was widely perceived as a reaction to the criticism of the presidential and parliamentary election campaign levelled by the metropolitan French media in October of the same year. As noted earlier, the French TV channel, *France 2*, was shut down and several French papers and magazines were censored. The local debate came to the fore then and intensified early in 2000 in the wake of renewed criticism by the French media. Relations with the French media are still tense, and diplomats on both sides have been trying to raise diplomatic relations between the two countries above the fray, but these incidents clearly reflect the centrality of the language issue in Tunisia today with respect to relations with France and to the political, economic, educational and cultural choices that the ruling elite is making.

In a news conference in February 2000, the French foreign minister emphasised the atmosphere of trust and concord that characterises the relations between the two countries and eventually addressed the language issue. He initially avoided a question about the fact that French universities were requiring Tunisian applicants to take a French proficiency test when membership of the *Francophonie* Organisation waves this requirement. Then, commenting on the plan to establish a US-Maghreb economic partnership, which would compete with the already signed EU-Tunisia partnership accord (see Mekki, 1998), he surprised everyone by explaining, in the words of a reporter (Ghbara, 2000: 3), that

> there was a need for a complementary relationship between *francophonie* and *anglophonie*, adding that the French language is still strong in Tunisia and that it is an enriching element in the culture of the country. He conceded that the worldwide spread of English had to be recognised because it has become the language of science and technology, and he thought that French was not under threat in Tunisia, stressing that the issue is not a bilateral one for it to raise concern in France. (author translation)

In fact, France has always shown concern over any effort to promote English in Tunisia. Its strong reaction to establishing English-medium educational institutions like the Ariana Pilot School and the Carthage Institute of Technology (see below) is a good illustration of this. The French-style institutions that eventually supplanted them benefited from considerable French financial and academic support. Battenburg (1997: 9) reports that

> in spite of budget reductions, in 1996 the American government contributed an estimated US$600,000 and the British government allocated about US$400,000 for language, cultural and educational activities. The French government, in contrast, spent US$20 million for such programs within Tunisia.

The rivalry between French and English

While Arabic-French rivalry continues, English has begun to spread, particularly in education and more recently in business, and has, therefore, constituted a challenge to the predominance of French in areas where Arabic is unlikely to spread in the foreseeable future. The growing demand for English has been motivated by a desire to access scientific and technological information directly from original sources, rather than through French which has come to be seen as a handicap in the quest for faster modernisation, development and integration in the global community. Jourchi (2001: 3) argues that the linguistic/economic/cultural struggle is likely to be complicated further by the interference of a third factor, namely

> the silent and powerful spread of the English language, propelled by its supporters, thousands of graduates from American universities and global multinational companies, in addition to a plan for an American-Maghrebi partnership with a US$5 million fund to counter the partnership accord with the E.U.

A review of the effort to promote English in education will help us to reassess the present and future position of this language in Tunisia. As shown in Table 6, there has been a growing interest in English since independence, but the major developments occurred in the early 1960s, 1980s and, more significantly in 1996. In 1964, the *Institut Bourguiba des Langues Vivantes* (*IBLV*) was established with U.S. and British assistance. The IBLV played a key role in reorienting studies and research in the university English departments towards linguistics and foreign language teaching, was the main promoter of English for Specific Purposes (ESP) and currently continues to teach English to the public throughout the country.

The early 1980s were marked by four significant developments: the start of the Transfer of Technology Program (TTP) in 1981; the establishment of the Ariana Pilot School; the planning of its logical follow-up institution (the Carthage Institute of Technology, CIT) in 1983; and the start of the ESP Resource Center Project in the same year. These undertakings received financial and academic support from the U.S. government, the Ford Foundation and the British Overseas Development Agency (ODA) through the British Council, as indicated in Table 6. The TTP was motivated by the focus of the Sixth Development Plan (1982–1986) on providing greater and faster access to science and technology directly through English in the interest of time and effective human resource development. In this programme, which ended in 1994/95, nearly one thousand of Tunisia's most promising *baccalauréat* holders were sent to some of the best American universities in order to obtain advanced degrees in a variety of science and technology disciplines and were expected to return home to help transform the local research and work environment. About 60% of these students eventually returned to work in the university system and the private sector.

No studies have been done to evaluate the impact that these graduates have had on the local environment, but anecdotal information indicates that the majority initially faced resistance from well-positioned senior faculty who tried to block their promotion, and from junior colleagues who viewed them with envy and suspicion. In time, some of them have been promoted to higher positions in the university system (as deans and directors of faculties/institutes, heads of departments and professors) or in government (e.g. one was appointed as *Secrétaire d'Etat* or Deputy Minister, in charge of promoting computer technology). Others have succeeded in the private sector as researchers/managers or private businessmen/women. As indicated by one of them who works for a local drug company, their contribution to the local work and research environment is currently valued for the ease with which they use English to facilitate interaction with most foreign companies, including Italian and German ones, but much more so for the North American management skills they are helping to promote in the business environment.

The second significant development in 1983 was the Ariana Pilot School, where mathematics and science were taught in English from the seventh year. As this programme was underway, and in parallel with the TTP, plans were being drawn for establishing the CIT, which was meant to provide an English-medium university education to the graduates of the Ariana School as well as other students from the Arab World and neighbouring African countries. The project was abandoned in 1987 in unclear circumstances following the change of leadership in November of the same year. Battenberg (1997) speculates that the new

Table 6 Chronology of decisions concerning English in education

Dates	Decisions/declarations
1958	First educational reform of national education, English taught for 5 years in 6-year secondary school cycle (age 13+)
Early 1960s	• Establishing the *IBLV* (1964) • The earliest ESP programmes start in several higher education institutions around the country • Plan to reduce reliance on teachers of English from France (recruitment of Peace Corps volunteers and teachers of different nationalities)
1970	• English taught for 4 years in 7-year secondary school cycle (age 15+) • Tunisification of English textbooks (British ODA and Ford Foundation support)
1978, 1979	First Tunisian ESP textbooks introduced in secondary school • English for Secretaries (October 1978) • English for Science and Technology (October 1979)
1981	• Start of Transfer of Technology Programme (US aid assistance) • Start of English broadcasts on radio/TV
September 1983	• Establishing the Ariana Pilot School • Planning the Carthage Institute of Technology Project (1983–87) • Establishing the ESP Resource Center at the IBLV (ODA)
September 1989	Ariana Pilot School stops enrolling students to study in English, becomes French-medium *Lycée pilote*
June 1993	Last graduating class of Ariana Pilot School educated in English
1994–95	English introduced in 5th year of basic education
1995	• President Ben Ali visits South Africa, finds political and economic negotiations hindered because of inadequate English (April) • ESP Resource Center becomes a department for the promotion of teaching ESP (December), ODA funding for Center ends (July)
1996	• ESP Resource Center funding resumed through British Partnership Scheme (BPS) till March 1999 • English introduced in 8th year of basic education (5th year course cancelled) • Three-year BPS programme to train supervisors, teacher trainers and teacher training assistants for secondary school (1996–99) • English required in vocational training (1.5–2 years) • English generalized gradually in higher education • IBLV branches reinvigorated and increased to teach English to the public • Establishing the *diplôme d'études supérieures spécialisées* (DESS) programme in Applied Linguistics/ESP at the IBLV (turned DEA, MA equivalent in 1998)
September 1997	English introduced in 9th year of basic education
1998–2002	Latest reform of the national *maîtrise* (BA equivalent) in English along with other university specialties (goal: employability of graduates)
September 2000	English introduced in 7th year of basic education

leadership was not keen on pursuing a project developed by the former President's son and that French influence was a key factor in its demise. While this may be true, those of us who worked in the Ariana School and were paying close attention to the development of the CIT project were not very hopeful about it. Irrespective of outside French influence, the project seemed to be plagued by inertia, poor planning and resistance of the bureaucrats from the Ministry of Education and from other departments to the Ariana School itself, and we could anticipate the same fate for the CIT.

The third development in 1983 occurred when the ESP Resource Center was established at the *IBLV*. The main objective of the centre was to promote the teaching of ESP in tertiary education by providing teaching resources to teachers and training them in course design and implementation. The centre became a department within the *Institut Supérieur des Langues de Tunis* and continues to serve ESP practitioners as well as graduate students of applied linguistics (see Daoud, 1996; 2000).

The developments in 1996 were even more significant because of their wider scope. English instruction was introduced earlier in basic education, became a required subject in vocational training, was generalised in higher education, and was offered by the state-owned *IBLV* to the general public at very affordable fees. In addition, there were attempts to improve the planning and evaluation aspects of ELT in basic and secondary education through trainer training, and in vocational training, through systematic curriculum design (see Daoud *et al.*, 1999; Daoud, 2000).

Since September 2000, English has become a required subject from the seventh year in basic school to the final year in vocational training or university education for all Tunisian students, in addition to its spread to the public through classes offered by the *IBLV* and through British and US agencies (the British Council and Amideast), several private educational institutions and major businesses. Thus, with basic education being compulsory until the ninth year, every Tunisian is now guaranteed at least three years of English language instruction, potentially four more in secondary education, a minimum of two additional years in vocational training for those who drop out of high school and two and a half to six years in higher education, plus whatever supplementary ESP instruction individuals may seek outside the state school system. The result would be a strict minimum of six years of English for nearly all Tunisians by age 16 and a maximum ranging between 10 and 13 years for university graduates at the rate of two to four hours per week, or 60 to 120 hours per year. If this trend continues, and if the passing rate at all levels of education keeps improving as it has in the last few years,[16] many more Tunisians will develop some degree of proficiency in English. For instance, it is projected that, for academic year 2001–2002 alone, 20.3% of the 20–24-year-old cohort will be attending university (see *Neuvième Plan*, 1997–2001) and, therefore, taking English.

It remains to be seen whether the teaching dispensed at the various levels of education will help develop the critical level of competence necessary for making English a widely used educational and work language in its own right, or promoting it to replace French as the first foreign language, a possibility that has been taking shape since the early 1980s and is expressed more forcefully today. There have been notable improvements in ELT/ESP in Tunisia; however, teacher training, assessment and evaluation remain the weakest links. The strengths and weaknesses may be summed up as follows (see Daoud, 1999: 134–5):

Strengths

- general English/ESP courses are required at all levels of education and in all the disciplines;
- public demand for English, particularly ESP, is strong;
- more English departments are offering pre-service teacher training;
- a coordinated programme has been developed for (1) graduate applied-linguistics research and (2) sustained professional support for ESP practice;
- ESP is established as an independent entity in the country, with its own community resources, practices and concerns.

Shortcomings

- there is no coherent policy for ELT/ESP;
- there is a high level of inertia about ELT/ESP curriculum design, implementation and evaluation;
- there is irregular or no input from stakeholders (applied linguists, specialist teachers, professionals, employers and learners);
- the three curricula in basic and secondary education, vocational training and higher education are not coordinated; their cumulative effect is not measurable;
- teacher trainers and teachers are not receiving adequate training;
- testing lags far behind; achievement testing is generally unreliable and test design has not changed sufficiently to match new syllabi;
- programme evaluation is still a foreign concept, in many respects;
- the higher-education context, in particular, lacks a full curriculum structure for ESP, and teachers are generally unprepared for the wide range of responsibilities involved in ESP practice (see Dudley-Evans & St John, 1998);
- the time allotted to ESP in vocational training and higher education is insufficient.

Regional and international influences

In addition to the Tunisian government's role in language-in-education policy and planning, several regional and international agencies have had a variable degree of influence on the promotion of languages in the country. The one language that is receiving no support from abroad is Arabic. The Arab League's Educational, Cultural and Scientific Organisation (ALECSO), which promotes cooperation among Arab countries in the linguistic, educational, scientific and cultural domains, is only playing a cosmetic role with respect to Arabisation. ALECSO's effectiveness depends on the member countries' commitment to, and implementation of, the wide array of decisions and resolutions already agreed to by these countries (see Ammar & Al-Khoury, 1966).

In contrast, the French government devotes huge resources, and often economic pressure, to the promotion of French, mainly through the *Institut Français de Coopération* in Tunis and the *Organisation Internationale de la*

Francophonie, which draws on considerable resources from France and Quebec (see Ager, 1996; Francophonie, 2000; *Jeune Afrique*, 2000). The reader should note that Tunisian francophiles take pride in the fact that former President Bourguiba was one of the founding fathers of the organisation, along with former Presidents Leopold Sedar Senghor of Senegal and Hamani Diori of Niger, in 1970. The organisation has been heavily involved in the current structural reform in Tunisia, namely in higher education, scientific research, vocational training, manufacturing (textiles and mechanical goods, the country's major exports in this category) and telecommunications.

This involvement is in the form of substantial financial resources (mostly low-interest loans) to upgrade programmes, procedures and management; scholarships for Tunisian students; funds to build and sustain joint research teams; and academic/professional expertise, with short- and long-term stays by experts in Tunisia to develop curricula and human resources. French support goes as far as offering a number of scholarships (5 to 10 annually) for Tunisians to pursue English graduate studies in French universities, some of which go unclaimed because Tunisians would rather do this in the US or the UK. In addition to its educational and economic involvement, the *francophonie* movement reaches deep into the social fabric of Tunisia, as it does in other member countries. *Francophonie* runs an international satellite television channel, *TV5*, and has a comprehensive agenda to target specific groups, such as the youth, women, NGOs as well as activists for democracy and human rights, for involvement in international, regional and local activities (seminars, conferences, cultural events, etc.) (see *Fancophonie*, 2001).

British and US involvement in promoting the English language and culture pales in comparison to this comprehensive francophone 'campaign' for the French language. British and US support, through the British Council and the Regional English Language Office (RELO) for North Africa and the Gulf (within the US Department of State, Bureau of Educational and Cultural Affairs), respectively, has decreased to less than a trickle in recent years, as Britain shifted its focus to the huge ELT market in Asia and to Eastern Europe after the collapse of the Soviet Union, while the United States has seemed to turn inward (at least as far as cultural and educational aid is concerned) under the influence of conservatives in the Congress. Because of the great demand for English worldwide, one notes a mercantilist approach to promoting it that has become predominant in the last decade or so and is very likely to be reinforced (Graddol, 1997: 63, uses such terms as 'brand management').

One also senses a certain neglect of this part of the world by the powers that seem to set the agenda for promoting English because they seem to consider it irrevocably within the French sphere of influence. It must be said that the generous support for French has worked against the promotion of English at a psychological level as well, because it has often led policy makers to do little for the language, arguing that if the British and the US really cared about English, like the French do about French, they would support its growth. But this view is losing ground. More and more Tunisians accept the fact that English is a commodity and the government has devoted much of its resources to increasing the amount of English language teaching, while the public is willing to pay to learn English. Still, programmes like the British Partnership Scheme, which helped sustain the ESP Resource Center can, with very limited funding, achieve a great deal, particularly if the focus is put on developing ELT research and management skills that can be easily passed on by a small number of trainees to a larger local student population (see Daoud, *et al.*, 1999).

Adult literacy

According to documents published by the Ministry of Social Affairs (see *Ministère des Affaires Sociales, MAS*, 1993, 2001), the Tunisian government launched an ambitious and carefully planned literacy campaign in 1992 in keeping with the eighth development plan for economic and social development (1992–96), the recommendations of the 1990 World Congress on Education For All held in Thailand and those of the Pan-Arab Plan to Guarantee Universal Education and Erase Illiteracy. The campaign ran alongside the reforms of the educational and vocational training systems previously described.

The *MAS* documents do not provide a clear definition of literacy, but one can be gleaned from an internal document published by the National Agency for the Eradication of Illiteracy (NAEI) (see Memorandum, 1993: 1–3) which describes the target population as the Tunisians who:

(1) cannot read, write and count (presumably in MSA because none of these documents specify the language(s) of literacy);
(2) cannot function in a given work situation in such a way as to hinder production and / or rendering a service; and
(3) in comparison to the literate people, feel inadequate, negative, and hopeless about changing their current living and work situation in terms of acquiring new skills and knowledge and improving them. (author translation)

According to MAS (1993: 2), the literacy campaign has four objectives:

(1) to erase linguistic and cultural illiteracy by developing basic reading and writing ability and improving the quality of life,
(2) to strengthen basic literacy skills among early school dropouts to save them from relapsing into illiteracy,
(3) to impart to the beneficiaries of regional development programmes the information, skills and techniques necessary for them to preserve the capital, tools and materials given to them and
(4) to erase illiteracy in the 15 to 44 year old group by the end of the ninth plan period (1997–2001), while reducing the illiteracy gap between males and females as well as urban and rural areas.

Implementation started officially on 13 September 1993 with the creation of the NAEI which includes representatives of seven ministries (Ministries of the Interior, Education, Agriculture, Public Health, Youth, Culture, and Professional Training and Employment) as well as national agencies and professional organisations concerned with literacy and development. The literacy programme was designed in such a way that it would be planned and implemented as an integral part of the consecutive socioeconomic development plans, and it targeted primarily the individuals between 15 and 29 years of age because they constitute the most active / productive part of the workforce and comprise the parents who would raise the future generations. The design included:

- providing the legal means to regulate the work of the various parties involved in the NAEI;
- undertaking two surveys, one to identify the human and material resources available to implement the campaign, and the other to identify the needs and attitudes of the target population (completed in February 1993);
- developing a suitable instructional approach and literacy materials for reading, mathematics and social interaction;
- training literacy teachers; and
- establishing 31 literacy centres, one in each department plus four regional centres for teacher training and materials production.

In 1999, the student population reached 14,749 (*MAS*, 2001) and the literacy rate rose from 68% in 1994 to 73% in the 10+ age category, while it rose from 87% to 91% in the 10–29-year-old group (see Table 1 which shows illiteracy, rather than literacy, rates). To achieve better results, the campaign was reinvigorated in April 2000 with the National Programme of Adult Literacy which is set to lower the illiteracy rate to 20% by the end of 2004 (note that the worldwide illiteracy rate for the year 2000 was 20.6%; see UNESCO, 2001). This programme encourages literacy students to attend classes at times that suit their work schedule and to obtain literacy materials to study at home with the help of a literate member of the family. It helps businesses to set up their own adult literacy units, while the government has taken measures to hire and train 2500 new teachers.

It is interesting that the government's literature and the advertising campaign in the audiovisual media do not specify the language(s) of literacy. The most recent advertising leaves one with the understanding that this language is MSA. However, it is to be expected that the diglossic / bilingual continuum (see Figure 2) is represented in literacy classes and that TA is used as a reference for the lexical content of literacy materials (see Ezzaki & Wagner, 1992; Maamouri, 1983). Furthermore, given the focus on 'information, skills and techniques necessary for the literacy students to preserve the capital, tools and materials given to them' (objective 3, above), it is very likely that French technical vocabulary is incorporated in classroom interaction. It was not possible to ascertain this at the time of writing, but judging from the language use which characterises basic and secondary education classrooms, the literacy context is all the more prone to encourage TA/EA use and French code-switching, bearing in mind that TA already borrows a substantial number of technical words from French. Finally, the reader will recall the argument developed in the section on the language profile of Tunisia about the changing normative range of literacy (Kaplan & Palmer, 1992). The fact that the literacy programme incorporates basic technical and management knowledge and skills is further support for this argument.

This section has dealt with language policy and planning in education, government administration and literacy. It is clear that Arabisation has had a boost thanks to government intervention; however, it has yet to penetrate the seemingly inaccessible scientific, technological and business domains where French is beginning to be challenged by English. While the question remains as to why the government has not set up an agency to take care of Arabisation, and perhaps ELT/ESP as well, as it has for literacy, it remains to be seen whether the position of French as the dominant language in these domains will be further challenged by either Arabic or English, or both, as more and more young Tunisians are taught (in) these languages.

Language Maintenance and Prospects

Intergenerational transmission of TA and the death of Berber

Tunisian Arabic is the only native language in Tunisia which is transmitted from one generation to the next, but the diglossic/bilingual continuum in which Tunisians partake to various degrees at home, school, work and in the ambient environment causes TA to change constantly. Still, this vernacular manages to preserve a distinctive (regional, urban, or rural) core – or more accurately, a set of distinctive (regional, urban, or rural) features (mainly phonological/prosodic and lexical) of a common Tunisian core – that any newborn acquires as his/her native language. Soon, parents, siblings, peers, family friends and other contacts begin to expose the newborn to the changes in that variety being acquired, and thus the socialisation of the young acquirer is initiated until he goes to preschool (or *kuttab*), then to school, etc., and thus too a very subtle change takes place in the TA that is acquired by each Tunisian child from one generation to the next. For instance, the TA variety that Tunisians of my generation acquired as children is not the same as the variety that our children have recently acquired, the latter reflecting a wider range on the diglossic continuum and a different bilingual mix, both of which are due not only to the current socioeconomic status and level of education, but also to exposure to new and varied sources of input (namely, audiovisual and multimedia sources).

The only other language that may involve a similar acquisition process in Tunisia is Berber, but it is dying. Only a small number of children living in isolated communities may still acquire it as their true native language. I have come across no more than ten students of Berber origin in nearly ten years at the University of Tunis and found that only one of them was a native speaker of Berber (Amazigh), the others mostly saying that they do not know the language nor do they hear it spoken around them. This student, who grew up in an isolated community in a village called Oursighen on the island of Jerba, started learning Arabic only at school at age six. The map of Tunisia (Figure 1) shows the areas where there are entire Berber-speaking villages in the south of Tunisia (Guellala, in Jerba; Taoujane, Tamezret and Zrawa on the departmental boundary between Gabès and Mednine; and Chenini and Douiret near the city of Tataouine, itself a Berber name; see Battenburg, 1999). A close look at a more detailed map of Tunisia, in particular the southern part, reveals several localities with names that do not sound Arabic and usually begin with /ta/, /te/, or /se/, /ze/, and other allophonic variants, which indicate the Berber origin of these places.

As for the number of Berber speakers, current estimates put it at less than 0.5% of the Tunisian population, based on what seems to have been the one and only study of this language (Pencheon, 1968) until Battenburg (1999) addressed the subject again. Battenburg confirms this estimate, suggesting that there are 45,000–50,000 Berber speakers at present; however, the student identified above gave a much lower estimate of 5,000–10,000. Battenburg reports that there is a big concentration of Berbers in Tunis who dominate certain services (newspaper vendors, market porters and Jerbian grocers, some of whom may be Berber), but they all seem to have been entirely linguistically assimilated in the Arabic-speaking population. It is interesting to note that Berber language/cultural identity was not a question on the 1994 census.

It may be that some people still identify themselves as Berbers, but no longer speak the language. However, this phenomenon is hardly noticeable in Tunisia, where the few students previously mentioned did not seem too anxious to claim or assert their Berber ethnicity. Considering an ecology of language perspective, the situation of Berbers in neighbouring Algeria and Morocco, with estimates of 15% and 40% Berber speakers respectively (see Katzner, 1986), is very different. I vividly remember two instances in Morocco: one where university colleagues were quick to assert their Berber ethnicity when I said that we were Arab brothers, and another where two taxi drivers were fighting over my luggage, nearly causing me to miss my plane, because one of them, an Arab, felt he was being robbed of a client as a result of connivance between two Berbers, the hotel receptionist who had called him first and the second taxi driver.

Prospects for a Changing Language Situation

The current language situation is largely the outcome of four and half decades of socioeconomic development policies that have, sometimes by design and sometimes by coincidence, set the educational and linguistic agenda for the country. This has resulted in discontinuities in language mastery and use and different attitudes towards the languages on the scene among the generations and social classes living in Tunisia today. Although in recent years language and literacy policy and planning have been better thought out, problems remain at the level of commitment to these policies and their implementation. This is so largely because political priorities often take precedence over applied linguistics requirements for successful implementation and because financial and human resources do not always match ambitious plans for language promotion. The recent drive for universal education, pragmatic higher education and improved adult literacy is salutary; however, the success of socioeconomic development and the generalisation of its benefits will eventually depend on the success of this drive.

Figure 3 (inspired by Kaplan & Baldauf, 1997: 312) illustrates the evolution of the language situation in Tunisia from the year of independence (1956) until 1996, when the latest reform was well underway. Based on this, we can perhaps imagine what the language situation will be like in the next decade or so. An important variable to consider and which could not be easily incorporated in this schematic representation is the changing level of literacy, so the reader should look at Table 1 at the same time.

In 1956, illiteracy was widespread. There were a few Tunisians who were educated only in Arabic at the *Zaitouna*, and even fewer who belonged to the elite and who were educated in French or bilingual Tunisian schools. This early MSA-French bilingualism is captured in the illustration by the overlap between MSA and French, while the diglossic relationship is captured by the overlapping circles representing TA and MSA. MSA-TA-French trilingualism was very

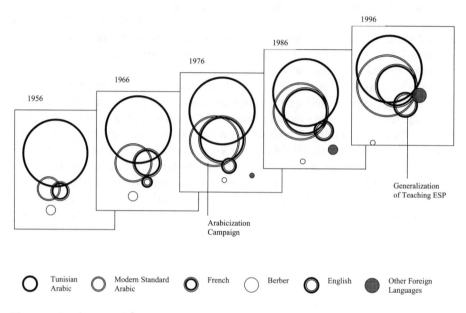

Figure 3 Evolution of the language situation in Tunisia (1956–1996)

limited. Berber was not an important language even then, so it is kept outside the overlapping areas although a few Berber speakers may have been bilingual (Berber + TA), trilingual (+ MSA) or even quadrilingual (+ French).

For 1966, which coincided with the end of the first educational reform, the figure shows an improved situation. In the 1960s, the socialist government of the time organised a literacy campaign which contributed to this improvement and provided the first illiteracy figures (see Table 1). MSA spread a little more than French because of an early drive to Arabise the educational system (see Table 5); however, French continued to spread because it was used to teach the sciences and even the humanities, given the lack of Tunisian teachers. English appears in the illustration at this time even though it had been taught since 1958, but recall that in the middle of the 1960s the government decided to stop hiring English teachers from France and the first Peace Corps volunteers started coming (see Table 6).

By 1976, the Arabisation campaign spread to secondary education (history, geography and philosophy were Arabised at once), but French remained as the medium of instruction of most subjects. Other foreign languages were introduced to cater for the needs of the growing tourism sector, while Berber was not given any consideration. Note that the MSA-French overlap increased, as did their overlap with TA. This was due to the spread of bilingual education and its contribution to lowering the illiteracy rate to 54.9%.

By 1986, the spread of French began to slow down as Arabisation was pushed further, while English started to spread a little faster thanks to the projects launched in the early 1980s and the growth of ESP (see Table 6). Note that English started to overlap with the other languages as it came to be seen more as a functional language, rather than a mere school subject, in science and technology, business (e.g. banking), and tourism. Other foreign languages were promoted, particularly by the *IBLV*, to satisfy the need in tourism and translation services.

The last set (1996) illustrates the early impact of the latest educational reforms and shows the growing rivalry between MSA, French and English. ELT/ESP was generalised while Arabisation was reinforced, thus causing some curtailment of the French language. More and more Tunisians were required or chose to take English plus an additional foreign language, which explains the more complex overlapping situation. At the same time, the illiteracy rate fell to its lowest level thanks to the drive for universal schooling and higher adult literacy.

Given this historical perspective and taking into consideration the forces at play in the Tunisian linguistic eco-system, it seems that language rivalry is not likely to subside. Future developments will continue to revolve around two dimensions: first, the rivalry between MSA and French and the extent to which Arabisation may be pursued; second, the growing rivalry between French and English as to which language would better serve the interests of the country. The current situation is very likely to prevail for the next decade, with the exception that English will spread a little more in education and in the business sector. However, there is no reason to believe that English will represent a serious challenge to French in the foreseeable future. Foreign trade (even when the EU partnership comes into effect in 2008) and cultural affiliation with France are not likely to change soon. Even if the EU uses English more widely than French, Tunisia is expected to deal with the EU mostly through France. Proficiency in French will continue to suffer if Arabisation is maintained at the current level or reinforced, but higher proficiency is likely to be achieved by a narrower section of the population (the one enjoying a higher socioeconomic status). This same section is very likely to seek to achieve higher proficiency in English as well.

As for MSA, it is not likely to penetrate the science and technology domains in the near future unless intensive corpus planning work is done and high quality training is provided, both of which require time, or unless a drastic decision is made to Arabise the higher levels of education should, for example, relations with France deteriorate for one reason or another. On the other hand, French could be reinstated to teach the sciences in years 7 to 9 in order to resolve the dilemma related to the language switch that is forced in year 10. This would, of course, present us with a situation similar to that which prevailed in the second half of the 1980s (see Table 5), except for a higher overall literacy rate. Let us consider these scenarios in more detail and explore the opposing forces at play.

To Arabise or not to Arabise: Arabic vs. French

While Arabisation may continue in the administration and in certain areas of the ambient environment that the government can control (billboards, signs, etc.), it seems to have run its course in education, at least for now. French will remain the medium of instruction for science, technology and business subjects in secondary and tertiary education in the foreseeable future. Any language switch is educationally untenable because the adequate language skills and instructional materials needed for this switch will require a great deal of time and resources. Educational institutions cannot be put on hold until a critical level of adequacy is reached. Furthermore, the system and the teaching staff, in particular, are too Frenchified in their training and educational outlook to be able to change.

Arabisation is highly unlikely to be pursued any further than the current level for another reason. Concern is expressed more and more openly about the deteriorating level of French which is expected to have a negative impact on the achievement and ultimate qualifications of university graduates. This concern will not encourage further Arabisation and may even lead to the reinstatement of French as the medium of instruction for mathematics and science in years 7–9 of basic education. This move would make educational sense as it would give students time to improve their French in order to cope with more complex scientific, technical and business courses in secondary school, and it can be implemented very easily given the availability of teachers and materials; however, it would be politically untenable, because any step back from Arabisation will be incompatible with the nationalist agenda upheld so far by the leadership and may even be seen as a breach of the *National Pact*, and ultimately the spirit of the constitution.

Another factor that works against Arabisation is the lack of a coherent long-term policy and the will to implement it and factor it into the economic activity in the Arab World, which makes the issue a pan-Arab one and takes it out of Tunisia's hands (see Ammar & Al-Khury, 1996, on the various agreements and resolutions that were signed by the Arab governments to promote Arabisation as far as university). It is totally unrealistic to expect Tunisia (or any other Arab country) to succeed in this endeavour because Arabic is a pan-national language and Tunisia by itself is too small. Even if Tunisia tried to develop and succeeded in developing a generation of university graduates and professionals who were perfectly functional in Arabic, it would be unable to make full use of their talents and be too limited a space for them to have productive careers or even find jobs. Tunisian trade figures with the MENA region show a meagre rate of 3% of imports and 12% of exports in 1998 (*Middle East Magazine*, 1999). This is an instance of the language policy and planning dichotomy (Kaplan & Baldauf, 1997) in that Arabisation cannot achieve ultimate success if it produces a generation of unemployable people. Tunisia under Former President Bourguiba actually tried this in secondary school in the 1958 reform only to produce Arabic-monolingual *baccalauréat* holders ('Section A', A for Arabic) whose chances for a university education and/or employment were not very good. Needless to say, the policy was abandoned after the first class graduated in 1964 (see Daoud, 1991a).

English vs. French

The promotion of English in Tunisia, almost exclusively through education, could not be spared in the political debate over language policy and planning. Since the early 1980s, some prominent politicians, businessmen and journalists have hoped that English would become the first foreign language, instead of French, as documented by Battenburg (1997). More recent calls, such as the one reported by Akkari (2000: 28), have been more straightforward and have, for the first time, come from opposition members of parliament who 'called for making English the first foreign language, instead of French, since the French themselves have begun to realise the inadequacy of their language and its loss of international prominence'. This was justified by 'the great demand for English classes outside the school system', and the fact that 'some private schools have introduced it in the early years of basic school'. In addition, 'many businesses have begun to require proficiency in English', which has prompted the National Employment Fund-21/21 (a government programme to tackle unemployment, particularly among university graduates) 'to schedule complementary courses in English to improve the employability chances of economics and management graduates within the country and abroad' (adapted, author translation).

These arguments in favour of English indicate a changing perspective on French which has been taking shape since the early 1980s when concrete action was taken in an apparent attempt to promote English to the same level as French in the Ariana Pilot School. This school, together with the plan to establish the CIT (see Table 6), prompted the French to react to the spread of English, and thereby to British and US influence in Tunisia. Having served as Deputy Director of the Ariana School, I can say that French influence could be felt as early as 1981–82 when the Ariana School had to be delayed a year so that it opened at the same time as the French-medium *Lycée Bourguiba* in Tunis, which was funded and staffed to the level of 40% by the French. As for the CIT project, it was abandoned initially in favour of the *Institut Préparatoire aux Etudes Scientifiques et Techniques* (established in 1992), then the *Institut National des Sciences Appliquées de Technologie* (1996), and finally an institution with a name and educational style in the best French tradition: the *Ecole Polytechnique de Tunis* (1994–97), all in the context of Tunisian-French cooperation.

Some 20 years later, there is a growing sense that French is seen more and more as a handicap, rather than an asset, on the way to modernisation and prosperity, and more and more Tunisians (businesspeople, educators, parents and students) are able to say with more confidence, and less deference to France, that our interests would be better served by promoting English, but not enough confidence to say in the same breath one of two things: (1) 'While promoting English, we feel we can gain a great deal by maintaining a high functional ability in French (which is what the rich and the most frenchified Tunisians are doing with their children by sending them to study in the US' (see Walters, 1999); and (2) 'We are going to promote English to a first-foreign-language position, without worrying too much about French, and hope that the partnership agreement we have signed with the EU will shelter us from the dreaded French backlash, given that France is our biggest trade partner (27%)' (see CIA, 2000).

In a speech commemorating the 45th anniversary of independence on 20 March 2001 (which coincided with the International Day of *Francophonie*), President Ben Ali spoke with confidence in favour of the first option, highlighting, first, the primacy of Arabic as the national language that 'shapes the personality' of Tunisian youth, then underscoring his effort to promote the knowledge of foreign languages, 'particularly French to which we have devoted the rank of the first foreign language in our educational system'. The President added that '[w]e consider French an important link to a civilisation to which we are united by ancestral historical relations'. The President also spoke about the recent promotion of English in educating the youth, noting their 'openness to foreign languages and cultures' and their 'awareness' of the greater importance of the communication media and of the requirements of globalisation (*Jeune Afrique*, 2001: 1, author translation).

It is fair to argue that the concern about French is more of a Tunisian problem than a French one, which is apparently what the French foreign minister meant when he recognised the worldwide spread of English and felt that 'French was not under threat in Tunisia, stressing that the issue is not a bilateral one for it to raise concern in France' (see Ghbara, 2000: 3). What he seemed to be saying was that French was in good hands that would defend it for a long time to come. Irrespective of French pressure, which is a reality, it is obvious that Tunisia cannot make the switch for legitimate educational reasons, mainly because of the lack of instructors with adequate ability in English. Of course, teachers, particularly in tertiary education, will draw on English references more often. They may also appreciate some of the advantages of the Anglo-American system, such as team work which was noted by a Tunisian medical professor who, upon attending his first ever conference in the US, was 'very impressed' by the fact that an 18-member team of US researchers could present a paper that was so coherent that it sounded like the work of only one person. In light of this experience, he commented that the French system represented a handicap for the Tunisian medical profession. Yet, these material and motivational factors will not be strong enough to cause a switch to English.

Assuming that a decision were made to switch to English, resistance to it would naturally be strongest from the French-trained academic community, for they would try to preserve their influence and protect themselves from having to adapt to an English-dominant environment. The proof of this lies in the resistance shown to the young PhD holders who returned from the US and Canada within the Transfer of Technology Program. The next line of resistance would be the bureaucrats who are not only francophile academics, for the most part, but also typically resistant to change. A case in point is the attempt made by a Tunisian-British team to ensure policy level support for the sustainability of the ESP Resource Center Project after British funding had run out in 1999. After several attempts to involve the Ministry of Higher Education in a systematic evaluation of the project (Daoud *et al.*, 1999), the former Director of the British Council (personal communication) concluded: 'I see no sign that the Ministry has a policy on language teaching for specific purposes and the only conclusion I can draw from this at present is that it is not (and possibly has never been) a major priority.'

Finally, perhaps the biggest obstacle facing the spread of English is political/ economic realism, given the greater economic relationship between Tunisia and its EU partners (France: 27%, Italy: 21%, Germany: 12% and the EU as a whole: 72%) as opposed to the very limited trade with English-speaking countries (US: imports 5%, exports 1%; UK: 2%). English may very well be the global language of trade and science and technology, but if Tunisia continues to deal mostly with non-English-speaking partners, it will have little incentive to promote English more than necessary. Thus, in an oddly similar way, the case of English in Tunisia is, like the case of Arabic, another illustration of the language policy and planning dichotomy, except that English stands a much better chance than Arabic of being promoted further in the business sector because it is the second most commonly used language after French by Tunisian companies involved in international trade (see, Bach-Baouab, 2000); that is, if we consider not only the trade partners, but also the volume of trade.

Conclusion

Making predictions about language change is a hazardous undertaking that is often inaccurate because language-related decisions are frequently taken on non-language-related grounds. Also, language-related decisions are often too ambitious to realise in the life span of one, two or more governments. However, by trying to understand the past and current situation, we may, as applied linguists, be better prepared to cope with whatever scenario eventually comes to pass. The signatories of the *National Pact* (cited above) signified in this document their determination to 'upgrade the national language (Arabic, meaning MSA) so that it becomes a language of science and technology, encompasses contemporary thought, and contributes in its own right to human civilisation', and in so doing, avoid the development of 'a split between the elite and the popular masses which might render the elite sterile and isolate the masses from modernity'. They considered Arabisation 'a pressing civilisational requirement and one of the best guarantees to transform modernity into a popular asset and to make it part of the general consensus'. These are noble objectives to which every Tunisian would wholeheartedly subscribe; however, for the applied linguist interested in language policy and planning they will constitute a fertile ground for research for a very long time.

Correspondence

Any correspondence should be directed to Mohamed Daoud, Institut Supérieur des Langues de Tunis, 14 Avenue Ibn Maja, Cité El-Khadra, 1003 Tunis, Tunisia (mdaoud@gnet.tn).

Notes

1. The information summarised in this section was drawn from the following sources: the main server on Tunisia (in English) at http://www.tunisiaonline.com; the World Bank Group at http://wbln0018.wrldbank.org/mna/mena.nsf/Countries/Tunisia; the *CIA* World Factbook (2000) at http://www.odci.gov/cia/publications/factbook/index/html; the African Development Bank Group at http://www.afdb.org/news/countries//basic-indic.html; and the United Nations Development Programme, Human Development Report, 1999 at http://www.undp.org/hdro/HDI.html.
2. The World Bank (2000) *Country Brief, Tunisia* suggests a correction of the official 16.2% rate down to 11.2%, noting that, unlike other countries, Tunisian labour statistics count a set of people, mostly household workers, as unemployed.
3. The system of life-long learning was eventually instituted by presidential decision on 20 July 2000 (*La Presse*, 21 July 2000: 1, 4).
4. Work on the *Atlas Linguistique de Tunisie* (*Linguistic Atlas of Tunisia*) started in 1997 and its results will soon be published, according to Taieb Baccouche, the team leader (personal communication, see Baccouche & Mejri, 2000). The goal of the project is to describe the phonology, morphology, syntax and lexicon of Tunisian Arabic (TA) and to produce a linguistic/ethnographic map of Tunisia. The work has included: (1) a thorough survey of the relevant literature; (2) the collection of questionnaire data from 1000 informants sampled according to region, age, sex and socioeconomic status; and (3) the recording of 3000 hours of TA in 250 locations around the country. According to Baccouche, there is work in progress on the *Linguistic Atlas of the Maghreb*.

5.   The survey consisted of two parts: (1) a small case study of local grocery shops in the region of Nabeul, involving the consultation of invoices and oral interview questions addressed to the grocers themselves and some delivery personnel working for whole-salers who happened to be present at the time of the interview about the languages used in the invoices and their impact on the business; and (2) a question about the importance of languages for one to live and prosper in Tunisia, which was posed orally to several secondary school and university teachers as well as students in basic and secondary education (two groups/78 students) and university (three groups, two undergraduate and one graduate/144 students).

6.   The expression 'eradicate or erase illiteracy' is translated from the Arabic expression *maHwu al-ummiyyati* which literally means the erasing of illiteracy. The expression is used regularly in official documents and speeches to imply that illiteracy is a disease that has to be cured, or a handicap to be eliminated. Some documents also use the expression *al-taHarruru min al-ummiyyati*, meaning 'freedom from illiteracy'. While the medical metaphor may seem absurd given the complex sociolinguistic nature of literacy, illiteracy is indeed perceived as the main reason for producing people who are a burden on society; i.e. people who (1) cannot read, write and count; (2) cannot function in a given work situation; and (3) feel inadequate, negative, and hopeless about changing their current situation in comparison to the 'educated' and are, there-fore, in need of some sort of treatment to become productive, positive members of society (Memorandum, 1993: 1–3). Note that the relevant documents produced by the Ministry of Social Affairs do not specify the language of literacy, but the assumption is that it is MSA.

7.   These statistics in Table 1 relate to what the *INS* (2000) calls 'one language', without specifying the language, which is an interesting understatement about the value of Arabic and French. I interpret the label as a reference to Arabic (or French in some cases) because the percentage of respondents who might have claimed English or another language besides Arabic or French would be insignificant.

8.   For complete details on the educational system in Tunisia, including reforms, figures, programmes, assessment, etc., see Daoud (in press b).

9.   As explained earlier in the monograph, although basic school has been extended to the ninth year, in order to make education compulsory for nine years, years 7 to 9 are really part of secondary education given that subjects are taught by specialised teach-ers with the same degrees and secondary school status and who are required to teach any level among the years 7 to 13.

10. *PRICAT* stands for *Projet de Renforcement Institutionnel Canadien en Tunisie* (Canadian Project for Institutional Reinforcement in Tunisia). The project, which ends this year (1996–2001), aims to promote working from objectives in the planning, design, imple-mentation and evaluation of various programmes/projects. The sectors concerned include vocational training, higher education, scientific research, telecommunica-tions, and industry (e.g. textiles, mechanical industry) (M. Grami, personal communi-cation).

11. The weekly newspapers are spread over the days of the week so that four different ones appear on Mondays, Thursdays and Saturdays, respectively; two on Wednesday and one on Tuesday.

12. 850,000 Tunisians were connected to the Internet in 1999 (nearly 10% of the popula-tion), and the stated objective for 2001 is to reach 1.4 million connections, or more than 14% (see Nehmé *et al.*, 2000).

13. North African scholars writing in English have consistently used the term 'Arabisation', rather than 'Arabicisation' because the policy and its implementation have not been limited to promoting the Arabic language as a linguistic phenomenon (language use in education and the wider environment, corpus planning and literacy), but involved the reassertion of Arab-Muslim identity. Arabisation continues to be used as a means to counter the former colonial power's interference in national affairs. In education, the switch to Arabic has influenced the course content and teaching approach, particularly in the humanities and social sciences. 'Arabicization' is the correct English derivation from 'Arabic', but for the above reasons, and perhaps

because of consonance with the French term *Arabisation*, we prefer the derivation to be from 'Arab'.
14. Tunisification refers to the effort to ensure that Tunisia retains its character as a nation in view of its geographical position, national history, civilisation, heritage, religion and language. It means neither a split from Arabism nor the suppression of foreign languages. Salem (1984: 188) cites a former minister of culture and close colleague of Mzali as writing: 'It has never been possible to separate the issue of Tunisification from the issue of Arabisation, or vice versa, on condition that the term *arabiation* does not carry any connotations of specific political tendencies contrary to the will of the Tunisian people to remain Tunisian; in other words, in control of their destiny and not melted into another people whoever they may be' (author translation).
15. This expression is favoured by francophiles who include academics, scientists, doctors and other professionals educated in French in Tunisia and/or France. This was illustrated in a recent colloquium entitled *La Tunisie d'Hier et de Demain* (Tunisia of Yesterday and Tomorrow) and organised by the Académie Tunisienne des Sciences, des Lettres et des Arts (Tunisian Academy of Sciences, Letters and Arts) Beit Al-Hikma, 9–12 January 2001. All the speakers, including the former Secretary General of the Arab League who had also served as Minister of Culture, presented in French.
16. Passing rate increase: Basic School Certificate (end of ninth year) 1998: 67.8%, 1999: 68.7%; *baccalauréat* 1998: 49.5%, 1999: 59.5%; university graduates: 1997: 13,600, 1998: 17,099, 1999: 19,646, projected increase for 2001: 21,270 (see *Ministère de l'Education*, 1999/2000; *Ministère de l'Enseignement Supérieur*, 1998/99, 1999/2000; *Neuvième Plan*, 1997–2001). University figures for 2000 become available in July/August 2001.

References

Ager, D. (1996) *'Francophonie' in the 1990s: Problems and Opportunities*. Clevedon: Multilingual Matters.
Akkari, N. (2000) hal tusbiHu al-angliziyyatu al-lughata al-ajnabiyyata al-uula? [Will English become the first foreign language?]. *Al-Shuruuq* 21 January, 28. Tunis.
Al-Eroui, A. (1989) *Hikayaat Al-Eroui [Tales of Al-Eroui]*. Vols 1&2. Tunis: Maison Tunisienne d'Edition.
Al-Sabah (2000) [Arabic daily newspaper] 19 February, 3. Tunis.
Al-Shuruuq (2000) [Arabic daily newspaper] 28 April, 28. Tunis.
Ammar, S. and Al-Khury, S. (1996) *Al-ta3ribu fi al-waTani al-3arabiyyi: waaqi3uhu wa mustaqbaluhu [Arabicization in the Arab World: Its Reality and Future]*. Tunis: Arab League Educational, Cultural and Scientific Organization (ALECSO).
Baccouche, T. (1994) *L'Emprunt en Arabe Moderne [Borrowing in Modern Arabic]*. Tunis: L'Académie Tunisienne des Sciences, des Lettres et des Arts, Beit Al-Hikma and Institut Bourguiba des Langues Vivantes, Editions du Nord.
Baccouche, T. (1998) La langue arabe dans le Monde Arabe [The Arabic language in the Arab World]. *L'Information Grammaticale, N° Spécial, Tunisie* [Grammatical Information, Special Issue, Tunisia], 49–54.
Baccouche, T. (in press) Tunisie (langues) [Tunisia (languages)]. *Encyclopédie de l'Islam*. Tunis: Author draft document.
Baccouche, T. and Mejri, S. (2000) Injaazu al-aTlasi al-lisaaniyyi al-tunisiyyi: ta'Silan lihuwiyyatin wa 3aamila tanmiyatin [Preparation of the Tunisian linguistic atlas: An assertion of identity and a factor of development]. In *Les Langues en Tunisie: Etat des Lieux et Perspectives [Languages in Tunisia: State of the Art and Perspectives]* (pp. 293–9). Tunis: Centre de Publications Universitaires.
Baccouche, T. and Skik, H. (1978) Aperçu sur l'histoire des contacts linguistiques en Tunisie [Perspective on the history of linguistic contacts in Tunisia]. In *Actes du Deuxième Congrès international d'Etudes des Cultures de la Méditerrannée Occidentale*, vol. 1 (pp. 157–95), and Discussion, vol. 2 (pp. 181–91). Alger: SNED.
Bach-Baouab, S.L. (2000) A survey of English in the sector of international trade in Tunisia. Unpublished DEA thesis, Faculté des Lettres La Manouba, Tunis.

Bakir, A. (2000) Al-lughatu al–3arabiyyatu wa xaTaru al–3awlamati [The Arabic language and the threat of globalization]. *Al-Sabah* 19 February, 10. Tunis.

Bannour, A. (2000) Brève mise au point sur la Lingua Franca en Méditerrannée [Brief review on the Lingua Franca in the Mediterranean]. In *Les Langues en Tunisie: Etat des Lieux et Perspectives* [*Languages in Tunisia: State of the Art and Perspectives*] (pp. 241–59). Tunis: Centre de Publications Universitaires.

Battenburg, J. (1996) English in the Maghreb. *English Today* 12, 3–14.

Battenburg, J. (1997) English vs. French: Language rivalry in Tunisia. *World Englishes* 16, 281–90.

Battenburg, J. (1999) The gradual death of the Berber language in Tunisia. *International Journal of the Sociology of Language* 137, 151–65.

Ben Ali, Z.A. (2000). Presidents' speech on 7 November. On WWW at http://www.tunisiaonline.com/news/071100-1.html.

Brahim, A. (1994) *Linguistique Contrastive et Fautes de Français* [*Contrastive Linguistics and French Errors*]. Tunis: Université de Tunis.

Central Intelligence Agency (2000) *The World Fact Book – Tunisia*. On WWW at http://www.odci.gov/cia/publications/factbook/index.html.

Chaabane, S. (1999) *Les Défis de Ben Ali* [*The Challenges of Ben Ali*]. Paris: Editions de l'Orient.

Chraiet, A. (2001) Universités: Le pourquoi d'une restructuration [Universities: The reason for a restructuring]. *La Presse* 3 January, 3–4. Tunis. On WWW at http://www.orbit-media.com.tn/.

Crowley, T. (2000) The language situation in Vanuatu. *Current Issues in Language Planning* 1, 47–132.

Daoud, M. (1991a) Arabization in Tunisia: The tug of war. *Issues in Applied Linguistics* 2, 7–29.

Daoud, M. (1991b) The processing of EST discourse: Arabic and French native speakers' recognition of rhetorical relationships in engineering texts. Unpublished PhD dissertation, University of California, Los Angeles.

Daoud, M. (1996) English language development in Tunisia. *TESOL Quarterly* 2, 598–605.

Daoud, M. (2000) LSP in North Africa: Status, problems, and challenges. In W. Grabe *et al.* (eds) *Annual Review of Applied Linguistics, 20: Applied Linguistics as an Emerging Discipline* (pp. 77–96). New York: Cambridge University Press.

Daoud, M. (in press a) Teaching, learning and testing in the disciplines as motivational factors in ESP. In M. Bahloul and M. Triki (eds) *Proceedings of the Second Maghreb ESP Conference: The ESP Teacher as an Agent of Change*. Sfax, Tunisia: Faculté des Lettres et Sciences Humaines. Paper presented at the same conference, 4–6 April 1995.

Daoud, M. (in press b) Education in Tunisia. In Leslie S. Nucho (ed.) *Education in the Arab World*. Washington, DC: America-Mideast Educational and Training Services.

Daoud, M. and Labassi, T. (1996) ESP and the real world: Some answers to new requirements. Paper read at the Second National ESP Seminar. Tunis. March 2.

Daoud, M.; Weir, C.; Athimni, M.; Barbaoui, K. and Oueslati, Z. (1999). *Evaluation of the English for Specific Purposes Resource Center Project: Executive Summary*. Tunis: ESP Resource Center. IBLV.

Djité, P. (1992) The Arabization of Algeria: Linguistic and sociopolitical motivations. *International Journal of the Sociology of Language* 98, 15–28.

Djité, P. (2000) Language planning in Côte d'Ivoire. *Current Issues in Language Planning* 1, 11–46.

Dudley-Evans, T. and St John, M.J. (1998) *Developments in English for Specific Purposes: A Multidisciplinary Approach*. Cambridge, UK: Cambridge University Press.

Ezzaki, A. and Wagner, D. (1992) Language and literacy in the Maghreb. In W. Grabe *et al.* (eds) *Annual Review of Applied Linguistics, 12: Literacy* (pp. 216–29). New York: Cambridge University Press.

Fantar, M.H. (2000) Mu3Tayaatun Hawla al-waaqi3i al-lughawiyyi fi Tunis min Qartaj ila al-Qayrawan [Data on the language reality in Tunisia from Carthage to Kairouan]. In *Les Langues en Tunisie: Etat des Lieux et Perspectives* [*Languages in Tunisia: State of the Art and Perspectives*] (pp. 43–62). Tunis: Centre de Publications Universitaires.

Fellah, M.J. (2000) TaHaalibu 3aaliqatun bi-ssafinati [Algae clinging to the ship]. *Al-Shuruq* 24 February, 10. Tunis.

Fishman, J. (1968) Nationality-nationalism and nation-nationism. In J. Fishman, C. Ferguson and J. Das Gupta (eds) *Language Problems in Developing Nations* (pp. 39–51). New York: John Wiley and Sons.

Francophonie (2001) Tunisie. On WWW at http://www.francophonie.org/oif/francophonie/membres/FICPAYS/RUBS/0103061.html.

Garmadi, S. (1968) La situation linguistique actuelle en Tunisie: Problèmes et perspectives [The present language situation in Tunisia: Problems and perspectives]. *Revue Tunisienne des Sciences Sociales* 13, 13–24.

Ghbara, F. (2000) Waziru al-kharijiyyati al-faransiyyu yarfa3u al-iltibasa [The French Minister of Foreign Affairs clarifies] *Al-I3laan*, 11 February, 3. Tunis.

Graddol, D. (1997) *The Future of English?* London: British Council.

Grandguillaume, G. (1983) *Arabisation et politique linguistique au Maghreb (Arabisation and language policy in the Maghreb).* Paris: Maisonneuve et Larose.

Hamzaoui, R. (1970) L'arabisation du Ministère de l'Intérieur: La brigade de la circulation de la Garde Nationale [Arabicization of the Ministry of the Interior: The traffic brigade of the National Guard]. *Cahiers du CERES* 3, 11–73.

Ibn-Khaldoun, A. (1988) *taarikhu Ibn Khaldoun [The History of Ibn Khaldoun]*, Vol 7 (2nd edn). Beirut, Lebanon: Dar Al-Fikr.

Institut National de la Statistique (INS) (1996) *Recensement Général de la Population et de l'Habitat de 1994: Caractéristiques d'Education, Tableaux Statistiques [General Census of the Population and Habitat of 1994: Characteristics of Education, Statistical Tables]*. Tunis: Ministère du Développement Economique.

Institut National de la Statistique (INS) (2000) *Statistiques Economiques et Sociales [Economic and Social Statisitics]*. On WWW at http://www.ins.tn/_private/idc/.

Ismail, A. (1992) *L'Ecole de Base [Basic School]*. Tunis: Association Tunisienne de l'Ecole Moderne.

Jeune Afrique (2000) La Lettre de l'Agence Intergouvernementale de la Francophonie [The Letter of the Intergovernmental Agency of Francophonie] no. 2036, 18–24 January, 23–26. Paris.

Jeune Afrique (2001) Le Président Ben Ali souligne l'importance du français en Tunisie [President Ben Ali underscores the importance of French in Tunisia]. On WWW at special/impression/editorial.php3?doc = /data/actu_afp/2001.

Jeune Afrique L'intelligent (2001) Confidentiel: Succès Tunisien à Tokyo [Confidential: Tunisian Success in Tokyo] no. 2097, 20 March, 18. Paris. On WWW at http://www.jeuneafrique.com/special/impression/editorial.php3?doc=/data/jaf/2097.

Jourchi, S. (2001) Al-ta3reebu ummu al-ma3areki al-thaqafiyyati fi al-maghribi al-3arabiyyi [Arabicization the mother of cultural battles in the Arab Maghreb]. Islam Online Web Site on WWW at http://www.islamonline.net/iol-arabic/dowalia/fan–19/alqawal.asp.

Kaplan, R.B. and Baldauf, R.B., Jr. (1997) *Language Planning from Practice to Theory.* Clevedon: Multilingual Matters.

Kaplan, R.B. and Palmer, J.D. (1992) Literacy and applied linguistics. In W. Grabe and R. B. Kaplan (eds) *Introduction to Applied Linguistics* (pp. 191–209). Reading, MA: Addison-Wesley.

Katzner, K. (1986) *The Languages of the World.* New York: Routledge and Kegan Paul.

Kefi, R. (2000) Quel avenir pour le français? [What future for French?]. *Jeune Afrique* 2036, 30–32.

Labassi, T. (1996) A genre-based analysis of non-native chemistry research article introductions. Unpublished DEA thesis, Faculté des Lettres La Manouba, Tunis.

Labassi, T. (in press) ESP: A market-oriented approach. In M. Bahloul and M. Triki (eds) *Proceedings of the Second Maghreb ESP Conference: The ESP Teacher as an Agent of Change.* Sfax, Tunisia: Faculté des Lettres et Sciences Humaines.

L'Action (1958) The president's speech at Al-Sadiqiyya High School. 26 June, 1, 2. Tunis.

L'Action (1986) The prime minister's speech at the Francophonie summit (Paris, 17–18 February). 18 February, 3. Tunis.

La Presse (2000) 21 July, 1, 3. Tunis.

Lopez, A.J. (1998) The language situation in Mozambique. *Journal of Multilingual and Multicultural Development* 19, 440–86.

Maamouri, M. (1973) The linguistic situation in independent Tunisia. *American Journal of Arabic Studies* 1, 50–56.

Maamouri, M. (1983) Illiteracy in Tunisia. In P.M. Payne (ed.) *Language in Tunisia* (pp. 203–26). Tunis: Institut Bourguiba des Langues Vivantes.

Mekki, N. (1998) A US–Maghreb economic partnership in the making. *Tunisia News* 284, 3, 9. Tunis.

Memorandum (1993) Muthakkartun fi al-namaTi al-jadidi linashaaTi maHwi al-ummiyyati we mutaTallibaatihi wa-l-khuTTati al-muqtaraHati litaTbiqihi [Memorandum about the new design for the activity of erasing illiteracy, its requirements and the proposed plan for its implementation]. Tunis: Ministère des Affaires Sociales, National Program for the Eradication of Illiteracy. 14 pp. Internal document.

Middle East Magazine (1999) Tunisia Online Web Site at http://www.tunisiaonline.com/pressbook/africasia3/index.html.

Ministère de l'Education (1999/2000) *Statistiques Scolaires 1999–2000: 2ème Cycle de L'Enseignement de Base et Enseignement Secondaire* [*School Statistics 1999–2000: 2nd Cycle of Basic School and Secondary Education*]. Tunis: Bureau des Etudes, de la Planification et de la Programmation.

Ministère de l'Enseignement Supérieur (1998/1999) *L'Enseignement et la Formation Supérieures en Chiffres* [*Higher Education and Training in Figures*]. Tunis: Bureau des Etudes, de la Planification et de la Programmation.

Ministère de l'Enseignement Supérieur (1999/2000) *L'Enseignement et la Formation Supérieures en Chiffres* [*Higher Education and Training in Figures*]. Tunis: Bureau des Etudes, de la Planification et de la Programmation.

Ministère des Affaires Sociales (1993) Al-khuTTatu al-waTaniyyatu li maHwi al-ummiyyati: MunTalaqaatuha wa injaazaatuha [The national plan for the eradication of illiteracy: Its origins and achievements]. Tunis: National Program for the Eradication of Illiteracy. 6 pp. Internal document.

Ministère des Affaires Sociales (2001) At http://www.ministeres.tn/html/indexdonnees/sociales.html.

Nehmé, M. *et al.* (2000) Tunisie – nouvelles technologies, nouvelles économies, nouveaux emplois [Tunisia – new technologies, new economies, new jobs]. *Le Nouvel Afrique Asie* 126, 27–53.

Neuvième Plan de Développement (1997–2001) At http://www.tunisie.com/developement/.

Pacte National (1988) Identité [Identity]. On WWW at http://www.tunisieinfo.com/indexreference.html.

Pencheon, T. (1968) La langue berbère en Tunisie et la scolarisation des enfants berbérophones [The Berber language in Tunisia and the schooling of Berber-speaking children]. *Revue Tunisienne des Sciences Sociales* 13, 173–86.

Premier Ministère (1999) *Arabization in the Administration*. Circular 45 (29 October). 3pp.

Price Waterhouse (1998) *Investment in Tunisia: Information guide*. Groupe MTBF-CAF, Price Waterhouse correspondent. Tunis: Imprimerie Signes.

Salem, N. (1984) *Habib Bourguiba, Islam and the Creation of Tunisia*. London: Croom Helm.

Salhi, R. (1984) *Language Planning: A Case Study of English in Tunisia*. Tunis: Université de Tunis. Unpublished DRA thesis.

Salhi, R. (2000) Language shift: The language situation in Tunisia, revisited. In *Les Langues en Tunisie: Etat des Lieux et Perspectives* [*Languages in Tunisia: State of the Art and Perspectives*] (pp. 31–42). Tunis: Centre de Publications Universitaires.

Shili, S. (1997) inTilaaqu al-sanati al-jadidati wa iqbalun mkaththafun 3ala-l-angliziyyati [Start of the new year and intense demand for English]. *Al-Shuruuq* 15 October, 3. Tunis.

Skik, H. (1976) Aspects du bilinguisme à l'école primaire tunisienne [Aspects of bilingualism in the primary school in Tunisia]. *Revue Tunisienne des Sciences Sociales* 44, 73–116.

Tsao, F-F. (1999) The language planning situation in Taiwan. *Journal of Multilingual and Multicultural Development* 20, 328–75.
UNDP (1999) The United Nations Development Programme, Human Development Report. At http://www.undp.org/hdro/HDI.html.
UNESCO (2001) At http://unescostats.unesco.org/.
World Bank (2000) Tunisia – Country Brief. On WWW at http://wbln0018. worldbank.og/mna/mena.nsf./countries/tunisia/.
Walters, K. (1999) 'New year happy': Some sociolinguistic observations on the 'anglicization' of Tunisia. In M. Jabeur, A. Manai and M. Bahloul (eds) *English in North Africa* (pp. 33–63). Tunis: TSAS Innovation Series, TSAS and British Council.
Walters, K. (2000) 'Ça y est?' 'Maçayesh': Some observations on language contact in contemporary Tunisia. In *Les Langues en Tunisie: Etat des Lieux et Perspectives* [*Languages in Tunisia: State of the Art and Perspectives*] (pp. 103–11). Tunis: Centre de Publications Universitaires.
Zaitouni, A.N. (1995) *Al-iSlaaHu Al-idariyyu* [*The Administrative Reform*]. Tunis: Centre des Etudes et de Recherches Administratives, L'Ecole Nationale d'Administration.

Biographical Notes on Contributors

Efurosibina Adegbija (formerly of the Ilorin University, Nigeria) was well-known for his research on endangered languages in Africa, especially Okó, his native tongue and on African language policy and planning in general. His major books *Language Attitudes in Sub-Saharan Africa* (Multilingual Matters) and *Multilingualism: A Nigerian Case Study* (Africa World Press) were widely adopted. He passed away on 7 January 2005 aged 52.

Mohamed Benrabah is Professor of English Linguistics and Sociolinguistics at 'UFR Etudes Anglophones', Stendhal-Grenoble III University (France). He was educated at the University of Oran (Algeria) and University College London (United Kingdom) where he received his PhD in linguistics in 1987. From 1978–1994, he was Lecturer and Senior Lecturer at the English Department at Oran University where he was Director of the Institute of Foreign Languages between 1980 and 1983. He settled in France in October 1994. He has published more than forty articles in journals and chapters in books as well as ephemeral pieces in popular publications in Algeria and France. His publications include a contribution to *Les Violences en Algérie* (Paris: Editions Odile Jacob, 1998), and a book *Langue et Pouvoir en Algérie: Histoire d'un Traumatisme Linguistique* (Paris: Editions Séguier, 1999). His research interests include applied phonetics/phonology, sociolinguistics, and language policy, language planning and language-in-education planning with a particular interest in the Maghreb and the francophone world.

Mohamed Daoud holds a PhD from the University of California, Los Angeles, and is a professor of Applied Linguistics at the *Institut Supérieur des Langues de Tunis (ISLT)*, Tunisia. He has been a member of the Advisory Board of ARAL since 1992. He has led several EFL/ESP syllabus design projects and co-authored textbooks in ESP and EOP in Tunisia. His research interests include language policy and planning, reading and testing in EFL/ESP.

Paulin Djité teaches sociolinguistics, linguistics, French, interpreting and translation, and research methods in languages and linguistics in the School of Humanities and Languages at the University of Western Sydney, Australia. His research focus lies in the areas of language-in-education policies and planning, language management and the spread of French outside of France.

Jean-François Y.K. Kpli teaches linguistics in the School of Languages, Literature and Civilization at the University of Cocody, Abidjan, Côte d'Ivoire. His research focus is in the areas of French and English grammar analysis and language spread in Côte d'Ivoire.